9.50/01 EC

D0923103

WITHDRAWN
UTSA LIBRARIES

LEONID ANDREYEV

[PAINTING BY U. ROSSINSKY]

LEONID ANDREYEV

A CRITICAL STUDY by ALEXANDER KAUN

AMS PRESS
NEW YORK

Reprinted from the edition of 1924, New York
First AMS EDITION published 1970
Manufactured in the United States of America

International Standard Book Number: 0-404-03638-4

Library of Congress Catalog Card Number: 75-126652

AMS PRESS, INC.
NEW YORK, N.Y. 10003

TO
VALERIA EDUARDOVNA

ACKNOWLEDGMENTS

This work has been accredited by the University of California as a thesis for the degree of Doctor of Philosophy in the department of Slavic Languages. To the members of the Committee on my candidacy I am indebted for their many-sided help. I am particularly grateful to the Chairman, Professor George R. Noyes, for his indefatigable effort to clear my essay from errors and gaucheries.

I am deeply beholden to Mme. Anna Ilyinishna Andreyev for her kindly interest in my work, for giving me invaluable personal information, and for permitting me to study her husband's unpublished writings, diaries, and letters. Among those who encouraged my trip to Europe for research purposes I wish to mention especially Miss Ethelwyn Wing and Mr. Albert Bender.

Acknowledgment is due to the *Freeman* and to the *New Republic,* in whose columns appeared originally the material incorporated in the sections of this essay pertaining to the general characteristics of Andreyev's art, and to the last days of Andreyev's life.

CONTENTS

ix

PART II

THE MOTIVES AND BACKGROUND OF ANDREYEV'S WORK

Contents

INTRODUCTION

INTRODUCTION

I

A brief survey of literary tendencies in Russia.—Dominating motive in Russian literature: Service.—Intelligentsia.—Serfdom.—Narodnichestvo.—City versus village.—Chekhov, as a transitional writer.—Gorky's new note.—"Pure" art.—The nineties, and their divergent currents.—The voice of Andreyev.

UNTIL the end of the nineteenth century Russian literature possessed a distinct motive: Service. It had been instrumental in propagating or popularizing certain causes, which varied with the time, the régime, the mood and cultural level of society. During the Kiev and Moscow periods of Russian history the written word had been ecclesiastic in content and in spirit. Even such secular productions as theatrical plays and syllabic verses, which began to appear about the middle of the seventeenth century, were definitely tinged with a religious hue. The advent of Peter the Great signified the subjugation of all national forces and sentiments, church and literature included, to the service of the State. He secularized Russia, at any rate externally. His drastic reforms and revolutionary changes formed the subject of literary propaganda and eulogy during his reign and throughout the eighteenth century. The sermons of Prokopovich, the satires of Kantemir, the odes and dramas of Tredyakovsky, Lomonosov, Sumarokov, Derzhavin, and their lesser brethren, were overwhelmingly dedicated to the service of the new order of things. Thus we find that Russian literature preserved a governmental or a semi-official character from the time of the Conversion (988) until the latter part of the reign of Catherine II, serving, with a very few exceptions, the powers that be. It is only with the appearance of the Intelligentsia, late in the eighteenth century, that Russian literature acquires the

3

oppositional character, which has remained its dominant trait, and thus transfers its service from the rulers to the people.

The somewhat vague term of Intelligentsia may be applied to the unorganized group of Russian men and women who, regardless of their social or economic status, have been united in a common striving for the betterment of material and spiritual conditions. Only such a broad definition of the Intelligentsia can indicate the scope of its interests and activities. Eschewing considerations of personal gain, disregarding and even combating class interests and privileges, in the name of the common weal, this group is bound to present a minority in an age of practical common sense, and, furthermore, an opposition to existing authorities. Until we arrive at ideal conditions, the fact remains that any government voices the desires of certain portions of the population, which desires it fosters and supports often at the expense of other portions of the population. Hence the Intelligentsia, in championing the equality of individuals and of classes, has condemned itself to the position of a perpetual opposing minority under any government, be it the tsaristic order bestowing favors upon the propertied classes, be it the Bolshevist régime which discriminates in favor of the propertyless.

Isolated thinkers, idealists, rebels against things as they are, Russia had had earlier, though in a very inconspicuous number. Not until the latter part of the eighteenth century, however, did there appear in Russia a group of such individuals, cogitating and acting somewhat coördinately. Such a thinking and articulate element, the Intelligentsia, began to show signs of existence three or four generations after the promulgation of Peter's reform, when a limited portion of society had been able to absorb Western ideas and doctrines, notably those of the French philosophers and encyclopedists of the eighteenth century. With the initial encouragement of Catherine II, a friend of Voltaire and Diderot, contemporary ideas of equality and democracy penetrated the minds of her advanced subjects, provoking inevitable resentment against the existing conditions of political, social, and economic slavery. With the writings of Novikov and Radishchev, both severely punished by Catherine, both therefore the first martyrs of the literary Intelligentsia, Russian literature freed itself from the fetters of Court and State, and entered upon its natural path—nonconformist, oppositional, denunciatory. Thenceforth Russian writers, if we consider the most representative of them, have performed a task similar to that of the prophets of Israel, in its loftiness and arduousness, and in the hardships and perils with which it is fraught. No longer serving authorities, whether secular or ecclesiastic, Russian literature during the last one hundred years has been largely dedicated to the service of the oppressed people.[1]

Not ungermane to the idealistic and altruistic character of this literature has been the fact that nearly all its conspicuous makers belonged to the very class against whose privileges and hardness they have pleaded on behalf of the masses. In other words, from Radishchev to Chekhov the bulk of Russian literature presents the gentry's attitude toward the peasant. Liberal-minded landowners and serf-holders, like Grigorovich or Turgenev, were typical of the pre-emancipation authors, whose chief purpose was to prove that the serf had a soul, and thus to arouse shame and repentance in those responsible for the enslavement of millions of fellow beings. Since both the writers and the readers were non-peasants, the subject matter did not escape idealization. To the "repentant nobleman" the abused

---

[1] My definition of "Intelligentsia" is inclusive, and is therein different from the prevailing definitions of this word, which are for the most part controversial (an elaboration of my view may be found in *The Freeman*, of March 29 and April 19, 1922). My definition does not exclude from the Intelligentsia even such seemingly "conforming" writers as Gogol and Dostoyevsky. For whatever their personal views may have been, their productions had a profoundly subversive significance, as far as existing institutions were concerned. However conservative in their last days, Gogol and Dostoyevsky revealed in their works the corruption of the political, social, economic, and moral state of contemporary Russia, and thereby contributed to the negatory outlook of the reading public. It may be noted, in passing, that under the Soviet régime Russian writers for the most part fare no better than under the tsars: they continue their nonconformist attitude, and proceed to denounce the ruling class, at the risk of persecution and even death. One need only recall the occasionally fearless stand of Gorky, *The Twelve*, by Blok, the execution of the poet Gumilev, and the generally precarious conditions of the Intelligentsia in Bolshevik Russia.

peasant appeared crowned with all virtues and endowed with unlimited potentialities. The Narodnik school dominated Russian letters through the latter half of the nineteenth century. "Narod"—that is, the people—from an object of pity and sympathy was raised to an object of worship and emulation. The peasant's suffering and humility, faith and kindliness, simplicity and poesy, were eulogized in prose and in verse, by Nekrasov, by Dostóyevsky, by Tolstoy, and by less artistic but more vehement Narodnik writers. At the same time the peasant institutions of the village system, the Mir and the Obshchina, with their main features of communal ownership and mutual responsibility, formed the alpha and omega of "Russian Socialism," from Herzen and Chernyshevsky, through Mikhailovsky, to the present day Social Revolutionists.

Narodnichestvo, or the cult of the people of the soil, in belles-lettres as well as in religious, political and social-economic thought, has owed its enduring effect in a large measure to the predominantly rural quality of Russian life. The late appearance of capitalism (large private industries were exceedingly few before the middle of the nineties) accounted for the preservation on Russian soil of traits and institutions which long ago became archaic and disappeared in the West. Of these institutions the village commune was in the eyes of the Narodniki most characteristically Russian, destined to serve as the foundation stone for a socialistic order. The village lent its flavor to literature. Rustic air and vastness permeate the best Russian novels, excepting those of Dostoyevsky. But though late, capitalism did arrive. The expectations of the Narodniki notwithstanding, Russia failed to "skip" the capitalistic stage in its march toward Socialism. The city became a factor in Russian life, it acquired a physiognomy and a voice.

Moreover, the village sanctuary no longer appeared infallible. Even among the Narodniki one could discern discordant notes regarding the saintliness and inherent communistic notions of the peasant. Thus during the eighties, Glyeb Uspensky wrote a series of village pictures which were most disparaging. Himself an ardent Narodnik, Uspensky went to live among peasants,

and the impressions he gathered were so disheartening that they
actually drove him to insanity. Uspensky's peasants differed
from Turgenev's gentle, poetic souls, as they differed from
Tolstoy's perfect Christians. Uspensky depicted them as
slaves of the soil, monomaniacal in their interests and aspirations, which were limited to the question of land, and more
land, to the exclusion of any other thoughts and sentiments.
At the same time Uspensky observed that, given an opportunity,
the peasant easily became a "fist," that is, a callous exploiter of
the Mir—the commune. The aching note in Uspensky's writings was the more convincing since the author belonged no
longer to the gentry but to the people. After the emancipation
of the peasants (in 1861) the field of literature was invaded by
"commoners," who treated the people from personal knowledge
and experience, not through the idealizing prism of the penitent
noble. The ranks of the Intelligentsia began to be interspersed
with direct representatives of the people, who discussed the
peasant with brutal frankness and unvarnished realism. After
Uspensky and Reshetnikov came Chekhov, who dealt the
Narodniki a severe blow with his *Peasants* (1897), an objective
presentation of rustic stupidity, callousness, drunkenness, and
ignorance. Still later, after the revolution of 1905, there appeared a special genre of literature, presenting the peasants as
drunkards, rogues and brutes. Notable among these productions were Bunin's *Village* and Rodionov's *Our Crime*.

Narodnichestvo had owed its success in thought and in action to a combination of interdependent circumstances. The
romantic idyl of an intrinsically Socialistic and Christian village,
accepted as an autochthonous Russian institution, and signifying
a peculiar road of development for Russia, could exist in the
minds of the Intelligentsia as long as this Intelligentsia (1)
consisted of penitent gentry apt to idealize the source of their
sick conscience, who (2) worshipped the "Communistic and
Christian" Mir and Obshchina from hearsay and pure theory,
and (3) believed that it was the destiny of Russia to remain
forever agricultural, rustic, non-capitalistic. The downfall of
Narodnichestvo came in consequence of the change which had

taken place in that combination of interdependent circumstances. Toward the end of the nineteenth century (1) Russian writers and readers were of heterogeneous class-composition, and among them the non-gentry element was strongly represented; (2) the economic and moral disintegration of the village had become a grave commonplace; the rapidly growing capitalistic industry, which the Government lavishly endowed, protected, and fostered, blew to pieces the Narodnik myth about Russia's "peculiar destiny," inundated the cities with swarms of starving peasants seeking employment in factories and foundries, and thus created a soil ready to receive the seed of Marxian, proletarian Socialism.

In Chekhov we find reflected the transition period between the village and city motive in literature. Of peasant stock, Chekhov at the same time represented that Intelligentsia in which the moods and attitudes of the gentry prevailed. To his very end (in 1904) he remained a Vosmidesyatnik—that is, a writer of the eighties, of that "gray" decade of soilless men split by inner contradictions, worn out by futile strivings and aimless whining, defined by a contemporary satirist (Saltykov-Shchedrin) as "boiled souls" and "neither fish nor flesh." Though by no means a rural writer, Chekhov in his descriptions of practically all walks of Russian life preserved in a measure the attitude of a noble, the point of view of a Turgenev, the twilight sadness that characterizes a moribund race. For the Russian gentry was doomed both as an economic factor and as an intellectual force, giving place to the third estate for the former function, and merging, as an Intelligentsia, in the multitude of "commoners." Chekhov's last drama, *The Cherry Orchard,* sounded the swan song of rural Russia, Russia of the ancestral estates, of the "Noblemen's Nests," of the Tatianas and Lizas, of the Lavretskys, Oblomovs and Rostovs. Lopakhin, an upstart capitalist, had driven out the gentle, helpless, impractical hereditary possessors of the estate, to transform it into a soap factory. The curtain fell to the sounds of the ax hewing down the sentimentalized, useless trees of the cherry orchard. Chekhov tolled the requiem for all that Russia which lived, felt, thought and acted according to the traditions of a patriarchal nobility, of an aristocratic Intelligentsia.

Meanwhile the new age, the city voice, was announced—not with sad regrets, but with triumphant shouts—by Maxim Gorky. Free from traditions, from cultural associations and bonds, and enamored of open, unfettered, unconventional life, Gorky ushered into the melancholy salon of Russian literature his band of tramps and vagabonds. With their mud-covered boots, or more often barefooted, this golden brigade unceremoniously trampled the literary parquet, and with lusty lungs roared defiance to existing conditions and conventions. Gorky's first heroes belonged not to the gentry, nor to the bourgeoisie, not even to the fourth estate, but to the fifth estate, to the Lumpenproletariat. In these Gorky found a suitable mouthpiece for his negative burden. He wished to disperse the melancholy, Chekhovian atmosphere of passive whimpering, of neurasthenic introspection, of Hamlet-like rumination, of dabbling in old slogans and in outworn truths. His care-free philosophers neither pleaded nor asked for sympathy, but hurled their contempt into the faces of smug possessors of property, declaring that the only thing which mattered was individual freedom, and that this freedom could be attained under any political or economic conditions. They sang hymns to Man who can make life what he wills it to be, and they despised those who were chained to their occupations, particularly the peasant, slave of the soil. It was a new and vigorous note, and fell on willing ears during the nineties. For although individualism seemed out of place in a decade of triumphant Marxism, the ultra-individualistic young Gorky won the hearts of his countrymen with the unheard-of freshness and energy of his protesting message. Acclaimed as a leader, as a stormy petrel of the revolution, Gorky, indeed, modified gradually his extreme individualism, combining it with collectivism, and finally dedicated his muse to the toiling masses. He became the centre of a large group of young writers (Kuprin, Bunin, Serafimovich, Gusev-Orenburgsky, Teleshev, Chirikov, Veresayev, Youshkevich, Skitalets and others), who for the most part depicted city life, the factory, the railroad, the seaport, dwelling upon the new phase of Russian reality—capitalistic industry and its concomitant issues. This cursory survey of Russian literary tendencies brings us to the twentieth century. To make this outline complete, a word may be said about those few artists who have stood apart from all movements and endeavored to serve "pure" art. Such poets as Tyutchev, Fet, Merezhkovsky, Minsky, Hippius, Balmont, Bryusov, Bely, Blok and a dozen others, remained in their lofty towers through whose stained-glass windows they visualized a world of their own. Deliberately they divorced themselves from reality, from the "street," and consequently life, the "street" reciprocated.[2] We may therefore pass over the "art for art's sake" movement in Russia, as an exotic plant of great beauty, which had an extremely limited appeal and influence. Aside from this phenomenon, Russian literature, we may now state by way of a résumé, has had for its motto: Service. Service to the established church and to the theocratic throne, to the end of the seventeenth century. Beginning with Peter, to the latter part of the eighteenth century, literature served the new order in the rôle of a hired courtier. Novikov and Radishchev introduced the anti-government tendency, in the service of the people. This tendency has remained in power to the present day, with certain variations in its application. Thus, till 1861 literature served the cause of the emancipation of the serfs. The peasant, freed on paper, but economically and politically disabled, required the service and worship of the Narodniki through the larger second part of the nineteenth century. With the advent of capitalism and industry, Russian literature became largely dedicated to the service of the city proletariat, of its problems, struggles and aspirations. What saved Russian literature from becoming a didactic sermon, was the genius of its creators who remained artists under all circumstances.

During the nineties Russian society underwent grave search-

---

[2] In times of great public events the ivory tower of the Russian "pure" artists would shake perceptibly. The revolution of 1905 provoked response on the part of Merezhkovsky, Minsky, Bryusov and others. Bely and Blok abandoned later their splendid isolation, and have directed the attention of the young generation, within the last decade, toward social and political problems.

ings of the heart. Compared with the preceding decade of stagnation, of "petty deeds," of cowardly slogans, of pseudo-Tolstoyan nonresistance and self-perfection precepts, this period was one of storm and stress. On one hand, economic changes revolutionized prevailing attitudes and conceptions. The great famine of 1890–1891, which, complicated with epidemics, devastated whole rural districts, awoke the somnolent Intelligentsia to the realization of the need of action, not merely of words, for the destruction of the order responsible for starving the granary of Europe. The revolutionary spirit was enhanced by the simultaneous growth of industries and the swelling of the ranks of the proletariat by multitudes of famine-stricken peasants. The Intelligentsia found a grateful field in secretly organizing workmen, propagating Marxian Socialism among them, and waging political and economic warfare through strikes and demonstrations. On the other hand, powerful currents of thought stimulated mental activity. The Marxians, represented by such brilliant publicists as Plekhanov (Beltov), Struve, Tugan-Baranovsky, Bulgakov, Lenin (Tulin, Ilyin), and other significant names and pseudonyms, carried on a lively and victorious campaign against the Narodniki. The Intelligentsia seemed overwhelmingly converted to the materialistic interpretation of history, yet they gravitated, with Russian inconsistency, toward individualistic thinkers. Gorky's sketches and Ibsen's plays enjoyed an immense popularity and wielded a mighty influence. Toward the end of that decade the Russian intellectual atmosphere had become saturated with Nietzsche.

Life was full of contradictions. Modern capitalism under an archaic absolutist despotism. A wistful generation eager for thought and action, overbrimming with energy and idealism, forced into silence and inactivity, crammed into the Procrustean bed of the censored word and of a clipped, distorted education. The dominant doctrine of Marx, reducing history and life to purely economic processes, and scoffing at the rôle of the individual, and at the same time numerous heroic deeds by revolutionary sons and daughters of aristocratic and bourgeois families, sacrificing their lives against the elementary economic wisdom of class interests and class consciousness. Perhaps in no other country could there exist such a *contradictio in adjecto* as Nietzschean Socialism. How can one reconcile Nietzsche's aristocraticism, his hatred for democracy, his contempt for the rabble, his glorification of inequality, with the levelling collectivism of the Socialist teaching! But the Russian intellectual has ever been eclectically synthetic. He gathers honey from various flowers, mixes it, and concocts a composite meal to his taste. One may add that his taste is nearly always of the negative variety. In the twenties and thirties the Russian intellectual borrowed from Byron his note of revolt against society, the only Byronic feature which appealed to him. Of Marx he eagerly adopted the negative side, namely, his critique of the capitalistic order, while finding difficulty in digesting his positive doctrines, such as his interpretation of history. Gorky's tone of rebellion won admiration, regardless of the positive tendencies one might infer from his writings. The rugged Scandinavians, from Ibsen to Hamsun, always found in Russia an audience eager to drink in their words of protest against the monster of organized society and public opinion. In Nietzsche, too, the Russian perfunctorily saluted the superman, but ardently embraced the philosopher's negative teaching, his transvaluation of accepted values relative to institutions and beliefs.

In this chaotic jumble of ideas and attitudes a voice was needed, which would emanate from one "above the battle." Not a voice of one who dwelt in a stained-glass tower, but of one who, while remaining with both feet on earth and intensely living through its tribulations and tragedies, could analyze and vivisect life with a keen eye and a sharp lancet. A voice of one who stood outside parties and movements, and could therefore be a merciless observer, not bothering about service to any institution or to any class or group of people. A voice which would not be drowned in popular outbursts and blinding passions, but would ring clearly and constantly a note of interrogation, a why and wherefore as to life and its value, as to man, his destinies and beliefs and quests.

Such a voice came from Leonid Andreyev.

II

General characteristics of Andreyev as a writer.—Philosophic problems.—
Unanswered questions.—Lack of detachment.—Gravity.—Un-
evenness.—Multiplicity of styles.—Reason for his influence.—
One of the rank and file.—Perpetual tocsin.—Lunacharsky's
estimate of Andreyev's position.

UNLIKE the majority of his predecessors and contemporaries,
Leonid Andreyev advocates no definite political or moral creed.
His problems are not those of particular individuals under
particular conditions. Nearly every story or play of his presents an illustration or postulation of some universal and general
philosophic question, the plot and the dramatis personæ serving merely as incidental accessories. He is mainly occupied
with the problem of life, of its purpose and value, and he approaches his problem with no ready solutions or definite formulas
and prescriptions. Everlastingly querying and setting forth
questions, he quails before the task of answering them. Usually
he leaves them open. Only rarely, and then hesitatingly, does
he hint at a possible solution, in a veiled and ambiguous manner. The solution itself does not appear to be of import to the
author.

Andreyev fails to give a definite answer because he lacks a
fixed philosophic system. To create, or even to embrace and
follow to the end, a philosophic theory, one must possess the
faculty of detachment, one must be able to regard things in
perspective. Andreyev is capable of searching into the reason
and nature and law of things only while in the very midst of
things, crying his "Wherefore" *de profundis*. He cannot
divorce himself from fleeting reality in order to adopt and faith-
fully adhere to a complete philosophic system, which aspires to
settle all difficulties once and for all. His mistress is neither
philosophy nor art, but fickle, ever-evolving life. This mistress

13

he serves and contemplates, adores and hates, doubts and denies, repudiates and glorifies—from close observation. Hence Andreyev's meditation is grave, too grave for the non-Russian reader. He is never at ease in Zion. His is not the joyous wisdom of Nietzsche, one of his most kindred spirits. Still less does he suggest the Gallic gracefulness of Anatole France, who contemplates our human follies from a lofty tower, and chuckles amusedly at the silly comedy of life, minding Montaigne's aphorism: "How sweet to recline on a pillow of doubts!"

This gravity, this proximity to his subject matter, weighs heavily on Andreyev's art. His art suffers from too much earnestness, from lack of light-footed springiness, from lack of the sense of humor which comes with aloofness.[1] His works are not evenly artistic. At times he shrieks, horrified, and wishing to horrify his reader. Nature is to him usually, as it always is to Thomas Hardy, blind, evil, fatal. But while Hardy suggests this notion, Andreyev drives it into your head with a sledgehammer. He often succumbs to words, and heaps up adjectives and similes connoting terror, horror, evil, madness, to the point of dizziness. "Madness and horror!"—the refrain recurring in *The Red Laugh*, might stand as a motto for many of his works. In his weak moments he toots and bangs and waves dazzling fustian rags—and then he is least convincing. At any event, such truculent readers as Tolstoy sneer at screams: "Andreyev says 'Boo!' But I am not scared." He sorely lacks the chaste subtlety of Chekhov's medium, and he knows nothing of the early Maeterlinck's words bathed in silence. Has Andreyev a style? If he has one it is as fluid, as changeable, as variegated as his themes and motives. He is interested primarily in conveying his ideas, or rather his question marks; and as to the medium, the vehicle—all means are justifiable. Thus we find in Andreyev a wide range of

---

[1] Such of his attempts as *The Pretty Sabine Women, Ben Tobit, Love to Your Neighbor*, and a few others, are exceptions, and most of them are too heavily laden with satire to be humorous.

stylistic variations, from extreme realism bordering on naturalism to a symbolism at times impenetrably obscure. Occasionally he even employs mutually contradictory methods in one and
the same work, as in the allegorical *Life of Man,* where amidst
a symbolistic setting we are treated to the most realistic shrieks
of a woman in travail.

Why, then, is Andreyev one of the most compelling of
modern writers? We have indicated that he bears no definite
moral or social message, that he has not created any philosophy,
that he has not discovered any new truths, that he is afflicted
with lack of detachment and perspective, with lack of reserve
and of a uniform style, that he is, in short, neither an inventive
thinker nor a perfect artist. What is the reason for his growing influence? Why has he enjoyed such an important place
among his compatriots, that most exacting, most expectant, most
subtle audience?

The reason for his compelling influence lies in the very mi-
nuses enumerated. He addresses us not from above, not with
the decalogue tone of a Tolstoy, not as an Olympian Goethe,
not as a condescending scoffer of Anatole France's calibre, not
as an artist *par excellence* like the early Maeterlinck, not as a
Nietzsche hurling his thunder over our heads into future generations. Andreyev speaks to us as one of the rank and file. He
dwells in our midst, in this vale of tears, a fellow-sufferer, a
fellow-doubter. He is more articulate than most of us are,
hence he utters aloud our whys and wherefores. But he is not
too articulate, not too artistic, not too perfect in employing his
medium, to aggrandize this medium at the cost of the issue.
He is too near to us mortals to be given a place in the Pantheon.
His is the human voice, the voice of the average intellectual of
the twentieth century, restless, questioning, evaluating, sick at
heart of disappointment and disparagement, yet ever seeking,
always searching—if only for the sake of the quest itself.

Andreyev is a compelling author, but not one who can be
"adored," who is "popular" with the masses. For he neither
flatters nor sugar-coats. Unlike Dostoyevsky, he does not even

pity the victims whose misery and pain he depicts without reserve. Pity usually has to come down, whereas Andreyev is on the level of the victims. In Russia, where the writer has been looked up to as a guide in all walks of life, political creeds included, Andreyev made no effort to utter popular slogans. He considered Gorky "the most honest, the most sincere Russian writer," but he resented Gorky's political sentiments and penchants as endangering his artistic freedom. Andreyev, until he began to fail as an artist, stood aloof from political parties, remained outside the Revolution. To be fettered with a definite "Aye" is not the lot of the eternal questioner. A tocsin he remained to the very end, a perpetual alarm clock disturbing his fellow men, forcing them to wakeful introspection, to an alert transvaluation of accepted values.

The failure of the abortive revolution of 1905 brought about a dual reaction in the ranks of the Intelligentsia. On one hand, an attempt was made to replace frustrated idealism by an appeal to the instinct of the gratification of the flesh. Artsibashev's Saninism, or glorification of the amoral male, Sologub's sadistic lyrics and prose, Kuzmin's fragrant panegyrics to sodomism—such were some of the currents in vogue after the fall of the Moscow barricades. On the other hand, a revival of mystic religiosity was to be observed among the so-called Bogoiskateli (God-seekers), the group of Dmitri Merezhkovsky, his wife Zinaida Hippius, Philosophov, Bulgakov and others. These sought after a synthesis between heaven and earth, between Christ and Dionysus, between Greek Catholicism and Western culture. During this noisome period Andreyev held his own, and went on ringing his alarm bell, spurring man's conscience to a merciless analysis of life and its illusions, tearing off the veils and masks from luring phantoms, complacent beliefs, narcotic doctrinairism and cocksure isms.

A. Lunacharsky, for years a pillar in the Bolshevik faction, and a keen though one-sided critic of art and letters, has attacked Andreyev time and again for his "philistinism" (read: anti-Socialism). Yet in the collection of essays, *Literary Disinte-*

gration,[2] Lunacharsky has this to say concerning the significance of Andreyev during the morbid years following the revolution of 1905:

> While some of us, scenting the breath of the Plague, carry on a loathsome orgy of perverted instincts, and endeavor to warm up their benumbed sensuality by means of sodomy, Sadism, and all sorts of abomination; while others burn candles and send up smoke to heaven and into the eyes of their neighbors, lisping variegated psalms and sermons—Leonid Andreyev, in a leathern mask, black and terrible, with a long hook in his hands, goes up and down the city streets, rummages in heaps of corpses and semi-corpses, hurls the rotten flesh into a large pit, pours lye on it, burns it. Should he at this performance perchance deal with his plague-hook a final blow to one who still rattles—what matter? Burn the corpses. Purify life.

This passage, suggestively indicative of Andreyev's rôle in Russian life and letters, fittingly concludes our outline of his general characteristics.

[2] *Literaturny Raspad,* St. Petersburg, 1908.

PART I

THE LIFE AND PERSONALITY OF
ANDREYEV

I

ANDREYEV'S CHILDHOOD, BOYHOOD AND YOUTH

Eventfulness of Andreyev's lifetime.—Adumbrative traits.—Life in Orel.
—Non-conformity and discontent.—Death of father.—At the St.
Petersburg university.—Hunger, and first literary attempts.—
Suicides.—Addiction to drink.—At the Moscow university.—
Painting.—Failure as a lawyer.—Journalism.—Ideal court re-
porter.—Feuilletons.

LEONID ANDREYEV died in the year 1919. The proximity of
this date limits somewhat our perspective, and diminishes the
chances for absolute objectivity and sureness with which we may
approach events historically crystallized. Yet the available
material enables us to draw a fairly comprehensive picture of
the author's life and career, without pretense to perfection.
Andreyev's life and work are so interwoven, so inter-reflective,
that neither can be adequately understood without a comple-
mentary study of the other. The forthcoming pages attempt
to portray his life, on the basis of autobiographic material and
of trustworthy testimony by those who knew him.

The forty-eight years of Andreyev's life mark significant
decades in the development of modern Russia. The year of
his birth (1871) ushered in the decade of active Narodnichestvo,
when the Narod, the people—that is, the peasantry—was deified
and worshipped in literature as in life. In his teens he witnessed the grayness of the eighties, the decade of "small deeds
and petty souls," which came in the wake of the romantic repentant noble and of the romantic terrorists who climactically
crowned their era with the execution, in the name of the Narod,
of Alexander II (1881). In the nineties, his college years and
first literary steps coincided with the *fin de siècle* currents of intellectual Russia, stamped with the influences of Marx, Nietzsche
and Ibsen, influences which paradoxically intermingled. An-

dreyev's talent ripened in the first decade of the present century, years pregnant with hopes and disappointments, years of "madness and horror," of war and revolution, of polluted ideals and sacrifices rendered vain. Finally, his last nine years passed under the accumulating clouds of doom, of the pending collision between the two Russias—the privileged and the disabled. He lived to see the discharge of the storm cloud, the crash of the old structure, and the clumsy attempts at rebuilding by the groping new ruling class. Then his heart burst, to the accompaniment of cannon and bombs baptizing the new Russia.

A photograph of Andreyev at the age of three or four years presents the child sitting in the relaxed posture of a tired old man, with drooping arms, with a disproportionately large head, with dark close-set eyes of a grave, almost inverted look, with a large, somewhat pouting upper lip tightly shutting on the lower one. Lvov-Rogachevsky quotes Andreyev's mother to the effect that even in his early childhood her son looked "very serious," this seriousness taking later on the character of melancholy, which alternated with moments of stormy gamboling and reckless escapades. Thus he was fond of skating on the most dangerous places of the town river, which was close to his home, at times when "the ice cracked and gave way under foot." [1] Mme. Anna Andreyev quotes her husband's recollections of his early life, from which it appears that outside of his melancholy moments he was a regular "bad boy," fighting bloody battles with the neighborhood lads, stealing apples in orchards, gambling with buttons, skittles, and even cards. According to his mother, among the boy's hobbies was a passion for the stage, manifested already in his sixth year. They took him to all first performances, and he was the pet of the leading actresses. At home he would gather the children of the vicinity, and arrange dramatic spectacles.[2] Mme. Andreyev qualifies the last statement with the remark that most of these "spectacles" were played by Leonid solo, himself personifying all the dramatic characters. She adds that his "first passionate love"

[1] Lvov-Rogachevsky, *Two Truths (Dvye pravdy)*, p. 17. Petrograd, 1914.
[2] *Ibid.*

was for a circus Apollo, a bareback rider, whom he watched through a crack in the wall; he embodied this impression in Bezano, in *He Who Gets Slapped*. If to these traits we add the hunger for books, which developed in him with his sixth year,[3] we may construct an image of the boy Andreyev—his serious, pensive disposition, his melancholy brooding alternating with outbursts of vivacity, his literary interests, his histrionic predilection. Here is an adumbration of Andreyev the writer, the denier and lover of life, the personifier of multifarious characters.

The city of Orel (pronounced: Aryól), the capital of the province of the same name, is a typical small town in central Russia. Turgenev lived in that province, and one may visualize it through the sad, chaste landscapes of the *Notes of a Huntsman*. The open spaces of Orel left in Andreyev a craving for broad vistas, for the unwalled outdoors. "We of Orel" is the title of a chapter in *The Seven That Were Hanged*, where Tsiganok, the brigand, expresses through his savage, bloodfreezing whistle the freedom and abandon of Andreyev's native province. In *The City, The Curse of the Beast, Savva,* and wherever he deals with urban life and civilization, Andreyev invariably voices his hatred for the stifling atmosphere of the big city, with its depersonalized, callously indifferent human beings. When Andreyev the reporter leaves Moscow for a short vacation to the country, his style acquires an unwonted freshness, vigor, fullness,[4] just as it does in *Peter in the Country*, when the "boy" of the barber shop faces real nature for the first time in his life. At the height of his success, Andreyev carries out

---

[3] In his autobiographic sketch given to Fidler for *First Literary Steps* (*Pervyie literaturnyie shagi*), p. 28 (Petrograd, 1911), Andreyev wrote: "Reading books I began at the age of six, and I read an extraordinary amount, whatever came to hand; in my seventh year I subscribed to a library. With years my passion for reading grew ever stronger, and at the age of ten or twelve I already experienced the feeling familiar to the provincial reader, which I may call nostalgia for a book." In his later life Andreyev showed his love and even reverence for books on many occasions. One may recall his sketch, *The Book*, or the dialogue of Professor Storitsyn, in the play by that name, with his degenerate son.

[4] "In the South," "Volga and Kama." Written about 1909 for *The Moscow Daily Courier,* and later included in volume I of *Works*, pp. 177–208 (Prosveshcheniye).

the dream of his life,[5] and builds for himself a "castle" in spacious Finland, with unlimited horizons, far from the noisy city. His love for nature and for unfenced spaces was coupled with an inherent reluctance to conform to prescribed regulations and standards. In the Orel gymnasium, the author tells us, he was "a poor pupil . . . always at the bottom of his class."[6] One can hardly ascribe this circumstance to Andreyev's stupidity. His poor standing in that secondary school was recorded not only in his scholarship but also in his conduct—a phase of nonconformity which subsequently tinged nearly all of his important writings. Young Leonid evidently chafed under the ferula of the "classicists," the officially sanctioned educators during the administration of Count Dmitri Tolstoy.[7] From the drab walls of the classroom, from the dull pages of thought-deadening textbooks, the boy yearned for air and sun and skies. In his autobiography quoted above Andreyev asserted that the "most pleasant moments" he could recall of his gymnasium years were the intervals between hours of instruction and those occasions when he was "sent out of the classroom":

In the long empty corridor there was a sonorous silence playing with the monotonous sound of footsteps. On both sides were doors closing off the classrooms, full of people. A ray of sunlight, a free ray, would burst through a crack and play with the dust raised during one of the shifts

[5] . . . "I mean to build a castle in Norway among the mountains: far below, the fiord; high up on the steep cliff, the castle . . . I will build a castle fit for an emperor." *The Life of Man*, Act II (*Works,—VII*, pp. 76, 77).

[6] From his short autobiographical sketch, *From My Life* (*Iz moyey zhizni*), in the January issue of the Petrograd monthly, *Everybody's Magazine* (*Zhurnal dlya vsekh*).

[7] Since 1866, and practically till 1905, the main purpose of the Russian Ministers of Public Instruction consisted in occupying the minds of the students with the study of "harmless" subjects, and thus preventing them from pursuing "dangerous" reading and thinking. In Tolstoy's classic gymnasia, Greek and Latin took the most prominent place. "The students were to gain a thorough knowledge of the grammatical and syntactical peculiarities of the ancient languages, and to be capable of rapidly translating under dictation difficult passages from Russian into Latin or Greek. . . . Instruction in Church Slavic was introduced at the expense of Russian. Natural science was eliminated, the hours for history, geography, and modern languages were contracted, and the study of modern languages was declared of secondary importance."—A. Kornilov, *Modern Russian History—II*, pp. 168, 169. New York, 1917.

and not yet settled. All this was mysterious, interesting, and full of a peculiar, hidden meaning.[8]

This retrospective account may have been couched in terms too complex and labored for the actual experience of a small boy, but it fits well with Andreyev's temperament, his predilection for solitary meditation and for discovering "hidden meanings" in everyday occurrences. It is evident that at an early age he developed a dislike for his humdrum environment, and sought to transport himself into a different world created in his imagination. Thus he recalls in 1908:

When I was a child I loved America. Perhaps Cooper and Mayne Reid, my favorite authors in my childhood days, were responsible for this. I was always planning to run away to America.[9]

Fate, however, forced Andreyev to turn his attention from the romantic Indians to prosaic reality. His father, a surveyor by profession, "of tremendous physical power," died suddenly, at the age of forty-two, leaving the family in poverty.[10] Orphaned while still a gymnasium student, Andreyev had an early taste of material privation, but it was while attending the university of Petrograd, where he studied law, that he "suffered extreme want." [11] He went hungry for days, brooding, alone,

---

[8] *From My Life.*

[9] Conversation recorded by Mr. Herman Bernstein, in his preface to *Satan's Diary*, p. xii (N. Y., 1920). Mme. Andreyev tells me that as a boy her husband did run away to America, but he went only as far as Petrograd, whence he was brought back to Orel, to face his angry parents.

[10] *From My Life.* Also in *First Literary Steps* (p. 28), where he wrote: "My late father was a man of a clear mind, of a strong will, and of great fearlessness. He had no inclination for art in any form, but books he loved and read extensively, while nature he regarded with the profoundest interest and with the warm love which was due to his peasant-squire blood. He was a fine gardener, dreamt of the country all his life, yet died in the city . . . very early, at the age of forty-two (suddenly, from hemorrhage of the brain); in the country he might have lived to a hundred years." One will note that Leonid Andreyev met with a similar death.

Regarding the "peasant-squire blood" of his father: A footnote on Page 245 of Vengerov's *Russian Literature of the 20th Century* (*Russkaya literatura XX vyeka*) states that Andreyev senior was the son of a marshal of nobility and a peasant (serf) girl.

[11] *Ibid.*

self-centred, unable to approach his comrades or acquaintances with any request for assistance.[12] One can trace the impressions of those days in most of Andreyev's early stories dealing with the life of poverty-stricken, solitary individuals, also in his *Days of Our Life,* the play portraying student life, where the character of Onufry is autobiographical (according to Mme. Andreyev). "I then wrote my first story, about a hungry student," he relates.[13] "I cried when I wrote it. In the editorial office they returned me the manuscript with laughter. So the story was never published." In another place Andreyev writes of the same incident: "My first literary experiment was due not so much to my infatuation with literature as to hunger. It was during my first year at the university of Petrograd; I suffered severe hunger, and in despair wrote an atrocious story— *Concerning a Hungry Student.* At the office of *The Week* (*Niedielya*), whither I brought my story in person, they returned it to me with a smile. I do not remember what has become of it. Later I made a few earnest attempts at breaking into print: I sent stories to *The Northern Messenger* (*Syeverny Vyestnik*), to *The Field* (*Niva*), and I cannot recall to what other periodicals, and from everywhere I received rejections, on the whole justifiable—the things were wretched. These failures affected me in such a way that by the time of my graduation from the university—that is, at the age of twenty-seven—I gave up all thought of literature, and decided in earnest to become an attorney." [14]

In view of his boyhood dreams, the discouragement which Andreyev met at his first literary attempts must have pained him sharply. We have mentioned the fact that he was a voracious reader even before his teens. At the age of thirteen or fourteen his reading assumed encyclopedic dimensions. "My conscious attitude to books I consider to have begun," he recorded later, "with my reading of Pisarev, soon followed by Tolstoy's *What Is My Faith?* This took place while I was in the fourth

12 *Ibid.*
13 *Ibid.*
14 *First Literary Steps,* p. 30.

or fifth class of the gymnasium, and I then became simultaneously a sociologist, a philosopher, a natural scientist, and everything else. I bit into Hartmann and Schopenhauer, and at the same time learned by heart Moleschott's book on food. At twenty I was well acquainted with all of Russian and foreign literatures (translated). Certain authors, as, for instance, Dickens, I reread about ten times." [15] The desire to emulate his favorite authors, a desire common to youthful readers, was for a time checked by a rival passion for painting, of which more presently. "For the first time I began to think about becoming a writer," we read in his autobiography, "when I was in my seventeenth year. To this time belongs a characteristic entry in my diary: it outlines with wonderful correctness, though in puerile expressions, the literary path which I have followed and am still pursuing to this day. . . . I recalled the diary by accident, when I was already a writer, with difficulty found that page, and was struck by the preciseness and the far from childish seriousness of the prediction which has been fulfilled." [16] He adds that I. A. Belousov, the director of the gymnasium, who was also teacher of Russian, regarded Andreyev's compositions very favorably.

Andreyev cites an interesting detail as to his literary fiascos during the Petrograd period of his university years. He relates the substance of a story he sent to the *Northern Messenger*, then the organ of modernist literature:

My student years were passed in poverty. To this time belongs one of my first attempts at fiction. I wrote a story under the title, *A Naked Soul*. . . . As far as I am able to orient myself in modern tendencies, the story was characteristically decadent, and curiously enough, it was written before Russian Decadence had manifested itself in any noticeable way. I remember that there was portrayed a very old man who had acquired the tragic faculty of reading men's hearts. There was nothing hidden for him in any person. Naturally, the more this "naked soul"

[15] *Ibid*, p. 29. According to Mme. Andreyev, Alexandre Dumas remained her husband's favorite to his very end; he reread him a number of times.
[16] *Ibid*, p. 30. This is probably the entry of which he speaks in his diary shortly before his death. *Infra*, p. 75.

came in contact with men, the more tragic grew its impressions. As far as I recall, there was nothing left for him in the end but to commit suicide. Among other things I remember this detail: The old man saw a fellow throwing himself under a passing train. And, mind, he visualized what the severed head was thinking. I sent this story to the *Northern Messenger,* and I remember the letter of the critic, A. Volynsky, in which he rejected my manuscript for the reason that it was "too fantastic, too out of the ordinary," or something to this effect.[17]

A Naked Soul suggests much of the later Andreyev, both in its fantastic element, and in its treatment of thought as a powerful, clairvoyant force. Suggestive, too, is the end of the hero. Suicide as an attempted solution of life's problem figures in some of his early stories, and also in his personal life. In his first autobiographical sketch Andreyev states that in 1894 he tried to shoot himself, as a result of which attempt he contracted a heart disease, "not dangerous but obdurate and troublesome."[18] We know of at least two other such attempts, presumably one before and one after the shooting. Lvov-Rogachevsky laconically states that "one time he lay across the ties of a railroad track, and let a train pass over him; another time he tried to shoot himself, and still later he wounded himself in the chest with a knife."[19] Of the first adventure we have Andreyev's own story, as quoted by Brusyanin:

I became infatuated with Tolstoy's *What Is My Faith?* and ploughed

---

[17] Quoted by A. Izmailov, in his *Literary Olympus* (*Literaturny Olimp*), pp. 243, 244.

[18] *From My Life.* Andreyev's heart trouble was more serious than it might appear from his own account. Says Lvov-Rogachevsky: "Andreyev's weak heart explains in part his convincing portrayal of the sensation of horror. I purposely inquired of the author concerning his ailment. It has tormented him for more than twelve years. Now [written in 1914] his heart attacks have almost ceased. He would often wake at night with the notion that presently he was to die. At times he began to write a story, obsessed with the idea that it had to be finished promptly, in view of the approach of death. The heart attacks used to be excruciating."—*Two Truths,* p. 26.

Mme. Andreyev has told me that her husband's heart trouble was of a "purely psychological, nervous nature." Granted that this ailment was not physiological, but the result of self-suggestion, the fact remains that Andreyev suffered from it mentally, at any rate. His letters and diary toward the end of his life abound in complaints about his "poor heart."

[19] *Two Truths,* p. 25.

through this book of great seekings. . . . I read it, studied it, but was not converted to Tolstoy's faith. The positive part of his teaching—his faith in God, the perfection of one's personal life for the sake of a single aim, God—did not appeal to me, and I rejected it as something foreign to myself. Thus I retained only the negative side of Tolstoy's teaching. I kept asking myself: What is the purpose of my life, since I have no yearning for God, in accordance with the substance of the system of "the great writer of the Russian land"? [Turgenev's words addressed to Tolstoy.] Well, on a certain clear May night I was in a youthful company. The party had been jolly, noisy, interesting. We were returning along the railroad tracks. Some of the crowd were still arguing, unable to part with the subject discussed at the picnic. Some sang songs, others gamboled, pushed one another, played "leapfrog." I lagged behind the company, and felt gloomy in my solitude. I kept on asking myself: For what purpose do these sing, and those argue? Wherefore and why do they do it? Wherefore and why do we walk along the railroad track? For what purpose was this road built? For what purpose do they, my friends, make merry and live? Suddenly, in view of the coming train, the thought of suicide gripped me poignantly, and I stretched myself in between the rails of the track, deciding that if I remained alive, then there was sense in living, but if the train crushed me, then, consequently, such was the will of Providence. . . . My head and chest were bruised, I was all scratched, my jacket was torn away from me, my clothes were tattered, but still I remained alive. . . . I was then sixteen years old.[20]

Professor S. A. Vengerov adds an interesting touch to this story. Andreyev told him that while testing his fate at that moment, he knew that there were two kinds of engine running cn the Orel-Vitebsk railroad, one with a furnace high from the ground, the other with a low furnace. The latter furnace would have reduced him to a heap of torn flesh, but on that occasion the engine had a high furnace, and the youth remained unhurt.[21] Young Andreyev was evidently a typical Rus-

---

[20] V. V. Brusyanin, *Leonid Andreyev*, p. 38. Moscow, 1912.

[21] In *Russian Literature of the 20th Century*, p. 249. "I cannot answer these questions: let fate answer them," was the way the boy reasoned, according to Andreyev's reminiscence in a conversation with his wife. Curiously enough, Gorky listened to Andreyev's account of this adventure without surprise: he had practiced that trick as a regular sport. The following passage may be of interest as an example of Russian stoicism:

"In Andreyev's account there was something vague, unreal, but he adorned it

sian intellectual, gravely introspective, uncompromisingly self-
analyzing, and ready to translate his ideas into actions, the sort
of youth Artsibashev portrayed in Youri, of the notorious
Sanin.[22]
We do not know what was the immediate cause of Andreyev's second attempt at suicide, by a revolver. We may assume it to have been the combination of his material wretched-
ness and spiritual loneliness, during his early student years in
Petrograd. It was in Petrograd also that his third attempt
took place, as recorded by Brusyanin from the words of an eye
witness. Andreyev was present at a student party, with its regular songs, dances, drinking, and . . . discussions. Though
the year of the affair is not given, we can easily imagine during
the nineties a heated exchange of views among Russian youths
on the burning problems of the day. The oppressive policy of
the Government, the persecution of those university professors
who had the courage of independent opinion, the growth of the
labor movement, the controversy between Marxism and Narod-
nikism, these and many more problems aroused endless discussions at any gathering of Russian students in Andreyev's college
years. Brusanin gives no details regarding the circumstances
which led Andreyev, at the end of the party, to strike himself in

with an amazingly brilliant description of the sensations of a person over whom
thunder thousands of tons of iron. This sensation was familiar to me—at the age
of ten I used to lie down under a moving ballast train, vying in daring with my
playmates; one of them, a switchman's son, performed it with particular coolness.
This diversion is almost safe, provided the furnace of the engine is sufficiently
high above the road, and when the train moves uphill. . . . For a few seconds
you live through a creepy feeling, endeavoring to press to the ground as closely as
possible, and being hardly able to overcome by a strain of your will the passionate
desire to make a move, to raise your head. You feel the torrent of iron and wood
rushing over you, sweeping you off the earth, trying to carry you off somewhere,
and the rumbling and clanging of the iron seems to ring in your very bones.
Then, after the train has passed, you remain lying for a minute or more, unable
to rise. You feel as though you were swimming in the wake of the train, and
your body stretches out endlessly, it grows, becomes light, airy, and you are about
to fly above the earth. This is a very agreeable feeling."—Maxim Gorky, in A
Book on Andreyev (Kniga o L. Andreyeve), p. 7. Petrograd, 1922.
[22] "Perpetual sighing and whimpering, and incessant questionings such as: 'I
sneezed just now. What was the right thing to do? Will it not cause harm to
some one? Have I, in sneezing, fulfilled my destiny?'" Sanin, p. 263. Berlin,
1921.

the chest with a knife,[23] but they were undoubtedly similar to those of the Orel picnic, which resulted in the adventure on the railroad track. The boisterous merriment, drink and dance and song provoked in Andreyev a contrary reaction, a gloomy concentration on the issues discussed, and a reflex expression of his disgust with life and with its unanswerable questions.

Depressed by poverty, self-centred and shy, impressionable and analytical, Andreyev the student felt keenly life's contradictions, and in those days sought an easy solution in escaping from life. It is interesting to note that with all his susceptibility and responsiveness, Andreyev did not belong to the regular type of the "political" student who settled his doubts and queries by joining a revolutionary party, in whose perilous activity he might drown everything personal. Professor Vengerov states that Andreyev "lived the debauchee life of the student Bohème, which he later presented in his plays, *Days of Our Life* and *Gaudeamus.*" [24]   In one of his feuilletons in the *Moscow Daily Courier,* Andreyev recalled one celebration of a university holiday at Petrograd, at which instead of the regular drink and noise he was treated to speeches by famous writers and educators; he was deeply moved by the oratory which appealed to the students' dignity and responsibility.[25] The tone of surprise and enthusiasm with which that event was described, showed that it was an extraordinary occurrence in the otherwise nonpolitical and nonsocial life of young Andreyev. "On the whole," remarks Professor Vengerov, "he remained all his life typically apolitical, untouched by political problems. Even the year 1905 failed to intoxicate him." [26] Of this trait of his more will be said presently.

Drink was to Andreyev probably one of the means for escaping from consciousness. In Russian life it was difficult for a sensitive person to remain a calm onlooker at the political and

[23] Brusyanin, *Leonid Andreyev,* p. 36.
[24] *Russian Literature of the 20th Century,* p. 246.
[25] *University Day (Tatianin den), Works—I,* pp. 167–173.
[26] *Op. cit.,* p. 247.

social national tragedy.   One had to take sides, or else to forget oneself in cards, in vodka, or in death.   The number of
Russian artists—their sensitiveness is patent—who sought sol-
ace in one of these ways, or who have lost their reason, is imposing.[27]   Andreyev was addicted to drink in his student years,
and also in subsequent periods of his life.   Of this he spoke in
a letter to his mother,[28] reviewing his past.   His drunkenness
would come in fits, lasting at times several days.[29]   E. Chirikov
tells of Andreyev's "fits of sadness" which "would end in an
effort to forget himself in the cup." [30]   B. Zaytsev quotes a letter from Andreyev, in which he speaks of his yearning for the
"other reality," the one born by imagination: "this is why . . .
I used to like drunkenness and its wonderful and terrible
dreams." [31]

We do not know for what reason Andreyev transferred himself to the University of Moscow,[32] where he received his di-
ploma in 1897.   At Moscow he was better off materially, being

[27] It would be difficult to enumerate these victims, without falling into literary
gossip. Suffice it to mention Pushkin, Belinsky, Nekrasov, Pomyalovsky, Mus-
orgsky, Garshin, Vrubel, Blok, a few representative artists, now dead, whose tragic
frailties have been substantiated documentarily. Of the great Russian writers,
Goncharov alone could boast of an even and "happy" disposition, at all events,
placidly complacent. Gogol regretted that his revered master, Pushkin, gave so
much of his time to cards, but neither was Gogol spared the need of an "escape."
He was driven into a *mania religiosa* by his keen eye, which saw, in spite of himself, nothing but evil in Russian life. Dostoyevsky found "divine harmony" during
his epileptic fits. Of Turgenev's brooding melancholy over his native land, one
may judge from his *Poems in Prose* and *Senilia*. Tolstoy had to hide the rope
and the gun, lest he be tempted to commit suicide—until he found his panacea in
God-good. Some of the living Russian authors would corroborate my statement
through their personal "vices," were it proper to discuss living men.
[28] *Infra*, p. 156.
[29] G. Chulkov, in *A Book on Andreyev*, pp. 68, 69, 72.
[30] In *Russian Miscellanies (Russkiye Sborniki)*, No. 2, p. 62. Sofia, 1921.
[31] In *A Book on Andreyev*, p. 86. According to Mme. Andreyev, during their
married life (1908-1919) her husband very seldom turned to drink as a refuge
from reality. The declaration of war by Germany caught him in the midst of a
"fit." He immediately became sober, and hardly touched a drop of wine till his
very death. Mme. Andreyev relates another instance of her husband's ability to
rise above his habits and vices. An inveterate smoker, consuming numerous cigarettes during his work, he would occasionally decide to test his will power, and for
several days resist the tempting cigarettes which remained on his desk and in his
pocket.
[32] "Closer to Orel, and more of the Orel atmosphere," is the suggestion of Mme.
Andreyev.

aided by the students' committee, and also through painting portraits for the fee of three to five rubles apiece, but sometimes for as high a remuneration as ten or twelve rubles.[33] He loved painting from his childhood. "I felt a passionate affection for painting," he wrote in his autobiography, "even when an infant. I drew a great deal (my first teacher was mother, who held the pencil in my hand)." [34] As a mature and famous writer, Andreyev still turned longingly to his brush. He said to Izmailov: "To this day [about 1909] I ask myself at times: Which is my real vocation, that of a writer or that of a painter? At any rate, writing I began in my youth, while I do not recall myself without a drawing pencil in my earliest childhood." [35] It may be presumed that the brush served Andreyev as one of the means for escaping into the fantastic world of "another reality," beside such means as the contemplation of a stray sunbeam in the school corridor, or the communion with the heroes of Reid and Cooper, or vodka, or such of his subsequent infatuations as color photography, or seafaring, or the war. For his paintings were not at all realistic, as he admits in his autobiography: "Nature I did not like to copy. I always drew 'from the head,' committing at times comic errors." [36] In fact, he never gave up his brush. There were periods in his later life when he devoted himself entirely to painting, ignoring all other interests and problems. The critic Chukovsky describes Andreyev as he appeared during such a stage, on one of his visits to the author's village in Finland:

. . . Now he is a painter. His hair is long and wavy, he has the small beard of an æsthete, and wears a black velvet coat. His study is transformed into a studio. He is as prolific as Rubens; he does not lay his brushes aside all day. You walk with him from room to room, and he shows you his golden, green-yellow paintings. Here is a scene from *The Life of Man.* Here is a portrait of Ivan Belousov. Here is a large Byzantine ikon representing with naïve sacrilege Judas Iscariot and

[33] *From My Life.*
[34] *First Literary Steps,* p. 29.
[35] *Literary Olympus,* p. 244.
[36] *First Literary Steps,* p. 30.

Christ. . . . All night long he walks back and forth in his huge study, and talks of Velasquez, Dürer, Vrubel. . . .[37]

Andreyev had been complimented on his canvases by such authorities as Repin and Serov. The Academician Nicolas Roerich has told me that although Andreyev's technique was obviously amateurish, he displayed an indubitable talent, "quite Goyaesque." Lvov-Rogachevsky also speaks of Andreyev's fondness for Francisco Goya, particularly for the Spaniard's "Capriccios." Andreyev was probably attracted by Goya's keen power for detecting the beast in man, in consequence of which the faces of his sitters invariably resemble some quadruped—an ass, a goat, a wolf, an orang-outang, or a rabbit. Andreyev, no doubt, appreciated such a gift, a gift which he himself possessed in no small degree. Not fully satisfied with the verbal presentation of his characters, he apparently sought to complement it through another medium at his command— brush and paint. A passage from Lvov-Rogachevsky may shed some additional light on this accomplishment of Andreyev:

In recent years Andreyev has come back to painting, and in 1913 his canvases even appeared at the exhibition of the Independents, and were regarded very favorably by the critics. At present on the gray walls of his castle, alongside of numerous caricatures out of Goya's "Capriccios," hang Leonid Andreyev's pastels, some of which are harshly realistic things, like the portrait of a Finn with an icicle-covered face and with muddy-blue eyes, others—schematic symbols, like the musicians in *The Life of Man,* or the Black Maskers marching in a crowd toward the castle of Duke Lorenzo, lured by the inviting lights [*The Black Maskers*] . . . In his study hangs a large auto-portrait, and in the niche one sees a picture representing Tolstoy in his last days. This painting is a reproduction from a photograph, but Andreyev has succeeded in lending an extraordinary power to the piercing, utterly penetrating eyes of the dying man. These eyes you cannot forget for a long time.[38]

[37] Reprinted with some changes from *Literary Messenger* (*Literaturny Vestnik*), Petrograd, 1920, in *A Book on Andreyev,* p. 43.
[38] *Two Truths,* pp. 33, 34. Mme. Andreyev corrects Lvov-Rogachevsky: the picture in the niche was a copy of a photograph of Tolstoy while he was sick in the Crimea, some years before his death.

While at the university of Moscow Andreyev made his first acquaintance with the "printing press": he was in charge of the department of "information" on the daily paper, *The Russian Word (Russkoye Slovo)*; he had to indicate on what days and hours certain institutions were open to the public. "For this literary work I received thirty copecks a day." [39] It would be wrong, however, to assume that as a student at Moscow Andreyev did nothing more serious than drink, paint portraits, and set up stereotyped information for a daily newspaper. The youth who as a boy had "bitten into" Schopenhauer and Hartmann, Pisarev and Tolstoy, was sure to continue his search for truth among the world thinkers. Unfortunately we find no record of his intellectual interests in those days, but we do find an indirect reference to the fact of his study of Nietzsche at that period. In his story, *Sergey Petrovich*, published in 1900, he wrote of a student, Novikov, who changed the drab existence of the hero by initiating him into *Also sprach Zarathustra*. According to Lvov-Rogachevsky, Andreyev used as a prototype for this Novikov a fellow student who was "extremely gifted and well read, and subsequently became a distinguished scholar. With this 'Novikov' Andreyev at one time tried to translate Nietzsche." [40]

Upon his graduation, in 1897, he began to practice law, but, he states, "I got off the track at the very outset. I was offered a position as court reporter for the *Courier*. I did not succeed in getting any practice as a lawyer. In all I had one civil case which I lost at every point, and a few criminal cases which I

Andreyev's pictures, including the one he considered his masterpiece, "Judas and Jesus," are at the museum of Viborg, Finland. At the Berlin residence of his widow I saw one large copy of a Goya "Capriccio," and was struck with its intense expressiveness. No mere copyist could have put into the work so much genuine feeling and graceful force. One should not exaggerate, however, Andreyev's talent as a painter. Painting was with him, after all, a side issue, one of his hobbies, a recess from his true work, his literary art, which was his life. That in his letters and in his diary Andreyev gave so much space and attention to his paintings, need not be taken seriously. I am told by Mme. Andreyev that when her husband and Roerich came together, the writer insisted on discussing his canvases, while the painter endeavored to turn the conversation on his, Roerich's, bits of writing. Idiosyncrasies of artists!

[39] *Literary Olympus*, p. 244.
[40] *Two Truths*, p. 44.

defended without pay." [41] His failure as a lawyer becomes comprehensible when one reads such of his sketches as *His First Fee, The Defense, Christians,* or the court scenes in *The Seven That Were Hanged* and in *Tsar Hunger.* Like the young attorney in the story of the first title, Andreyev could not stomach the cynical attitude of men of the legal profession to the question of the client's guilt or innocence. His noble intention of championing justice and truth in legal trials was mocked by his experienced colleagues and by the defendants themselves. Whenever he mentions in his works court proceedings, he invariably underlines the presumptuousness of the judges, the sham quality of the ceremonies and the ordeal, and the dominant cynicism of the initiated. It is legitimate to presume that Andreyev was constitutionally unfit for the legal profession, and that he gladly chose the direction of lesser resistance though of lesser remuneration [42]—that of a court reporter.

He must have been a remarkable reporter. At least his editor testifies that "with every day Andreyev's accounts became more and more noted, not only among professionals, but even with the general public. One felt in them a belles-lettrist rather than an ordinary chronicler." [43] We may judge retrospectively what an ideal reporter Andreyev was apt to make, with his detachment of a sympathetic observer. His characteristic trait as an author consisted in his faculty of approaching problems and issues not so closely as to distort the perspective,

---

[41] *From My Life.* In a later statement Andreyev described his journalistic vicissitudes before he obtained his position on the *Courier.* Here is an eloquent detail: "There lived in Moscow an attorney, Malyantovich [subsequently member of Kerensky's cabinet]. *The Moscow Messenger (Moskovsky Vestnik),* . . . invited him to write for it. In his turn he let me attend trials and write reports, while he merely "went over" them, and handed them to the newspaper. My honorarium amounted to four copecks per line. At the office they were quite satisfied with the reports, as long as they believed they were written by an experienced attorney. But one fine day they learned that I was writing them. My prosperity was gravely threatened. It happened, however, that just then they could not find a man for the job, and I was retained."—*Literary Olympus,* pp. 245 ff.

[42] One of the editors of the *Moscow Courier,* I. Novik, states that the fee Andreyev received for his accounts did not cover his expenses, in view of which he was permitted to contribute similar material to the *Moscow Messenger.*—In his article, "Leonid Andreyev," *The Russian Emigrant (Russky Emigrant),* No. 4, p. 10. Berlin, November, 1920.

[43] *Ibid.*

and yet with such keen interest and deep sympathy as to make one feel that he personally had lived through the situations, peripetia, dramas of his characters. In fact, years later a leading critic reproached Andreyev with having preserved the peculiarity of a court reporter, who is interested in presenting the case, the proceedings, the persons involved, but who does not bother a whit about the sentence: "The verdict will be announced tomorrow," [44] as the customary conclusion of Russian court reports goes. Andreyev the doubter, the indefatigable raiser of questions, usually left them open, reluctant, and perhaps unable, to offer solutions. He remained the ideal reporter attending the complex trial which is life, an objective observer who is yet not alien to the parties involved.

Novik and his colleagues urged Andreyev to widen the range of his subject matter. He made a few clumsy attempts, produced a long story of fantastic contents, wrote an essay on the ethics of the legal profession, none of which proved suitable for a daily paper, either in size or in substance. [45] Gradually, however, he adapted himself to the rôle of a feuilletonist, a most important functionary in the pre-revolutionary press of Russia. The Russian reader eagerly looked to the lower part of his newspaper's page for the discussion of the burning problems of the day, in politics as well as in art. Writing in a light vein, the feuilletonist had to perform the delicate task of dodging the lynx-eyed censor by masking his thoughts, at the same time rendering them decipherable for the reader trained in the gentle art of reading between the lines. It is natural that censor-ridden Russia should have produced the most subtle and keen feuilletonists on the Continent. Among them Andreyev could hardly aspire to a rank higher than second. For one thing, he never succeeded in concealing his inherent gravity, he lacked

[44] Vladimir Kranichfeld, in his monthly review in *The Contemporary World* (*Sovremenny Mir*), January, 1910, pp. 86 ff. A. Izmailov quotes I. Novik: "Andreyev's court reports were not the customary press stuff concerning trials in the court room. He approached the question not in the regular journalistic way. The indictment did not interest him at all. The accumulated evidence moved him not in the least. All his attention was concentrated on the characterization of the defendant and of the environment in which he lived."—*Literary Olympus*, p. 246.

[45] *The Russian Emigrant—IV*, p. 10.

the ease, the lightness of laughter that kills, for which faculty were famous such of his compatriots as Doroshevich, Amfiteatrov, Yablonovsky, Kugel (Homo Novus), and many other artful dodgers on the slippery arena of Russian journalism. Still Andreyev, under the pen name of "James Lynch," occupied the lower story on the page of the *Courier* for several years, occasionally contributing to this department even after he made his reputation at a writer of fiction.[46]   Evidently he was a drawing card, for the editors would not have kept him on a salary for such platonic reasons as his beautiful dark eyes.

Some of his feuilletons were subsequently published in the first volume of Andreyev's collected works (1911).   They deal with a wide variety of topics, from meditations on the Christmas-eve suckling pig to bitter denunciations of the whimpering Intelligentsia, from such hackneyed themes as the tribulations of suburbanites to reviews of important plays.   In spite of the puerility and half-baked wisdom which characterize many of these writings, they are valuable as roadstones in the course of the author's evolution.   They show us the young journalist in his shirt sleeves, discussing things directly, not through the veil of art.   Here he is more outspoken in his views and preferences, which foreshadow the hidden and masked meanings of his later works, and which also show much more clearly the influences contributary to their formation.

[46] As late as 1903 he contributed to the *Courier* a feuilleton under the regular title of "Life's Trifles"; though in January of the same year he stated: "Now I devote myself exclusively to fiction. I rarely write articles of a general nature." —*From My Life.*

II

ANDREYEV'S FEUILLETONS

Motives in Andreyev's feuilletons.—*The Sphinx of Modernity.*—Ibsenite individualism, and contradictory notes.—Buoyancy.—Denounces Chekhovian melancholy.—Greets Gorky.—Love for life, in spite of its drawbacks.—Avowed influences.—Nietzschean motives.— Illusionism.—Desire to escape responsibility.—Andreyev's view of the writer's mission.—Intense sincerity in his creations.

THE future analyst of the modern soul became early aware of the complexity and contradictoriness of his subject matter. In *The Sphinx of Modernity* [1] Andreyev draws the difference between the harmony in the ethical, social and mental life of the ancient man, and the chaos reigning within the modern individual. How definite and consistent were relations in pagan Rome, in comparison with our day, when "there are no pagans or Christians, but a mixture of both; no masters or slaves, but a mixture of both." Our thoughts and acts, moods and principles are mutually contradictory and hostile, yet intertwined and inseparable like a "many-colored skein."

Who is he—this citizen of the twentieth century, this sphinx of modernity?

He weeps over a book describing the suffering of the destitute, demands these books and these tears, yet with every tread of his sole he crushes living beings. He augments vice to a degree which would astonish Rome and decadent Byzantium, and demands of art chastity and shrinking modesty, approving only of plays ending with the triumph of virtue. He cries insistently and peremptorily, "Thou shalt not kill," and goes forth to kill, and weeps while killing.

Impotent in vice as well as in virtue, perpetually warring with a thousand foes that nestle in his head and heart, with one hand giving bread, with the other taking it away—he weeps without grief and laughs with-

---

[1] *Works—I*, pp. 53, 54.

out joy. His tongue has split into a thousand tongues, and he does not know himself when he lies and when he tells the truth—this unfortunate sphinx of modernity, who vainly attempts to solve his own riddle and who perishes without solving it!

This chaos of the modern mind Andreyev was to gauge in his art. In the meanwhile, as a journalist, he merely juxtaposes conflicting elements and attitudes, unable to reconcile contradictions or to adopt a definite, uncompromising point of view. He is torn between individualism and collectivism, between optimism and pessimism, between realism and symbolism—but throughout these flounderings one feels his earnestness and sincerity: the writer is not so much instructing his audience as he is trying to find himself, to clarify his own doubts.

The effect of Ibsen on young Andreyev is shown in the latter's enthusiastic reviews of *An Enemy of the People, The Wild Duck, When We Dead Awaken,* the plays presented by the recently established Moscow Art Theatre at the end of the nineties. The artistic production of the plays by the troupe of Stanislavsky enhances the admiration of the young reviewer. In the fourth act of *An Enemy of the People*

the power of suggestion coming in waves from the stage into the auditorium, reaches the highest strain. The drama of one man is transformed into the drama of all mankind. Before the eyes of the indignant spectators honor, justice and truth perish under the onslaught of a mad, egotistic, blinded mob. Stockman gains in stature . . . he is the suffering spirit of mankind, pining in the fine net of commonplace, stupidity, and cheap malice.[2]

He quotes and paraphrases Ibsen's heroes, comments and philosophizes on the questions involved with the devotion of a disciple. Ibsen and Stanislavsky succeed in pervading the audience with hatred for the mob, for the tyrannical majority, and with admiration for the solitary free spirits who perish gloriously in the unequal battle. And though this very public is probably a criminal mob when outside the theatre, throwing

[2] *Works—I,* p. 275.

stones at the Stockmans, and stifling them with trivial stupidity, yet for a moment they are regenerated.

Is it not precious to live through such a moment of spiritual purgation, and then, perhaps for the rest of your life, remember that at least for a few minutes you have succeeded in living, feeling, and thinking like a man, instead of bleating and wagging your ingratiating tail like one of the great herd.[3]

Ibsen's individualistic note struck a sympathetic ear in Andreyev, most of whose feuilletons, even the earliest, voice contempt for the spirit of gregariousness, for the "tyranny of conventional pettiness," for the common aspiration to be "like everybody else." The future author of *The Life of Man, The Curse of the Beast* and other works exposing the bane of our life, sameness, is anticipated in his *Courier* philippics against the machine-made, stereotyped interiors of modern homes,[4] the fear of the average citizen to be the first in any new undertaking or departure from convention, his "agoraphobia," manifested in his dread of doing things alone, as an individual,[5] his perpetual gossip on similar themes, in similar expressions, with similar jokes, tinged with the same feeling of hopeless ennui.[6] Andreyev suffocates in the stale atmosphere of herd psychology and herd action, and he yearns for the sharply outstanding individual, for the "enemy of the people."

Andreyev, as will appear later, seldom showed any consistent adherence to one theory or point of view. His contempt for the mob, for the average, did not lift him to the isolated peaks where dwell such aristocrats as Nietzsche. To the end he was torn between hatred and love for the human mass.[7] Alongside such diatribes as those quoted above, which voice the Doctor Stockman attitude to the "majority," we find in his feuilletons quite "democratic" passages. By such we mean not the

[3] *Ibid*, p. 277.
[4] *Ibid*, p. 38.
[5] *Ibid*, p. 63.
[6] *Ibid*, pp. 77–87, passim.
[7] Recall his different and contradictory treatment of the masses in *To the Stars, Savva, Thus It Was, The Seven That Were Hanged, Tsar Hunger, He Who Gets Slapped*.

expressions of sympathy and compassion for the submerged, for Dostoyevsky's "humiliated and offended" [8] : pity does not exclude contempt. But one hears the note of respect in his reference to "the ordinary, gray crowd, which composes the very kernel of life, while those culturally refined are only its showy side . . . The gray, stubborn crowd, which moves inexorably and heavily, while those culturally refined hop over it like fleas, and shout with importance: Right! left!" [9] And one feels not only respect but love and affection for just "people" in the passage where Andreyev recalls an incident from his boyhood days, when one winter morning he rode on his skates beyond the town, and from the ice-covered river envisaged a limitless snowy expanse. The majesty of the stillness and lifelessness gripped the boy's heart, and a mortal terror filled him. He tried to shout, but the sound died in his throat. At this moment, when he regarded himself even as a particle of the dead waste, the tolling of the church bells in the town reached his ears, and brought him back to life, to the realization that

There are people! Dear, good, live people! 'Tis people who toll the bells there, beyond the high snowy hill; 'tis they who have now gathered at church, or sit around and drink tea, or still rub their sleepy eyes, but whatever they do and wherever they be, they are all the same dear, good, live people. They call me to come to them out of this icy desert, and presently I shall fly to them, because I love them. I shall throw myself into their arms, I shall press myself to their warm hearts, and shall kiss their bright, speaking eyes . . . I shall tell them how afraid I was in this waste, under the glances of white dead eyes, how stillness enwrapped me as though with a white shroud. . . . They will understand me, the good, dear people, and together we, full of life, shall laugh over that which is dead. I shall fly to them, because I love them, because I am *not dead*. . . . Toll on, summoning bells.[10]

As he lived on, Andreyev heard the summons of these bells ever more seldom, and he rarely succeeded in spanning the gulf

[8] E. g., *Poor Russia*, in *Works—I*, pp. 117–125.
[9] *Ibid*, p. 252.
[10] *Ibid*, pp. 264, 265.

of his solitude and isolation. But in those years, at the close of the nineties, he endeavored to fall in tune with the nascent song of joy, sounded by Gorky. He craved for a relief from the Chekhovian mood which had been in vogue among Russian intellectuals for more than a decade. With bitter sarcasm he described the fashionable hypochondriacs of the time, who tried to look like "wet hens," in order to have success in the press, in society, among friends and women. He protested against the popular line, "Gray life, tedious life, gray with drops of blood on it." But his protest concerned only the first part of the phrase, for he could not deny the tragic nature of Russian life under the autocratic régime. And though he proclaimed the beauty, colorfulness, and many-sidedness of life, he was unable, for reasons of censorship, to say anything in regard to the drops of blood which bespattered this life. Thus his attacks upon his melancholy contemporaries left a good deal that was unsaid though it could be surmised, as was the case with most of the public utterances in pre-revolutionary Russia.[11] While employing a large arsenal of invectives against the inactivity of the Intelligentsia, he could only hint remotely at what he considered it their duty to do. Russian publicist literature was in the main negative, for it was easier to dodge the censor in adverse criticism than in positive precepts. Thus Andreyev had no difficulty in upbraiding the Russian "Intelligent" for his pitiable and ridiculous position:

Isolated from the toiling mass of the people, elevated to some limitless height, oversated to the point of indigestion with spiritual food, inebriated with the vinegar and gall of his aimless and pathless existence, numerically insignificant yet regarding himself as of sole importance, lean as Pharaoh's cow, and like her insatiable—he sits in a quaint steam bath, and with all his might flagellates himself with the rods of perpetual and wild penitence.[12]

11 In this respect conditions under the Bolsheviki have deteriorated. Dissenting sentiments can be voiced with more difficulty and at greater risk than under the tsars. To be sure the authorities offer a plausible reason for the rigidity of censorship in Soviet Russia: the conditions of enforced dictatorship, which amount to a state of constant war on all fronts.
12 *Works—I*, p. 48.

Gorky's barefooted brigade had already sounded their contempt for the smug citizen as well as for the whimpering, conceited Intelligentsia. Andreyev echoed this new note of impatience with the theatrical pose of protestant passivity, of Tolstoyan nonresistance, of hypertrophied introspection, of self-enamored melancholy, assumed by the Intelligentsia since the collapse of the revolutionary Narodniki in the eighties. But what was the Intelligentsia to do? All open public activity, unless subservient to the Government, was forbidden. Clandestine revolutionary propaganda among the people, the peasants, had been proved futile by the heroic Narodniki. The reply of Gorky and his circle could not be stated openly, but its implied meaning was transparent: A new class clamored for attention and guidance—the proletariat. of the cities. The decade of the nineties witnessed the artificially rapid growth of Russian industries, and its resultant industrial crisis. The first condition was responsible for the increase in the number of factory workers, while the second condition made these workers susceptible to revolutionary propaganda. Hence Andreyev's indignation at the passive whining of the Intelligent anent the "gray, tedious life," at a time when "at his very side, into his very ears, sound summoning voices: 'Men, give us men, for behold, here is a good cause, here is good work; but there is no one to undertake it.' " [13]   The hypochondriacs slandered life, shrouded Russia in gloom, made all leaves on all trees "rustle something sad, transformed all curly birches into weeping willows, all oaks into cudgels." [14]   This melancholy was perhaps due, as we may interject, to isolation and ignorance of the people on the part of the Intelligentsia. Since Peter the Great there had existed two Russias, the cultured minority and the illiterate masses, and as time went on the abyss between them grew wider and deeper. The brooding, bored intellectual does not know, insinuated Andreyev, that

Below—far below—abysmally separated from this hapless Do-nothing, lives and powerfully breathes the toiling mass. For us it is asleep; for us

[13] *Ibid.*, p. 49.
[14] *Ibid.*, p. 51.

its breathing is only a sign of senseless force. But do we know of what this mass is dreaming? Were we to know, we might find something joyous and invigorating in these dreams, might find them less misty than they seem to those who look from above.[15]

The note of joy and vigor recurs throughout Andreyev's feuilletons on the threshold of the twentieth century. In his descriptions of spring, of the Volga, of Russian Easter, in his dramatic reviews, he sings praises to life and to the joy of living. "One should live joyfully. One should live joyfully," he reiterates and italicizes these words,[16] so unusual in the Russia of the nineteenth century. And with assurance he states that "the song of pessimism is sung and buried," adding the reservation that he refers not to philosophic pessimism, but to "the pessimism of the average burgher, which is dull enough to kill flies."[17] He is far from justifying life as it is, but while mercilessly attacking evil and ugliness he regards them as excrescences which dim but do not annul the value of life. With all his dislike for Chekhov's characters (if this term can be applied to his will-less, boneless, characterless individuals), because "they are destitute of an appetite for life,"[18] Andreyev pays a glowing tribute to the performance of *Three Sisters* at the Moscow Art Theatre. The pathos of the thwarted hopes and dreams of the three women brings tears to his eyes and haunts his mind for days, but it does not disparage his love for life. He reiterates:

What a pity about the sisters. How sad . . . And how madly one yearns to live![19]

For, indeed, the sad story of Chekhov's three sisters is saturated with deep craving for life, for beauty, for light. What if the strivings remain unfulfilled, the dreams are shattered, the hopes broken! The hymn of life sounds in the very tragedy of the sisters, "and only he who has not been able to hear the triumphant cry of life in the groans of a dying person, can fail

---

[15] *Ibid.*, p. 49.
[16] *Ibid.*, p. 39.
[17] *Ibid.*, p. 60.
[18] *Ibid.*, p. 255.
[19] *Ibid.*, p. 254.

to perceive this." [20]   Here we find a clue to Andreyev's attitudes in their variations in the course of his evolution.   In spite of his reputation as an "apostle of gloom," he invariably manifests his love for life, with all its conflicts, sufferings, disappointments.   He considers erroneous the prevailing conviction that "if a person weeps, is ill and tormented, it follows that he does not wish to live and does not love life; but if he laughs, is healthy and stout, then he wishes to live and loves life." [21] After seeing the heartbreaking tragedy of the three sisters, Andreyev feels his love for life enhanced and whetted.   A similar feeling he experiences when the curtain drops on Ibsen's disenchanting *Wild Duck,* a play which he regards as surcharged with the joy of life, perhaps against the wish of its author.   Both Chekhov and Ibsen are painfully aware of life's folly and vulgarity, falseness and violence, pettiness and futility, but, according to Andreyev, pessimism may reach a fatal line at which it crosses "most innocently" into optimism. "In condemning all life, one becomes its involuntary apologist. I never believe so much in life as when reading the 'father' of pessimism, Schopenhauer.   Here is a man who thought as he did—and lived.   Consequently, life is powerful and invincible." [22]

The reference to Schopenhauer at this formative stage of Andreyev raises the question of the literary influences exerted on the young writer.   In a letter written in 1908, Andreyev acknowledges the "strong influence of Pisarev, then of *What Is My Faith?* (*My Religion*), then of Hartmann and Schopenhauer, then of Nietzsche." [23]   No Russian intellectual of the latter part of the nineteenth century escaped altogether the influence of Pisarev, the champion of Nihilism during the sixties, who called upon the youth to destroy all conventions, to smash right and left, and to uphold only those things which are capable of surviving the general smashup.   The influence of Tolstoy was also primarily of the negative category, for while very few

---

[20] *Ibid.,* p. 255.
[21] *Ibid.,* p. 255.
[22] *Ibid.,* p. 285.
[23] *Two Truths,* p. 24. See also *supra,* pp. 26, 27.

accepted his positive teaching, his criticism of established institutions and beliefs found a ready soil in the minds of the quizzical and ever doubting Russian youth.[24] Similarly widespread had been the influence of Schopenhauer, particularly since the eighties, when the passivity of the Intelligentsia sought justification in such doctrines as nonresistance (Tolstoy) or the denial of the will to live, the latter doctrine superficially corresponding with the prevailing melancholy mood of the Chekhovian variety. Less known at that time was Nietzsche, for in its Russian translation *Also sprach Zarathustra* appeared as late as 1900.[25] Andreyev evidently read this work in the original. The first direct mention of Zarathustra and the superman occurs in Andreyev's story *Sergey Petrovich* (published in 1900), where the Nietzschean termination of an unsuccessful life through "voluntary death" is suggested. Nietzschean motives are evident in some of Andreyev's dramatic reviews of that period, definitely and explicitly in the review of Gerhart Hauptmann's *Michael Kramer*, implicitly in the review of Ibsen's *Wild Duck*, which was presented somewhat earlier.[26] Thus he sententiously states in the latter review that "one of the most desperate 'wild ducks' manufactured by the human race is so-called 'truth.'"[27] Or again, discussing the question of falsehood and truth, he comes to the conclusion that "truth is that which justifies life and intensifies it, while that which harms life is always and everywhere false, though it be mathematically proven."[28] He is not dismayed by Ibsen's dethronement of human truths, he is not terrified by the interminable conflicts and

24 See *supra*, p. 28 ff., for Andreyev's account of Tolstoy's influence on him.

25 Ivan Lavretsky, in *A Sketch of L. Andreyev* (*Independent*, 67: p. 242) asserts that Andreyev was responsible for the first Russian translation of *Also sprach Zarathustra*. I have been unable to verify this statement, which seems doubtful, if only for the reason that Andreyev's knowledge of German was slight. See *supra*, p. 35. In 1900 there appeared four Russian translations of *Zarathustra*, as recorded by *The Book Messenger* (*Knizhny Vyestnik*), for 1900, pp. 66, 134, 146, 165.

26 Both plays were given at the Moscow Art Theatre during the season of 1901-1902. The repertoire of this theatre is given by Oliver Sayler, in his *The Russian Theatre under the Revolution*, pp. 25-27. Boston, 1920.

27 *Works—I*, p. 286.

28 *Ibid.*, p. 284.

struggles which men carry on in the name of "wild ducks," lame illusions, tattered ideals.

I rejoice at this struggle. Victorious will prove neither truth nor falsehood. That will conquer which is in alliance with life itself, that which strengthens its roots and justifies it. Only that which is useful for life survives, all that is harmful for it perishes sooner or later, perishes fatally, irretrievably. To-day it may stand firm as an indestructible wall, against which the heads of the most noble men are smashed in fruitless struggle; to-morrow it will fall. It will fall, because it has presumed to arrest life itself.[29]

There is a striking resemblance between the substance of the quoted passage and Nietzsche's attitude toward life, as it is epitomized by Professor Henri Lichtenberger:

. . . du moment où je vie, *je veux* que la vie soit aussi exubérante, aussi luxuriante, aussi tropicale que possible, en moi et hors de moi. Je dirai donc "oui" à tout ce qui rend la vie plus belle, plus digne d'être vécue, plus intense. S'il m'est démontré que l'erreur et l'illusion peuvent servir au dévelopment de la vie, je dirai "oui" à l'erreur et à l'illusion; s'il m'est démontré que les instincts qualifiés de "mauvais" par la morale actuelle—par exemple la dureté, la cruauté, la ruse, l'audace téméraire, l'humeur batailleuse—sont de nature à augmenter la vitalité de l'homme, je dirai "oui" au mal et au péché; s'il m'est démontré que la souffrance concourt aussi bien que le plaisir à l'education du genre humain, je dirai "oui" à la souffrance. Au contraire, je dirai "non" à tout ce qui diminue la vitalité de la plante humaine. Et si je decouvre que la verité, la vertue, le bien, en un mot toutes les valeurs reverées et respectées jusq'a present par les hommes sont nuisible à la vie, je dirai "non" à la science et à la morale.[30]

The review of the next play, *Michael Kramer*, Andreyev writes more definitely "under the sign" of Nietzsche, as one may judge from the very title of the article, *If your life is a failure, let your death be a success.*[31] He justifies the death of

---

[29] *Ibid.*, pp. 287, 288.
[30] *La philosophie de Nietzsche*, pp. 105, 106. Paris, 1905.
[31] *Works—I*, pp. 291–299. The title is a paraphrase of Nietzsche's aphorism: "Manchen misräth das Leben: ein Giftwurm frisst sich ihm an's Herz. So möge er zusehn, dass ihm das Sterben um so mehr gerathe." *Also sprach Zarathustra*: "Vom freien Tode."

Arnold Kramer as the best solution for one who is unfit for life. Men, like wolves, kill their wounded mates.

Both men and wolves act unconsciously, but while wolves perform this simply and naïvely, men mask it with words and with fruitless feelings of pity and compassion. He who is unfit for struggle becomes unfit also for life, its synonym, and no matter how many compassionate hands extend to support the falling man, they will prove fatally impotent. Even worse: intending to support, those same compassionate hands will most surely push him into the waiting pit.[32]

Later Andreyev will turn again and again to the question of the place of the weak in life (*Life of Vasily Fiveysky, Darkness, Savva*), and also to the value of pity (*Darkness, Savva, Judas Iscariot, The Seven That Were Hanged*). Voluntary death as a Nietzschean solution of an unsuccessful life will be suggested in *Sergey Petrovich*.

Without going into analysis, it is sufficient at this juncture merely to indicate wherein Andreyev the journalist anticipates Andreyev the artist. For the same purpose one may mention here two other motives suggested in the feuilletons and repeated in later works. Illusion as a panacea, as a means for lending life sense and intensifying it, is advocated in the review of *The Wild Duck*. Man's power consists not in his logical reasoning, but in "his wonderful elasticity, in his exclusive faculty of discovering for himself everywhere and always a 'wild duck.' "[33] We shall find this note repeated a number of times in his stories and plays, in *The Little Angel, The Foreigner, The Life of Vasily Fiveysky, Savva, Anathema,* and elsewhere. Another motive is foreshadowed at the conclusion of the review of *An Enemy of the People*. The title of the review is *Dissonance*, suggested by the stolid stupidity of the droshky driver, with whom the writer tries to enter into conversation, under the influence of Ibsen's drama just witnessed.

And each of us performed his mission. He drove me, and I thought about him. About him and the like of him, beasts and domestics, about

[32] *Works—I*, p. 295
[33] *Ibid.*, p. 288.

their stupidity and bestial feelings, about the gulf which separates them from us, loftily solitary in our proud striving toward truth and freedom. For a single moment (it was a strange sensation) there flamed up in me a hatred for Doctor Stockman, and I had a desire to part with my free solitude and to dissolve in this gray, dull mass of semi-humans. Possibly I might have in another moment mounted the driver's box, but luckily we came to the end of the journey.[34]

This morbid desire to renounce the responsibility of a cogitative and noble life in exchange for comfortable abandon in the mire of the lowly and the degenerate, recurs in *Darkness*, in *Sashka Zhegulev*, in *Professor Storitsyn*, in *He Who Gets Slapped*, in *Samson Enchained*.

Before parting with this stage in Andreyev's career, it is interesting to note his early attitude to the reader, and his early conception of the mission of the writer. These two points are illuminated in the two articles printed at the end of the first volume of his *Works*. He frankly tells the reader that though he writes a feuilleton for him day after day, he does not love him—that "mail box into which you daily drop a letter." [35] The reader picks up indifferently that which may have been written with blood and tears, he wants first of all to be amused and diverted. Andreyev mitigates his harsh words by consoling himself with the hope that there may be from ten to a score readers "akin to him in thought, mood, and feeling," [36] to atone for the prevailing indifference and lack of congeniality. He is evidently annoyed by the necessity of entertaining the public. "Ah, my reader," he exclaims, "trust not the feuilletonist when he simulates merriment and displays all sorts of verbal somersaults for your amusement. He is deceiving you, because this is what you want. In truth, he is your jester, don't you know this? A real, genuine jester, of the kind your respectable ancestors employed. Trust him not! One cannot trust the mirth which you may buy for five copecks, as one cannot trust mercenary kisses." [37] As a *pro domo sua* observation, this es-

[34] *Ibid.*, p. 280.
[35] *Ibid.*, p. 307.
[36] *Ibid.*, p. 312.
[37] *Ibid.*, p. 305.

timate of the feuilletonist's rôle is certainly exaggerated: Andreyev never plays to his audience, at any events not in the substance of his writings. He is apparently disgusted with the gayety of the tone which he is forced to employ for the concealment of his grave contents. As a writer of fiction Andreyev usually goes against the grain of the public mood, provoking unpopularity, and enjoying the freedom of saying what and as he pleases. In a letter to Lvov-Rogachevsky he says: "I know, the readers hate me; they are facing the sun, while I have turned my back on it . . . But, to be sure, I cannot be insincere, I cannot write about what I do not live through, I cannot renounce my individuality merely because from every direction they shout: 'Step gayly!' " [38]

That a writer must not aspire for success and popularity, was Andreyev's conviction at the very dawn of his career. In the concluding article of the first volume of his *Works,* he speaks *About the Writer.* True, the words emanate from the mouth of a phantom visitor, with whom the author is ostensibly irritated and displeased; but this is the conventional strategy of the feuilletonist who introduces a bogus spokesman for his personal views. In substance, the article discusses the prevailing opinion that there are two beings in the artist, one who creates and one who lives his private life, and that the two may be quite different and divorced. The "visitor" vehemently protests against this view, which he holds responsible for the abundance of mediocre writers who "shine as do the moon and the stars: they illuminate life's pits and caverns, but give no warmth and germinate no new life." [39] They may have talent, which is a necessary thing, just as four legs are necessary for a horse.

But in the same way as four legs will by themselves not make a steed out of an ordinary horse, so will talent *alone* not make one a writer. Through its creative power talent may invent a number of situations never experienced by the author himself: in a state of satiety one may excellently picture the pains of hunger; while perspiring from heat, the horrors of death from freezing; in greatest bliss, misfortune. But these

[38] *Two Truths,* p. 12. The date of the letter is not given.
[39] *Works—I,* p. 318.

will be dead pictures, however skillfully made. They will resemble life as much as a wax doll resembles a living person. Of course, many will be deceived by the similarity: did not certain crows peck the grapes painted by Apelles? Peck they did, but their hunger was not appeased. The word of the writer must be sharp as a lancet and hot as fire. . . .[40]

The artist by grace of God is bound to learn and experience everything in his own person, to starve and humble himself and suffer torture and commit suicide and die—in a word, he must go through the Golgotha of the universe before he can fulfill Pushkin's admonition "with his word to burn the hearts of men." Zola's *Germinal* is unconvincing because Zola was essentially a sated bourgeois who was "capable of saving up five million francs, five million dinners!" Similarly, Gogol's Poprishchin (in *Notes of a Madman*) is but a "wax figure." On the other hand, Dostoyevsky drew his Raskolnikov and his Prince Myshkin and his numerous outcasts and sufferers with the terrible convincingness of one who lived through all the hells he pictured. Garshin gave us the pathos of madness, because he knew the flashes of insanity, and Glyeb Uspensky was able to present with such vivid force the peasant "in the grip of the soil" precisely for the reason that he renounced the life of comfort, went to live in the village, and "wandered across the bosom of Russia's earth as its alarmed conscience."[41] The queer "visitor" would fain have the writers appear as "knights of the spirit," poor in earthly possessions, suffering privation and want, following their inner call with no prospect of material gain. Of course there will be very few who will undertake this thorny road, but these few shall purify the temple and drive the vendors out of the holy precincts. Andreyev says in conclusion:

Well, I have chased him out. But he is persistent. He will come again. Again he will torment me with these unnecessary, absurd conversations—he is persistent and ruthless. And even the consideration of the fact that my visitor is only an hallucination does not console me, for it is more difficult to get rid of an hallucination than of a tangible person.[42]

[40] *Ibid.*
[41] *Ibid.*, p. 322.
[42] *Ibid.*, p. 324.

This was a significant visitation on the threshold of Andreyev's literary career. Indeed, the visitor proved persistent. To the very end Andreyev regarded the writer as the bearer of a high and responsible mission. And though he achieved material success and comfort, he never lost his faculty of experiencing suffering and destitution. The "visitor's" demand that the writer live through madness, hunger, horror, even death, was in a large measure fulfilled by Andreyev. He *lived* the tragedies of his characters. According to Chukovsky,

he did not simply write his works; his subjects seized him as if with a flame . . . for a time he would become a maniac under its spell. . . .

. . . While creating his Leiser, the Jew of *Anathema*, he would involuntarily lapse into the biblical intonation of speech, even in private conversations, at tea. For the time he became the Jew himself. And when he was writing *Sashka Zhegulev*, in his voice were heard the Volga notes of bold abandon. Unconsciously he adopted the voice, manners and the entire spirit of his characters, and became their embodiment, like an actor. I remember how one evening he astonished me with his care-free merriment. It appeared that he had just finished the description of Tsiganok, the daring Orel Gypsy of *The Seven That Were Hanged*. While picturing Tsiganok, he became transformed into him, and by inertia he remained Tsiganok till next morning: the same words, intonation, gestures. He became Duke Lorenzo, while writing *The Black Maskers,* and a sailor when writing *The Ocean*.[43]

The convincing power of Andreyev's art, which renders some of his most extraordinary characters so terribly real and not mere wax figures, emanates probably from this spontaneous faculty of his—to merge body and soul with his characters. Mme. Andreyev tells me that in planning aloud a newly conceived story or play, her husband would saturate himself with the life of each prospective character, mentally investigating his past history, his environment, examining minutely his probable manners, habits, idiosyncrasies and predilections. While molding each imaginary life, he would be carried away by his creation, and would gradually begin to act it, to personify it. Even *The Red Laugh*, which is not evenly persuasive, and where one sus-

[43] *Native Land (Rodnaya Zemlia)*—III, pp. 31, 32, 33.

pects some labored efforts on the part of the author, is reported to have affected him so deeply that upon finishing it "his nerves were utterly shattered, and for some time he was unable to work." [44] Andreyev told Lvov-Rogachevsky that for a long time he could not make himself write down the chapter, "Kiss Him and Be Silent," in *The Seven That Were Hanged*. The scene where the old couple Golovin are saying good-by to their son on the eve of his execution cannot be read without emotion in spite of or perhaps because of the reserve with which it is presented. Andreyev began this chapter several times, unable to continue. "Sobbing prevented him from writing." [45] It is precisely for this hysteria, for this inability to detach himself from his subject matter, that Merezhkovsky truculently questions whether Andreyev is an artist: "In contemplating monstrosity, he succumbs to monstrosity. In contemplating chaos, he becomes chaos." [46] Be it as it may, the quaint "visitor" would have no reason to reproach his host with lacking sympathy with his creatures, with not experiencing the sensations portrayed by him.

Andreyev's impersonating faculty was apt to produce the impression of affectation. We have seen that even as a child he

[44] *Two Truths*, p. 67.

[45] Ibid. p. 120. In his description of the first private reading of *The Seven That Were Hanged*, at the author's residence, A. Izmailov quotes Andreyev as follows: "I have just completed a new work which has exhausted me . . . Only *The Red Laugh* had wearied me as much as this story. After that I found no strength in myself to undertake any new work for nearly half a year. Now the same will probably happen again. Then the impressions of the war settled in my heart so arbitrarily that they excluded everything else. At present it's the impressions of being confined in prison, in the grip of a single thought—the impending execution. . . . By constant thinking about it, by placing myself continuously in the position of the condemned, I have created for myself an atmosphere of hellish suffering, which has grown extremely heavy these last days. On waking up I felt myself in the throes of a depressing thought. It seemed to me that I was expecting something, that presently something dreadful and oppressive would take place, that some one would come in and announce that a misfortune had occurred. Only a few days ago I suddenly understood what was the matter. I had simply fixed my thought on the unfortunate seven convicts to such a degree that involuntarily I shared their deathly anguish."—*Literary Olympus*, p. 285.

[46] *In the Paws of an Ape,* January issue of *Russian Thought* (*Russkaya Mysl*) for 1908. Reprinted in his *Works,—XII,* p. 202. Petrograd, 1912.

displayed histrionic predilections.[47] There is something theatrical about Andreyev's expressions, hobbies, photographs, even private letters. But it would be a superficial judgment to regard him as deliberately theatrical, as a poseur.[48] One is rather inclined to suppose that all his life Andreyev desperately sought an escape from reality, now in suicide, now in illusory rôles. With his aptness for divesting himself of his everyday self and assuming a new one, he had no difficulty in entering whole-heartedly into a fresh rôle, and playing it with the utmost sincerity. This explains not only the convincingness of his characters, who are so many Andreyevs; the need of enacting an illusion may also explain the restlessness in his personal life, his ardent periodical infatuations, now with color photography, now with painting, now with sea voyages, now with the war, in which he wished to find a panacea for ugliness, smugness, pettiness. He seemed always to crave for an illusory Beyond, for a world other than the one in which he physically lived, for "another reality." Says Chukovsky:

. . . contradictory opinions exist concerning Andreyev. Some said he was conceited. Others, that he was an open soul. One visitor would find him acting the part of Savva. Another came upon him as he personified the student from *The Days of Our Life*. Still another, as Khorre the pirate. And every one imagined that he saw Andreyev. They forgot that before them was an artist who wore hundreds of masks, and who sincerely, with ardent conviction, regarded each one of his masks as his genuine face.[49]

Such were the motives suggested in Andreyev's feuilletons, with the occasional awkwardness, hesitancy, inconsistency, and

---

[47] *Supra*, p. 22.
[48] Yet precisely such was the opinion of most of Andreyev's acquaintances. J. V. Gessen, editor of *The Rudder* (*Ruhl*), a Russian daily in Berlin, confessed to me that he did not take seriously Andreyev's complaints of ill-health, during his stay at Gessen's home in Finland, shortly before his death. "I took it for one of his customary poses," said Gessen in a tone of astonishment that for once Andreyev's acting was "genuine."
[49] *A Book On Andreyev*, p. 49.

even banality, which may be ascribed to youth and inexperience. They have been dealt with at some length here, because they possess the value of an overture, which now dimly, now clearly, anticipates the melodies and motives of the main work.

III

EARLY STORIES

Andreyev's first story.—Gorky's response.—The *Znaniye* group.—Andreyev's unpartisanship.—Success of his first book.—The "Wednesdays."—His solitude among writers.—Broadening problems: *The Abyss* and *In Fog.*—Attacks and praise, symptomatic attitude of the public.—His first wife.—Her death.—His gloom.—Growing opposition to his writings.

OF Andreyev's main work, *Bargamot and Garaska* was the first story to be published (1908). It was written for the Easter issue of the *Courier,* at the request of Novik.[1] This, and four or five of the stories that followed it, though displaying indubitable talent, possessed little originality. One felt in them the traditional humane warmth of Russian literature, the capacity for understanding the lowly, and hence for *tout pardonner,* the endeavor to discover the eternally human at the basest rungs of the social and ethical ladder. Bargamot is the awe-inspiring policeman of the "bad" neighborhood, and Garaska its incurable drunkard and scrapper. To have these two meet on Easter morning, become reconciled and mutually respectful—what a typical Easter story, and what a typical Dostoyevsky theme! Andreyev's early stories were more modern than Dostoyevsky's in that they were written in a more impressionistic vein, following closely in the footsteps of Chekhov. Yet, though lacking in originality, they attracted the attention of leading Russian writers, and first of all that of Gorky.

Andreyev's relations with Gorky are worth recording. His senior by two years, Gorky was an international celebrity at the time of the "James Lynch" writings. Time and again Andreyev in his feuilletons mentions Gorky with admiration and rever-

[1] *From My Life.*

57

ence. In his article denouncing the whimpering Intelligentsia, he
consoles himself with the fact that "the time of Maxim Gorky
has come, of him who is the most vigorous of the vigorous, and
with this the market rate of melancholy and its representatives
is falling irresistibly." [2] For one of his articles he uses the title
"Madness of the Brave," followed by the motto: "To the madness of the brave we chant a song," from Gorky's *The Song of
the Falcon*.[3] He devotes a special article to the condemnation
of the curious crowd which annoyed with unceremonious gazing
and whispering the writers Chekhov and Gorky, when the two
sat in the foyer of the Moscow Art Theatre, drinking tea. On
this occasion Gorky addressed the crowd with a few energetic
remarks which voiced his annoyance at its ill-mannered curiosity.
Gorky's conduct was discussed in the press, on the whole sneer-
ingly. Andreyev came out boldly as the champion of the unconventional, blouse-clad singer of the fifth estate.[4] The phantom visitor, while bitterly reproaching the majority of writers
for their superficial, *opéra bouffe* descriptions of the suffering
people, says: "All hail to Maxim Gorky: He has come from
the bottom of life, bringing thence some fresh information on
his stevedore's back, in his horny hammer-man's hands, in his
broad chest, the chest of a freedom-loving hobo." [5]
    Of his first acquaintance with Gorky, Andreyev related the
following to Izmailov:

   . . . It so happened that when the Government suspended the publication of *The Nizhni-Novgorod Leaf* (*Nizhegorodsky Listok*), its sub-
scribers received in its place the *Courier,* by an arrangement of the publishers. Owing to this, my very first story fell into the hands of Gorky
[probably during Gorky's administrative exile to the city of Nizhni-
Novgorod, 1898–1899]. One day, on coming to our office, I was told
that Gorky had written to an acquaintance (to N. P. Asheshov, I think),
asking him who was hiding under the pen name of "Leonid Andreyev."
To this inquiry I replied in a personal letter.
   Thus began a correspondence between us, and somewhat later took

[2] *Works—I*, p. 50.
[3] *Ibid.*, p. 126.
[4] *Ibid.*, pp. 157–161.
[5] *Ibid.*, p. 322.

place our meeting in person. Alexey Maximovich [Gorky] happened to pass through Moscow on urgent business, and made an appointment with me to meet him at the railroad station. He was then at the zenith of his fame. I recall with what excitement I hurried to the depot, fearing to be late, and I remember especially that first moment when I perceived his face, so familiar to me from his portraits, his lamb-wool cap, and the tight overcoat on his tall figure.

To him I am infinitely obliged for the clarification of my world outlook as a writer. Never before my talks with him had I regarded so earnestly my work and my gift. He was the first to speak to me of my talent—a dubious subject for me—and of my responsibility for the use of that talent. He was the first to teach me respect for the loftiness of a writer's profession.[6]

Andreyev has expressed his gratitude to Gorky in warm terms. In his first autobiographical sketch he states: "Maxim Gorky helped me a great deal with his advice and instruction, which I have always found excellent."[7] This was written about 1903. Though there is reason to believe that in subsequent years the relations between the two writers became less congenial, as we shall see presently, Andreyev declared in 1911 his indebtedness to Gorky in even more enthusiastic words:

For the awakening in me of a genuine interest in literature, for the consciousness of the importance and strict responsibility of the writer's vocation, I am beholden to Maxim Gorky. He was the first to pay earnest attention to my fiction (namely, to my first printed story, *Baragamot and Garaska*). He wrote to me, and then for many years he lent me his invaluable support through his ever sincere, ever wise and severe counsel. In this respect I consider my acquaintance with Gorky as the greatest bit of good fortune that has happened to me as a writer. If anything at all can be said about persons who have exerted an actual influence on my literary destiny, then I must point out only Maxim Gorky, that ever true friend of literature and men of letters. It is because of an obvious reserve on my part that I am obliged to refrain from a more ardent expression of gratitude and of a deep, singular respect for him.[8]

[6] *Literary Olympus*, p. 248.
[7] *From My Life*.
[8] *First Literary Steps*, p. 31. Lvov-Rogachevsky adds an interesting detail re-

Gorky, a self-made man, rising from the lowest social stratum to the heights of literary achievement and leadership, was very sympathetic toward young writers, ever on the lookout for some latent talent among the timid débutants. His endorsement of Andreyev opened for the latter the pages of the Petrograd monthlies, those parliaments of public opinion, which in the absence of an open political rostrum in the country served as clearing houses for 'the ideas and ideals surging in society. Gorky "adopts" Andreyev, spends a vacation with him,[9] and draws him into the family of his publishing house, Znaniye (Knowledge). Znaniye becomes the centre of the militant literary youth, the "constellation of Big Maxim," in the contemporary parlance. Gorky gathers around him such writers as Chirikov, Skitalets, Teleshev, Serafimovich, Gusev-Orenburgsky, Veresayev, Aizman, Zaytsev, and even the solitary Chekhov blesses the young braves, and contributes his swan song, *The Cherry Orchard,* to the *Sbornik (Miscellany)* of *Znaniye.*[10] Andreyev finds himself in an at least superficially congenial company. Though of different temperaments and world outlooks, these writers had a common attitude of negative criticism toward existing conditions and institutions, in their external forms,

garding the mutual attachment and congeniality of the two writers at one stage of their career: "During a certain period Maxim Gorky and Leonid Andreyev were planning jointly a play, *The Astronomer.* The idea was not carried out, though Gorky wrote his *Children of the Sun,* and Andreyev *To the Stars.* The chemist armed with his microscope, and the astronomer armed with his telescope, are two answers to one question."—*Two Truths,* p. 38. Gorky's play appeared in 1905, Andreyev's in 1906. The chemist in the first drama, and the astronomer in the second, represent alike the detached scientist who regards the world *sub specie æterni.* On the whole, however, Andreyev's play is more optimistic and revolutionary, strange as it may seem in the light of the political stand of these writers. While Gorky's play was produced throughout Russia, that of Andreyev was not allowed by the authorities to appear on the stage.

9 *Works—I,* pp. 187–190. In a description of a trip to the Crimea, Andreyev relates to the readers of the *Courier* his comical adventures on horseback, in company with a friend, "whose loud voice resounded distinctly, pronouncing his o's in the Volga fashion." In a footnote to this feuilleton, as it appeared in the collected *Works,* the author identifies this friend as M. Gorky.

10 The *Sborniki* appeared from time to time in the form of neatly printed books containing stories, plays, novels, occasionally poems, by contemporary writers. Later translations were added, notably of Verhaeren, Schnitzler, Knut Hamsun, Sholom Asch, Walt Whitman. Altogether forty *Sborniki* were issued beginning with the year 1903, and terminating with the war.

and toward the nineteenth century moods and sentiments extant amidst the Intelligentsia.[11] The *Znaniye* circle and publications bore a definite stamp of a revaluing tendency. In the reminiscences of one of the last Mohicans of that group, Evgeni Chirikov, we find the following observations:

> ... the erection of the literary-revolutionary fortress of *Znaniye,* where gathered under the leadership of Gorky almost all the fiction writers of the time who had revolutionary leanings. I must say that for a time this fortress remained unpartisan, in view of the fact that alongside of representatives of the new faith [Marxian socialism] there convened writers from various shipwrecks of revolutionary thought [Narodniki of all shades], as well as writers merely opposed to the régime.
>
> ... How could the young, militant Andreyev, bewinged with success, help joining this militant group of writers?
>
> ... Having received in heritage the testament of world revolution, about which Dostoyevsky wrote, and which was bequeathed by one generation to the next; burning with a glowing hatred for reaction and despotism, with which the conception of the "old world" was associated, Andreyev joined Gorky, who, on the one hand, had smashed all bourgeois values through his Nietzschean tramps, and, on the other hand, sang hymns to the "madness of the brave" and to the "lofty sounding name of man" (*chelovyek*) ... Gorky belonged as yet to no party, but was just a free lance in the struggle against the "old world," which trait made him akin to Andreyev. The latter entered *Znaniye,* and since that time the names of Gorky and Andreyev have been linked together by their readers and admirers. If they speak of Andreyev, they are sure to mention Gorky likewise, and vice versa.[12]

There was nothing new or unusual in the tendency of the public to regard as a unit writers of different views and allegiances. To the Russian reader the names of Pushkin, Lermontov, Gogol, Turgenev, Nekrasov, Dostoyevsky, Belinsky, Tolstoy, Chernyshevsky, Dobrolyubov, Pisarev, Mikhailovsky, Korolenko, Chekhov, Gorky, Andreyev signify an artistic and ethical unit, an expression of the national consciousness and conscience, a united struggle against oppression and pettiness, regardless of the individual leanings and mutual contrasts of these men.

[11] *Supra,* p. 9 ff.
[12] *Russian Miscellanies—II,* pp. 64, 65.

They were all ramming the same hostile wall, they were all sowing seeds of doubt, discontent, and criticism, even when they were conservatives like Gogol, Slavophils like Aksakov, religious seekers like Vladimir Soloviev, Nihilists like Pisarev, or principleless egoists like Artsibashev. As negators, they were a unit. But when it came to saying "Aye," their differences were many and irreconcilable.

The difference between Gorky and Andreyev, a difference of natures and temperaments, inevitably came to the surface in connection with the choice of a positive ideal in the immediate present. To use Turgenev's classification of individuals, Gorky proved a Don Quixote, eager for action by all means, whereas Andreyev showed his Hamlet temperament. In his story, *Ghosts*, Andreyev portrays two inmates of an insane asylum, one of whom spends all his time in knocking at doors, while the other, Yegor, is bustling with activity around the place, helping the doctors and nurses, caring for the patients, and making himself generally useful. Gorky quotes Andreyev's admission: "The madman who knocks, is myself, and the active Yegor is you. It is in you to feel confident of your power: that is the central point of your madness and of the madness of all your kindred romanticists, idealizers of reason, who are divorced from life through their dream." [13] Both hated the oppressive régime, but while Gorky translated his hatred into deeds, and actively supported the revolutionary movement, Andreyev found himself in no position to subscribe definitely to any party or movement. According to Chirikov, Gorky joined the Social-Democratic party as early as 1903, and in 1904 he "was appropriated for special use by its Bolshevik faction, which guarded him in strict paternal fashion, protecting him" against their opponents and Marxian heretics. Chirikov goes on to say:

As long as Bolshevism remained a family affair within the Social-Democratic party, everything was calm in the fortress of *Znaniye*. But with the advent of the revolution of 1905, the situation changed. M.

[13] *A Book on Andreyev*, p. 20.

Gorky, who had joined Lenin's first attempt at rendering the revolution permanent, left Russia after the bitter failure of this attempt, and settled on the island of Capri, where he shut himself up definitely within the Bolshevik party circle. He retained his rights as editor and "boss" [of *Znaniye*], and the group of writers began to feel the quite transparent guardianship of the Bolsheviki. An effort was made to shake off this protectorate from the island of Capri: the group of writers, under the pretext of the inconveniences connected with editorship from a distance, elected Andreyev as editor of the *Sborniki*. At first Gorky consented, but soon he changed his mind. Then all the writers, headed by Andreyev, abandoned the fortress, which fell under the exclusive management of the Bolsheviki. The quite accidental companionship of Andreyev and Gorky broke off abruptly. . . .[14]

The roads of the two young and successful writers parted. One of them threw himself heart and soul into the revolutionary movement, exalting the all-powerful Narod in a neo-Narodnik manner, and championing the cause of the toiling masses against their political and economic oppressors as *the* solution of all doubts and problems. The other remained "with his back

[14] *Russian Miscellanies—II*, pp. 67, 68. E. Chirikov has enjoyed an established reputation as a writer of stories and plays, and as a reviewer of provincial life for the daily and monthly press. With all due respect for his fame and achievements, one is inclined to accept some of his present utterances with a considerable grain of salt: the embittered exile speaks in him. Maxim Gorky has never been a fanatical adherent of one faction or another. While having faith in the programme of the Bolsheviki before the revolution, he vehemently attacked their policy and tactics after their victory in November, 1917 (a collection of his denunciatory articles appeared in 1918 in Berlin, under the title, *The Revolution and Culture* (*Revolutsia i kultura*). Nor was he controlled by the Bolsheviki. During his Capri sojourn Gorky contributed stories and articles to such organs as the Menshevik monthly *The Contemporary World* (*Sovremenny Mir*), and the Social-Revolutionary monthly *Legacies* (*Zavyety*). Again, it requires a fantastic imagination to detect any Bolshevik "guardianship" or "management" in the *Sborniki* of *Znaniye*, before or after the revolution of 1905. A perusal of the novels, dramas, stories and poems—that is, of all the material which was published in these books—disproves Chirikov's statement. The only tendency that can be discovered in some of these writings may be called socialistic in the sense that the city workmen, their struggles and aspirations, are extolled. But E. Chirikov himself would have signed his name to those contributions, since he was a converted Marxian, according to his admission in the article quoted (p. 61). Then, too, not "all" the writers left the "fortress." Ivan Bunin, for example, also a bitter exile at present, continued to contribute to the *Sborniki* to the end. Even Andreyev, in spite of his secession and his joining a rival publication, *Wild Rose* (*Shipovnik*), in 1906, appeared in the *Sborniki* with his *Savva* (1906), with his *Judas Iscariot* (1907); and as late as 1908 he shared with Knut Hamsun the twenty-sixth *Sbornik*, with his *Days of Our*

against the sun," a "Nay" sayer *par excellence,* a doubter, a merciless examiner and prosecutor. It required courage and unblinking sincerity for a member of the Intelligentsia, a young writer admiringly listened to by an expectant audience, to stay aloof, "above the battle," nay, to question and disparage the revered ideal. "Unpartisan" [15] he remained both in life and in art, binding himself to no platform or programme, and therefore in a position to preserve objectivity and perspective.

In spite of their acute differences, Gorky and Andreyev did not break all relations, as Chirikov's statement might lead one to believe. "There was hardly a single fact, a single question, which Leonid Nikolayevich and I regarded in a similar way, yet our numerous divergences did not prevent us—for entire years—from feeling for one another . . . the profound concern and interest which do not often come as a result of even

Life. Andreyev's attitude toward Gorky even six years after the alleged break —that is, in 1911—may be seen from his autobiographical note quoted on p. 59.

[15] See Vengerov's statement, *supra,* p. 31. According to Gorky, "in the essence of his spirit Andreyev was profoundly indifferent toward politics, only rarely displaying fits of external curiosity for them. His basic relation to political events he expressed most sincerely in his story *Thus It Was"* (*A Book on Andreyev,* p. 25). This story, as will appear later, voices an utter skepticism in regard to political revolution and popular freedom.

E. Chirikov states: "Andreyev never was a member of a party. A man of broad mental and artistic horizons, he felt an instinctive repugnance for our Social-Democrats. They seemed wingless to him, because they limited man's thought and will by various frontier posts and ditches. Of all the varieties of revolutionists, he regarded the Social-Revolutionists with most sympathy: in them there was heroism, there was triumph of the spirit over death itself, there was an approach toward that *man* which "sounds loftily." (*Russian Miscellanies—II,* p. 67.)

A curious detail: Early in 1905 Andreyev "discharged the universal Russian duty" (as he expressed himself in *The Shield* (*Shchit*—p. 4, Moscow, 1916, 3rd edition) ; i. e., he spent a month in jail. Lvov-Rogachevsky names the port of Taganrog as the place of his arrest (*Two Truths,* p. 68), but there is reason to give more credence to Gorky's statement that it was in Moscow, where "at the residence of Andreyev the meeting of the central committee of the Social-Democrats (Bolsheviki) used to take place. Once the entire committee together with the host were arrested and haled to prison" (*A Book on Andreyev,* p. 27). Of course this fact does in no way indicate Andreyev's adherence to that party: under the old régime it was customary for unpartisan but sympathetic persons to assist revolutionary organizations with their residences and mailing addresses. Yet he would hardly have acted in this manner had he felt a "repugnance" for the Social-Democrats, as Chirikov alleges.

The fact of Andreyev's aloofness from all parties is not absolutely without doubt, as far as the last years of his life are concerned. *The London Times* for October 17, 1917, has the following brief dispatch: "Andreyev elected member of

an old friendship." [16]   These are the words of Gorky, spoken retrospectively, after the passing of his old enemy-friend. Aside from their views, the two men were honest and sincere enough to recognize one another's talent and literary mission, to regard themselves as members of the same guild, as fellow artists by the grace of God. Even during the war, when their attitudes became most antagonistic, Andreyev sent his collected *Works* to Gorky (in 1915), with the inscription: "Since *Bargamot* of the *Courier* days, everything here has been written and created before your eyes, Alexey. In many respects my work is the history of our relations." [17]   The Bolshevik coup threw the two men still further apart; Andreyev, lonely and sick in his exile, hurled invectives at Gorky for compromising with the "butchers," for having "sold" himself. Gorky did not "blame him for this attitude," "for he [Andreyev] had been such as he desired and was able to be—a man of rare originality, of a rare talent, and of no little manliness in his quest after truth." [18]   The relations between the two writers were mutually significant and eventful, even if not always congenial and friendly.

To return to Andreyev's first steps, it is worth noting the encouragement he received as a new writer. With the aid of Gorky, the "James Lynch" of the *Courier* became a contributor to the leading monthlies, and his stories roused discussion and

the preliminary Parliament." This took place in the last days of Kerensky's régime. Mr. Gregory Zilboorg, an official in the Ministry of Labor at that time and the author of *The Passing of the Old Order in Europe* (New York, 1920) told me emphatically that Andreyev was elected on the ticket of the Cadets, the party of Prince Lvov and Milyukov, which he had ridiculed in *The Pretty Sabine Women*. In reply to my inquiry, Professor Milyukov wrote that he was unaware of Andreyev's membership in his party, but that Andreyev's views at that time were very close to those of the Kadets. Mme. Andreyev assured me that her husband was elected to the pre-parliament as a representative of the Petrograd newspaper editors. In a letter to Goloushev, written about that time, Andreyev confirms the last assertion. In those days, however, the case was not so much of party issues as of a national problem. To Andreyev the disintegration of the army and the spreading influence of the Bolsheviki appeared as a national disaster, to avert the consequences of which he was willing to support all those whom he regarded as patriots and pro-ally.

[16] *A Book on Andreyev*, p. 8.
[17] *Ibid.*, p. 18.
[18] *Ibid.*, p. 38.

polemic. That his rapid fame was not due to any "pull," but to the intrinsic quality of his work, may be seen from the following incident retold many times.[19] After the appearance of the story *Once There Lived* (*Zhili-byli*) in the Marxian monthly, *Life* (*Zhizn*), for March, 1901, the fastidious critic, Merezhkovsky, inquired in an agitated tone whether it was Gorky or Chekhov who was hiding under the pseudonym of Leonid Andreyev. This story was noticed also by A. Izmailov, a critic catering to the popular taste, who praised the author's "fine sense of stylistic beauty," his "concise and vigorous language, perfectly truthful and sustained in dialogue," and concluded that "if he be indeed a beginner, one may regard him with hopes." [20] In September of the same year there came out the first volume of Andreyev's stories, dedicated to Maxim Gorky, and published by *Znaniye*. The success of this volume is illustrated by the following figures, furnished by Lvov-Rogachevsky.[21] The first edition of four thousand copies was sold out in two months; the second edition of eight thousand, which included two additional stories, *The Wall* (*Stena*), and *The Abyss* (*Bezdna*), was exhausted in two weeks. In all, *Znaniye* issued nine successive editions of this volume, forty-seven thousand copies, a goodly number for a beginner, if one considers the small and discriminating reading public of Russia. The triumph of the young writer was further enhanced when his first book was favorably reviewed by the dean of Russian publicists, N. K. Mikhailovsky, for thirty years the dictator of Russian criticism. His monthly article, *Literature and Life*, in the leading Narodnik monthly, *Russia's Riches* (*Russkoye Bogatstvo*), for November, 1901, Mikhailovsky devoted to Andreyev's first volume, comparing its impression on him with that produced by Dostoyevsky's *Poor Folk* on Nekrasov and Dostoyevsky. The critic found "indubitable, genuine originality" in the stories, with a consistent *leit-motif* defined by Mikhailovsky as the "fear of life, and fear of death." [22] He predicted a

---

[19] Cited in *Two Truths*, p. 44.
[20] *Bourse Gazette* (*Birzhevyia Vyedomosti*), April 9, 1901.
[21] *Two Truths*, p. 45.
[22] It should be observed that the first volume did not include *Bargamot and*

great future for the author, with one grave provision: that he rid himself of the dangerous predilection for "disembodied abstractions," shown in *The Lie* (*Lozh*). This was the only piece in the volume which "disturbed" the veteran realist, who consistently waged war against "fog" and "vagueness" in literature, condemning not only the Decadents of the nineties, but even Dostoyevsky's "abstractions." [23] On the whole the critics were remarkably unanimous in their optimism about the fate of the new writer. Beside Izmailov and Mikhailovsky, he was warmly greeted by Mirsky (E. A. Soloviev),[24] by A. Bogdanovich,[25] by Botsianovsky,[26] by Skabichevsky,[27] by Protopopov,[28] by Shulyatikov,[29] by Burenin,[30] by Yasinsky,[31] to name only the metropolitan critics. He was hailed as a keen observer of life, while Yasinsky considered him a "psychologist-explorer,"

Garaska, From the Life of Captain Kablukov, Young Men, and *Defense.* These stories had the traditional "good" note of Russian literature, each one showing man's better feeling prevailing against his evil impulses. Without these, the volume gave a uniformly gloomy impression.

[23] In a set of his *Works* presented to Andreyev, Mikhailovsky inscribed: "To Leonid Andreyev from the author who loves him in spite of *The Lie* and *The Wall.*" Andreyev acknowledged his indebtedness to Mikhailovsky for "establishing his reputation." After his article in *Russia's Riches,* Mikhailovsky wrote to Andreyev, gave him some suggestions, and requested a story for his monthly. Andreyev sent him his *Thought* (*Mysl*), but the veteran critic evidently regarded this story as negatively as he did *The Lie,* for he rejected it. "He returned it to me," said Andreyev, "with a letter in which he stated that he failed to understand such a story. What ideagenous meaning did it contain? And if it was merely a clinical picture of a person's mental débâcle, then he did not feel sufficiently competent to judge how correctly I drew the psychology of the sick man. Only a psychiatrist could judge in this case."—*Literary Olympus,* p. 250. The story *Thought* was published in 1902 in another leading monthly, *God's World* (*Mir Bozhiy*). During the same year Mikhailovsky published in his magazine Andreyev's story *The Foreigner* (*Inostranets*), which was free from "abstractions."

[24] *Everybody's Magazine,* November, 1901.

[25] *God's World,* November, 1901.

[26] *Literary Messenger,* January, 1902.

[27] *News* (*Novosti*), January, 1902.

[28] *Russian Thought* (*Russkaya Mysl*), March, 1902.

[29] *The Moscow Courier,* October 9, 1901.

[30] *New Times* (*Novoye Vremya*), January, 1902.

[31] *Monthly Writings* (*Yezhemesyachnyia Sochineniya*), December, 1901. J. J. Yasinsky, an old and popular writer, said among other things: "I had no knowledge of Andreyev. On the night when I began to read his stories, and could not part from them till dawn, till I finished the whole book, I perceived that a new star had risen. Of this I am convinced. It flared up in a bright silvery light across the horizon, and pierced the gloom of the early Petersburg morning with its beautiful and mysterious radiance."

though he, too, like Mikhailovsky, took exception to *The Lie,* finding it "un-Russian."

There is no external or autobiographic evidence as to the effect of these critics on the young writer; it is doubtful whether the effect could have been profound or fruitful (the question of outside influences on Andreyev will be discussed later). We have cited his acknowledgment of Gorky's beneficial guidance, but until the publication of the correspondence between the two men (probably not before Gorky's death) we are unable to trace the direction of Gorky's criticism. In later years Andreyev recalled with gratitude the Moscow "Wednesdays," an informal gathering of authors, where they discussed one another's works. He was received into the circle about the year 1899, and continued to attend the "Wednesdays" as long as he lived in Moscow (to the end of 1905). Among the regular members of these assemblies were the brothers Bunin, Belousov, Teleshev, Goloushev, Timkovsky, Goltsev, Serafimovich, Shalyapin (the singer); less regular visitors were Gorky, Skitalets, Yelpatyevsky, Veresayev, Chirikov, Zlatovratsky, Boborykin, Zaytsev, Chekhov, and even the Symbolist poets, Balmont and Bryusov. Every Wednesday some new production would be read by one of the authors, followed by frank and at times harsh criticism on the part of those present. According to Zaytsev, the most frequent reader was Andreyev.[32] The first story of his to be read at the "Wednesdays" was *Silence.* The author was too timid, and Gorky read the story with deep emotion, which was shared by the entire gathering.[33] Andreyev needed sympathy and support, but as any beginner he was in even greater need of restraint; at the "Wednesdays" he received a generous portion of both favorable and adverse criticism. "Once," he relates, "I read there a story, *Furniture.* They reviled it so earnestly that I never attempted to have it published." [34] Teleshev recalls a similar case, with a story of

[32] *A Book on Andreyev,* p. 78.
[33] *Ibid.,* pp. 93, 94. Teleshev's reminiscences.
[34] *Two Truths,* p. 213.

Andreyev, which he names *The Shrew* (*Buyanikha*). It is likely that they refer to the same case, one of them erring about the title. Seven or eight years after that incident Teleshev requested Andreyev to donate a story for some charity book, and since the latter had nothing ready on hand, Teleshev asked for the story rejected by the "Wednesday" group. This Andreyev refused to do, in an indignant tone, but promised to send him a fresh story.[35]

It is doubtful whether Andreyev felt intrinsically at home with the circle of the "Wednesdays," though he appeared with them in various photographic groups, and always recalled them with warmth.[36] The majority of those writers (Chekhov, of course, must be excepted; but he was a rare guest) belonged to the "constellation of Big Maxim,"—that is, they were vigorous believers in the efficiency of the socialistic movement, and in the grandeur and heroism of the nascent proletariat. Andreyev was constitutionally a doubter, a "court reporter" who could see both sides of the case, an observer with a perspective. The year 1905, replete with grandiose upheavals, ardent hopes and black disappointments, demonstrated Andreyev's inability to be carried away by the reigning enthusiasm. After his release from prison,[37] Andreyev wrote *The Governor,* a dispassionate psychological study suggested by the Bloody Sunday of January 22, 1905. In October of the same year, the month of the general strike, of mad hopes, blinding achievements, important concessions by the tsar, and manifestations of popular ecstasy and power, Andreyev composed his *Thus It Was.* "Thus it was, thus it will be" was the refrain of this narrative of a revolution, picturing the pettiness and helplessness of human masses, inward slaves and cowards regardless of political changes. This must have been the last story read by Andreyev for the "Wednesdays," judging from the impression it produced on its hearers, recorded by V. Brusyanin:

[35] *A Book on Andreyev,* p. 94.

[36] In his diary (undated entry in 1919) Andreyev spoke of the "Wednesdays" as his "second childhood period," from which he retained the memory of being regarded as a *Wunderkind.*

[37] *Supra,* p. 64, footnote 15.

The story *Thus It Was,* just completed, was read by the author at one of the literary "Wednesdays," and I remember with what a distraught sense of expectation we rode through the Moscow streets toward the house where the reading was to take place. The streets were empty, timid lights flickered in the houses [the strike was on], military patrols rode to and fro, and at the corners policemen stood in twos . . . and I recall what a dissonance the concluding lines of the story seemed to the hearers. Thus it was, thus it will be: men will conquer their king, then shout over his grave: "Long live the Twenty-first!"

And I remember that many of those present attacked the author: Why was he trying to destroy the illusions on which we then lived? . . . And I cannot forget with what sadness in his eyes Leonid Andreyev, his face pale, defended his lack of faith. He said to us: "Live through your lack of faith, overcome it, in order that you may live and believe." [39]

He must have felt a stranger among his fellow writers, with his keen discernment of delusions, with his determination to approach life, and embrace it, through doubt and denial, after having perceived it with the eyes of Schopenhauer.[40] Moreover, he differed from the men of the "Wednesdays" in that, as Chukovsky suggests, "they were genre-writers, agitated by questions of passing everydayness and not of existence, while he was the only one in their midst who meditated about the eternal and the tragic." [41] The "disembodied abstraction" which appeared to Mikhailovsky as "a small black cloud," and which, he hoped, would disperse, grew crescendo as a motive in the art of Andreyev. After the "disturbing" *Lie* (1900) came *The Wall* and *The Tocsin* (both in 1901), *Thought* (1902), *The Red Laugh* (1904), written in a similar tone and manner. At the same time even those of his stories which were not "disembodied abstractions," but dealt with flesh-and-blood individuals in a realistic style, acquired a broad significance, involving

---

[39] V. Brusyanin, *L. Andreyev,* p. 12. When Andreyev had read the manuscript of *Thus It Was* to Gorky, the latter queried with some annoyance whether the story was not "a bit precipitate" (*A Book on Andreyev,* p. 27). Subsequent events proved the correctness of Andreyev's misgivings.

[40] *Supra,* p. 46.

[41] *A Book on Andreyev,* p. 51.

universal problems of perpetual value. While most of his predecessors and contemporaries in Russian literature interpreted a certain section of life, within limits of space and time, Andreyev began to indulge more and more in treating life *sub specie æternitatis,* in setting forth broad problems, where individuals and places serve as mere algebraic symbols. He begins to display this tendency as early as 1902 (*The Abyss*) and 1903 (*Life of Vasily Fiveysky*).

The frankness with which Andreyev put forth the questions and doubts that troubled his mind, shocked even the Russian reading public, long accustomed to a gloveless treatment of delicate issues. Thus his *Abyss* and *In Fog,* both published in 1902, aroused a storm of protests in the press. He tried to show that our ego is terribly complex and mysterious, that it may contain brutal elements of which we are not aware until the moment when unexpectedly they emerge and manifest their power. But his demonstration of evil was interpreted by a part of the public as enjoyment and advocacy of evil, while others accused him of slandering the human race, and in particular the noble, idealistic Russian youth. Andreyev became the centre of a polemic. He was vehemently attacked not only in such a conservative organ as the *New Times,* but even in the ultra-modernist review, *The Balance (Vesy),* and in the monthly of modern mystics, *The New Path (Novy Put').* The wife of Leo Tolstoy in a letter to the editor of the *New Times* [42] thanked its contributor, Burenin, for stigmatizing Andreyev as an erotomaniac,[43] and proceeded to point out the danger to society of such a writer as Andreyev, who clips the wings of the readers, "wings given to each one of them for lofty flights toward spiritual light, beauty, charity, and God." She further admonished the modern authors that even in depicting evil they must follow in the footsteps of Dostoyevsky and Tolstoy, and "should not illuminate the aspects of filth and vice, but should combat them through illumining the highest ideals of good and truth, and their triumph over evil, weakness, and vice." The

[42] January, 1903, No. 9673.
[43] In No. 9666.

Countess typified the nineteenth-century attitude of Russia toward literature as primarily an uplifting factor. More surprising was the reaction of Anton Krayny (pseudonym of Zinaida Hippius, wife of D. S. Merezhkovsky), a leading Symbolist poet and critic, on the pages of *The Balance,* at that time the organ of the most extreme literary tendencies and of the most indifferent moral standard.[44] A. Krayny portrayed Andreyev as sitting on the bank of a river after an autumn rain, slowly scooping the slush with his hand, and watching with glee how it smacks and creeps down his compressed fingers.[45] The label of "filth" was applied to Andreyev's work also by V. Rosanov,[46] a brilliant sensuous essayist, while Professor Manasseyin took Andreyev to task for some inaccuracies from the medical point of view, shown in his *In Fog.*[47]

On the other hand, Andreyev's merciless analysis of human nature found vigorous defenders in such public-spirited critics as A. Bogdanovich,[48] E. Soloviev,[49] E. Anichkov,[50] A. Bostrem,[51] Father Michael,[52] P. Ivanov,[53] V. Botsyanovsky,[54] and in the larger part of the young generation. Two prominent daily papers, the Moscow *Russian Gazette* (*Russkiya Vyedomosti*), and the Petrograd *News* (*Novosti*), opened their pages for a discussion of Andreyev's two stories. A large number of letters appeared there during the month of January, 1903, for

---

[44] *The Balance* published not only poems and prose glorifying sexual experiences, but also panegyrics to Lesbian love and sodomism. The editor, V. Bryusov, has written powerful erotic verse and prose, while a novel by one of his contributors, M. Kuzmin, *Wings* (*Kryl'ya*), was withdrawn from circulation by order of the authorities, because of its open praise of homosexual relations.

[45] *The Balance,* March, 1903.

[46] *The New Times,* January, 1903, No. 9677.

[47] *The New Path,* August, 1903.

[48] *God's World,* January, 1903.

[49] Under the pseudonym of Andreyevich, in *An Essay on the Philosophy of Russian Literature* (*Opyt filosofii russkoy literatury*), pp. 509–511. Petrograd, 1904.

[50] In *Literary Images and Opinions* (*Literaturnyic obrazy i mnyeniya*), p. 184 ff. Petrograd, 1904.

[51] *Education* (*Obrazovaniye*), December, 1903.

[52] *To Fathers and Children* (*Otsam i dyetyam*), Moscow, 1904.

[53] *To the Enemies of Leonid Andreyev* (*Vragam Leonida Andreyeva*), Moscow, 1904.

[54] *Leonid Andreyev,* Petrograd, 1903.

the most part by university students.[55] Nearly all of these agreed with the critics who took the author's side, namely, that in the first place, the presence of the brute in man is a probability, and not a slander, and secondly, that by showing us evil as it is, without dilution or adornment, Andreyev was benefiting his readers rather than corrupting them. During the early stages of the discussion the author himself took part in it. Under the pen name of James Lynch, he devoted a feuilleton to the abusers of *The Abyss*, in which he said in part:

> In this naïve complacency of cultured people, in their ignorance of the boundaries of their own ego (or more precisely, in Nietzche's terminology, of their self), I see danger for their further development and for the humanization of their imperfect species.[56]

In reply to those who accused him of slandering the race, he wrote:

> How can one "slander" those on whose conscience lies, to say the least, the Anglo-Boer war, or the Chinese campaign? They boast of the fact that there have been prophets among men—but is it not true that they have slain their prophets? . . . The horror of our false and deceptive life lies precisely in the fact that we do not notice the brute. When he stirs and raises his voice, we regard the sound as the yelp of a lap dog, which we take for a walk and treat good-humoredly with a lump of sugar: "Eat, dearie, and calm yourself." And when on a certain nasty day the pampered beast will tear the little chain, break loose, and devour both ourselves and our neighbors, then we are amazed and stunned, and refuse to believe: it must be an infamous invention![57]

"James Lynch" concluded with an appeal to the lovers of man that they "mercilessly bait the brute," for "all beasts are afraid of light." He was echoed somewhat later by the critic E. Soloviev, who ended his essay in praise of Andreyev with the following words:

> One should endeavor to destroy the prejudice that all is well and safe; one should tear the mask of complacency and propriety from a life which

---

[55] Particularly in the issues 53, 59, 67 of the Moscow daily, and in the issues 46 and 47 of the Petrograd daily.
[56] *The Moscow Courier*, No. 27, 1902.
[57] *Ibid.*

hides in itself corruption, hypocrisy, spiritual pauperism. What Andreyev did was to point out how our most precious possession—the children—perish, perish as victims of vulgar and filthy vice, in the very society which turns its back on whatever contains freedom and truth.[58]

The year 1901 brought unrelieved praise to Andreyev; the critics greeted him warmly, with an occasional note of reservation in regard to the further steps of the young writer, who was still in the stage of finding himself. But within the next year, 1902, Andreyev revealed his real face to the public, which became thenceforth divided in its reaction to the merciless analyst. The reception of *The Abyss* and *In Fog* was to be typical of the response aroused by his subsequent works. Only such *littérateurs par excellence* as A. P. Chekhov were able to consider Andreyev's productions from the purely artistic point of view, regardless of their subject matter and "problem." [59] To the great majority of his readers and critics, nearly every new story or play by Andreyev was a challenge, a shock, a blow, provoking violent revulsion or intense admiration. His solitude among his fellow writers became poignantly marked. In his diary [60] he recalls the impression he made on his contemporaries: "A queer head emerged on a snakelike neck, with a pale face and eyes that were not good: I have come." He goes on relating the effect which the reading of *In Fog* produced on the "Wednesday" gathering. "They bit their lips maliciously, they grew inwardly pale." Some one spoke of a rumor concerning a youth who committed suicide after reading *In Fog*. Malignant looks at the author. What would he say, they asked him, if that rumor proved correct? "I should be gratified," he answered, and recalled that once before he had said this. Indeed, he discovered among his early diaries an entry,

---

[58] *An Essay on the Philosophy of Russian Literature*, pp. 510–511.

[59] In those days of noise and fuss around the name of Andreyev, Chekhov wrote to him in one of his letters: "Your *Foreigner* I like very much. This story and *In Fog* are two serious steps forward. These already possess much calm, and show the author's confidence in his power; there is very little of the writer's nervousness in them. The dialogue between the father and the son in the story *In Fog* is done calmly, and deserves not less than excellent-plus."—A. P. Chekhov, *Letters* (*Pisma*), Petrograd, 1911, dated January 2, 1903.

[60] Dated June 16, 1918.

during the year 1891, in which he outlined his literary ambition.[61] In substance, he expressed there his desire to show to man, "on the basis of the past thousands of years of science, art, history, etc.," that life is folly, destitute of freedom, death being the only freedom. "I desire that those who read me should grow pale and commit suicide, that I should be hated and cursed, yet read nevertheless. When I hear of the first death on my account, I shall be glad." With all due allowance for the exaggerated expressions of a bombastic youth, one has to agree with Andreyev that his early forecast proved correct on the whole. As he grew mature, he freed himself from the puerile desire to *épater les bourgeois,* but his writings continued to cause "inward pallor" and violent jolts to his readers and critics.

The number of Andreyev's adverse critics grew with the increase of the gods he denied. Religionists attacked him for his *Life of Vasily Fiveysky,* for his *Savva, Judas Iscariot,* and other "heretical" productions; Vyacheslav Ivanov, Rosanov, Merezhkovsky, Filosofov, abused him in the secular press, and the clergy succeeded in procuring the Government's suppression of *Savva* and *Anathema* for stage presentation. While the conservative press, notably *The New Times,* called Andreyev a firebrand of the revolution, the socialistic organs accused him of anti-revolutionary sentiments; both sides could cite abundant instances in favor of their indictments. Among his Marxian opponents, Adamovich, Orlovsky, and Lunacharsky, the last named was the most formidable enemy, since he skillfully employed his dialectic method of argument, and, while praising Andreyev for some merits, attacked him vehemently for what he considered his incurable "philistinism." Thus while noting with approval that Andreyev zealously attempted to destroy, Samson-like, the temples of the Philistines, the future Bolshevik Commissar of Education was alarmed to see that the author began to "shake the pillars of the temples of true gods," that he raised his hand against genuine values.[62] In another article

---

[61] *Supra,* p. 27.
[62] In *News from Abroad* (*Zagranichnaya Gazetta*), No. 3, 1908.

during the same year Lunacharsky branded Andreyev "Herostratus," condemned his *Judas* as a slander against humanity, and his *Darkness* and *Tsar Hunger* as defamations of the revolution and of the working class.[63] Andreyev was evidently hurt by the attack from the "left," as one can judge from the tone of the interview he gave to A. Izmailov:

> Because of *Tsar Hunger* party critics accuse me of lack of faith in the victory of Socialism. In the book, *Literary Disintegration,* dedicated to the struggle with the monstrosities in modern literature, from the point of view of the proletarian world outlook, Lunacharsky accuses me of a calumnious portrayal of the working class. The idea of *Tsar Hunger* has been interpreted as the bankruptcy of the revolution. Perhaps I am myself to be blamed in a certain measure for being so understood. I have not made it sufficiently plain that this was a picture of mere mutiny, and not of a real revolution. True, one of my personages says there: "Do not insult the revolution—this is a mutiny," but such a remark is, indeed, not sufficient. If the public knew the whole plan of my work, if they knew that after "War and Peace," over which I am thinking at present, was to follow a special part, "Revolution," they would not taunt me with this reproach. Rather would they reproach me with excessive optimism.[64]

The Modernists of *The Balance* continued to regard Andreyev with diffidence and contempt. Bryusov credited him with possessing talent, but considered him stupid and uncultured, and jeered at the popularity of *The Life of Man,* which vied with the vogue of Lehar's comic opera, *The Merry Widow.*[65] Zinaida Hippius carried the battle abroad, and introduced Andreyev to the French public as a pompous mediocrity.[66] Among the few critics who endeavored to analyze Andreyev *sine ira,* one may mention A. Redko, of *Russia's Riches,* who reviewed every work of the author with profound impartiality; Professor Ovsyaniko-Kulikovsky, who gave an objective estimate of *The Life of Man;*[67] Ivanov-Razumnik, in his book

[63] *Literary Disintegration,* pp. 163, 176.
[64] *The Russian Word (Russkoye Slovo),* a Moscow daily, for April 8, 1908. The optimistic part never came to light, however, remaining one of the illusions Andreyev carried to his grave.
[65] *The Balance,* January, 1908.
[66] *Mercure de France,* pp. 74, 75, January, 1908.
[67] In *Heat-Lightnings (Zarnitsy),* No. 2, pp. 197–214. Petrograd, 1909.

on Sologub, Shestov, and Andreyev; [68] Professor M. Reisner, in his somewhat labored sociological study of the author; [69] and, with some reservations, K. Chukovsky, whose critical writings suffer from too much cleverness.[70]

Andreyev owed a good deal to the critical help of his first wife, Alexandra Mikhailovna, née Veligorsky, whom he married in 1902.[71] According to Lvov-Rogachevsky, next to Maxim Gorky she exerted the strongest influence on his art: "She was the first to whom the young artist read his works, and the first to tell him words of truth, at times severe words. . . . Those who knew her agreed as to her fine taste, sense of proportion, and tact." [72] She died on December 10, 1906, in Berlin, where she lived with her husband most of her last year. During this year Andreyev completed his first symbolical play, *The Life of Man*, which appeared in the first issue of the *Wild Rose Almanacs* (*Almanakhi Shipovnik*), with the inscription: "To the radiant memory of my friend, my wife, I dedicate this composition, the last on which we worked together." In a letter to Lvov-Rogachevsky, written in 1908, Andreyev said:

My late wife was an active collaborator in my work, a sensitive and impartial critic, who often made me change both the form and the tendency of my writing. My latest things, *Judas Iscariot, Darkness, The*

[68] *About the Sense of Life,* second edition. Petrograd, 1910.
[69] L. *Andreyev and His Social Ideology* (L. *Andreyev i evo sotsialnaya ideologia*). Petrograd, 1909.
[70] Chukovsky's method consists in discovering an author's characteristic peculiarities, and tracing them through his works with the persistency of a Sherlock Holmes. *From Chekhov to Our Days* (*Ot Chekhova do nashikh dney*). Petrograd, 1908. Pages 129–140 deal with Andreyev, rather flippantly. A book by the same author, in the same year and place, *Big and Little Andreyev* (*Andreyev bolshoy i malenky*), has appended a collection of abusive epithets used against Andreyev by various critics.
[71] Mme. Andreyev has told me that Alexandra Mikhailovna had a beneficial effect on her husband. Among other things, she helped him check his drinking propensity.
[72] *Two Truths,* p. 71. All those who have written about her, and those with whom I have spoken on the subject, agree with Lvov-Rogachevsky. Says Brusyanin: "Like a beautiful, sad shadow, Andreyev's first wife passed through his life . . . Gentle, fragile, with a certain quiet sadness in her eyes, she seemed to be aware of the short time she was to live, and expressed anxious care for the fate of the productions of her husband, who needed friendship and encouragement."—L. *Andreyev,* p. 35.

Curse of the Beast, Tsar Hunger, were written after she had gone, and, if this be of any significance to you, they bear the traces of the most depressing mood I have lived through.[73]

Andreyev was solitary by nature, yet he was not strong enough for solitude. Alone, he could not face reality, and was threatened by fits of drunkenness or by thoughts of suicide. He was in need of a companion who would combine the comrade and the nurse. In Gorky's description of Alexandra Mikhailovna we find this happy combination:

> . . . Leonid Nikolayevich introduced me to his bride—a thin, frail young lady, with lovely, clear eyes. Modest and silent, she impressed me as lacking personality, but soon I became convinced that she possessed a wise heart.
>
> She quite understood the need of a motherly, watchful relation toward Andreyev; she perceived at once and deeply the value of his talent, and the tormenting vacillations of his moods. She was one of those rare women who while capable of being passionate mistresses do not lose the faculty of loving with a maternal love. This double love had equipped her with a fine sensitiveness, so that she could discern between the genuine complaints of his soul and the jangling words of a whimsical mood of the moment.
>
> . . . She lived in constant anxiety about him, in an incessant strain of all her powers, completely sacrificing her personality to the interests of her husband.[74]

To complete the portrait of Andreyev's first wife, it is worth while to quote V. Veresayev, a veteran member of the "Wednesdays." He speaks about the wonderful congeniality of the Andreyevs' married life, about her jealous care for her husband's comfort and proper mood, and of her "great intuitive understanding of what her artist-husband wished to do and could do, in which respect she was the living embodiment of his artistic conscience." [75] Veresayev states from the words of Andreyev that he wrote his *Red Laugh* three times before his wife approved of it. Veresayev emphasizes this exclusive power of

---

[73] *Two Truths,* p. 72.
[74] *A Book on Andreyev,* p. 26.
[75] In *Morning Breezes (Utrenniki)*—I, p. 82. Petrograd, 1922.

Alexandra Mikhailovna over her husband, adding that at the "Wednesdays" Andreyev eagerly listened to criticism, but- "out of a hundred suggestions he accepted perhaps one or two." [76]

The loss of his wife cast Andreyev into a mood of such depression that his friends feared lest he should take his life.[77] He survived his sorrow by completely saturating himself with

[76] *Ibid.,* p. 83. Veresayev's version sheds a curious light on Andreyev's methods and moods. He writes: "Andreyev worked at night. She never went to bed before he finished and read to her all he had written. After her death Leonid Nikolayevich told me with tears in his eyes how he composed the *Red Laugh*. He finished the story, and read it to his wife. She lowered her head, and said with an effort: 'No, it is not right!' He began to write the story all over. A few days later he finished it. It was late in the night. Alexandra Mikhailovna was then in the period of pregnancy. She was weary, and fell asleep on a couch in the room adjacent to the study, after making her husband promise that he would wake her up. He did so, and read to her the story. She burst into tears, and said: 'Leonichka, it is still not right!' He grew angry, and began to argue that she was a silly and did not understand anything. She cried, and kept on insisting that it was not right yet. He quarreled with her, but . . . he sat down to write it for the third time. And only when he heard the story in its third version did Alexandra Mikhailovna brighten in face and say joyously: 'Now it is right!' And he felt that now, indeed, it was right" (p. 82).

I have written to Mme. Anna Andreyev about Veresayev's story, and asked for her opinion. In a recent letter to me she speaks of Veresayev's version with considerable reserve. "It is hardly possible to associate 'rewriting' with Leonid Nikolayevich's work; at any rate, such cases were exceptional. . . . I might reproduce in minutest detail the mode of his compositions, beginning with *The Seven That Were Hanged,* and I cannot recall a single instance when his work was not purely intuitive. Do you remember what he wrote himself in his Diary?" (see *infra,* pp. 118, 119).

One may suggest that the composition of the *Red Laugh* belonged to those "exceptional cases" of which Mme. Andreyev reluctantly admits; indeed, this story of horrors bears the stamp of laboriousness. My correspondent questions Veresayev's story from still another point: "Alexandra Mikhailovna was a good wife and friend, she loved him, and therefore could not express her general disapproval for his work, because she must have known or felt that such a disapproval might *hurt* his work. Adverse criticism could be useful for such an artist as Andreyev only when it was accompanied by definite reasons; on the whole, it was a delicate point. . . ."

At all events, it is clear that Andreyev sought in his wife a sensitive and receptive audience, by whose opinion and judgment he tested his work. It is curious to note that while he read his compositions to his first wife, he had his second wife read them to him, anxiously watching her every intonation. Mme. Andreyev is a fine reader, yet she tells me of the nervous agitation that gripped her every time she had to read aloud a new work by her husband, especially if it was a play. For she knew how sensitive he was to her reaction, how easily he might grow diffident as to the intrinsic reality of his composition should she fail to grasp the tonal shades of the characters.

[77] Gorky, in *A Book on Andreyev,* pp. 29 ff.

it, in accordance with his general view on living and thinking.[78]
The period of depression was followed by a period of feverish
literary activity, which was stamped by his melancholy state
of mind, "bearing the traces of his mood," as he stated in his
letter to Lvov-Rogachevsky, quoted on pp. 77–78. Indeed, when
one compares *The Life of Man* with most of Andreyev's immediately succeeding writings, one feels how the gloom thickened
in the mind of the artist, how pain and despair extinguished
the faint ray of light which still glimmered in the earlier work.
The Life of Man, pessimistic though it is, still contains scenes
imbued with the joy of life; the affectionate scenes between Man
and his Wife have probably an autobiographic tincture.   In
the end Man dies with a proudly uplifted head, almost victorious over senseless Chance.[79]   This faint ray does not recur till
much later, and then as a rare dissonance—in *The Seven That
Were Hanged,* for instance.   Andreyev's normal key becomes
invariably minor, his color unrelieved black.   His reputation as
that of the "apostle of gloom" is established.

[78] *Supra,* p. 46.
[79] In 1908 Andreyev published a new version of the last scene, "Death of Man."
Man no longer towers with his lionine gray head, as in the first version, but lies
flat in a conventional bed.

IV

MATURITY AND SOLITUDE

Singular success of *The Seven*, etc.—Life in Finland.—Expanse and freedom.—Hobbies.—Andreyev's second wife.—Tolstoy and Andreyev.—Tolstoy's letter.—Andreyev in Yasnaya Polyana.—The points of criticism in Tolstoy's letter applied to Andreyev.—The style is the man.—Andreyev's subjectivity.—Flaubert vs. Moderns.—Andreyev's strength and weakness.—His realistic method.—His ability to express the individuality of things and the inexpressible.—His employment of symbols. Stimmungssymbolik and universal symbols.—Lack of unity in his symbolic plays.—Intermixture of realism, symbolism, and allegory.—Obscurity.—Hurried writing.—Surplusage.—Inspirational intuition.—His work more a deliverance than a joy.—Intuition vs. normality and reason.—Pan-psychism in his later works.—Andreyev on form.—Merezhkovsky's judgment.—Andreyev's growing isolation.—His attachment for the Moscow Art Theatre.—Reserved reciprocity.—Andreyev's "cruel reputation."—Andreyev and Blok.—Andreyev's "substance" curtly defined.—Pleading with Nemirovich-Danchenko for the need of tragedy.—Andreyev's unborn works.

ONLY once did Andreyev regain the unanimous acclamation of 1901—with his story of *The Seven That Were Hanged*, published in 1908, and republished numerous times by various houses for several years in succession. It was praised by all, even by Merezhkovsky,[1] as a masterpiece both in technique and in emotional power. But Andreyev was apparently tired of men and their affairs.[2] During the same year he retired to Fin-

[1] In his *In a Still Slough, Works—XII*, pp. 232–242.
[2] A. Izmailov, describing the first reading of *The Seven That Were Hanged*, at the St. Petersburg residence of the author, observed that Andreyev was weary of people and the city. Soon after that reading Andreyev moved to Finland. Of his St. Petersburg apartment Izmailov gave a few interesting details: "He lived then on the Kamenny-Ostrov Prospect, in a large, magnificent building of modern

land, where he lived in seclusion and in communion with nature. In a letter to Lvov-Rogachevsky, written at that time, he spoke somewhat lyrically about his moods and sentiments:

This spring I am going to settle in Finland definitely, for summer as well as for winter. My purpose is: to come close to nature, which I love boundlessly, and to find more suitable conditions for my work than the city can offer. A few words about nature. Behold the first and only book which I have read through, and which I can always read without boredom! The full significance of nature for me, I cannot define as yet. Balancing myself on the tightly stretched rope, which is my life and my work, I should have broken my neck a score of times, were it not for nature. Nature and nature alone brings me back to the lost equilibrium. Nature serves me as an inexhaustible source of joy, of spiritual health. Nature, too, gives me a vague but firm assurance that some day I shall succeed in discovering the first cause of life the strength-giver, and in understanding why life is after all, joy, and not sorrow.[3]

In the Finnish village Vammelsu, near the Black Rivulet, Andreyev built for himself a villa, the fulfillment of the dream of Man.[4] Korney Chukovsky describes this villa as an expression of the author's love for the colossal. "The fireplace in his study was as large as a gate, and the study itself like a public square. His house loomed above all other buildings in the village; each beam was gigantic; the foundation was a mass of Cyclopean granite piles."[5] Mme. Andreyev recalls how her husband exasperated the architect by insisting on enormous plate-glass windows, which were out of keeping with the otherwise Northern style of the building. Andreyev's plan was probably more in harmony with the Norway house pictured by Man, when he was day-dreaming with his beloved wife:

architecture. . . . It was somewhat gloomy in his enormous study, with its leather furniture in "modern style," and the dreary painting by Roerich, presenting in dry and severe colors a group of seven ravens perched on a hill [Izmailov probably refers to the painting known as "The Ominous"—*Zlovyeshcheye*] . . . Of portraits there hung only those of Gorky and Shalyapin. On the bookstand could be seen a single photograph, the autographed portrait of Baroness von Suttner, which he received after the publication of his *Red Laugh*."—*Literary Olympus*, p. 284.

[3] *Two Truths*, pp. 20–21.
[4] *Life of Man*, Act II.
[5] *A Book on Andreyev*, p. 45.

WIFE: How cold it is there, and how the wind blows!

MAN: Ah, but I shall have thick walls, and there will be huge windows of one large pane, and on winter nights, when the blizzard rages and the fiord is roaring below, we shall draw the curtains and kindle a fire in the huge fireplace. There will be great andirons, on which will burn whole logs—whole forests of pitchy pines.[6]

In this "castle" of his Andreyev spent nearly all of the last ten years of his life. Within a few hours' ride from Petrograd, he was nevertheless cut off from the hubbub of the capital. The quiet village inhabited by rough taciturn Finns afforded Andreyev the freedom and expanse he had craved for since his boyhood in the town of Orel. Here he could give full sway to his whims and hobbies. Now he would engage in painting, to the exclusion of everything else; now he abandoned himself to experiments in photography, particularly to color photography, obtaining at times astonishing results;[7] now he would plunge headlong into writing, consumed by the creative impulse, deaf and blind to all other issues and interests, impersonating each one of his characters with the sincere abandon and spontaneity of a child playing at make-believe. The painter Repin compared Andreyev to Duke Lorenzo, the main character in *The Black Maskers*, and Chukovsky found that the writer played that last rôle more naturally than his numerous other parts. "It suited him," he wrote, "to be a magnate; in every gesture he was a grandee. His fine, chiseled, decorative face,

---

[6] *The Life of Man,* Act II.

[7] Some of the colored landscapes he photographed belie the medium of their reproduction: so artistic do they appear in composition and tone effect. I also had the good fortune to look over a large collection of photographs taken with a stereoscopic camera by Andreyev and by those about him. These glass rectangulars showed me the author in various moods and situations, often caught unawares by the camera—at his desk in the study, at the helm of his small yacht, in the Finnish harbor, dressed in a spruce naval uniform, on the seashore—sometimes without any dress on—in the family circle, or with friends. I have carried out a vivid impression of the writer's appearance, as that of a person of middle height, a bit stocky but agile, with a marvelous head, which Repin wanted to replicate on canvas in John the Baptist. Most memorable are Andreyev's eyes: dark, they glow with an intense light, both penetrating and introverted, always grave. Because of these eyes Andreyev's face does not lose its earnest, almost stern expression in any of his pictures, except two: one, with his favorite child, Savva, where his face is transformed by a joyous paternal smile, and one other, after his death, with the black torches extinguished, and a great calm lending the face a wise gentleness.

his graceful, somewhat full figure, his aristocratic light gait—
all this harmonized splendidly with the rôle of the magnificent
duke, which he played so superbly in his last years."[8] His
restlessness found an outlet in the sea which was close to his
village. From early spring till late autumn he cruised in his
yacht through the treacherous skerries off the coast of Finland,
returning home weathered and bronzed, refreshed and invig-
orated. His love for the sea and understanding of it appear
with particular impressiveness in *The Ocean*, the tragedy permeated with the tingling saltiness of sea air. According to
Mme. Andreyev, her husband's moods depended on the direction of the sea winds: He felt elated when the west wind blew,
while the north wind filled him with depressing thoughts of
death. His sense of smell was one of his best developed senses,
and he enjoyed everything which smelled of the sea; for hours
he would loiter with his little Savva in the harbor, inhaling the
various odors, and enlarging on their significances. One of his
cherished possessions was a piece of tarred rope which his wife
jestingly presented to him as a bouquet, and which always hung
by his bed. His nostalgia for the sea Andreyev considered one
of his organic characteristics. He said to a newspaper correspondent:

I have loved the sea for a long time, since my childhood, from books.
And I have been awaiting it. And never have I experienced such joy as
at the moment when for the first time I stepped on a deck swaying under
my feet. I felt the fulfillment of that which was to be fulfilled.[9]

The last ten years of his life Andreyev spent in close union
and comradeship with his second wife, Anna Ilyinishna Denisevich, whom he married in April, 1908, while composing his masterpiece, *The Seven That Were Hanged*. Relatively little has
been written about this period, and almost nothing about Mme.

[8] *A Book on Andreyev*, pp. 45–46.
[9] An interview in the weekly, *Russia's Morning* (*Utro Rossii*), September 8,
1913. Mme. Andreyev tells me that on his first arrival at Petrograd, he immediately boarded a steamer for the port of Kronstat. Andreyev's nostalgia for the
sea reminds one of the same urge in Joseph Conrad, who was also born in an
inland country.

Andreyev.[10] The reason for this is suggested in the following lines written to me by her in February, 1922:

Strange as it may perhaps seem, during the ten years of his life with me he drifted apart from his former chums and colleagues. He continued to love them tenderly, but as one loves one's childhood playmates, or one's old couch. . . .

By the time of his second marriage Andreyev had become tired of his fellow men, and keenly aware of his solitude among contemporary writers. In his wife, Anna, he found the friendship which gives unreservedly, asking in return nothing but the joy of being able to give more. "My ears," he called her in a letter to his brother, Andrey. He needed her sympathetic ears, her fine response, her delicate sensitiveness, her unflagging alertness, and her constant, watchful presence, in order to overcome the depression of his black solitude, and to be in a position to create. With the selfishness of a genius or of a child (he possessed the elements of both) he monopolized all her time,[11] all her attention and interest, all her strength and energy.[12] During his creative periods he would dictate his productions to her all night long, striding up and down his huge study, smoking incessantly, consuming quantities of strong tea from the always

[10] In Vengerov's work (*op. cit.,* p. 250) I find one line: "Later Leonid Nikolayevich married the daughter of A. I. Denisevich, an Odessa journalist." Denisevich was neither A. I., nor an Odessa journalist, but I. N. and a social worker in St. Petersburg. At his home met prominent politicians and revolutionary leaders, and it was in that atmosphere that Andreyev conceived the type of Werner, in *The Seven That Were Hanged.* In the various reminiscences written about Andreyev after his death I find only one reference to his second wife, in those of Skitalets (Petrov), He speaks of the secluded life of the Andreyevs in their "enchanted castle, where, according to rumor, they never received any guests and gave no parties, but were engaged all year round in writing gloomy fantasies." Despite the rumor, Skitalets was invited by Andreyev to his villa where he met the hostess, "a beautiful young woman of a pronounced southern type" who impressed him "as a serious, clever, balanced person."—In the Harbin daily, *Russia's Voice* (*Golos Rossii*), February 21, 1922.

[11] For a long time she was unable to attend to her teeth, because whenever she set out for Petrograd, Andreyev would exclaim: "But how shall I get along without you!"

[12] Persons who have known the Andreyevs, like the writer, Mme. A. Damansky, told me that a few years after their marriage it was difficult to recognize in the physically worn Mme. Andreyev the erstwhile "striking beauty" of the popular Mlle. Denisevich.

active samovar, and utterly oblivious of the fatigue and exhaustion of "his ears." Yet though indifferent to her physical weariness, he was exceedingly sensitive about her inner reaction to his dictations, and would stop in the middle of a passage on becoming suspicious concerning the sympathy of his audience.[18] The importance of Mme. Andreyev in the life of her husband can be appreciated after reading the following lines from his diary, written shortly before his death:

> My relations with Anna are a theme of such enormous importance and value, that it is with difficulty that I decide to approach it. It is as though I conceived a desire to define all my attitudes toward life; it is like the request of a certain lady reader to explain in a few words the meaning of my works. I am not writing about my relations with Anna because, in the first place, I generally do not write about the most important things, and in the second place, because I speak about these things to Anna, and speak unreservedly, without the need for transferring anything into secret documents. Isolated, brief entries merely serve as the thermometer of a given day. The weather, compared with nature itself.
>
> .   .   .   .
>
> She [Anna] forms an inseparable, essential part of my soul. She is my best and only friend, with whom I always find it interesting and important to share my ideas, whether it be about life, or about my works and plans. My first desire on seeing something, is to tell Anna about it: only after passing through Anna does everything seen, experienced, and contemplated by me become a fact of my soul. Without that—all is but a dream and oblivion.

The year of Andreyev's second marriage coincided with what he later regarded as the climactic development of his talent, the "attainment of the peak," in his words written in a letter to Goloushev (in 1918). "In 1906," he recorded in that letter, "I wrote *Lazarus, The Life of Man, Savva*. In 1907, *Judas* and *Darkness*, while in 1908 alone, *The Seven That Were Hanged, Days of Our Life, My Memoirs, Black Maskers,* and

---

[18] Needless to say, Andreyev was able to create in this fashion because his wife enjoyed his tyranny not as the bearing of a cross, but as a great happiness, infinitely proud of her lot, and responding to the beats of his talent's wings with all the fibres of her soul.

Anathema. In general, 1908 was a wonderful year in vital activity: I married Anna, built my home, lived through memorable experiences, and wrote so many of my best works." Each one of the writings enumerated was a literary event of national dimensions, generating heated discussions in the press and at various gatherings, and endowing Andreyev with a renown which had the element of scandal about it. With the exception of *Days of Our Life,* the understandable realistic play based on student life, which enjoyed a continuous popularity throughout Russia, all these productions assaulted some established fetich, and thereby provoked the resentment and protest of the offended worshippers. At any rate, Andreyev became the most-talked-of author in Russia, whose plays were produced at the best theatres of Petrograd, Moscow, Kiev, Odessa, and other big cities, and whose works were eagerly commented upon in lectures and articles.

At the height of his fame Andreyev paid a visit to Yasnaya Polyana. Thinking Russians found themselves impelled at one time or another to come into the presence of the great man, to draw strength and consolation from the "conscience of Russia," as Tolstoy has been called by his countrymen. Writers, among other pilgrims, were attracted to the author of Russia's *Iliad* and *Odyssey,* to the artist whom Turgenev addressed from his deathbed with the words, "Great writer of the Russian land." This in spite of Tolstoy's renunciation of his art, his condemnation of his own best novels and stories as well as of all famous artistic productions created by the few for the few. The artist and keen critic never died in Tolstoy. The works he produced after 1880, the year when he definitely embraced his new faith, including his last novel, *Resurrection,* and his posthumous plays and stories, amply testify to the failure of Tolstoy the preacher in his effort to destroy Tolstoy the artist. In reading his letters, diaries, and his remarks recorded by his friends and contemporaries, one learns how vitally interested he was to the end in questions of literature, how pointed were his critical observations, how keen his likes and dislikes.

Tolstoy regarded Andreyev's talent skeptically. I have already noted the saying attributed to him: "Andreyev says, Boo! But I am not scared." Upon hearing of the plot of *Darkness*, Tolstoy praised the idea of the story, but after reading it he was disappointed. "They praise him," he said, "so he permits himself to write God knows what. Absolute lack of the sense of measure—the main thing in any art, whether poetry or music or sculpture. As soon as the artist overdoes, I become at once aware of it. Ah! he wants to catch me!—and I keep myself on guard against him." [14] On another occasion he also suggested that "the chief trouble with Andreyev is that he has been so profusely glorified that now he strains himself to write extraordinary things." [15] In this respect Tolstoy agreed with Merezhkovsky, who compared the effect of the public on Andreyev to the deathly hug of a gorilla on an infant.[16] *Tsar Hunger* impressed Tolstoy as "an accumulation of horrors and effects." [17] He expressed amazement at the success of Andreyev, who was less talented than Kuprin, Serafimovich, Artsibashev.[18] Of *The Life of Man* he said: "It is naïve, affected pessimism, when life does not run according to your wish. . . . I receive many such letters, particularly from ladies. It has neither new ideas nor artistic images." [19] Still more sweepingly did he state his opinion one evening during a discussion of modern literature: "I cannot read Andreyev. I read one page and feel bored. I see that it is false. The same as in music: when the player strikes a false note after every three notes, I am unable to listen, I go out, or stop my ears." [20] He failed to see any meaning in Andreyev's symbols and allegories.

[14] *Two Years with Tolstoy* (*Dva goda s Tolstym*), notes by his secretary, N. N. Gusev (Moscow, 1912), p. 77, entry for February 6, 1908. Gusev, and his successor, V. F. Bulgakov, enjoyed the confidence of Tolstoy and of his intimate associates. At present they are both connected with the Tolstoy Museum, and with its various publications.

[15] *Ibid.*, p. 98, March 8, 1908.

[16] *In the Paws of an Ape* (*V obezyannykh lapakh*), *Russian Thought*, January, 1908. One should remember that if Andreyev was at all influenced by the public, the effect of its praise was neutralized by that of its abuse.

[17] *Two Years, etc.*, p. 104, March 18, 1908.

[18] *Ibid.*, p. 105, March 22, 1908.

[19] *Ibid.*, p. 132, May 8, 1908.

[20] *Ibid.*, p. 139, May 19, 1908.

"I have read the prologue to Andreyev's *Anathema*," he said. "It is insane, perfectly insane! Absolute nonsense! A certain Guardian, certain gates. . . . It is astonishing how the public likes this incomprehensibility. Nay, it demands such stuff, and searches for some special significance in it." [21]

As a victim of Tolstoy's merciless criticism Andreyev found himself in a rather prominent company. In his *What Is Art?* and in his later articles Tolstoy wrought havoc in the ranks of the world's great, slaughtering Shakespeare and Wagner, Beethoven and Nietzsche, and with especial vehemence the moderns. In literature Tolstoy abhorred obscurity and finicalness, mysticism and symbolism, art for the sake of art, and beauty for the sake of beauty. He demanded of a work of art that it should be reasonable, clear and accessible to the common reader, and that it should contain an uplifting message. It was natural that he should disapprove of Andreyev, both for his symbolic style and for his purely negative tendency in destroying all beliefs and moral values.[22] Andreyev dedicated his *Seven That Were Hanged* to Tolstoy, evidently feeling that this work of his would meet with the approval of the valiant fighter against capital punishment. Along with the dedication he must have sent a letter, for we find this mentioned in a letter from Tolstoy, dated "Yasnaya Polyana, September, 1908." Tolstoy's letter is worth translating, as presenting not only his last expression of the writer's catechism, but also his veiled references to what he considered weaknesses in Andreyev, notably, the latter's affected outlandishness, excessive speed in composition, and alleged playing to the gallery.

I have received your good letter, my dear Leonid Nikolayevich. I have never known the meaning of dedications, though methinks I have myself

[21] V. F. Bulgakov, *With L. N. Tolstoy, in the last year of his life* (*U L. N. Tolstovo v posledny god evo zhizni*), p. 184, entry for May 26, 1910. Moscow, 1911.

[22] According to Mme. Andreyev, Tolstoy expressed his unreserved approval of Andreyev's *Christians*. In this satirical sketch of a court room, a prostitute refuses to take the oath as a witness, arguing that her profession precludes her adherence to the Christian faith, while the judges and the prosecutor endeavor in vain to persuade her that one may remain a Christian even when engaging in fraud, thievery or murder.

done some dedicating to some one. I only know that your dedication signifies your good feelings toward me, which I have noted also in your letter to me, and this pleases me greatly. In your letter you judge your writings with such sincere modesty, that I shall allow myself to express my opinion, not about your own writings, but about writing in general— ideas which may perhaps be of use to you too. I think, in the first place, that one should write only when the thought he wants to express is so persistent that it will not leave him in peace until he has expressed it as well as he can. All other inducements to write, vainglorious ones, particularly those of the hideous pecuniary kind, though allied with the chief prompting—the need of expression, can only interfere with the sincerity and dignity of writing. One should be on constant guard against this. In the second place, there is often the desire to be peculiar, original, to astonish and surprise the reader; of this our contemporary writers in particular are often guilty (the whole Decadent movement is based on this desire). This trait is even more pernicious than those side considerations of which I spoke first. It excludes simplicity, and simplicity is the necessary condition of the beautiful. The simple and artless may be poor, but that which is not simple and is artificial can never be good. Thirdly: hurried writing. This is both harmful and a sign that the writer has no genuine need for expressing his thought. For if there be such a genuine need, then the writer will spare no labor or time in order to bring his thought to full definiteness, clearness. Fourthly: the desire to respond to the tastes and demands of the major part of the contemporary reading public. This is particularly harmful, and it ruins in advance all the significance of what the author intends to write. For the significance of any literary product consists not in its being instructive in the direct sense, like a sermon, but in its revealing to men something new, unknown to them, and for the most part contradictory to that which the large public considers indubitable. And it is precisely this [significance] that is necessarily excluded here [in the fourth case].

Perhaps something out of all this may be of use to you. You write that the merit of your works lies in their sincerity. I admit not only this, but also that their aim, too, is good: the desire to contribute to men's well-being. I think that you are sincere also in modestly judging your productions. This is the more worthy on your part, since the success which they enjoy might have prompted you, on the contrary, to exaggerate their importance. I have read too little of you, and too carelessly, as I read little in general, and am only slightly interested in belles-lettres [literally: artistic productions—"khudozhestvennyia proizvedeniya"]; but from what I remember and know of your writings, I should advise you to work longer over them, bringing their underlying ideas to the last degree of precision and clearness.

I repeat that your letter has pleased me very much. If you happen to be in our vicinity, I shall be glad to see you.

Lovingly,

LEO TOLSTOY.[23]

Andreyev did visit Yasnaya Polyana, in the last year of Tolstoy's life. Bulgakov records this event in his diary, 4–5 May, 1910. In his description Andreyev appears as somewhat affected, as a poseur—the usual impression of those who saw him for the first time. The first things Bulgakov noticed were "his handsome swarthy face, a little restless, his white hat, fashionable cape." While being introduced to the count's family, Andreyev's "hands trembled." He was very "timid and mild, and agreed in everything with his hosts." Andreyev was on the way to his Finland villa from a trip south, on which he saw Gorky at his Capri home. He told them of his infatuation with painting and with color photography. Unfortunately, the most interesting part of his visit, the conversation of the two writers during an afternoon stroll in rain and hail, was not recorded. In the evening, Bulgakov observed:

Andreyev sat with the ladies in the drawing-room. He wore a cream-colored knitted jacket which went very well with his dark complexion and pitch-black locks, and with his full figure; he was, apparently, perfectly conscious of the effect. "May I? At home I always wear this," he innocently inquired. We spoke of his works. Personally he liked most of all *Lazarus* and *The Life of Man,* was "beginning" to like *Judas Iscariot.* Concerning the stories *The Abyss* and *In Fog* [which the countess had attacked in 1903: *supra,* p. 71], Leonid Nikolayevich declared that "such" stories he no longer wrote. He told us that at the beginning of his literary career he "studied the styles" of various writers—of Chekhov, Garshin, Tolstoy, analyzing their writings syntactically, and trying to write à la Chekhov, à la Garshin, à la Tolstoy. He succeeded in all cases except that of Tolstoy. . . .

[23] *Letters of L. N. Tolstoy* (*Pisma L. N. Tolstovo*), 1848–1910, No. 269, pp. 334-336. Moscow, 1910.

Lev Nikolayevich came in. He offered Andreyev a chance to write
for the one-copeck publications of *The Mediator* [*Posrednik*: a popular
publishing house, in which Tolstoy took great interest]. But Andreyev
declared that he could not do it, to his regret, because he "had done like
Chekhov": he had sold to a certain concern not only his past but also
his future works. At tea he talked to Lev Nikolayevich about the critic,
K. Chukovsky, who had raised the question of a special dramatic literature for the cinematograph. Andreyev was very enthusiastic about this.
Lev Nikolayevich listened at first skeptically, but later he apparently became interested. "I shall most certainly write for the cinematograph!"
he announced at the end of the conversation.[24]

Bulgakov is one of those faithful worshippers who involuntarily belittle those who appear within the radius of their sun.
Hence his somewhat patronizing tone about Tolstoy's visitors.
That night, when alone with his master, he spoke rather doubt-
fully of the young author who was so popular and apt to be
complacent. But Tolstoy retorted that from their conversation on that afternoon he knew that Andreyev was "thinking of
moral questions"; and that Andreyev had produced on him
"a good impression. Clever, such kind thoughts, a very fine
person. But I feel," he added, "that I must tell him straight-
forward the whole truth: he writes too much." [25] It is interesting to learn that Tolstoy who was keener and deeper than any
of his satellites, who was very sensitive and abhorred sham and
affectation, found Andreyev agreeable. On the other hand, the
younger writer, who had expressed on previous occasions his
opposition to Tolstoy's views, and whose *My Memoirs* (1908)
was regarded as a caricature of the Yasnaya Polyana hermit,
was deeply moved by his contact with the great man. There
is a touching significance in the parting of these two outstanding
figures of Russian life and letters, as recorded by Bulgakov:

In the doorway leading from the study into the drawing-room, Lev
Nikolayevich met Andreyev. The latter thanked L. N. with emotion.
L. N. asked him to come again. "Let us be more intimate," he said, and
added: "Permit me to embrace you."

24 *With L. N. Tolstoy*, pp. 143–144.
25 *Ibid.*, p. 144.

And he was the first to extend a kiss to his young colleague. . . .
When Andreyev and I went out, I observed how deeply he was agitated
by the leave-taking.

"Tell Lev Nikolayevich," he spoke in a halting voice, as we were de-
scending the stairs, turning his excited face to me and scarcely seeing the
steps, "tell him that I . . . feel happy, that he is . . . so kind." [26]

Gulliver's Death, written in 1911, was Andreyev's last tribute to the memory of his great compatriot and fellow writer.[27]
The bereaved author described the Lilliputians clambering over
the dead body, and making vain efforts to estimate the only
giant that ever appeared in their puny midst. In the concluding
paragraph he expressed what practically all Russians have felt
toward Tolstoy, adherents and opponents alike:

From the world has forever departed the great human heart which had
hovered over the land and filled the days and dark nights of the Lilliputians with its resounding beats. Heretofore, whenever a Lilliputian awakened in the midst of the night from a terrible dream, he would hear the
habitually even beats of the mighty heart, and, reassured, he would again
fall asleep. Like some faithful guard, the noble heart watched over him,
and sounding its ringing beats, it sent down to the earth good will and
peace, and dispersed the terrible dreams with which the dark Lilliputian
nights are so replete.

And the great human heart has forever departed from the world. And
stillness reigned. . . .[28]

Tolstoy's letter to Andreyev voiced the writer's literary ten-

[26] It is worth while to quote a few more lines from Bulgakov, the jealous disciple who is loth to praise an outsider, and who, unlike his master, judges from
the exterior: "Andreyev produced a favorable impression on everybody at Yasnaya Polyana. All the time he held himself with extreme modesty, even timidity.
About Lev Nikolayevich he spoke with reverence. His speech is simple, at times
somewhat coarse, in contrast to the easily understood yet beautiful and grace-
fully precise language of Lev Nikolayevich. He was posing a bit, it seemed to
me. Even his costume was, as they say, 'simple but elegant'—a picturesque cape,
a black windsor tie in his shirt, then his effective jacket. He probably thinks that
his handsome exterior is in need of all these accessories."—*Ibid.*, p. 146.

[27] Somewhat earlier Andreyev wrote an obituary note, under the title, *Half A
Year Before His Death*, in which he emphasized the impression of gentleness and
goodness produced on him by "the blessed ancient."—*Works—VI* (Marx edition,
Petrograd, 1913), pp. 302–304.

[28] *Works—XII*, p. 239.

ets, and, by implication, his chief misgivings concerning Andreyev's talent. By applying to Andreyev the four points set forth in the letter, we shall throw light on the essential traits of his artistic personality. The last point—as to the conformity of the author with the prevalent public taste—may be dismissed in a sentence. From what we have already observed (see, e. g., *supra*, pp. 51, 74–76), and from our further discussion, it must appear clear that Andreyev was decidedly nonconformist in his views, a consistent *enfant terrible* in his relations with the public. In regard to the first point—the nature of the author's impulse for writing—Andreyev (except for a few attempts in his last year, of which we shall speak later) complied with Tolstoy's demand that one should write only when prompted by an irresistible urge for self-expression. Chukovsky tells us how Andreyev would give himself up to writing "with an intensity that was exhausting," oblivious of every one and everything.[29] Also Gorky describes Andreyev during a period of devastating activity at Capri, when he abandoned himself to writing, sitting at his desk day and night, "half dressed, dishevelled, but happy," consumed by the fire of his imagination.[30] More serious are the charges against Andreyev, implied in the second point—anent lack of simplicity—and in the third—concerning hasty composition. Indeed, Tolstoy rounds up his "general" precepts by a direct, personal counsel to Andreyev to "work longer" over his writings for the sake of "precision and clearness." These points are connected with the author's mode and methods of writing—that is, with the way he perceived, felt, digested, and reflected the experiences which formed his artistic world—in a word, with Andreyev's personality; and they must be considered at some length.

Andreyev did frequently display a lack of simplicity, and occasionally he was, indeed, guilty of hasty composition. But his former sin was not due to a desire "to be peculiar, original, to astonish and surprise the reader," just as his latter fault did not betray a want of a "genuine need for expressing his

[29] *A Book on Andreyev*, p. 48.
[30] *Ibid.*, p. 32.

thought." Andreyev's stylistic peculiarities and flaws reflected the traits of his character, amply illustrating the truth of the old but not antiquated definition of style as "the man himself." The variety of methods, and the multiplicity of forms he employed, the exaggerations, superfluities, and obscurities of which he was guilty—these and other traits composed his style, his intense, seething, contradictory, unpoised personality.

One of his conspicuous features was subjectivity, a feature whose merit or demerit for the artist is still debated by the adherents of Flaubert's view that the duty of art is to be impersonal,[31] on one hand, and by the more numerous modern critics who accept the opposite view, as for instance, Remy de Gourmont,[32] or Benedetto Croce.[33] After all, the difference between the two views is more of degree than of essence. Impersonality in art is well-nigh unattainable, the individuality of the author being of necessity felt in one place or another of his work. Even *Madame Bovary,* the highest example of detached art, implies a certain attitude toward life in general, an attitude which is unmistakably Flaubert's. Chekhov's objective types and sketches cannot help expressing indirectly the author's sad outlook upon a world in which he depicts the ridiculous and the futile. In a work of art we welcome the presence of the creator hovering over it, just as the believer feels the omnipresence of God, if one may proceed with Flaubert's comparison. The question is, to what extent is the author's presence felt. As a guide through the soul chambers of his characters, the author must not be too obtrusive, nor too subjectively elusive. He must not

[31] From his letter to George Sand: . . . "dans l'idéal que j'ai de l'art, je crois qu'on ne doit rien montrer des siennes, et que l'artiste ne doit pas plus apparaître dans son œuvre que Dieu dans la nature. L'homme n'est rien, l'œuvre tout!"— Gustave Flaubert, *Correspondance—IV,* pp. 219-220. Paris, 1904.

[32] "L'œuvre d'un écrivain doit être non seulement le reflet, mais le reflet grossi de sa personalité. La seule excuse qu'un homme ait d'écrire, c'est de s'écrire lui-même, de devoiler aux autres la sorte de monde qui se mire en son miroir individuel" . . . —Remy de Gourmont, *Le livre des masques—I,* p. 13, Paris, 1896.

[33] "We do not ask of an artist instruction as to real facts and thoughts, nor that he should astonish us with the richness of his imagination but that he should have a *personality,* in contact with which the soul of the hearer or spectator may be heated."—Benedetto Croce, *Æsthetic,* p. 389 (translated by Ainslie). London, 1909.

shout over our heads through a megaphone, forcing upon us labels, epithets, and points of view, nor must he hint at these with arbitrary obscurity; in either case he would invite uncalled-for intimacy. The author ought to respect his reader's intelligence and faculty of self-orientation, step politely aside, and permit him to form his own inferences and conclusions. Otherwise the author's personality may become an annoying nuisance.

Andreyev projects his personality in all his writings, with all its peculiarities, merits and drawbacks. His subjectivity is manifested otherwise than in the choice of subjects familiar to him. Indeed, like Flaubert,[34] he is fond of penetrating unknown regions, of painting strange environments, of dissecting alien natures. He probes the state of mind of high bureaucrats, of tramps, policemen, priests, revolutionists, prostitutes, merchants, and of numerous other categories foreign to his personal mode of living and thinking. Where he differs from Flaubert, is that he creates the unfamiliar characters not "de tête," but from his heart. Flaubert tried to make the characters in *Madame Bovary* think and talk in their own way, as he himself would under no circumstances think or talk. Moreover, he did not let us see in the least degree his personal opinion of the persons he created, nor surmise his preferences and choices. In Andreyev we often feel that the characters serve as mouthpieces for the author. A lyrical note runs through all of his works, making the author's presence felt strongly. The lepers in *The Wall*, the lonely wretch in *At the Window*, Judas the traitor, Augustus encountering Lazarus, Anathema storming heaven, Samson torn between flesh and spirit, these and their very antipodes speak the familiar Andreyev language—many-sided and variegated yet definitely individual. Even the dog, in

---

[34] In a letter to Mme. X: "Les livres que j'ambitionne le plus de faire sont justement ceux pour lesquels j'ai le moins de moyens. *Bovary* en ce sens aura été un tour de force inouï et dont moi seul jamais aurai conscience: sujet, personnage, effet, etc., tout est hors de moi . . . ; je suis en écrivant ce livre comme un homme qui jouerait du piano avec des balles de plomb sur chaque phalange." —*Correspondance—II*, p. 128.

Later he wrote to the same lady: "Ce qui fait que je vais si lentement, c'est que rien dans ce livre [*Madame Bovary*] n'est tiré de moi, jamais ma personnalité ne m'aura été plus inutile . . . : tout est *de tête*. . . . Juge donc, il faut que j'entre à toute minute dans des *peaux* qui me sont antipathiques . . ."—*Ibid.*, pp. 198, 199.

Snapper, strikes the reader as an incarnation of Andreyev.
Again, there is never any doubt as to the author's attitude toward his characters; although he does not employ the out-
of-date "author's comment," we invariably know his sympathies and antipathies. In most cases he sympathizes, for the
simple reason that nearly all his main characters (and his works
usually centre in one character) are none others but Andreyev
himself in various editions. But when he hates or despises, he
shows his sentiment with unmistakable intensity, though not directly. We feel his contempt for the father of Pavel (*In
Fog*), his animosity toward the Governor's son (*The Governor*), his mocking scorn for the twelve Apostles (*Judas Iscariot*), his bitter hatred for the old man of *My Memoirs.*

Andreyev's subjectivity is both his weakness and his strength.
His art suffers from lack of detachment. Where the cold eye
of a scientific investigator is required, he may fall short. The
chapter "Kiss him and be silent," in *The Seven That Were
Hanged,* despite its tremendous appeal, ends with an admitted
failure to describe what has taken place. Tears did not let the
author record the final embrace between the parents and their
son doomed to be hanged on the morrow. An artist has no
right to shirk his responsibility of expressing in significant form
that which we, ordinary mortals, are too tongue-tied to utter
adequately. He is a weak artist who grows hysterical over the
terrible and tragic in his workshop, life, who yields to monstrosity and succumbs to chaos, according to Merezhkovsky's accusa-
tion.[35] At the same time Andreyev's subjectivity lends his
works a human appeal of such profound sincerity that it atones
for the artistic weakness. His creations are, indeed, not merely
"of the head." In the words of Chukovsky, quoted previously,[36] "he did not merely write his works; his subjects seized
him as if with a flame. Each theme consumed him to the end;
for a time he would become a maniac under its spell." While
creating a character he became saturated with its psychology,
acted and lived like this character, with the abandon and ear-

[35] *Supra,* p. 54.
[36] *Supra,* p. 53.

nestness of a child playing some make-believe game. He had the faculty of assuming various personalities and thus actually experiencing the emotions, passions, sufferings of his numerous creations.[37] Hence the tremendous power of conviction and truthfulness that his works possess even when describing the extraordinary. A. Izmailov relates the effect of *The Seven That Were Hanged* on Novodvorsky and Morozov, two "experts of death," in the sense that both experienced in their early revolutionary activity the agony of awaiting execution. Released after nearly a quarter of a century of solitary confinement in the awful casemates of the Schlüsselburg fortress, the punishment to which their death sentence had been commuted, these two veterans were present at the first private reading of the story by Andreyev. Said Novodvorsky:

"I am amazed how you, not having actually lived through the anguish of inevitable death, could become imbued with our moods to such wonderful verisimilitude. Astonishingly true."

Morozov, too, wondered at the "truthful, poignant, and profound" way in which Andreyev "surmised so much." [38] Only an author writing with the blood of his heart can attain the almost uncanny realism of Andreyev in reproducing some of the rarest and most racking human experiences. No wonder that upon completing his *Red Laugh*, "his nerves were utterly shattered, and for some time he was unable to work." [39]

In order to clarify further Andreyev's personality as seen through his subjective art, a few observations of his literary methods will be helpful. "They wonder why I write certain things in a peculiar style," Andreyev is quoted as having said after the presentation of *The Black Maskers* (in 1908). "The

---

[37] *Supra*, pp. 54, 55. Flaubert, with all his admiration for impersonal art, regretted his inability to experience any genuine sympathy with his characters. Thus, while working "scientifically" and objectively over *Salammbô*, he wrote to Ernest Feydeau: "Je donnerais la demi-rame de notes que j'ai écrites depuis cinq mois et les 98 volumes que j'ai lus, pour être pendant trois secondes, seulement, réelement émotionné par la passion de mes héros."—*Correspondance—III*, pp. 103, 104.

[38] *Literary Olympus*, pp. 289 ff.

[39] Quoted *supra*, p. 54, from *Two Truths*, p. 67.

explanation is very simple: every work should be written in the style which it demands. *Tsar Hunger* could not be written without symbolism; *The Seven That Were Hanged* could be written only in realistic tones . . . I am not a slave of either symbolism or realism, but they are my servants—now the one now the other, according to my theme." [40] Indeed, Andreyev consistently regarded the medium of expression as a "servant," as an instrument for the purpose of conveying an idea, selected solely for its fitness, never as an aim in itself, or for the sake of being "original," as Tolstoy hints. In accordance with the nature of their themes, Andreyev's productions are, stylistically, realistic, or symbolistic, or "pan-psychic," to use his own term.[41]

Intrinsically, all art possesses the elements of realism and symbolism. In order to appeal it must create an actuality, a persuasive reality, no matter whether reproduced from tangible life, or hewn from the imagination. At the same time a work of art cannot help being symbolical, implying a significance beyond the limits of immediacy. Andreyev is both a realist and a symbolist, and his works differ only extrinsically, in the relative prominence given to visible reality or to its underlying meanings. In this limited sense the major part of his writings is composed in the spirit of the traditional Russian realism.[42] He follows his great predecessors who since Pushkin and Gogol have regarded as the artist's field of observation actual life, with its everydayness, its trivial situations, gray events, and

[40] An interview quoted by V. V. Brusyanin, in his introduction to *Plays by L. Andreyev*, pp. xxi–xxii. New York, 1915. I am unable to locate the original.

[41] These remarks are not intended as a detailed study of what Mr. Spingarn calls "dead lumber," referring to the old paraphernalia of rhetoric (*The New Criticism*, p. 19. New York, 1911). Like Mr. Spingarn, I agree with Croce's view that "form and content cannot be separated from one another and considered apart" (*Ariosto, Shakespeare and Corneille*, p. 274. New York, 1920); and, like him, I approve of Oscar Wilde's dictum that "technique is really personality" (in "The Critic as an Artist," *Intentions*, p. 206. Putnam edition, 1913). This brief survey of Andreyev's literary methods is undertaken precisely as a part of the study of his personality, not as a separate entity.

[42] Arthur Symons draws a clear distinction between Russian realism and French naturalism: "In a page of Zola and in a page of Tolstoy you might find the same minuteness; and yet in reading the one you might see only the filth, while in reading the other you might feel only some fine human impulse."—*Plays, Acting and Music*, p. 117. New York, 1909.

commonplace individuals, not merely copying this life (a function whose relevance to art is similar to that of a player sitting on the piano, to borrow a terse simile from Whistler [43]), but reproducing it "through the veil of the soul," in the old-fashioned words of Poe.[44] Russian realists, in depicting ordinary life and ordinary persons, have succeeded in discovering the eternal human beneath the most brutal exterior, in revealing the pathos of tragedy even in sordidness and banality, in giving us what Maupassant calls more than reality.[45] Andreyev is such a realist, when he deals with concrete life, his distinct trait being that of sublimating visible reality by means of thought which pervades his individuals and raises them above mere vegetation, as we shall see later.

Andreyev employs the realistic method in his early stories, and in practically all his *nouvelles*,[46] or long stories, including

[43] *Ten O'Clock*, p. 12. Portland, 1912.

[44] "Art is the reproduction of what the senses perceive in nature through the veil of the soul."—*In Marginalia*, p. 226 (v. VII of Works, Stone & Kimball, Chicago, 1895).

[45] "Le réaliste, s'il est un artiste, cherchera, non pas à nous montrer la photographie banale de la vie, mais à nous en donner la vision plus complète, plus saisissante, plus probante que la réalité même."—"Le Roman," preface to *Pierre et Jean*, p. xv (Paris 1897, 61st edition).

[46] An analysis of the distinction between the short story, *nouvelle* and novel lies outside the scope of this essay. The term "nouvelle" is used here to denote those tales of Andreyev which, though possessing the quality of sustained unity, sin against the canon of brevity—the essential condition of "totality," according to Poe (*The Philosophy of Composition*, in v. VI, p. 34, of *Works*). As Mr. Arthur Ransome puts it, "the short story must be a single melody ending with itself; the *nouvelle* a piece of music, the motive of whose opening bars, recurring again and again throughout, is finally repeated with the increase in meaning that is given it by the whole performance. (*A History of Story Telling*, p. 309. London, 1909.) The *nouvelle* is a suitable name for Andreyev's longer writings, in which there may be many scenes, each one important in itself, yet all of them knit together by one motive, one plot. The *nouvelle* has flourished in Russian literature. To this type belong most of Pushkin's and Gogol's prose tales, Korolenko's *Blind Musician*, Chekhov's *Ward Number Six*, *The Orlovs* of Gorky, while the novelists *par excellence* were not less famous for their *nouvelles*. Suffice it to mention Turgenev's *Spring Freshets* or *Asya*, Dostoyevsky's *A Gentle Soul* or *The Gambler*, Tolstoy's *Cossacks* or *Sevastopol Tales*. With Andreyev, too, the *nouvelle* was a favorite form of composition. His primary interest lying in neither plot nor setting but in character, in the evolution, experiences, and transformations of the individual, it is evident why he preferred the scope of a *nouvelle* to the novel's complexity of plot and counterplot. He takes an individual, as, for instance, Father Vasily, and presents him to us in the various stages of his tragic life, each stage more or less complete in itself, yet forming an inseparable link in the chain

his very last work, *Satan's Diary*. A keen psychologist, possessed of that rare gift of expression which Croce regards as the independent and autonomous "intuitive-expressive knowledge," [47] Andreyev makes us visualize the world of reality in its full significance. As an artist he has the power of revealing to us the nature of individuals, things, emotions, of which we have only a vague impression, and whose *"individuality* escapes us," according to Henri Bergson.[48] With a few bold strokes he can draw an unforgettable portrait. He has the eye for discerning the essential and characteristic amidst the thousands of details which block and confuse our ordinary vision. And, again, it is his artist's discriminative power which selects the precise, felicitous word for the expression of his intuition. Suffice it to mention, as an illustration, *The Story of The Seven That Were Hanged,* where each one of the seven convicts is drawn at full length and depth with a great economy in means, and where even the minor characters, like the prison warden, or Kashirin's sentinel, or the officers at the execution, are indelibly stamped with the "individuality" to which M. Bergson refers. Not only does he succeed in making us visualize concrete persons and situations, but he also takes us into the misty regions of our inner selves, and by dint of convincing images he renders the abstract and, for us, inexpressible, into palpable reality. Such, for instance, is his treatment of thought, his favorite subject, in numerous places, but with particular poig-

---

of circumstances which build up the single motive—Vasily's doomed tragedy. Or he presents seven individuals, in *The Seven That Were Hanged,* each one a complete portrait, and all of them strung together like beads on a string, the pervading motive being death. In *Sashka Zhegulev* the hero is present in each of the numerous scenes described, being the sole motive of the evolving drama. Even when absent in flesh, as when his mother and sister discuss their lost dear one, Sashka Zhegulev dominates in spirit, the pivot of the conversation, the focus of all interests, memories, thoughts, emotions. The same unity of motive and variety of settings can be observed in *Lazarus, The Governor, Satan's Diary,* and in all of Andreyev's *nouvelles.*

[47] *Æsthetics,* p. 18.

[48] "*L'individualité* des choses et des êtres nous echappe . . . nous ne voyons pas les choses mêmes; nous nous bornons, le plus souvent, à lire des étiquettes collées sur elles." *Le rire,* pp. 156–158, passim (Paris, 1908). He comes to the conclusion that the arts alone may bring us face to face with reality, for "l'art n'est sûrement qu'une vision plus directe de la réalite."—*Ibid.,* p. 161.

nancy in *Thought* and *The Governor,* where human thought
looms as a terrible and autonomous entity, dynamic and uncon-
trollable. Or, to cite another example, his playful description
of "shaggy" sleep, in *Darkness,* a story as yet unknown in the
English language.[49] Without any visible effort or labor Andreyev, when at his best, produces the desired impression. Thus
he tells us (in *Ghosts*) that Yegor "displayed his gums when
he laughed, and for this reason it seemed as though his whole
self laughed, inside and outside, and as though his very hair
laughed." [50] He conveys the idea of Musya's physical frailty
and spiritual ardor by describing her excessively large prison
coat, out of whose rolled-up sleeves emerged her "thin, almost
childlike, emaciated hands, like flower stems out of a coarse,
filthy pitcher," and by mentioning the "hot pallor" of her face,
which spoke of her great inner flame (in *The Seven That Were
Hanged* [51]). He suggests to us the deathly loneliness of the
pickpocket (in *The Thief*), when spurned by all decent people
he stands on the platform of the speeding train, and sings in
unison with the noise of the wheels; he sings toward the setting
sun, across the boundless fields, and pours out the yearning and
anguish of a hunted animal in the simple motive of that twilight song: "Come. Come to me." [52] With what an unpre-
tentious image he transmits the feelings of Haggart (in *The*

---

[49] When the Terrorist, for three days and nights hunted by the police, finally
seeks immunity in a house of prostitution, his fatigue begins to show itself:
"He tried to think about Thursday [the day on which he was to carry out his
terroristic act] . . . but his thoughts rebelled, bristled, pricked one another. It was
because offended sleep began to fret. So soft and gentle out there, on the street,
here it no longer stroked caressingly his face with a hairy, shaggy palm, but it
wrenched his legs and arms, and pulled his body as though intending to tear it.
". . . And he lay down . . . And sleep, delighted, smiled broadly, pressed the
man's cheek now with one shaggy cheek now with the other, softly embraced him,
tickled his knees, and became blissfully quiet, resting a soft downy head on his
breast.
". . . Down in the salon the music played, frequent stubby sounds with little
bald heads began to prance swiftly, and he thought: 'Now I may sleep'—and at
once fell fast asleep. Triumphantly squeaked shaggy sleep, embraced him warmly,
and breathless, in profound silence, both of them sped into a transparent, melting deep."—*Works—IX,* pp. 139, 142, 144.
[50] *Works—V,* p. 35.
[51] *Works—VIII,* pp. 15, 57.
[52] *Works—V,* pp. 11, 12.

Ocean), who crouches in the dead of the night under the window of the church: "The first sounds of the organ. Some one sits alone in the dark, and in an incomprehensible language converses with God about the most important thing." [53]

The last words might well apply to Andreyev himself. His language became less "comprehensible" whenever he aspired to discuss the "most important things." "I have never been able to express fully my attitude toward the world by way of realistic writing," he admitted in a letter to Amfiteatrov. [54] The rapid success of his realistic productions, instead of tempting him to acquiesce in the applauded subject matter and medium, urged him on into unexplored regions. His ideas broadened, his quest deepened, and he found himself impelled to vary his medium. His ambition to postulate questions touching on universal values appeared fettered by realism. Realistic art deals with the concrete, it reproduces life as it is—that is, life composed of relativities, of lights and shadows. Abstractions, absolute conceptions, to be presented by story or play, must needs discard the forms of actual life, and replace them with conditional forms wherein nothing is any longer impossible or improbable. Intending, for instance, to present man's life as *essentially* stupid, as ruled *absolutely* by malignant chance, Andreyev was forced to abandon realism, the enemy of absolutes, and create a life schematized, simplified, conventionalized, with the aid of symbols and allegories. As a child of his age, Andreyev voiced the contemporary want of a symbolic approach to life, a want reflected in current Scandinavian and Franco-Belgian literature as a reaction against realism overdone, just as one hundred years before romanticism appeared to be a recoil from stiff classicism. Tolstoy's resentment of modern tendencies as "artificial" and coming from a desire to be striking and "original," was due to his life-long endeavor to think rationally and to write realistically. He failed to admit that Strindberg and Maeterlinck, Andreyev and Claudel, Bryusov and Verhaeren, employed symbols chiefly because the complex modern soul was

[53] *Works—XIII*, p. 95.
[54] Probably in 1916.

weary of tangible particulars and sought to embrace universal abstractions, to interpret life in its quintessential aspect.

The symbolic element is present in all of Andreyev's works. As a modern artist, he prefers suggestion to outspokenness. With his painter's sense for color, and with his general inborn feeling for rhythm, he usually endeavors to create an atmosphere, a mood, with the aid of suggestive backgrounds, of suggestive sounds and words, of Stimmungssymbolik, in the terminology of Professor Volkelt.[55] The mad thoughts of Father Vasily (in *Life of Vasily Fiveysky*) on the eve of his final catastrophe take place during a terrible night, to the accompaniment of a raging and howling snowstorm. While he reads aloud to his guffawing idiot son from the Scripture, the wind comes wailing in unison: "Ikh dvoye. Ikh dvoye" (two of them), the repetition of the word "dvoye" imitating the wail of the wind in the chimney. In *The Tocsin*, the entire nerve-racking scene of the conflagration passes under the continuous groans and frantic shrieks of the alarm bells, a theme that may have been suggested by Poe's poem. "Tak bylo. Tak budet," monotonously tick-tacks the pendulum in *Thus It Was*, the recurring refrain enforcing the idea of human incurable sameness. "Pokatilis, pokatilis," rumble the wheels of the train, arousing a feeling of terror and doom in the heart of the thief (*The Thief*). The mood of "madness and horror" in *The Red Laugh* is attained both by the repetition and reversal of these two words, and by means of coloring everything in red—the skies, the fields, the faces, the metal on the guns. Grayness is the prevailing color in *The Life of Man*, symbolizing the drabness of life and of man's interests and aspirations. Music is prescribed in almost every play of Andreyev, suggesting such ideas as philistine commonplaceness (the ball scene in *The Life*

[55] Johannes Volkelt, *System der Æsthetic.* v. I: *Grundlegung der Æsthetic,* chapter VII, pp. 151-155. Munich, 1905. The author differentiates three kinds of symbolism in art—Vorstellungssymbolik, verallgemeinernde Symbolik, and Stimmungssymbolik. To the first class belong such universally accepted notions as black being the sign of mourning; to the second, such all-human types as Shakespeare's personages, or Goethe's Faust; to the third, such means as color or sound employed for the suggestion of a certain mood. Andreyev has used all these classes.

of *Man*), social smugness and class contrasts (the quadrille in *Tsar Hunger*), the tragic mingling of beauty and ugliness, of chastity and vice (the Duke's song, in *The Black Maskers*), universal cacophony and disharmony (the barrel organ, in *Anathema*), man's longing for religion (Dan's pipe organ, in *The Ocean*), the burlesque of life (the tango melody, in *He Who Gets Slapped*), man's marionette-like impotence (the waltz of the dogs, in the play by the same title), the luring call of the flesh (the Egyptian music, in *Samson Enchained*).

Andreyev's symbols possess also the quality of universal applicability. His symbolic characters are for the most part generalized particulars, individual cases placed in such circumstances and situations as to lend them a universal, all-human significance. Vasily Fiveysky purports to be as universal a type as Job or Brand. Man, in *The Life of Man,* is intended to typify the average representative of the human race. The author of *My Memoirs* is a generalized rationalist. The Workmen in *Tsar Hunger,* as well as the Engineer, the Priest, the Bourgeois, the Hooligans, in the same play, represent respective human categories in their universal aspect. All great works of art possess this quality of implying a broad significance, for art, we may repeat, is essentially both realistic and symbolic. Where symbols predominate, however, where implication is made prominent at the expense of explicitness, we expect the symbol to stand the test required by Goethe, namely: "Das ist die wahre Symbolik, wo das Besondere das Allgemeinere repräsentirt, nicht als Traum und Schatten, sondern als lebendig augenblickliche Offenbarung des Unerforschlichen." [56] Andreyev aims at achieving this persuasiveness in his symbolic works, at embodying in convincing flesh and blood images, metaphysical abstractions out of the region of the "Unerforschliches," at presenting these as a "living momentary revelation." He instills probability into the presentation of such unfathomable questions as Judas's possibly high motives in betraying Christ, as the ultimate analysis of one's soul, with its known and unknown ele-

---

[56] *Sämmtliiche Werke—III: Sprüche in Prosa*, p. 184. Cotta edition, Stuttgart, 1850.

ments and factors, as the mystery of death, as the knowability of absolute wisdom and justice, as the feasibility of combining freedom with truth. But for a full achievement of this ambitious aim, Andreyev lacks the genius of Goethe. The main weakness in Andreyev's purely symbolic works, *The Life of Man, The Black Maskers, Anathema, The Ocean,* consists in their lack of a persuasive unity of tone and mood. What Andreyev says of Maeterlinck in one of his essays is curiously applicable to his own symbolic productions:

. . . the symbolic form is suitable for ideas, lending them unparalleled expanse, but it is dangerous for psychology: there can be no psychologic truth where a clear motivation is lacking, where the very *basis* of the soul's movements is symbolic, of double meaning and words. The symbolist does not bring his heroes to tears, he forces them to weep; he presents as a given fact that which still has to be proved—psychologically, of course. Granted that in *La mort de Tintagiles,* Maeterlinck's strongest piece, the feeling of fear is developed with marvelous truthfulness, yet it is not sufficiently motivated, it lacks gradation, it is given from the very outset on faith; and if I am personally afraid of death, I shall readily become frightened, but, if not, I shall remain calm. More than mathematics does psychology demand: Prove! One may begin to yawn while looking at some one yawning, or to weep at the sight of a weeping man, or become scared in view of some one scared—the crowd knows this—but this is mere physiology. Only *proven* tears can move us to genuine grief, can arouse deep emotions. Maeterlinck does not prove, he only commands—and a command may be disobeyed. . . .[57]

One is inclined to disagree with Andreyev's demand of the provability of symbols. In his own works as well as in those of Maeterlinck one is indeed often commanded to take things for granted, but one obeys the command by virtue of the mood created by the author, to which we succumb involuntarily. In *L'intruse* or *Les aveugles,* in many parts of *The Black Maskers* or of *Anathema,* the Stimmungssymbolik performs the function of drawing us under the influence of an atmosphere that is all-powerful and pervading. The fear of death suggested by *La*

[57] *Letters on the Theatre,* in *Wild Rose Almanacs,* No. 22, pp. 267–268, Petrograd, 1914.

mort de Tintagiles is a universal feeling which requires no "proof." Where proof is needed there the mood is not convincing. It is in this respect that Andreyev occasionally falls short, unlike Maeterlinck, whose early plays are irresistible in their sustained Stimmung. Andreyev often forces us to ask for proofs, because he destroys the unity of style, the unity of mood in his writings. *Anathema* in its Prologue and Epilogue is symbolic-allegoric, while through its five acts we are driven from rank realism (the masterly opening scene in the market-place) to incidental symbolism sandwiched between ordinary speeches (the motive of Rosa-beauty, the organ-grinder, Anathema's asides). In *The Life of Man* we are prepared for a conventionalized atmosphere, with a Someone-in-Gray, a flickering candle, an algebraic Man. Then the author of a sudden breaks the suggestive tone by bits of realistic outspokenness. The screams of the mother giving birth to a child do not harmonize with the symbolized stage, nor does the figure of the regular stage doctor, nor some of Man's ultra-realistic addresses to Someone-in-Gray. The reference to automobiles lends the play a chronologic finiteness, robbing it of its alleged fitness for all times and places.

Andreyev's lack of unity in the tone of his symbolic plays is evidenced also in his frequent failing to sustain the delicate subtlety of the symbol, and reducing it to allegory. The symbol bears an intrinsic value, is independent of its underlying meaning, and may be enjoyed for its apparent form as much as for its implied idea. The allegory, on the other hand, is not unlike a rebus, wherein every stroke and letter is indispensable for the construction of the whole idea, and is absolutely inseparable from the notion it formulates. Symbolism obviously requires more subtle art than allegory, the latter following closely upon the heel of the primitive fable. Andreyev is not the only artist who finds himself tempted to follow the direction of lesser resistance, and drop from the giddy edge of suggestive symbol to the plateau of demonstrative allegory.[58] Andreyev appears

[58] A striking instance may be cited from Ibsen's *The Lady of the Sea*, in which the author fails to sustain the symbolization of the lure of the sea, and introduces

at times torn between the two modes of presentation. In *The Life of Man* allegory prevails, introducing, as in *Everyman,* personifications of abstract ideas. Yet the Man and his Wife, in their conversations and in the peripeteias of their fortunes, form a plot in itself, of suggestive symbolic artfulness, which is vitiated by the interspersed allegoric banalities. In *Anathema,* Anathema is an allegory, personifying the Evil spirit accursed by God, but at times he rises to symbolize the universal thirst for knowing the absolute truth, sinking again into allegory as Nullius, the tempter. Even *The Black Maskers,* than which Andreyev has written few more striking pieces of poetic prose suffused with Stimmungssymbolik, suffers from the intrusion of allegoric figures, such as the castle-soul, as Thoughts, Heart, Hate, which render the play in places too transparent for symbolism, yet too complex and obscure for a morality play. The break of unity defeats the author's ambitious intention.

Obscurity is another trait of Andreyev's symbolic writings, hinted at by Tolstoy, and present not only in his plays, where clarity may be impeded by stage limitations of time and space, but also in some of his stories, the type of composition which allows scope for ample clearness of expression. Such of his works, as *Judas Iscariot, Lazarus, The Black Maskers, The Ocean,* have set the public and the critics guessing as to their true meaning, often arousing conjectures of various kinds. A noisy popular critic, K. Arabazhin, voiced the prevailing sentiment by exclaiming: "We decidedly protest against reducing literary criticism to the solution of new rebuses and charades, labeled Symbols." [59] One may agree with Pater concerning the "pleasurable stimulus" derived by strenuous minds from a style not too obvious,[60] and one can appreciate Andreyev's fastidious

in the end the Stranger, an obtrusive personification greatly impairing the delicate quality of the play.

[59] *Leonid Andreyev,* p. 228, Petrograd, 1910.

[60] " 'To go preach to the first passer-by' says Montaigne, 'to become tutor to the ignorance of the first I meet, is a thing I abhor'; a thing, in fact, naturally distressing to the scholar, who will therefore ever be shy of offering uncomplimentary assistance to the reader's wit. To really strenuous minds there is a pleasurable stimulus in the challenge for a continuous effort on their part, to be rewarded by a securer and more intimate grasp of the author's sense."—*Appreciations,* p. 17, London, 1911.

frown at the need for new things to get the "visé" of a "vulgar and mediocre Arabazhin." [61] Symbolic art has never been accessible to the broad public, appealing as a special delight and æsthetic adventure to those who are in no hurry to "understand" when they approach art. There are not many who share Edmund Gosse's pleasure in fathoming the obscurest of French Symbolistes, Stéphane Mallarmé, whose "desire was to use words in such harmonious combinations as will induce in the reader a mood or a condition which is not mentioned in the text, but was nevertheless paramount in the poet's mind at the moment of composition." [62] Andreyev's *Ocean, Black Maskers,* and many other productions, abound in such suggestive "harmonious combinations," considerably less cryptic than *Après-midi d'un faune,* whose obscurity aroused the somewhat vehement plea of Remy de Gourmont for the need of a greater number of obscure writers. [63] How Andreyev resented the public demands for "clearness" can be seen from the following extracts from his letter to the director of the Dramatic Theatre at Moscow, in reply to the latter's request for a slight revision of *The Black Maskers:*

For me *The Black Maskers*—the sad fate of Duke Lorenzo—is a thing complete, finished once and for all, which cannot tolerate any one's interference, not even the author's.

No matter how much I try to explain, he will never understand me,

---

[61] *Letters on the Theatre,* p. 269.

[62] *French Profiles,* p. 319, London, 1913. In regard to the quoted sentence of Gosse, Mallarmé wrote to him: "Il y a, entre toutes, une phrase, où vous écartez tous voiles et désignez la chose avec une clairvoyance de diamant, le voici: 'His desire was' [etc.] Tout est là."—*Ibid.,* p. 320.

[63] "Il y a trop peu d'écrivains obscurs en français; ainsi nous nous habituons lâchement à n'aimer que des écritures aisées, et bientôt primaires. Pourtant il est rare que livres aveuglément clairs vaillent la peine d'être relus; la clarté, c'est ce qui fait le prestige des littératures classiques et c'est ce qui les rend si clairment ennuyeuses. Les esprits clairs sont d'ordinaire ceux qui ne voient qu'une chose à la fois; dès que le cerveau est riche de sensations et d'idées, il se fait un remous et la nappe se trouble à l'heure du jaillissement. Préférons, comme X. Doudan, les marais grouillants de vie à un verre d'eau claire. Sans doute, on a soif, parfois; eh bien, on filtre. La littérature qui plaît aussitôt à l'universalité des hommes est nécessairement nulle; il faut que, tombée de haut, elle rejaillisse en cascade, de pierre en pierre, pour enfin couler dans la vallée à la portée de tous les hommes et de tous les troupeaux."—*La culture des idées,* pp. 127, 128. Paris, 1910.

to whom are foreign the torments of rebellious conscience, the sorrow of lost hopes, the grief of deceived love and of friendship trampled under foot. . . . He will never understand me, whose soul is comfortably peaceful, whose heart is thick with health and fat, whose ear is turned to the outside, but has never turned inward, has never heard the clang of clashing swords, the voices of madness and pain, the savage noise of the great battle, for which man's heart has served as a field since time immemorial. He will never understand me, who has not lit a fire on the tower of his reason and of his heart, and has not perceived the illuminated road along which approach strange guests, and has not grasped that great riddle of existence—the appearance of darkness in response to the call of light, the emergence of black, cold beings knowing neither God nor Satan, shadows of shadows, beginnings of beginnings. Born of light, they love light, yearn for light, and extinguish it inevitably. And not one word do I wish to add for him who does not and never will understand me. As to those who do understand me, for them another word is superfluous.[64]

One cannot gainsay the author's right to endow his works with an inner subtlety comprehensible only to those who possess a penetrating vision. Yet one cannot help accusing Andreyev of vagueness not only in regard to the hidden implications of certain symbols of his, but even of vagueness in their visible presentation. "All art hates the vague; not the mysterious but the vague," observes Arthur Symons.[65] *The Life of Vasily Fiveysky* is a realistic tale, clearly told, with the main character as a symbolic type. *The Life of Man* is an allegoric-symbolic modernized morality play, where both the visible images and their underlying meanings are as comprehensible as *Everyman* or as *Aglavaine et Sélysette*. Andreyev, like the early Maeterlinck, has the faculty of reducing universal problems and situations to simple, almost naïve formulæ.[66] The more is one ag-

[64] From a letter addressed to "Konstantin Nikolayevich," evidently Director Nezlobin. No date. Probably written in 1915, when *The Black Maskers* was presented at the Dramatic Theatre.

[65] *The Symbolist Movement in Literature*, p. 307.

[66] Compare the Prayers of Man and his Wife, for simplicity in expressing a universal human attitude, with the words of Maeterlinck's Aglavaine, stating one of the eternal tragic situations:
. . . "n'est-ce pas étrange, Sélysette? je t'aime, j'aime Méléandre, Méléandre m'aime, il t'aime aussi, tu nous aimes l'un et l'autre, et cependant nous ne pourrions pas vivre heureux, parce que l'heure n'est pas encore venue où des êtres humains

gravated by the ambiguities encountered in his later works.
Judas's motive in betraying Christ is not made clear by the
author, nor can we see our way clear in the labyrinthine symbols
or allegories of *The Ocean*, nor may we be sure of comprehend-
ing the sequence of events in *The Black Maskers*—is Duke
Lorenzo insane in the first act or in the last? Again, the
scene of the duel between the Duke and his double, as well as
the scene of the Duke standing at the head of his dead body,
are mystifying, to say the least, in regard to their visible probability. The author evidently takes for granted that the
reader or spectator knows what he knows, an assumption which
provokes a comparison used by Andreyev in regard to Maeterlinck, namely, that the spectator of the Belgian's plays resembles
"a perfectly sober person appearing at a party, where everybody has been drunk for a long time, and where, moreover, all
the wine has already been consumed: it is difficult to get intoxicated just from drunken embraces!" [67] Or perhaps the
author himself in not quite clear as to his ideas and intentions,
hence the obscurity of his presentation? [68] This is not an ir-
reverent innuendo, for we find Andreyev actually exalting the
artist's ignorance of his aims. Praising the Moscow Art
Theatre for its gropings and errors, he states that "the genuine artist, like the sinner, must never know what he doeth. . . .
The artist must be a *mystery* to himself, otherwise he may lose

puissent s'unir ainsi. . . ."—*Aglavaine et Sélysette,* Acte III, scène 3, p. 79 of v.
III, ed. *Théâtre.* Paris, 1905.

[67] *Letters on the Theatre,* p. 268.

[68] Schopenhauer, the one thinker whom Andreyev admired to the end, has an
incisive paragraph on this subject:
"Dunkelheit und Undeutlichkeit des Ausdrucks ist allemal und überall ein sehr
schlimmes Zeichen. Denn in neunundneunzig Fällen under hundert rührt sie her
von der Undeutlichkeit des Gedankens, welche selbst wiederum fast immer aus
einem ursprünglichen Missverhältniss, Inkonsistenz und also Unrichtigkeit desselben
entspringt. Wenn, in einem Kopfe, ein richtiger Gedanke aufsteigt, strebt er schon
nach der Deutlichkeit und wird sie bald erreichen: das deutlich Gedachte aber
findet leicht seinen angemessenen Ausdruck."—*Ueber Schriftstellerei und Stil,* in
v. IV of *Werke,* p. 481. Weichert, Berlin.
Essentially, this is also the view of Croce. He denies that we may have important thoughts, and yet not be able to express them. Our failure to express them
beautifully and fully testifies to the fact that we have not grasped those thoughts
clearly and completely. For "every true intuition or representation is, also, *expression.*"—*Æsthetic,* p. 13 ff., *passim.*

his sincerity, with the loss of which he will lose everything. And even if the Art Theatre has indeed committed mistakes because of not knowing itself, then even this is for the best: mistakes are necessary, truth will spring forth out of them, as the grain stalk out of manure." [69]   These words Andreyev may have applied to himself: the publication of his *Letters* coincided with his new departure—his "pan-psychic" productions, of which we shall speak presently.

Tolstoy's admonition against "hasty writing," and his direct advice to Andreyev to "work longer" over his compositions, touch upon another important side of the author's personality —his inability to create consciously and laboriously. "He could not change or polish up the things he had written," observes K. Chukovsky. . . . "His works were extemporaneous improvizations by their very nature." [70]   Maxim Gorky also reprimands Andreyev for his "slipshod" writing, for his lack of assiduity, for his aversion to "work." "He treated his talent," says Gorky, "as a poor rider treats his splendid steed— he galloped it mercilessly, but never cherished nor loved it. His hand could not keep up with his vehement fantasy in drawing its complicated designs, and he did not take care to develop the power and dexterity of his hand." [71]   The truth is that both Tolstoy and Gorky were guilty of occasional "slipshod" writing—few Russian prose writers have been immune from this sin. Yet Tolstoy, who rewrote his gigantic *War and Peace* seven times, and who taxed the patience of his family and his publishers with his numerous corrections and changes, [72] was justified in demanding fastidiousness on the part of the younger writers. While Chekhov still preserved the traditions of Turgenev's chiseled prose, his younger contemporaries displayed a hurried carelessness in their impressionistic compositions. The *Znaniye* group expressed their departure from the "gentry literature" not only in contents, but in tone and form as well, flaunting as it were their care-free manners and defiance of con-

[69] *Letters on the Theatre,* p. 247.
[70] *A Book on Andreyev,* p. 51.
[71] *Ibid.,* p. 33.
[72] See G. R. Noyes, *Tolstoy,* pp. 132–134. New York, 1918.

ventions. In direct contrast to these "savages" stood the group of the so-called Decadents or Symbolists, the small coterie of Russian followers of the Franco-Belgian Parnassiens and their successors, the Symbolistes. The writers of this group often placed form above content. Andreyev occupied his usual position among his contemporaries—a solitary position. Endowed with a natural feeling for rhythm, and with a fine sense for form and color (witness his not unsuccessful attempts at painting), Andreyev produced at times a prose which would have delighted even such an exacting stylist as Flaubert. But being an "inspirational" writer, he depended exclusively on his intuition, scorning the toil and travail recommended and practiced by such masters of technique as E. A. Poe. Certainly he was incapable of the amazing perseverance with which Gustave Flaubert labored over his style, painstakingly searching for the form that would precisely fit the idea.[73]

Because of the beautiful brilliance of Andreyev's style, its drawbacks and flaws are much more irritating than they would be in a modest, gray style. A tiny spot may be quite lost on drab material, but it bulges and looms in magnitude when on a bright cloth. In a masterpiece, psychological as well as stylistic, like *The Seven That Were Hanged*, one is particularly annoyed by a few points which show lack of reserve in the author. The final pages relating the arrival of the prisoners at the place of execution, their last words, and their death, are filled with

---

[73] "Possessed of an absolute belief that there exists but one way of expressing one thing, one word to call it by, one adjective to qualify, one verb to animate it, he gave himself to superhuman labor for the discovery, in every phrase, of that word, that verb, that epithet. In this way, he believed in some mysterious harmony of expression, and when a true word seemed to him to lack euphony still went on seeking another, with invincible patience, certain that he had not yet got hold of the *unique* word. . . . A thousand preoccupations would beset him at the same moment, always with this desperate certitude fixed in his spirit: Among all the expressions in the world, all forms and turns of expressions, there is but *one* —one form, one mode—to express what I want to say."—Walter Pater, *Appreciations*, p. 29, quoting "a sympathetic commentator."

Gorky states that occasionally Andreyev would become aware of his frivolous attitude toward his style, and then he would say: "Yes, I must read Flaubert. You are apparently right: He is, indeed, a descendant of one of those geniusmasons who built the indestructible cathedrals of the Middle Ages!"—*A Book on Andreyev*, p. 33.

subdued pathos, and are written in such a delicate language that one is hardly aware of it as of a medium. Yet carried away by an impressionistic sleight, Andreyev twice underlines the detail of Sergey's lost golosh looming black on the snow field: a shrieking detail in the hushed atmosphere. Or again: the concluding paragraph describing the dead bodies lolling in the coffins, with "elongated necks, bulging eyes, and blue tongues protruding from their mouths," is a crude bit of naturalism which adds nothing to the impressiveness of the story, but rather weakens the effect of surcharged, unuttered tragedy. In the chapter, "Kiss him and be silent," in the same story, Andreyev draws one of the most heartrending scenes in world literature. Few can read it without choking emotion. Yet the chapter contains not one loud word, not one emphatic phrase or simile. "Here took place that which one must not and cannot describe," is the somewhat disappointing conclusion of this chapter. But Andreyev's omission in this case is more pardonable, if not praiseworthy, than his failure to omit the obtrusive details of the golosh and the bulging eyes. Here and elsewhere he is guilty of a lack of selectiveness, a sin one could not attribute to Turgenev or Chekhov, a sin that would appear unpardonable to Walter Pater.[74] This weakness is demonstrated in such works of Andreyev as *The Wall, The Red Laugh, The Tocsin, The Curse of the Beast, Life of Vasily Fiveysky, Lazarus.* Each of these productions illustrates some powerful idea—life's cruelty and futility, the madness of war, the pathos of solitude, the horror of city life, the tragedy of faith colliding with reason, the paralyzing terror of death. Moreover, they all succeed in driving their central idea home, they persuade the reader. Yet each one of them suffers in a larger or lesser degree from what Pater calls surplusage. The reader is convinced not by way of sug-

---

[74] " 'The artist,' says Schiller, 'may be known rather by what he *omits*'; and in literature, too, the true artist may be best recognized by his fact of omission." And on the next page: "Surplusage! he [the true artist] will dread that, as the runner on his muscles. For in truth all art does but consist in the removal of surplusage, from the last finish of the gem engraver blowing away the last particle of invisible dust, back to the earliest divination of the finished work to be, lying somewhere, according to Michelangelo's fancy, in the rough-hewn block of stone." —*Appreciations,* pp. 18, 19, 20.

gestion, of æsthetic emotion, but rather by means of a verbal sledgehammer. The reader yields to the author's argument in a state resembling physical exhaustion caused by a cumulative succession of horrors. The inner idea is conveyed to him by means of external details which prepare him, one might say, physiologically, for the attitude which the author wishes him to accept. Thus his aversion for life is generated by a series of nauseating descriptions of malodorous lepers, in *The Wall*. His hatred for war is aroused with the aid of heaps of dead bodies and masses of demented beings, to the brazen accompaniment of the refrain: "Madness and horror. Horror and madness," in *The Red Laugh*. An uninterrupted series of misfortunes and accidents in the life of the pious Vasily Fiveysky leads you to doubt the justice of Providence. The horror of death creeps upon you from the livid motionless hand of Lazarus, "forgotten on the table." These methods of persuasion may be legitimate for purposes of propaganda, but to art they are as foreign as gore-filled slaughter houses or anatomical museums. Andreyev would probably reject them if he gave them a second thought, if he were not in a hurry to express his momentary intuition, which one could hardly expect to be always felicitous. It is this "hurry" that explains why he uses at times violent epithets and bombastic metaphors—a sheer "surplusage." Despite his wonderful mastery of the Russian language, his excellent utilization of the most intimate recesses of human speech, he sometimes sacrifices simplicity to such labored phrases as "each nerve resembled a rearing bent wire, on whose edge rose a little head with eyes madly bulging from horror, with a convulsively gaping mouth, speechless mouth" (in the first chapter of *The Seven That Were Hanged*) ; "The bell suffocated in torments of death agony, and it moaned like a person who no longer expected help, and had no more hope" (*The Tocsin*). He uses too unsparingly such expressions as "terror," "grave and enigmatic fate," "enormous, bottomless silence," "elemental boundless thought," "boundless calm," "silently enigmatic fields," "fatal inevitability," "boundless all-powerful darkness," "fiery liquid in a cup of sufferings"—all these epithets appearing in a single realistic work, *The Life of Vasily Fiveysky,* and typical of his occasional loud speech elsewhere. The brass music often detracts from the unity of tone, and weakens the hold of the main motive on your attention and interest. As Walter Pater remarks:

. . . the ornamental word, the figure, the accessory form or color or reference, is rarely content to die to thought precisely at the right moment, but will inevitably linger a while stirring a long "brain wave" behind it of perhaps quite alien associations.[75]

Gorky tells us of his futile efforts to persuade Andreyev to labor with care on his composition. Amazed at his energetic creative activity at Capri, soon after the death of his first wife, Gorky at the same time observed many inaccuracies in Andreyev's writings. But when Gorky protested that "Duke of Spadaro" (in *The Black Maskers*) would sound to an Italian as absurdly as "Prince Bashmachnikov" (shoemaker) to a Russian, and that in the twelfth century there had been no St. Bernard dogs, Andreyev was annoyed. "These are trifles," he retorted. And he considered "nonsense" the remark that one must not use the expression: "they drink wine like camels," that one should say: "as camels drink water." [76] Gorky admits, however, his admiration for his friend's brilliant talent. Regarding himself humbly as "a dray horse" rather than as "an Arabian steed," Gorky worked hard on the education of his mind, read quantities of books, endeavored to gather information, facts, precise knowledge. On numerous occasions Andreyev astonished him by divining at one glance the essence of some very complex matter, on which Gorky had spent much time and labor. "Leonid Nikolayevich," says Gorky, "was talented by his very nature, organically talented; his intuition was amazingly sensitive. In everything pertaining to the dark sides of

[75] *Ibid.,* p. 18. Andreyev's loud phrases would certainly have been scorned by his "master," Schopenhauer, who admonished the German writers, "dass man zwar, wo möglich, denken soll wie ein grosser Geist, hingegen die selbe Sprache reden wie jeder andere. Man brauche gewöhnliche Worte und sage ungewöhnliche Dinge."—*Werke—IV,* p. 480.
[76] *A Book on Andreyev,* p. 33.

life, to the contradictions in man's soul, to ebullitions in the region of instincts, he was uncannily perspicacious." [77]

It becomes evident that Andreyev created almost all his works not in the cool atmosphere of deliberation, but in the quick flame of inspirational intuition. Conceiving in a flash some image or idea, he would become impregnated with it, and be relieved only upon discharging it speedily, reluctant to prolong the pangs of travail. Skitalets describes his conversation with the Andreyevs, during which he expressed his wonder at the fact that "such a big and powerful thing" as *The Ocean* was written in so short a time as two weeks. Whereupon Mme. Andreyev retorted that in her opinion "that was the only way in which the tragedy could have been written—by inspiration." Her husband, while dictating it, "ran up and down the study like one possessed, his hair standing on end, his eyes burning . . . One might lose one's reason by writing such mad fantasies too long." [78] In the same way he created his other works, consumed by an inner flame which was urgent and permitted neither respite nor deliberation. Mme. Andreyev spoke to me of her feeling of wonderment during the period when her husband produced *Anathema*. "The work," she wrote to me on another occasion, "was genuine inspiration. Not a single correction was made in the manuscript. One night he dictated to me eight hours in succession." Once written and published, his production did not interest him: he did not think of it, regarded it with a certain coldness, "as though he was oversated by it," according to Chukovsky. [79] This was at any rate true during his artistic activity—that is, before the war. He did not like to discuss his former works, but was always looking forward to his next one, which he expected to excel everything he had done before. [80] One gains the impression that literary activity

[77] *Ibid.*, pp. 10, 11, 19, *passim.*
[78] *Russia's Voice*, February 21, 1922.
[79] *A Book on Andreyev*, p. 51.
[80] *Ibid.*, p. 51. In a letter to Nemirovich-Danchenko, director of the Moscow Art Theatre, Andreyev wrote, evidently in reply to some remark about his play which was running then at that theatre: "I am not thinking about *Katherina Ivanovna*, and I do not intend to. Why should I? To-day or to-morrow I set out to write a new play, and already these new people, with whom I am as yet

was to Andreyev not so much a positive joy as a liberation from fixed, obsessing ideas. How could Tolstoy or Gorky expect him to be slow and meticulous about his composition, when this process amounted to pulling an arrow out of one's wound! One should bear in mind, furthermore, that Andreyev's reasoning faculty hardly functioned in his creative moments. About one year before his death he entered in his diary the admission that nearly all his "best things were written at times of the greatest personal confusion, during periods of the most depressing mental experiences." Thus he wrote *Judas* shortly after the death of his first wife, when his thought was "completely in bondage to the images of her illness and death." His *Seven That Were Hanged* he composed while "sick and crazed after a spell of drunkenness." During his most productive period, in the autumn of 1908, he was living through a terrible tragedy. "It is beyond doubt that regarding my personal state of mind during those months I was in a condition of psychosis, of a serious semi-dementia." Yet it was then that he wrote "with unusual lightness and speed" his *My Memoirs*—"the work was interrupted by moods which were close to murder and insanity"; then *Days of Our Life, The Black Maskers,*[81] *The Son of Man,* and *Anathema.* "On the contrary, after a good sleep, in a balanced state of mind, in fair health and domestic prosperity, my writing was poorer." The conclusion at which Andreyev arrives in that entry is perhaps too sweeping, a reflection of his morbid physical and mental condition at the time of writing the diary, but like every exaggeration it contains an element of truth: "Hence the conclusion: My *thought* is the enemy of my work. It is necessary for me to think of something else, in order to let

but slightly acquainted, agitate me, draw me into their emotions and experiences, lure me. . . . To them, indeed, I am going."—(Written in the fall of 1912).   .

[81] Mme. Andreyev informs me in a letter that *Days of Our Life* was completed in seven days and *The Black Maskers* in the following seven days. It is remarkable how the author could transport himself from one mood to an altogether different one without pausing. Another illustration both of his speed and of his artistic reaction to "depressing experiences," is given by Mme. Andreyev: *"The Parrot* or rather *The Pessimist* [a one act symbolic play, about ten pages long] was written in three or four hours on a certain evening, when Leonid Nikolayevich became agitated by the high temperature of our boy, Savva . . ."

intuition get freed and boldly create its own work, not depending on reason, and not pursued by it." [82]

A word more must be said in connection with Andreyev's literary methods. His *Letters on the Theatre*, published in 1912–1913, are interesting both as a retrospect and as a forecast. He advocates there the need of reforming the theatre from that of external action to one of "soul," of "pan-psyche." Action, movement on a large scale, reproduction of visible, physical life, he relegates to the cinematograph. The "legitimate" stage must relinquish its outworn methods and conventional plots. The age of Benvenuto Cellini, with its numerous incidents, escapes, murders, surprises, is gone. The modern intellectual is more interested in the personality of a Nietzsche, externally uneventful, "yet of the most tragic hero of modernity." The theatre ought to satisfy the subtle requirement of the modern audience, by revealing the inner world of the soul, by displaying the interaction of thoughts, of moods. This view of Andreyev sheds light on his important works written before that time, in which he had intended to unveil the soul of modern man, and analyze his institutions, beliefs, doubts, seekings, aspirations. His criticism, in these *Letters,* of the symbolic drama, and in particular of Maeterlinck "commanding" symbolism, indicates perhaps the author's feeling of having partially failed in accomplishing his purpose in his own symbolistic plays. The weakness of these, discussed in the preceding pages, consisted largely in their lack of inner and exterior unity, in the clash between the visible reality and the underlying symbol, where the two should merge and harmonize. Andreyev's remark about the salutary effect of mistakes, with reference to the Moscow Art Theatre,[83] has a personal application. Indeed, his first *Letter* was published in 1912, one year after *The Ocean.* The plays which followed this Tragedy, *Professor Storitsyn, Katherina Ivanovna, Thou Shalt Not Kill, He Who Gets Slapped, The Waltz of the Dogs* (published posthumously),

---

[82] A fuller exposition of this remarkable entry is, unfortunately, considered premature.

[83] *Supra,* pp. 111, 112.

Samson Enchained (yet unpublished in the Russian), and some minor attempts, present Andreyev's departure from symbolism to what he labels pan-psychism. Still convinced that the stage ought to be an arena for the display of our inner experiences rather than of external "action," he succeeds in fusing both elements. His plays of this period are psychologically correct and "provable," and they are free from the obvious flaw of his earlier symbolic productions—obscurity. His later dramas, pregnant though they are with symbols, are understandable to the average audience. *He Who Gets Slapped* has been a theatrical success, even in the United States, the land of the tired business man. The reason for this success lies in the fact that though failing to grasp the hidden meanings and symbols in this play, the audience finds satisfaction in its visible, universally comprehensible element. A symbolistic, or "pan-psychic," work of art ought to have such a double appeal—to persons of a limited, superficial vision, and, over the head of these, to the chosen few who are congenial with the author. Writing to the director of the Moscow Art Theatre about *Samson Enchained,* Andreyev says: "Here is a formal tragedy, and at the same time a tragedy based on inner experiences, pan-psyche, psychic realism—call it what you will. My ideal: a tragedy over which Schopenhauer and his cook would weep together." [84]

Andreyev's personal attitude toward the form of his writings has been clearly expressed in his private letters, where he found it easier to dot the i's. Of particular interest is his letter to Alexander Amfiteatrov, a prolific journalist and novelist, popular with the pre-revolutionary radical readers. The external clarity of *Thou Shalt Not Kill* prompted Amfiteatrov to congratulate its author on his "return" to realism. Here are some excerpts from Andreyev's answer:

It is true, that *Thou Shalt Not Kill* is realistic in character, at least in its external form. But it signifies neither a deviation in the direction of "genuine" realism nor a renunciation of my mystic-symbolic seekings. The plain fact is that such a form was the only one which suited the

[84] Letter to V. I. Nemirovich-Danchenko, dated December 28, 1914.

particular mood (not my personal mood) and the particular idea . . . I have never kept to one form as obligatory, and, generally speaking, have never fettered the freedom of my form or tendency. . . .

In contrast to the prevailing categorical insistence on form as the primary source of the contents, to me form has been and is merely the boundary of the contents, determined by it, and issuing from it. Roughly speaking, man comes first, and his trousers afterward. . . .

It may be lack of power, but I have never been able to express fully my attitude toward the world by way of realistic writing. Most probably, this indicates that by my inner literary-human make-up I am not a realist. What am I, then? A mystic? I do not know. And, when all is said, I simply do not understand, and—pardon me—I do not accept *this* classification, it appears ridiculous to me. For, in my view, Alexey Maximovich [Gorky] is just such a mystic . . . and just such a mystic was the most realistic Ludwig Börne in the moment when with closed eyes he sang to the mystic joy of death on a barricade.

Life is a Mystery for all who think and live in earnest. The main question is, Where does man come in [in the artist's work]?—and not whether one employs "symbols" for the expression of his feelings, or the form of a Turgenev-Kuprin novel. Let him express himself by means of a cube . . . only let him express man, and not a hog in a skullcap.

. . . But sometimes form may arouse hatred and ardent desire to battle with it. This occurs in the case, unfortunately not too rare, when form becomes a dogma, an exclusive path into paradise. And when symbolism demands of me that I shall even blow my nose symbolically, I shall send it to the devil. And when realism requires that even my dreams be constructed after the recipe of Kuprin's stories, then I reject realism.[85]

In this letter we have Andreyev's creed. He expresses here his hatred for fetters and dogmas, his paramount interest in man, his complex make-up, his variegated modes of approach to life. In the last account he is a realistic writer, for when at his best he lends the quality of gripping actuality to the world of his creation, even if this world be woven out of the threads of his fantasy. Had he obeyed the admonition of Tolstoy, and "worked longer" on his writings, these might have been more evenly effective. But Andreyev would not have been Andreyev

[85] Letter, probably written in 1916. See *supra*, p. 103.

if he had emulated Tolstoy or Gorky or Flaubert. He must be taken for what he is, with all his shortcomings and idiosyncrasies. The flaws in his style diminish but slightly the value of his work as an expression of our questioning age. We may sum up with the words of his bitter opponent, Dmitri Merezhkovsky, who, after abusing Andreyev as an artist, has this to say in explanation of his interest in the latter's productions:

> At all events, in regard to his influence on the reader's mind, he has no equal among the contemporary Russian writers. All of them are candles under bushels, he alone is a candle on the table. They have infected no one, he infects everybody. Good or bad, this is so, and the critics cannot help considering this, if criticism consists in understanding not only that which is written about life, but also that which takes place in life.
>
> The æsthetes of the Roman decadence refused to read the Apostle Paul, because he wrote an imperfect Greek. Those were losers in the end who did not read Paul: they overlooked Christianity. I am not comparing Andreyev with the Apostle Paul, but I fear lest we overlook life in this case, too.[86]

Externally, Andreyev's life in Finland had the appearance of success and prosperity. He became the highest paid author in Russia, his contributions were solicited by editors, publishers, stage producers, and even directors of moving pictures. Yet, owing to his fastidiousness, he refused to cater to the public taste, to compromise for its sake at the request of those solicitors, and though well known and universally read, he enjoyed neither popularity nor affection. Hence he never attained financial success, and never made his income correspond with the large expenditures made necessary by his "broad" mode of living, with its Russian hospitality and Russian unpracticality.[87] He craved material independence, in order to afford the luxury of writing precisely what and as he pleased, ignoring the polite "suggestions" of publishers and producers, as well as the vituperations of "up-to-date" critics.[88] With the exception of *The*

---

[86] *In a Still Slough*, p. 205.

[87] He nicknamed his Finnish home "Villa Avance," because it was built and kept up by advances on his future productions.

[88] As late in his career as 1915 he had to fight for his freedom of expression, as can be seen from the following passage, taken from a letter to a director of a

Seven That Were Hanged, nearly every important work of his since *The Life of Man* met with abuse on the part of newspaper reviewers and popular critics, such as Arabazhin, and such professional theatrical reporters as Yartsev and Efros.[89] He was generally reproached for the obscurity of his symbols, accused of pornography, and relegated to the dustbin as out of date. The last murderous argument was advanced in view of Andreyev's persistently gloomy tone, in spite of the fact that during the half decade before the war all was apparently well in Russia.[90] Unmoved by the blatancy of the superficial mod-

theatre: "If they are not going to publish my work in a way I consider worthy, I shall simply give nothing for publication; if a play of mine cannot be produced in the proper way, it shall not be produced at all. And, in general, I prefer entirely not to be rather than to exist 'relatively.' "—Letter dated May 26, 1915.

[89] These two, writing for Moscow and Petrograd publications, were considerably more reserved in their tone than the provincial reporters. To cite an example: In 1910 Andreyev found himself forced to issue a public "explanation" in connection with the attack of the Kiev reporters against his work and personality. He quoted some of the epithets those gentlemen applied to him, such as "commercial artist," "pimp of his talent," and the like.—*Theatre and Art (Teatr i Iskusstvo),* No. 37, p. 679. Petrograd, 1910.

Andreyev's treatment by the conservative ecclesiastics is typified in an article by Bishop Hermogenes, during the same year, in which he labels *Anathema* "an infamous pasquinade against Divine Providence," citing numerous passages from the New Testament to prove that Andreyev has intended his play as a diatribe against Christ and Christianity, his other aim being "the replacement of Christianity by so-called Demonism, or the worship of the devil, as a basis for modern life." In regard to Andreyev's play, *Anfisa,* the bishop is "deeply convinced" that it "contains a patent and conscious advocacy of depravity and abominable vices." The bishop concludes that Andreyev presents "without doubt" "a certain dark and evil power emanating from Freemasonry or from some other revolutionary organizations."—*The Russian Banner (Russkoye Znamya),* No. 3, 1910; the most reactionary daily published in Petrograd.

[90] This point of view was fully expressed by Professor Peter Kogan in his *Notes on the History of Modern Russian Literature (Ocherki po istorii noveyshey russkoy literatury),* v. III, part II, pp. 1–61 (Moscow, 1912), in which he devoted to Andreyev sixty scathing pages. Considering literature as a direct reflection of contemporary social moods, this critic came to the conclusion that Andreyev was a superannuated writer, since he voiced the pessimistic views of the preceding decade instead of voicing the vigorous and joyous present. It may be objected, in the first place, that Andreyev's productions reflect not temporary moods for their own sake, but use them as a basis for eternal questions which have occupied thinking minds since time immemorial. Secondly, Professor Kogan's optimism in regard to the contemporary pulse of society was hardly warranted. The deep impression made on the public by Andreyev's plays of that period—*Professor Storitsyn, Katherina Ivanovna, Thou Shalt Not Kill*—was due precisely to the fact of their illuminating the reigning emptiness, pettiness, weariness and vulgarity of Russian society in the years immediately preceding the war. Indeed, there were Russians who ade-

ern prophets and seers, continuing to heed only the "voice of God"—his inner voice, Andreyev courted solitude and isolation. That he did not bear his position altogether indifferently may be seen from the following passages taken from a letter of his to Nemirovich-Danchenko (date of March 27, 1913):

> For five years, having neither allies nor sympathetic critics nor a single friendly press organ, I have been battling alone against my critics and my readers for my writer's Self. For five years I have been covered with incessant vulgar abuse, and bespattered with mud from head to foot—for everything I do. . . .
>
> All Russia, without exaggeration, lives on *Katherina Ivanovna,* as it did a while ago on *Professor Storitsyn;* the subscription list for *The Field,* owing to its giving my works as a premium, has risen to thirty-five thousand . . . and in the meantime Arabazhin reads lectures "On the causes of the wane of Andreyev's popularity."
>
> You [the Moscow Art Theatre] are staging *The Life of Man:* they praise you and scold me. You produce *Anathema*—they dub me idiot, while you and Kachalov [the player of Anathema] are exalted. The same happens with *Katherina Ivanovna.*

As we have observed before, Andreyev, though solitary by nature, was not strong enough to bear solitude. In his life he needed the comradeship of such ideal companions as his first wife and her successor. In his art he yearned for the support and encouragement of these and of those few fellow-artists whom he deemed capable of judging his works without bias of party or creed. As such he regarded with particular esteem the members of the Moscow Art Theatre, who have aided immeasurably the development of the Russian drama and stage, who have given an example of a group of men and women striving with the most disinterested devotion toward the highest artis-

quately appreciated Andreyev's dark reflections. Thus *Katherina Ivanovna* formed the topic of serious discussion at an evening of "The All-Russian Literary Society," at Petrograd, early in 1913, where the play was favorably analyzed by critics and dramatists and by its producer, V. I. Nemirovich-Danchenko (*Two Truths,* p. 146). The well-known painter and art-critic, Alexander Benois, published an article about the play (in *Speech* [*Rech*], No. 129, 1913), stating that public opinion had been deeply stirred by *Katherina Ivanovna* manifestly because it "touched on important contemporary problems," provoking "our dark despair, our hopeless sorrow," and reflecting the spiritual emptiness of our life.

tic goal attainable, and who, among other achievements, stimulated Chekhov to create plays by offering him an adequate stage with the proper Stimmung. Ever since his reporter days Andreyev had admired this theatre, and later he experienced the joy of seeing his best plays produced there. He had a dream of making this theatre his "own," of co-operating with it heart and soul, of using it as a free and supple springboard for his ideas, regardless of their unpopularity. "You are the only theatre," he wrote to Nemirovich-Danchenko (October 24, 1912); "this is true, but I assure you without shame or remorse that I, too, am the only one among the living dramatists who can *rise* to your height. . . . As far as I am concerned, I know that if I had the immutable support of such a theatre as yours, I should write *twice* as decently. . . . By Jove, I should even risk a podvig!" [91] Andreyev's ardent suit was reciprocated with reserve. The directors of the theatre, though brave and independent, were reluctant to face something like a public scandal with every play by Andreyev that they presented. *The Life of Man* was greeted by a hail of abuse and mockery, furnishing abundant food for cartoonists and burlesquers.[92] *Anathema* brought, indeed, fame to the actors, particularly to Kachalov, in the title rôle; but the author fared badly at the hands of the reviewers and the clergy, the latter succeeding finally in having the play forbidden by the authorities. When *Katherina Ivanovna* was presented, Andreyev—at that time in Rome, on a visit —was informed by Nemirovich-Danchenko in a telegram of "a regular battle between applause and protests" taking place in the auditorium. Andreyev commented on this reception in a letter to a friend (December 23, 1912): "The theatre from which even applause has been excluded [by the request of the directors], where the actors and the very curtain have become accustomed to respect and deference, where even a wry smile appears as an offense, this respectable theatre reverberates with hisses!" Indeed, violent reactions were out of place at that

[91] The word "podvig" signifies a heroic deed, whether a feat of physical prowess or an act of saintly asceticism.

[92] Simultaneously with the presentation of this play, a burlesque operetta was produced with great success at Petrograd, under the name *Life of Man Inside Out*.

theatre, where even the soldiers of the Red Army are impelled
to behave as though they were in a temple.   The directors evidently hesitated a bit before consenting to present, in 1914, Andreyev's *Thought,* for fear that its lugubriousness would provoke a fresh protest on the part of the public, which was prone
to trust in the assurances of the popular press that all was well
in Russia.   Andreyev found himself forced to plead for this
play.   He wrote to Nemirovich-Danchenko (probably in the
spring of 1914) : "As to the gloom of *Thought,* and the possibility of reproaches for its tone, I am not going to assure you
that this is quite impossible: anything can happen with us these
days. . . . An idea has become imbedded in many heads, like an
oaken stake, about a certain vigor and joy of life filling our
present days, but wherein this vigor and joy are manifested the
vehement optimists themselves do not know.   I may say even
more: if you try to give the public what it demands, it will leave
you.   For all those externally vivacious writings [of the protesting optimists] are in substance most melancholy and hopeless.   That is gloomy which is without talent and labored."

Thought was presented at the Moscow Art Theatre, but it
was the last of Andreyev's plays to be produced there.   The
playwright was presumably aware of the fact that his embraces
were not altogether salutary for the success of his beloved theatre, as one may judge from a letter of his to the same director,
in which he urged him to stage Alexander Blok's dramas: "I
am dangerous at present for your theatre, in view of my cruel
talent and my cruel reputation, while Blok will prove the exact
opposite for you.   He seems to be the only artist who has absolutely no enemies, who is loved by all dreamily and tenderly,
as he loves his 'Fair Unknown.'   Behold one who is in the highest degree artistically pure, proud, and untouched." [93]

It is characteristic that Andreyev should have recommended
Blok.   Andreyev disliked heartily the Russian Decadents and
Symbolists, but though Blok was one of the most prominent
Symbolists, Andreyev felt a certain nostalgia for the singer of
the "Fair Unknown," and even, according to G. Chulkov, knew

[93] Probably written in 1914.

some of his poems by heart.[94] In his reminiscences, Blok describes his two uneventful meetings with Andreyev, one of them at the latter's Petrograd residence, where he found "a large number of people, nearly all writers, many of them celebrities . . . With no bond between one another, they were separated by black gaps . . . and the remotest of them all, the loneliest of all, was Leonid Andreyev. The more amiable and kindly he appeared as a host, the lonelier he was." [95] Though the two men never became close to one another, they felt a mutual sympathy. Chaos called unto chaos, to paraphrase Blok's words. They were both pathetically lonely amidst their colleagues, and both felt that Russia, far from being well, was on the eve of a catastrophic bankruptcy of its institutions and ideals. Andreyev expressed this feeling in his "unpopular" plays, Blok voiced his presentiment in some of his mystic lectures before the "Philosophic Society" at Petrograd. The pathos of the sympathy between the two lonely writers was the more poignant, because they failed to bridge the "black gap," and died in solitude, without having clasped hands in mutual understanding.

Becoming ever more solitary and ever more misunderstood, Andreyev occasionally gave vent to his bitterness. "What have they written about me!" he exclaims in a letter to Goloushev. "It is both laughable and somehow shameful; and when you realize that this is Russia, that such is the intellectual metropolitan press, you become bitter and horrified. Altogether it is frightful. Where are men? This question sounds now everywhere, and there is no answer." [96] He felt that his voice resembled a call in the wilderness, unheeded and not understood, considered out of place and out of time, and yet he was convinced that his was the true and needed voice, merciless and unsweetened. Impatient with the prevalent misinterpretations of his point of view, he once defined it with cavalier brusqueness, in a letter to the same Goloushev: "The whole substance of me consists in that I do not accept the world as it was handed to me by my tutors and teachers, but in the most restless fashion I question it, dig into it, scrape it, turn it around and upside down, examine it not only from prescribed directions but also from its posterior. And while I am enthusiastic about the world's face, I turn my nose away from its foul posterior. This is all there is to my simple mechanism." [97]

In his growing isolation Andreyev turned again and again to the Moscow Art Theatre, making desperate attempts to retain his bond with the only artistic stronghold which he respected and which had the power to stimulate his creative life. His plays and playlets, produced at various theatres of both metropolises and in the provinces, before and during the war, meant but little to their author. In his intimate letters and in his diary he spoke slightingly both of those plays and of the manner of their execution. It was the Moscow Art Theatre that he craved, as a salvation and as an incentive. In his letters to Nemirovich-Danchenko he poured out his aching heart; he pleaded and fought, admonished and exhorted, appealed and demanded, firmly convinced that in championing his own case he was prompted by no other motive than the yearning after an art fearless and independent. He grieved over the fact that his favorite theatre continued to produce such of his harmless things as *Days of Our Life*, while his big dramas remained under the ban. For nearly four years (from the end of 1914) he argued with this theatre in favor of presenting his last two plays, *The Waltz of the Dogs* and *Samson Enchained*, receiving evasive answers which aggravated him exceedingly by their hesitating tone and indecision. "Concerning *The Waltz of the Dogs* and *Samson Enchained*—I fail to understand you," he wrote on one of these numerous occasions. "You say: another challenge to the public, another battle. But why have calm? Don't! Do have challenges, battles." And he reminded Danchenko that years before he, Andreyev, had reproached the Moscow Art Theatre for being a "theatre of spiritual calm." He rejected the argument that in time of war the public was not inclined to listen to "remote" subjects. On the contrary, to An-

[97] About the same time.

dreyev the war augured a revival of heroic aspirations and noble sentiments, rendering tragedy timely and desired. The following extracts are valuable for the understanding of Andreyev's state of mind early in the war (September 1, 1914):

As yet I do not know whether I am right or mistaken, but it seems to me that things are coming my way. I have in mind *tragedy,* which is inevitably destined to revive. See how sweeping is the gesture of the events, in what a pose the nations place themselves, hear how pathetically the cannon declaim! Small, intimate, local drama, with its parochial morality and parochial philosophy, the purely native drama—of what use is it now? For whom? The hero, the heroic in masses and in the individual, broad strokes and extreme stylization, the loudest words and the most risky poses, clarion blasts, hymns, miracles and revelations, Sinai and Sabaoth—this is our present and this will be our future for a good decade. . . .

Believe me: Now is the time for you to stage tragedy . . . Down with *Days of Our Life* and its like . . . and long live Lorenzo [of *The Black Maskers*], *Anathema, The Ocean, The Life of Man,* and others yet unborn . . . I am jesting, but earnestly: aside from anything else, the war makes my heart rejoice because of the resurrection of the tragic in literature—in which I revive myself. The last five years have been so sad for me, because my feeling of life's tragicness collided daily with the triumphant dramatization of life, my scale of a hundred miles to the inch appeared unsuitable for the short pedestrian paths, loopholes and moleholes, and with every day I felt myself to be more and more superfluous. . . .

At this stage of the war Andreyev was still enthusiastic and hopeful—we shall speak of this period presently. He wished the Moscow Art Theatre to rise with him, to share his passion for tragedy, and he was deeply wounded when that theatre proceeded to run such taffy "successes" as Surguchev's *Autumn Violins* or his own "proper" plays. "You may present a thousand times *Days of Our Life* and *Anfisa,*" he protested (August 27, 1914), but in not producing *Anathema,* in having forgotten *The Life of Man,* in spurning *The Black Maskers,* and in passing indifferently by *The Ocean,* you have sentenced me to death, you have left me my body, while my soul you have thrown over-

board." Still he believed in the approaching recognition of his
point of view and was full of plans for new tragedies. He concludes this letter: "And now I am going to the graveyard
where are buried my unborn children: *The Revolution, Peace
and War, Nebuchadnezzar, Ahasuerus, Samson* and I shout:
'Arise, children! We are summoned.'" But as the war pro-
gressed, Andreyev became convinced that arms and the Muses
are poor bedfellows. Of all his projected works he accomplished only *Samson,* and that he had practically completed in
January, 1914; it has not yet been published or produced. His
other "children" remained unborn. The encouragement he
craved and wanted so urgently did not come forth. One may
feel his impotent bitterness in the semi-jocular passage of his
letter to Nemirovich-Danchenko, written presumably in January, 1916: "My position is woeful. I am approaching my
jubilee, and still am at a loss where to have my works produced.
I write a play, and gaze at it as a ram at new gates: 'For what
good have you come into the world?' If I had money, I should
buy me a portfolio and deposit my manuscripts therein: 'Rest
in peace, dear dust . . .'"

Thus ends the period of Andreyev's artistic maturity—in utter solitude, weariness, and impotence.

V

WAR, REVOLUTION AND DEATH

Two aspects of Andreyev's attitude toward the war.—Public acceptance of it.—Journalism.—*King, Law, Liberty.*—*War's Burden.*—General enthusiasm.—Andreyev's illness, depression, material want, craving for an illusion.—War—Autocracy's doom.—Military nature of the March revolution.—Andreyev's hopes for war's results.—Predominance of gray soldiers.—Extremism of the masses.—Breakdown of fighting spirit and discipline.—Andreyev's disgust and dark prophecy.—Elected member of Pre-Parliament.—Bolshevik victory.—Andreyev's uncompromising opposition.—*S. O. S.*—Last trip to Petrograd.—His mother and his letter to her.—Retrospection.—Self-humiliation.—Andreyev portrayed by Roerich.—Work on *Satan's Diary.*—1919.—About Gorky.—Eager to head anti-Bolshevik propaganda.—Letters to Gessen.—State of mind and body.—Spurned by Whites.—Projected trip to America.—"Three roads."—"Threefold exile."—Disgust and despondency.—Bracing effect of nature.—Death of Man.—Last utterance.

THE war found Andreyev in a state of depression and of gloomy forebodings.[1] It wrought a notable change in his mood, causing his dimmed spirit to flare up, for a time, with dazzling enthusiasm of faith in men and in ideals. Outwardly Andreyev presented the aspect of a man who had been converted for the first time in his life to a positive belief, which he expressed and championed with unreserved ardor. Inwardly he was being devoured by the poisonous worm of doubt and diffidence. Before discussing both these aspects, we must note that

---

[1] According to Mme. Andreyev, her husband had a presentiment of the oncoming events. He usually mapped out in advance a year's work, travel, and other plans. But in 1914 he found himself unable to plan ahead. When pressed for a reason, he muttered darkly: "It is hard for me to speak now. I feel nothing but gloom in the future."

Andreyev's artistic activity ended with the war, hence the events of the war and the revolution will be treated in this part of the essay, in connection with his biography proper. The preceding political and social occurrences, such as the war with Japan, the revolution of 1905, terroristic acts, labor upheavals, waves of banditism and others, were reflected in one way or another in Andreyev's stories and plays, and will therefore be discussed along with the author's art. His productions after the fall of 1914 can hardly be ranked as art, a bitter truth which he himself admitted in a letter to Roerich.[2] The background of his last years should therefore be presented at this juncture.

In the same measure as the war with Japan, in 1904–1905, had been unpopular in Russia, the war against Germany was in the beginning—before the manifestation of the criminal mismanagement and corruption of the military and civil authorities—popular and stimulating. It appealed as a conflict of ideas, and of course there was no doubt in the minds of either side as to which ideas were right and just. Leonid Andreyev, skeptic and misanthrope, author of the *Red Laugh,* shared the fate of his European fellow writers who were engulfed by the mighty wave of patriotism. Jolted out of his social apathy by the formidable events, Andreyev unreservedly dedicated his pen to what appeared to him the cause of justice and humanity. The spectacle of the greater portion of the civilized world taking up arms in the name of high principles, possesses the irresistible effect of an elemental hurricane which sweeps away one's doubts and misgivings, and fans one's faith in man and in ideals, however faint that faith may have become. At such a time one's analytical faculty grows blunt, one is apt to become credulous, to indulge in exaggerations, in journalistic generalities. And if this state of mind be a weakness, it is one which brings, at the time, such men as Anatole France nearer to the heart of humanity than those who, like Romain Rolland, preserve the strength to remain *au-dessus de la mêlée.* Andreyev proved to be merely human, impressionable and inconsistent. To the correspondent of the London *Daily Chronicle* he expressed his attitude early

[2] *Infra,* p. 173.

in the war, in an interview from which the following lines are quoted:

> Though I am opposed to war on principle, and regard bloodshed with horror, I welcome war with Germany as necessary. This is a war for the soul, for spiritual liberty. The Germans are not murderers of the body; they are, to use a Russian expression, killers of the soul. . . .
> If Germany wins, the future of Russia will be dark and terrible. The reactionary forces of Russia have always been at once fostered and despised by Germany. If Germany be defeated, Russia will, I am convinced, enter upon a path of political and social progress on which the nation's heart has long been set. . . . Russia must win at any cost, and in the effort to obtain victory the people and the government must be absolutely united.[3]

Andreyev wrote numerous articles during the war, hardly any of which will survive the teeth of time, despite their forceful style and effectiveness for propaganda purposes. Neither can one rank as art his play, *King, Law, Liberty*, which appeared late in 1914, or his *nouvelle*, *War's Burden*, published in 1915. The play depicted the tragedy of Belgium, a tragedy which was too close at hand for adequate treatment.[4] The treacherous invasion of Belgium, the destruction of Belgian universities and libraries, the inhuman atrocities of the German troops—these and similar horrors were at that time presented through one-

---

[3] The New York *Times*, September 16, 1914, p. 1.
[4] Andreyev had his misgivings about this play. On August 27, 1914, he wrote to Nemirovich-Danchenko: "I intend to write a play—whose heroes are, sub rosa, Maeterlinck, Vandervelde, and others. . . . Naturally, it is far from a patriotic *mauvais ton*, but rather something like a 'dramatic chronicle of the war. . . .' To be sure, the present cannot serve as material for a purely artistic work, but it seems to me that by enacting the play in Belgium I shall lend it the distance which must separate the spectator from the stage. . . . I have hesitated a long time, but the fact is that I am somewhat ashamed to be ambiguous, while for purely artistic work I lack both the calm and the perspective." Andreyev used no such apologetic tone about his earlier productions. One feels a lack of self-confidence also in his letter written to the same friend somewhat later (October 13) when the play had been realized. "Dear Vladimir Ivanovich, do go over to the Dramatic Theatre. . . . I have attempted to develop a current theme in accordance with the principles of psychism, and it seems to me that I have succeeded in solving a difficult task. . . ." Less than four years later (April, 1918) Andreyev admitted in his diary that both that play and *War's Burden* were "weak things . . . presenting in substance poor publicist stuff."

sided information, of necessity biased. Consequently, when Andreyev repeated these themes in his play, he left the impression that he was an editorial writer for Allied propaganda. This, despite the fact that the plot in itself was very dramatic, presenting the decision of the King and the celebrated Belgian writer, Grelieu (who obviously stood for Maeterlinck), to destroy the dams, and thus to flood the country and drown the invaders. In normal times the author might have produced a masterpiece out of this subject. But *inter arma silent musæ.* In the fall of 1914 Andreyev the artist succumbed to Andreyev the journalist, of the *Courier* tradition, hence his play bore the stamp of "war literature." On one hand the unreal, maudlin Maurice, unable to comprehend how the Germans can be so cruel as to hang snipers; on the other hand German officers, as unreal as Maurice, though corresponding to the conception of them popular among the masses of the Allies. Blumenfeld speaks of the Commander:

> He has a German philosophical mind which manages guns as Leibnitz managed ideas. Everything is preconceived, everything is prearranged, the movement of our millions of people has been elaborated into such a remarkable system that Kant himself would have been proud of it. Gentlemen, we are led forward by indomitable logic and by an iron will. We are inexorable as Fate.[5]

This concoction is met by Blumenfeld's colleagues with shouts of "bravo." During the war it did not require much courage or originality to drag into the current issues some of the great German thinkers, and to link them with the war. Blumenfeld appears bookish, or rather journalistic, a hero of the Sunday supplement of an American newspaper. In real life one hardly encounters a German officer philosophizing on the uselessness of sleep, on the folly of paying heed to one's organism, on the indomitable power of will.

War's Burden barely misses being one of Andreyev's best stories. The diary of an average Russian paterfamilias, the

5 *Works—XVII*, p. 165.

evolution of his reactions to the war, his selfish resentment to the hardships inflicted on the civilian population, the gradual broadening of his outlook, his nascent patriotism and altruism, his final reconciliation with life "according to Schopenhauer"— this theme is developed by Andreyev in his early realistic style. The type, an ordinary clerk, resembles the hero of Dostoyevsky's *Poor Folk* in his mode of reasoning and his excessive sentimentality. What detracts from the value of the story, what renders it journalese, is its surcharge of current events. There are pages and pages of accounts taken from newspapers, pertaining to the victories and defeats of the Russian armies, to the sessions of the Duma, massacres of Armenians, high cost of living and other facts of the war. This element forms such a heavy ballast in the story that one is forced to relegate it to the limbo of "war literature."

In his enthusiasm for the war Andreyev voiced the sentiment of the Intelligentsia. In July, 1914, there were barricades on the streets of Petrograd, a revolution seemed inevitable,[6] but Germany's declaration of war deflected public opinion from internal questions to the grave problem of the defense of the country from foreign aggressors. The war with Germany was as popular in Russia as the war against Napoleon in 1812. Forgotten were party dissensions and class antagonism and the general opposition to the Government, in the united resolve to defeat the enemy. With the exception of a small group of defeatists living abroad, like Lenin and Trotsky, the Russian public was practically unanimous in championing the cause of the Allies. Such implacable fighters of Tsarism as Kropotkin and Plekhanov were as enthusiastic in their support of the war as were such reactionaries as Purishkevich and Bobrinsky, such conservatives as Guchkov and Stakhovich, such liberals as Milyukov and Rodichev, such radicals as Yablonovsky and Yordansky, such mystics as Bulgakov and Merezhkovsky, such æsthetes as Balmont and Bryusov, such solipsists as Sologub and Kuzmin,

---

[6] A. Kaun, *Russia under Nicolas II*, supplement to Kornilov's *Modern Russian History—II*, pp. 337-338. New York, 1917.

even such extreme futurists as Igor Severyanin. Germany, and particularly Prussia, symbolized for Russia everything despotic and reactionary. While the Russian imperialists saw in the war a means for defeating a rival imperialism, to the majority of the Russian people the war appeared as a crusade against the stronghold of European militarism and oppression, with the removal of which Russia's own despotic rule would inevitably give place to a more progressive form of government.[7] The alliance with the foremost democracies of Europe, England and France, was in itself a pledge for a better political future. Carried away by this sentiment, Andreyev went so far as to say in a public statement: "If the German be our enemy, then the war is necessary; if the Englishman and the Frenchman be our friends and allies, then this war is good, and its purpose is good.[8]

And here is the other side of the medal. On April 13, 1918, Andreyev registered in his diary the following significant lines:

The poisoning of my soul began with the war. The very fact of my accepting it, that is, of my transferring it from the all-human plane to the field of "fatherland" and politics, was due probably to the simple instinct of self-preservation. Otherwise the war would have remained for me only a "red laugh," and I should inevitably and before long have lost my reason. This danger of losing my reason existed for me throughout the war, and at times I felt it terribly. I fought this menace by way of publicistic writings. My two weak things, *King* and *War's Burden,* were weak precisely because (especially the latter) they presented in substance poor publicistic stuff. I had to live without going mad.

'Tis curious how I, half-consciously, restrained my imagination from picturing the essence of the war. This was a very difficult task, because my imagination is unrestrainable—it has been so all my life. Well-nigh independent, it subordinated both my thoughts and my will and my desires, and it was particularly strong in presenting pictures of horror,

---

[7] Deputy Kerensky of the fourth Duma, representing the socialistic Labor group which refused to vote for the war budget at the declaration of the war, said in a speech on that occasion: "Peasants and workmen, all who desire the happiness and well-being of Russia in these days of trial, harden your spirit! Gather all your strength, and, having defended your land, free it."—*Ibid.,* p. 340, quoted from W. E. Walling's *The Socialists and the War,* pp. 192, 193.

[8] *Ibid.,* p. 346.

pain, suffering, of the sudden and the fatal. I do not know how I managed it, but I actually succeeded in putting a bridle on my imagination, and rendering it in regard to the war purely formal, almost semi-official, not going beyond governmental communications and newspaper rubbish. But this was only half a salvation, preventing me from sinking at once into the dusk of chaos. For alongside the upper, governmental imagination, reduced to strict semi-official limits, there worked my secret (there is such a thing) underground imagination. And while on the main floor Allied hymns were played pompously and with decorum, down in the cellar something dark and terrible was going on. Thither were driven "madness and horror," and there they are abiding unto this day. And from there they are sending through my whole body these deathly poisons, these dizzy headaches, these piercing heartaches, this yellow sluggish virus which suffuses my organism so heavily and painfully. I have captured a devil, swallowed him, and he stays in me—alive.

These lines help to explain the paradox of Andreyev the doubter and denier, the perpetual prosecutor and disparager, turning vehement war propagandist. They suggest that the "virus" found a ready soil in Andreyev. His organism weakened, his spirit lustreless, he became susceptible to infectious microbes. During his active period he possessed the clear eye which could "see through" the popular nostrums, and the strong mind which rejected flimsy beliefs and thin panaceas, in face of unpopularity, opposition, and isolation. But by the latter half of 1914 Andreyev presented a fountain with its reservoir practically drained. His talent, however robust, had fed largely and rather extravagantly on his inner flame, which was by no means inexhaustible, and required fanning and nursing. The lack of response to his tragic notes, which was becoming ever more nearly general, gradually affected his energy and vitality, generating in him a sense of futility and impotence. After *Samson Enchained,* his last brilliant flash, Andreyev became artistically dumb, powerless to bring forth the ambitious ideas which had nestled in his mind awaiting the creative summons. With the atrophy of his creative faculty—that is, of the very essence of his being—began his rapid decay and disintegration, a process which Andreyev endeavored to check by desperate attempts at calling forth fresh illusions and clinging to them. Such an illusion was the war.

The diary entry quoted on pp. 136–137 illustrates amply Andreyev's mental and physical state during his last years. Coupled with the strain of his mind to preserve its balance, there were his bodily ailments. His strong organism finally began to give way under the combined stress of spiritual chagrin and physical over-exertion. One must remember his abnormal mode of living, his actively wakeful nights, his constant restlessness, his regular insomnia which Mme. Andreyev tried in vain to conquer by reading to him adventure stories. His letters usually contained some reference to his poor heart and wretched head. "My ill health," he wrote to Goloushev in January, 1916, "binds my hands. I am in need of money, and I have an offer to deliver eleven lectures for ten thousand rubles. Yet I cannot accept it: how can I with such a head!" The material problem rose in importance with the decline of the author's artistic power: he now wished to believe that with material independence he might resurrect his talent, might build "an Andreyev theatre, with its own public and its own order," as he whimsically threatened the Moscow Art Theatre in a letter (September, 1916). One can understand why he could not resist the temptation of joining the editorial staff of *Russia's Will* (*Russkaya Volya*), a large Petrograd daily founded in 1916 with a patriotic éclat, but suspected by a large part of the public as an organ of Protopopov, the Rasputin-made minister of interior. Braving scandal and calumny, Andreyev lent his name to the paper, taking charge of its departments of fiction, stage and criticism, at the salary of thirty-six thousand a year, beside fifteen hundred per printed sheet. Andreyev emphasized these details in a letter to Goloushev (June 26, 1916), adding: "This is important for me, because earning a sure and 'quiet' fifty thousand a year I shall be able to write plays *without the need of producing them,* I shall become independent of the market, of fussy critics, and the publishers' will." He gave still another reason for taking this step, a few months previous, writing to the same friend (September 7, 1915): "But my main purpose is—to become intoxicated with work, and to escape from the cursed reality, at least for a time." After having actually joined the paper, he wrote to Goloushev (June, 1916) in the same vein: "All these last years I have been oppressed by idleness, I have burned within myself, invisibly for others, like that perfected stove which consumes its own smoke, not letting it out. . . . My very illness was due mainly to idleness; now I am going to be well."

Within a few months Andreyev became disillusioned as to the salutary effect of the newspaper work, since he had discovered that the fire of the war, which he expected to purge the public and lift it to the heights of tragedy, proved a will-o'-the-wisp. In the first place, he was forced to forego his secluded régime, and to settle in Petrograd. The work itself demanded all his time, ruining his health, and extinguishing in journalistic drudgery the last flashes of his talent. Lastly, he found himself in uncongenial company, with the independence of his views jeopardized. How he suffocated in that atmosphere was evident from the new pet illusion about which he began to dream—an escape to the "south," of which he wrote frequently in his letters during the fall of 1916. "I yearn for south, south, south— passionately, unutterably," he wrote in November of that year (presumably to Nemirovich-Danchenko), "yet the south is so remote from us! To think that I shall never find myself in Los Angeles, whence I once received a graceful letter from a Spanish lady. Los Angeles, Brazil, Cuba, Jamaica, Porto Rico, Ceylon, Celebes, Java, Indo-China . . ." Again, as in his high-school days, he hated his stifling environment, and longed for romantic distances, or rather romantic names, like Los Angeles. His newspaper office oppressed him as much as his gymnasium classroom had done years before, as we may judge from his letter to Goloushev (?) (the same month): "But above all else—it is dreary, because of the lack of sun, fog, slush, darkness. I crave devilishly for the south, for the tropics, palms and darkies, for sea and expanse, for air and light. Here— the electric light begins to burn in the early morning, and continues to burn till the next morning." Fatigue and headaches were other invariable motives of his letters at that time. Yet in spite of weariness, sickness and disgust with his surroundings, Andreyev forced himself to manufacture a play, *Dear Phantoms*, with the young Dostoyevsky as its central character. "I am writing with the speed of lightning," he informed Goloushev. "Three acts in two sittings. I should have finished the play in two days if I had the time, if it were not for editorial meetings, or mother's birthday celebration, or crowds of visitors. Of course I can write only at night. . . . It goes without saying that the play is only forty-six per cent decent, not more." This attitude toward his production was a sure sign of the author's decline. Even more outspoken was his letter about the same time to Nemirovich-Danchenko, in connection with his *Dear Phantoms:* "As I have told you, I desire to earn some money through this play, in order that I may remain on the free path of a writer. . . . The newspaper is an unstable affair: a divergence in point of view may throw me overboard. I must make my material dependence on the newspaper as slight as possible. This is the main reason why I have worked on my play so stubbornly and perseveringly, overcoming sickness and fatigue." In admitting this motive for writing the play, Andreyev transgressed the first "thou shalt not" of Tolstoy's tetralogue,[9] and thereby doomed his work to insignificance. About two months after its presentation Andreyev in a letter to Goloushev (January, 1917) dubbed it "nonsense and rubbish." The success of the play was only partial; it was considered "out of time." Skitalets was present at its first production, in the Imperial Alexandrine Theatre, and thus describes his impressions:

I felt that the public received indifferently this fine play, which was, however, inopportune. . . .

"Friends and admirers" had arranged a false success. They prepared numerous laurel wreaths of enormous dimensions, called for the author, and in a body presented them to him. There were applause and shouts of Bravo, but one felt in the air the cold atmosphere of indifference. Andreyev himself, in his black blouse, wasted and exhausted, seemed to feel

[9] *Supra*, p. 89 ff.

it, when with a sad and diffident face he stood amidst these funereal wreaths, so to speak, on the brilliantly illuminated stage, stood motionless and also like a dear phantom of the irretrievable past. . . .[10]

Disappointed in the war and in its effects on mankind, broken in spirit and in body, Andreyev wearily dragged his shell down the sloping path. "Ah, I am so tired," he wrote in January, 1917, to Goloushev, a mediocre writer but a warm and constant friend. "It is difficult even to imagine how unwell I am . . . Yet I have so many big plans! Precisely—big: the pettiness and vanity of my surroundings generates, as an antithesis, a striving for great themes and for great men." But this ambition was like the effort of a wounded bird to flap its wings. In the same letter Andreyev cried out in a Galgenhumor: "Seryozha, let us buy for a poltinnik [half a ruble] some carbolic acid and drink it!" His personal disintegration was accompanied by a premonition of the catastrophic events which were to befall Russia in the near future. Thus in a letter dated November 16, 1916, he wrote: "A sweeping current, dragging us through whirlpools, carries us toward a precipice, an abyss, a smoking chaos, where everything is wild, dark, and formless." In March, 1917, Russia was in the grip of a revolution.

Consciously or unconsciously, the Intelligentsia supported the war because it foredoomed the autocratic régime. In a war which augured victory for the more highly developed technical skill, for the more adequately organized industry and transportation, for the more efficient and honest government, there was hardly a chance for official Russia, corrupt, lackadaisical, ignorant, in charge of a loose-jointed empire, with its industry in the state of infancy, its agriculture archaic, its means of transportation utterly inadequate, its army up-to-date and ideally equipped —on paper only.[11] By the end of February, 1917, Russia had been tested and found obsolete, corrupt, and rotten to the core. The overthrow of the tsar was not so much a revolution as the painless death of a thing which had been long lifeless, but went on existing by artificial means. One of the artificial props of

[10] *Russia's Voice*, February 21, 1922.
[11] *Russia under Nicolas II*, p. 348.

the autocracy had been the rigidly disciplined, unthinking army led by loyal servants of the throne. The years 1915–1916 confirmed in the minds of the Russian military leaders the necessity of removing the incapable monarch, for the sake of a victory for the Allies. In March, 1917, the army commanders not only did not attempt to quell the popular unrest, but supported the demand of the party leaders for the abdication of Nicolas II.[12] The practically bloodless liberation of the country from the yoke of the Romanovs was accomplished with the active connivance of the army, and largely in the name of carrying on the war more efficiently and to a victorious end. That this was the immediate aim of the revolution, appeared to be the opinion of the majority of the political leaders who voiced it in their speeches, in the declaration of the Provisional Government, in the notes of Foreign Minister Milyukov to the Allied Powers. The army was flattered and feared, the army was idealized and hosannahed, the army was regarded as the savior of Russia, of Europe, of the world. Andreyev, revived by the violent shock of the revolution, voiced this sentiment in his enthusiastic statement to a Reuter representative:

It is all too manifest that the brilliant and decisive victory over the autocracy could not have been won except with our Russian army . . . Until the great day of March 9, our army had at least the outer form of troops whipped into shape by the inexorable laws of the military code, but to-day it is an army of volunteers defending with guns its liberty and rights. . . . In the first days of the war . . . I put down in my diary the following words: "They call it 'war,' but it really means revolution. In its logical evolution this 'war' will bring the downfall of the Romanovs and will end not in the ordinary way of previous wars, but in a European upheaval. This upheaval will bring in its wake the destruction of militarism [and of] permanent armies, and the creation of the United States

[12] Numerous memoirs by generals and politicians of the old régime substantiate this statement. Professor P. N. Milyukov in his historical account of the revolution tells of the assent of General Alexeyev, Chief of Staff, and of the Commanders-in-Chief, Generals Russky and Brusilov, to uphold the stand of President Rodzianko of the Duma and of the delegation of the Provisional Committee which came to demand the abdication of the tsar.—P. N. Milyukov, *History of the Second Russian Revolution* (*Istoriia vtoroy russkoy revolutsii*), v. I, part 1, p. 50. Sofia, 1921.

of Europe. . . . The day is not distant when the house of Hohenzollern will collapse, and peace will be concluded by free peoples on terms of liberty, equality and fraternity.   After that day there will come more distant and still brighter days, when all Europe, having purged itself clean of blood, will become one brotherhood, and on the ruins of the old cities, monarchies, castes and privileges, there will be built a new and free humanity."   We are through with the military from this day.   We only have an armed Russian people, which is accomplishing its mission of defense of the country's liberties.   Once its work is done, it will don its civilian clothes.   After that it will cease to be an army once and for all, if human wisdom and consciousness will permit.   Build wooden barracks— we only want such for our temporarily armed and fighting citizens, so that we can easily remove them.   Do not build stone barracks, those jails of   militarism, the permanent bulwarks of the soldiery, the eternal dispensers of dissolution and blood." [13]

In 1923 Andreyev's enthusiasm and faith sound pathetic, but in those days they were shared by many, and not only in Russia.   One *wished* to believe in the purgative value of the war, in its hygienic effect, in its being a war to end war, in its ennobling consequences.   How else could one explain and atone for the array of a score of millions of human beings for mutual slaughter!   And the wish generated the thought.   Andreyev, in dire need of a fresh illusion, shared the wish of the Russian liberals and moderate socialists that the spring revolution of 1917 would serve primarily the purpose of a more vigorous and efficient campaign against the Central Powers, in the name of the high principles expressed in Andreyev's flowery statement quoted above.   Hence he, the author of *Thus It Was, Judas, Savva* and other works illustrating the stupidity, brutality and cowardice of the masses, felt now impelled to idealize the gray mass of the soldiers, to endow them with conscious bravery and intelligence, to sublimate them into free individuals voluntarily sacrificing their lives in the name of democracy.   Under this impulsion Andreyev wrote his propaganda articles,[14] which coin-

13 The New York *Times,* August 5, 1917 (Magazine Section).
14 A dispatch to the New York *Times* for April 28, 1917, page 1, states: "Andreyev has been enlisted by the Provisional Government as a writer of propa-

cided in the main with the oratory of the fiery Kerensky on his indefatigable trips to the front.

That the flattery of the soldier contained a considerable element of fear is obvious. When one reads the multitudinous memoirs of the men who took active part in the events of those days, military officers and civilians alike, one invariably gains the impression that a gigantic bluff was being carried on consciously and unconsciously by the Russian patriots in their attitude to the Army. One of these sources, which may be used with confidence, is the book of *Reminiscences* by V. B. Stankevich,[15] a scholarly jurist who volunteered early in the war, and served as an officer throughout the war and the revolution. Mr. Stankevich had been the secretary of the Labor group in the Duma, to which belonged Kerensky, and remained the latter's friend and assistant to the very end. His book has been quoted both by conservatives and by radicals as one of the few authentic accounts and profound analyses of the revolution. It is a disillusioning book for those who picture the early stage of the revolution in the romantic halo of universal brotherhood and voluntary coöperation among all classes of the population in the name of the sacred cause. According to Stankevich, the soldiery was felt from the outset to be the inexorable master of the situation, a master to be feared and appeased:

> Officially they celebrated, glorified the revolution, shouted Hurrah to the fighters for liberty, adorned themselves with red ribbons, and marched under red banners. . . . Ladies established feeding stations for soldiers. Everybody said, "we," "our" revolution, "our" victory, and "our" liberty. But in their hearts, in intimate conversations—they were terrified, they quaked, they felt themselves captives of a hostile element rushing in some unknown direction. The bourgeois circles of the Duma, which in fact had created the atmosphere that provoked the explosion, were utterly unprepared for "such" an explosion.[16] Unforgettable is the figure of Rod-

ganda." Mme. Andreyev wrote me that some of his articles were circulated "in millions of copies." At the same time he continued to contribute regularly to *Russia's Will*, until the advent of the Bolsheviki.

[15] *Vospominaniya*, Berlin, 1920.

[16] See *supra*, p. 142 ff. The "Progressive Bloc" of the Duma, led by President Rodzianko and Milyukov, and supported by the military commanders, in their anxiety to carry on the war more honestly and capably, were very moderate in

zianko, the corpulent squire and distinguished person, as he passed through the crowds of unbelted soldiers in the corridors of the Duma. He preserved a majestic dignity, but on his pale face was congealed an expression of deep suffering and despair. Officially it was stated that "the soldiers had come to support the Duma in its conflict with the Government," while in reality the Duma found itself abolished from the very first days. A similar expression could be noticed on the faces of all the members of the Duma Committee, and of those who stood close to them. I am told that representatives of the Progressive Bloc wept hysterically at their homes in helpless despair. . . . Even on my visits to the feeding stations, where the soldiers were fed day and night free of charge and with perfect cordiality, I observed that the hospitable hostesses endeavored to buy off the soldiery, as it were. They dined them and treated them lavishly, yet they felt the hopelessness of their efforts, since the soldiers sat in sullen concentration, chewed their food without letting the rifles out of their hands, not even conversing with one another, nor exchanging impressions; but conscious in a certain gregarious way of some common interests of their own, they meditated in their own fashion, in a manner different, incomprehensible, defying interpretation.[17]

The quoted passage epitomizes the nature of the Russian revolution. The century-long struggle against the autocratic régime resulted not in a political revolution, after the manner of the West, but in a social revolution. The third estate, which proved so strong and tactful in France and wherever it supplanted the feudal aristocracy, was found wanting in Russia,

their political demands. At first Rodzianko telegraphed to the tsar an urgent request for the appointment of a "responsible cabinet of ministers"—this was indeed the demand of the whole Progressive Bloc. Only after the revolt of the Petrograd garrison and the invasion of the Duma by rebellious regiments, did the Duma send a delegation to the tsar with the request for his abdication in favor of his son. Nicolas abdicated in favor of his brother Michael, an arrangement which was approved by the Duma Committee and by the Provisional Government. A constitutional monarchy was all that the Progressive Bloc aspired to. But the victorious soldiers hooted Milyukov and Guchkov, when these announced the candidature of Michael Romanov. The latter was persuaded to abdicate in his turn till the convocation of the Constituent Assembly, which would decide on the form of the national government. These facts are quoted after Milyukov's *History of the Second Russian Revolution*, pp. 40–55. Milyukov states that he was the only member of the Government opposed to the abdication of Michael (p. 54), and he considers this abdication as "the first capitulation of the Russian revolution" (p. 55), which inevitably led to the triumph of the Bolsheviki (p. 58).

[17] *Reminiscences*, pp. 70–72.

both in numbers and in social stamina. The third estate, through the Duma leaders, wanted *only* a political change, and solicited the aid of the army for the accomplishment of this change. But these leaders found themselves in the position of Frankenstein, when their intended tool began to "meditate." The Russian soldier had an ideal reputation in military annals, because of his endurance and unquestioning obedience. But now the stolid peasant mass, forming the bulk of the army, was jolted out of its mental stagnancy and passivity into the recognition of its power and importance. On one hand the soldier became aware of the corruption and weakness of the old régime which caused unnecessary slaughter through lack of sufficient and proper ammunition.[18] On the other hand, the soldier who broke his oath of loyalty to the tsar and brought about his downfall, was now hailed and glorified as the savior of Russia and of liberty. Since he became convinced that revolt was a virtue, he concluded in his naïve way of reasoning that the degree of virtue was in proportion to the thoroughness of the revolution. Compromise as a mode of thinking and acting implies a civilized stage, whereas the simple Russian comprehended only such an alternative as *aut Cæsar aut nihil.* The removal of the tsar signified to the masses the abolition of the symbol of authority emanating from an outside source, and implying blind obedience and unquestioning submission to a small group of privileged persons. The annulment of this authority meant to the common man the establishment of its antipode—the authority of the unprivileged. Hence: all land to the peasants, all factories to the workmen, all power to the Soviets of workmen's, peasants', and soldiers' deputies.

The efforts of the several provisional governments from March to November, 1917, were concentrated on modifying this simple reasoning of the masses, while on the other hand this reasoning was encouraged by the Bolsheviki. With his

[18] In his *Reminiscences* M. V. Rodzianko states that "the Army was fighting well-nigh with bare hands. During my visit to the front, in the spring of 1915, I witnessed cases when our soldiers repulsed attacks with stones. There was a project to arm the troops with axes."—*Archive of the Russian Revolution (Archiv russkoy revolutsii),* v. VI, Berlin, 1922.

fiery eloquence Kerensky appealed to the people for patience, for compromise, for the postponement of their demands till the convocation of the Constituent Assembly, which would have the power to legalize the social and economic changes. At the same time Kerensky engaged in the tremendous task of electrifying the disorganized and vacillating army with a fighting spirit and with a desire to continue the war against the Central Powers, in the name of democracy. Indeed, he succeeded in inducing a portion of the troops to advance against the enemy, to be followed before the end of June by a collapse of the military organization, and by an ignominious retreat of the armies on all fronts. Leonid Andreyev felt indignant and heartbroken: another illusion had burst. He published a scorching appeal to the Russian soldier, in which he said:

Soldier, what hast thou been under Nicolas Romanov? Thou hast been a slave of the autocracy. . . . Soldier, what hast thou been in the days of the revolution? . . . Thou hast been our love, our happiness, our pride. . . . And what hast thou become now, Soldier? . . .
Scoundrel . . . thou hast betrayed Russia.
Ah, how thou didst fly from the enemy, Russian Soldier! Never before has the world seen such a rout, such a mob of traitors. It knew the one Judas, but here were tens of thousands of Judases running past each other, galloping, throwing down rifles, quarrelling. . . .
Russia is dying, Russia is calling to thee.
Arise, dear Soldier! [19]

But neither the harsh "scoundrel" nor the caressing "dear" could stop the elemental disintegration of the gigantic body of the Russian army. When one reads at present the memoirs of the participants in the affairs of those months, written with the objectivity of a cooled-off, retrospective view, one can justify Andreyev's short-sightedness only by the pathos of proximity. Milyukov and Stankevich, in their works quoted previously, V. Nabokov,[20] General Krasnov,[21] General Lukom-

[19] Translated from *Russkaya Volya* in the *Yale Review*, January, 1918, pp. 225–228.
[20] "The Provisional Government," in *Archive of the Russian Revolution*, v. I, pp. 9–96. Berlin, 1921.
[21] "At the Interior Front," *ibid.*, pp. 97–240.

sky,[22] Peter Ryss,[23] to mention only a few of the active military and civilian leaders of that time, all agree that the offensive of the Russian army during the month of June was doomed to disaster. An army which had to be persuaded to advance, not by force of command but by eloquent speeches, was an absurd anachronism.[24] Hopelessly demoralized under the tsar's mismanagement,[25] the army became permeated from the very beginning of the revolution with such tendencies as inevitably followed the abolition of the custom of saluting officers, the establishment of "soldiers' committees" for the discussion and management of regimental affairs, and the incessant mass meetings at the front and in the rear, where a people cowed into submis-

[22] "From My Reminiscences," *ibid.*, v. II, pp. 14-44.

[23] *The Russian Experiment (Russky Opyt)*. Paris, 1921.

[24] The ardor of the French revolutionary troops was due to the fact that they fought in defense of the revolution and the fatherland against the foreign invaders. In 1917 the Russian soldiers had no such slogans, despite Kerensky's efforts to persuade them that they were fighting for precisely these values. The success of Trotsky's red army may be ascribed, in the first place, to the fact that, as in the case of France after 1791, Russia was threatened in 1919 and 1920 both by foreign invaders and by counter-revolutionary generals. The second reason for the superiority of the Bolshevik troops over those of Kerensky may be found in the rigid military discipline which was restored by Trotsky after it had been thoroughly debauched in 1917.

[25] Lack of ammunition and provisions, and the failure of the commanding officers to inspire respect and confidence, had destroyed the morale of the Army even before the revolution. Ex-President Rodzianko cites the following facts: "During 1915-1916 the number of soldiers who let themselves be captured amounted to two million; one million and a half deserted the front." Such were the *official* figures. "On August 26, 1914, after the battle of Gelchevo, there were left fifteen hundred men out of a regiment of thirty-five hundred. Three days later there gathered at the kitchens another fifteen hundred perfectly sound privates. I assert that such cases were not singular, and were absolutely verified." Before the revolution a group of officers headed by General Krymov arrived at Petrograd with a special report about "the Army getting decomposed, and the discipline being threatened by a complete breakdown. . . . The state of mind among the troops is growing so menacingly grave that the soldiers will most probably refuse to advance, and before this winter is over may abandon the trenches and the battlefield." It seems, in the light of these facts, absurd to blame the revolution or the Bolsheviki for the débâcle of the Russian army, and for the resultant separate peace with Germany. Rodzianko, a conservative and a monarchist, says: "I assert that the war would have been lost even if there were no revolution, and a separate peace would have been signed in all probabilities, perhaps not at Brest-Litovsk, but somewhere else, and it would have been even more disgraceful, because it would have resulted in Germany's economic domination over Russia."—*Archive of the Russian Revolution—VI*, pp. 22-45, *passim*.

sion and silence burst forth for the first time in a passionate, irresistible torrent of words. Says Stankevich:

> Military authority was the first to disintegrate. It had fallen to
> pieces immediately after the revolution, even under Alexeyev, Guchkov,
> and Kornilov. An army which had been built up on automaticity, me-
> chanicalism and strict formalism, found itself deprived of any prescribed
> regulations, of all authority. . . . Accustomed to answer only "Yes, sir,"
> "No, sir," and "I am unable to know," the army all of a sudden began
> to talk, to make a noise, to argue, to "self-determine." Built up on the
> contradistinction between private and officer, the army began to be self-
> governed on the basis of the most democratic quadripatrite formula [uni-
> versal, direct, equal and secret vote].[26]

Andreyev was slow in discerning the real state of affairs: the
systematic disillusionizer of yore was loth to part with the
bright illusion he had created out of the Russian soldier. But
when he did bring himself to the painful task of analyzing conditions, he once more revealed his unfailing sharpness of vision
and correctness of foresight. Late in the summer of 1917, in
an article called "Ruin and Destruction," he stated that the
country was "in mortal danger," and predicted the following
events: 1, starvation, caused by the inevitable conflict between
city and village; 2, the complete disintegration of the army; 3,
a separate peace with the Central Powers, which Andreyev regarded as treason to the Allies; 4, financial bankruptcy; 5, the
breaking up of Russia into numerous states. Andreyev not only
foresaw the fulfillment of his prophecy, but even prepared himself to meet the new situation philosophically, as may be seen
from the bitterly sarcastic conclusion of his article:

> And perhaps—perhaps there really ought not to be any Russia? Per-
> haps this is merely an old-fashioned term which it is time to destroy? If
> there is to be no Russia, there will be something else . . . "and at the
> coffin's portal young life shall play anew." Does it matter after all,
> whether it is Russian life or young German life? The people, too, will
> not perish. You cannot destroy at a blow one hundred million people.

[26] *Reminiscences,* p. 145.

They will get used to the new conditions. Who knows, perhaps there really ought not to be any Russia? [27]

Yet Andreyev was reluctant to acquiesce in passive grief. Late in October, 1917, after the Germans had occupied Riga and were threatening Petrograd, he appealed to the Allies for help. "Russia," he wrote in *Russia's Will*, "is going through a period of most dangerous sickness, and all further delay may prove fatal and irreparable." [28] He called on the British fleet to hasten to the Baltic Sea, in order to draw off the Germans from Russia's capital. But the Allies withheld all active support from the tottering government of Kerensky, hoping perhaps that with its fall there would be a chance for a strong order under the military dictatorship of the Kornilov group. [29] In October of that year Andreyev was elected by the Petrograd editors to the "Pre-Parliament," or "The Council of the Republic," convoked by Kerensky at the eleventh hour, in view of the oncoming Bolshevik wave. [30] This Council assembled a

[27] Quoted after Mr. L. Pasvolsky's translation in the *Review*, December 6, 1919, pp. 638, 639.

[28] The London *Times*, October 24, 1917.

[29] Such, at any rate, was the attitude of the Russian conservatives and liberals, backed by the British Ambassador and by the larger portion of the Allied press. The second part of his *History of the Second Russian Revolution* (Sofia, 1922), Milyukov devotes to the one question: "Kornilov or Lenin?" The author, an adherent of Kornilov, represented those who gambled on that alternative. Kerensky categorically states in his article "Gatchina" (*Contemporary Annals* [*Sovremennyia Zapiski*], October, 1922, p. 147, Paris) that the Kornilovist groups decided not to aid his government in case of a Bolshevik uprising. "Their strategic plan consisted in not interfering with the success of the Bolshevik armed insurrection, and in quickly suppressing the Bolshevik 'mutiny' after the fall of the hateful Provisional Government."

[30] In this connection may be cited a letter from Gregory Zilboorg, a loyal supporter of the Provisional Government, which he wrote in reply to my inquiry as to what he knew personally of Andreyev's political activity. I translate it from the Russian:

. . . "As to his political activity or political views, it is a lustreless story. . . . Since 1914 Andreyev, like the overwhelming majority of the Russian writers, had been silent. . . . His *King, Law, Liberty* is nothing but a hurriedly baked drama, in which there is everything requisite for a play of that sort, but in which there is nothing of Andreyev himself. It is evident that his social sympathies became dislocated and befogged. . . . In 1916 began the notorious epopee of Protopopov. . . . His newspaper, *Russia's Will* (Purishkevich nicknamed it *Prussia's Will*), proved a colorless, lifeless, short-lived sheet, in which Andreyev occupied a prominent position together with Amfiteatrov. . . . Then the revolution flamed up. An-

few times even during the Bolshevik uprising, accomplishing nothing beyond fine oratory. Andreyev cherished no longer any hopes. "Everything is upside down," he wrote to a friend during the growing domination of the Bolsheviki. *"They* rule Russia. They are going to direct the Academy of Sciences, the universities, to legislate. They, the illiterates. This is an insurrection of darkness against knowledge, of stupidity against reason." His faith in the people proved to be of short duration. In March of that year he had written (probably to Nemirovich-Danchenko): "I am sick as a clinic, and yet I rejoice like Isaiah, and regard the future with calm and confidence. Most important of all—I trust the people." A few months later his old contempt for the mob reëmerged, coupled with his mistrust in the value of all classes of the population. On October 29 he wrote to Goloushev: "An unprecedented triumph of stupidity . . . At present all democratic elements have separated themselves from the Bolsheviki, but this is of small avail. . . . How tedious life is becoming, brother! Everything personal has perished, is forgotten, while the social values —this is what they have become! Then this Council, where I sit: such faces, brother, that even before the uprising they reduced me to despair, to uttermost gloom."

The victory of Lenin and his adherents was due mainly to their making use of the popular slogans of the moment, promising immediate peace to a war-weary nation, land to a soil-

dreyev appeared nowhere with speeches . . . appeared at no workmen's meetings nor at any revolutionary gatherings. It seemed as though for the time he had dwindled away. He held (passively) a Cadet position—that is, he regarded the Provisional Government with hostility, sympathized with Kornilov, with old Alexeyev, with Milyukov, etc. When by the middle of October the party forces had definitely crystallized, and the Pre-Parliament opened under the name of the "Temporary Council of the Republic," or, as Kerensky once called it, "the council of the temporary republic," Leonid Andreyev took his place there with the Right, with General Alexeyev, Milyukov, Peter Struve, and others. He made not one speech, and voted all the time in unison with Alexeyev. Strange to say, it was difficult, impossible, to recognize in the Andreyev of those days, the former Andreyev, the stormy, turbulent, thunderous, fighting Andreyev. I saw him a few times in the corridors of the Maria Palace, where the Council met. It was not Andreyev, but a meek, taciturn, sullen middle-aged man, walking up and down the crowded hall. On November 9 the Bolsheviki replaced us. Andreyev disappeared from the scene, without having appeared on it. . . .'

hungry peasantry, and bread to a starving population. Even such a bitter enemy of the Bolsheviki as Professor P. N. Milyukov has come to regard that coup in the light of historical retrospect as a natural and inevitable phenomenon. In his lecture before the Lowell Institute, on October 28, 1921, he stated that "Russia was ripe for the revolution." He admitted that the dilatory policy of the moderate parties, their postponement of important reforms till the meeting of the Constituent Assembly, and their advocating the continuation of the war, were "a great mistake," and "fatal." [31] "The agrarian question and the control of the factories by the workmen were matters which had become firmly rooted in the masses. The soldier, it was soon discovered, did not want to wait till the Assembly met to divide his land . . . Furthermore, there was insidious propaganda to the effect that the Army was fighting for capitalists and imperialists. The Germans fraternized with the Russians over the trenches and caused havoc at the time of the greatest need. At the same time the extremists in Russia were quite willing to make use of the mind of the soldiers . . . The Bolshevik victory at Petrograd would have appeared slight in its effects had it not been received well everywhere. The uprising practically met with no resistance." [32]

But Leonid Andreyev refused to accept the Bolshevik victory as a historic inevitability. Ignoring the fact that the Russian army was in no position to carry on the war, he regarded the Bolsheviki as traitors for having concluded a separate peace with the Central Powers. Ignoring the fact that Kerensky's government was impotent and unpopular, he branded as usurpers and bandits the Bolsheviki who assumed authority without meeting resistance. He wished to remain uncompromisingly loyal to his illusion about the significance of the purpose of the war, hence he could not forgive the Realpolitiker who signed

[31] Milyukov elaborates the same view in his *Russia, To-day and To-morrow,* p. 32 (New York, 1922), where we find such a typical sentence as this: "It was a mistake on the part of the moderate groups not to pay enough attention to the consequences of their conscientious but dilatory methods."

[32] Quoted after the Boston *Evening Transcript,* October 29, 1921, part one, p. 4.

the disgraceful treaty of Brest-Litovsk. War against the Bolsheviki he came to consider as a sacred cause, in which all civilized nations were in duty bound to take part. Eagerly he awaited the fall of the Soviet government under the onslaught of its numerous foes—Russian, German, and Entente. From his Finnish abode he could hear the bombardment of Kronstadt, the port of Petrograd, and his heart craved for news of the fall of the red capital. When more than a year had passed with the power of the Bolsheviki still unbroken, Andreyev issued his *S. O. S.*, as he named his final appeal to the Allies to "intervene and stop bloodshed and anarchy" [33] in Russia. In fact, it was more a wrathful protest and a hopeless cry of agony than a practical appeal for help, though the latter note also sounded here and there in the article, as for instance:

> As a wireless operator on a sinking ship sends his last message through night and murk: "Help, come quickly! We are sinking. Save our souls!" so I, moved by faith in human goodness, fling into the dark distance my prayer for sinking men. Could you but know how dark is the night over us! . . .[34]

How faint must have been, however, Andreyev's "faith in human goodness" at this very time, while he was engaged in writing *Satan's Diary!* At the end of his outcry he seemed to realize the futility of it, and he addressed it to the chosen few: "Just as among bipeds there are men, so among journalists there are some who have long earned the name of knights of the Holy Ghost, and write not with ink, but with their nerves and blood, and to these I appeal. . . ." [35] Much firmer sounded his condemnation of the Allies whose position with reference to Russia he considered "either treachery or madness" (p. 1). Bitterly he advised his countrymen to forget that William II "had prepared to take his lunch at Paris, and that Mr. Wilson had taken his there only through the lucky chance of having crossed two oceans: the Atlantic, and the ocean of Russian blood poured out

---

[33] These were the words in the cable dispatch to the London *Times*, for March 1, 1919.

[34] *S. O. S.*, p. 11, of the pamphlet published in Finland in 1919.

[35] *Ibid.*, p. 18.

in defense of the Allied cause. . . . Forward, then, Russia, until thou comest to the very Cross! Guiltless of thy blood are Mr. Wilson and Mr. Lloyd George—has not all the world seen how they strove to wash their hands?" (pp. 5 and 8).

The task of examining the rightness or wrongness of Andreyev's stand in regard to the war and the revolution is beyond the scope of this essay. We are here concerned with his state of mind, with the explanation of his point of view, not with its justification. Regarded from this angle, Andreyev's attitude toward Soviet Russia presents for us a profound personal tragedy of shattered hopes and polluted ideals. It was, furthermore, a double tragedy, in the sense that while condemning the Bolsheviki and advocating merciless war against them, Andreyev found himself, as we shall presently see, isolated among the uncongenial counter-revolutionists.

The last years of Andreyev's life were full of mental and physical anguish. He suffered from material privation, from chagrin on account of conditions in Russia, and particularly from the consciousness of the atrophy of his creative faculty. Maria Yordansky, editor of the leading monthly, *Contemporary World,* in whose pages appeared Andreyev's *Thought* (in 1902) and other stories, described her meetings with the writer during 1918 and 1919. In February, 1918, she rode with him in a railway carriage from Petrograd to Finland. He told her that immediately after the Bolshevik coup he settled with his family in his Finnish villa, with no intention of returning to Russia so long as the victors were in power. But the news of his mother's illness made him undertake the dangerous journey to Petrograd:

"I stayed at my sister's" (he said) "in hiding. During this time my own residence was searched several times, everything was ransacked—books, papers, letters, clothes. They were looking for me. They tried to force my servant by threats to reveal my whereabouts. Very seldom, toward evening, I would go out to breathe some fresh air. They might have arrested me on the street, if I had been recognized." [36]

[36] *L. Andreyev's Emigration and Death* (*Emigratsia i smert L. Andreyeva*), in *Native Land* (*Rodnaya Zemlya*), No. 1, p. 45. New York, 1920.

We are not told for what precise reasons Andreyev was threatened with arrest. His views must have been widely known, judging from the fact that he "daily received heaps of letters in which he was called 'an abominable toady and lackey of the bourgeoisie,' 'traitor to the working class,' 'hireling of international imperialism championing the continuation of the world slaughter.' " [37] The letters bore such signatures as "a group of soldiers," "a group of sailors," "a group of workmen," or those of private citizens. His article, *To the Russian Soldier*, became evidently notorious, provoking anger and indignation. Andreyev remarked with bitterness that this was probably the only composition of his these people had read.[38] In proletarian Russia he felt even more isolated than under the autocratic rule.

This was Andreyev's last trip to Russia. As soon as his mother was strong enough to travel, she came to her Leonid, and shared to the last his poverty and tribulations, outliving him by nearly one year. The relations of Andreyev with his mother are worth noting. In his autobiography, written for Fidler, he mentioned that his "predilection for artistic activity belonged by inheritance to his maternal line"; also that his mother was his first instructor in drawing, "holding the pencil" in his hands.[39] She was of Polish descent (as were the mothers of many other Russian writers, notably of Nekrasov, Korolenko, Veresayev), née Pockowski, Anastasia Nikolayevna. Andreyev's sentiment for his mother can be seen from his letter to her written shortly after his last trip to Petrograd. A good deal of the intimate atmosphere is unfortunately lost in translation, but whatever is retained of the original has much biographical value. A full reproduction of this letter is justified by its being so characteristic of Andreyev. His style here, as occasionally in his fiction, is uneven, pictorial beauty alternating with exaggerations and bits of dubious humor. On the other hand, the letter reveals for us a corner of the author's intimate

---

37 *Ibid.*
38 *Ibid.,* p. 46.
39 *First Literary Steps*, pp. 28, 29.

self, showing him capable of warm affection and love, a trait which may surprise readers of his skeptical, destructive works. It also becomes evident how well Andreyev could play a part, wear a mask, appear jolly and poke fun, while his heart ached with grief and despair. Here and there the letter hints at the tragedy of the lonely foresaken writer, who forces a smile in recounting his little troubles and little joys, in growing enthusiastic over an old letter from the author Goloushev. He does not tell his mother of his anxious thoughts concerning Russia, though he is already contemplating his despondent *S. O. S.*[40]

Dear Little Mother! You still think it is a joke, but I tell you in the most serious manner that I love your letters *very* much, and that you are—how shall I say?—extremely congenial to me in your letters, both in their tone and in their contents. To be sure, your handwriting is terrible, and your orthography resembles the orthodoxy of an anarchist; indisputable is also the fact that your profound contempt for punctuation marks transforms your manuscripts into a continuous marasmus and cataclysm, forcing the reader to gasp for breath; everybody knows, too, that many a strong and healthy person has sobbed helplessly over your letters, despairing of finding a beginning and an end in these closely knitted stockings *sans* heels and toes—but all these things are trifles, the mere exterior. As to substance, you always write sensibly, cleverly, and finely, and somehow you always manage to tell an immense lot in a short letter.

Your last letter is one of the best specimens of your literary efforts. Again, little mother, I am not jesting in the least, and say this with the warmest affection for you, my semi-centennial friend. Fifty years, you will admit, is not a little, and you and I have been friends nearly fifty years, beginning with Pushkarsky Street [in Orel], and ending by the cold rocks of Finland. Before your eyes I have grown from a puss in boots and a ganglion into a writer of Russia, having passed through drunkenness, poverty, suffering. Before my eyes from a young woman you have become a "granny," having also passed through suffering, poverty, and so forth. And no matter what has happened to us, whithersoever fate has brought us, high up or low down, you and I have never lost the closest cordial bond. Persons came and went, but you always stayed with me, always the same—true, immutable, singular. I know some families where fine relations exist between parents and children, between

40 See Roerich's statement, *infra* p. 162.

mothers and sons, but such relations as between *you and me* I have not met. That is the truth.

I always write to you so much not because I am obliged to do so, and must perform a tedious duty, but because to write to you is both interesting and *needful* for me, needful for my own soul. I always know and feel that no one will understand me so well, will take such interest, will put so much love into reading my writings, as you do, and that no one will so grasp my jests and will laugh over my "funny" letters as you do, my unchangeable little Mushroom [a nickname Andreyev gave his mother when a child]. Of course I do not write you *everything*: sometimes I am afraid to disturb and distract you, sometimes—especially in matters involving philosophy and too complex problems—I naturally avoid too elevated a style; very often I even lie to you concerning my health and mood, presenting them in better color than they really are, but—you understand—even when I *lie* to you I feel a relief, I know that at all events you sense the truth and sympathize.

I do not like and do not know how to write sentimental things in letters, and for this reason I am not going to say *how* I love you, and how your illness has worried and frightened me. You know this yourself. I am stronger than others, and when necessary I am able to restrain myself and to keep a calm appearance, and this may sometimes deceive those who know and feel less than I do. But you know this, and I shall say no more about it. It is my misfortune that for this external reserve and calm I have to pay for a long time afterward with all sorts of pains, bodily and mental. Those who without restraint express themselves in words, in confusion, in tears, and so forth, manage to calm down and forget, while I remember everything.

Yes, I have a good memory, little mother, and though I may at times forget evil done to me, I never forget good deeds. I remember everything! But then surely I shall never, not even in my sleep, forget the endless good which you have shown me, your endless goodness and kindness. You have done so much for me in my life, more than any person can possibly do for another. Here again begins the sentimental, so I am not going to proceed, but I repeat—and do remember this: However much, in your opinion, I have done for you, I cannot repay you even a thousandth part, and shall thus remain your debtor. I have nasty nerves and an easily irritable mind. At times I am rude and loud, but if I grieve you, know that I myself suffer from it and feel ashamed at my boorishness. I am simply not a good enough man to pay you in full for all your goodness, and I am conscious of it. For example, how many times have I sworn before you that I shall never shout at you when playing whist, yet as soon as you deal wrongly I roar like one scalded.

And now, my dear little mother, my main wish is that you recuperate and grow healthy, without worrying and exciting yourself. I know that it is hard to be calm when we are in different places, and that it is hard not to be excited when both the Germans and the Bolsheviki push on, but here, forsooth, nothing can be done. Such terrible times not only Russia but the whole world has not seen for ages, and one must endure, with clenched teeth. If we could only manage to live through it! I think that Petrograd is threatened with no other calamities than hunger. The fact that the "government" has fled to Moscow will force those who have stayed to wake up and come to their senses. Everybody is in straits at present.

About us you need not worry. To be sure, it is our good fortune to own a house in the village, and to be known and treated well by every one around here. On my last arrival from Piter [the popular nickname for Petrograd], when late at night I had to walk from Tyursevo along the railroad ties, I asked an unknown Finn whom I met on the way whether it was against the rule to walk there. He said: "Others may not, but you may: everybody knows you."

So far everything is quiet here. Red Guards are scarce, most of them are fighting beyond Helsingfors. . . . I am afraid only of one thing—of hunger, which will come if the Reds and the Whites do not make peace but continue the senseless row.

The weather is remarkable. In the shade it is a trifle below freezing, but in the sun there is about twenty degrees [Réaumur; about seventy-seven Fahrenheit]. The children's rooms are not heated, and in Anya's [Mme. Andreyev's] study flies are buzzing. And it's so dazzlingly bright. The day seems as long as G's [probably Gouleshev's] nose illuminated by a searchlight. I stroll about, or find a little place in the sun, near the annex or by the front entrance, and closing my eyes I warm my muzzle. And I smell such a wonderful odor of something distant—of free expanses, of the sea, of Italy, of far-away blue skies. The other day I came out to the sea: a smooth sparkling white film, and on the horizon the aërial blue of the other shore. Such a deception: it appears as though over there, on that blue coast, they have not ice, snow, and winter, as we have here, but summer forests and meadows.

But the really happy ones are, of course, the children. The little idiots know nothing about Wilhelm or about Lenin, they eat to satiety, sleep soundly, laugh and play, and dive in the snow joyfully like cubs. And they always feel warm!

After dinner—this is a peculiarity of our bookish home—the nursery presents such a picture: beneath the lamp around the table sit Natasha [the widow of Andreyev's brother, Vsevolod], Emilia [the governess], Vadim [the eldest son of Andreyev by his first wife], Savva, Vera, Valentin [his three children by his second wife], and in deep silence they all read. They gobble up enormous books, of thousands of pages. To be sure, the funniest person is Tinchik [Valentin]. Not long ago Didishka [Vadim] got angry at him for something, and asked him, referring to his brain: "What have you got in your head?" Tinchik answered quickly: "Vanity!" He is very coy and affectionate with me, though after a kiss he immediately retreats into a corner; then from the corner he comes again for a kiss. Vadim works a good deal, has grown still bigger, and behaves very well: for him this year has proved very beneficial. In the evening we have talks.

Anna has been safely to the city and back, and she got very tired: a terrible lot of packing and transporting. She works too much, but I scold her all the same, lest she grow conceited. To tell the truth, she overworked during your illness.

I am tired writing, and shall finish to-morrow.

March 10, new style [1918. The Russian calendar was thirteen days behind the Western].

Life here is still quiet and peaceful. Were it not for the newspapers, which I receive daily through Sirki, I might forget about the Germans and the Bolsheviki. But then, the food reminds one, of course.

Still sunny, dripping from the roof, though the snow is firm and crisp. To-day after dinner—we eat all sorts of vile things, like sparrows—I sat on the upper terrace, in the sun. With your eyes closed, you might imagine yourself in India, in a tropical forest, amidst bananas, cocoanut oil, and crocodile purses. One thing is bad: my head aches from time to time, not seriously, but annoyingly. I don't know what it wants, it's hard to come to an understanding with it.

I receive no letters from any quarter. I worry a bit about Sergeyich [Sergey Sergeyevich Gloushev, by pen name Sergey Glagol; he died at Moscow in July, 1919]. Here is a dear man whom I love, and who regards me with sincere friendliness, unafraid of my talk and my influence. Yesterday I was looking over old papers and letters, and came upon these words from him—he wrote them after my departure from Moscow; "I miss you in the day, I miss you in the evening. In your society I lived with all the hidden fibres of my soul, and felt my brains working 'on all wheels.' The devil knows why it is that no one but you arouses such plans in my mind and such thoughts in my head."

Get well, little mother, do not excite yourself, drive away disturbing thoughts. Read more of Dumas and others like him, do not gnaw at newspapers, and let politics alone.

I embrace you firmly and tenderly, and I am always with you. At the first opportunity I shall send again some one with a letter to you. Don't be lonesome, little Mushroom. Regard everything as a hard trial sent not to us alone. We are far better off than millions of others. Let us endure!

                          Your *Little Puss in Slippers.*

The last two years of his life Andreyev ruminated a great deal. His nervous, feverish activity of former years was replaced by a self-conscious passivity which induced retro- and introspection. "It is dark in my soul," he wrote to Goloushev in the spring of 1918. "I am consuming the last particles of my energy . . . I wish to create, but am unable to, as though my talent had dried up." This notion naturally paralyzed whatever was left of his creative faculty, fettering his wings with diffidence. Mme. Andreyev urged him to write in his diary, as an outlet. She informs me that "he wrote his diary, because he was unable to compose anything creative. Tormenting and black were those last years." In his diary and in his letters Andreyev expressed all of himself, all which he wished and could express during those dying days. His motives were black, both in regard to the future and to his personal recent past. Thus in his diary and in a letter to Goloushev he wrote disparagingly about his last works: "The fundamental question is, Why has it so happened that during the first ten years of my literary career I rose with each work straight upward, like a rocket, rose swiftly, decidedly, and radiantly—then suddenly stopped . . . As though in the very air I had stumbled at some barrier, and I flutter beneath the ceiling like a bat. . . ." He proceeds to review his productions, and concludes that not one of his later plays comes up to his *Life of Man* or *Anathema,* and that in his stories he has not excelled *Judas* and *Darkness*. Even his superior writings he now regards as incomplete: *"The Life of Man* promises more than it actually gives. *Anathema* is more advanced in age, but is still immature." In this mood of self-flagellation Andreyev takes a morbid pleasure in abusing those of his works in which he appears somewhat constructive. "In short: I am strong and unique as long as I destroy, as long as I am Lazarus, in whose person I once drew myself. And I am weak, ordinary; I resemble many others and lose myself in the literary crowd, when I attempt to affirm, to console, to give hope, to pacify. Once born a Lazarus, I should remain one. . . . And what ruins me still further, is my most disgraceful lack of confidence in myself. In the depth of my soul I regard myself as rubbish, hence the pernicious effect of hostile critics on me." Whether Andreyev always held such an opinion of himself, it is hard to say. As far as his pre-war utterances go, they do not betray any inferiority complex; rather do they display a calm confidence in his intuitive power and in the value of his literary activity. The war poisoned him, as he admitted in his diary. As early as 1915 we find him indulging in self-humiliation, writing to a friend: "My soul is sick and frets at belonging to Leonid Andreyev. Ah, how I dislike him! At times tête-à-tête with myself is absolutely unbearable." Having lost his self-respect, he was no longer in a position to bear philosophically his unpopularity and isolation. On April 20, 1918, he mentions in his diary the fact that on this day, the twentieth anniversary of his literary début, he received not a single word of greeting, "not a sound." "Why am I disliked?" he queries, and somewhat irrelevantly he reproaches himself of treason: "Born to curse, I have distributed indulgences."

A telling portrait of Andreyev toward the end of that year is presented by the painter and clairvoyant thinker, Nicolas Roerich, in an article from which the following passage is quoted:

. . . His face had greatly changed. It had grown dark, had become a brown bronze, his nose appeared sharpened and pointed; his eyes, though they had not lost the vividness of their gaze, had become still deeper (much knowing). His hair fell low on his neck in long black locks. Exactly the face of a Hindu sage guarding mysteries. Thus Andreyev appeared to me when we managed to meet in October, 1918, after a whole year of our sojourn in Finland. . . . He was burning, he was all aflame with that same sacred thought with which he died on September 12, 1919. This thought was—to reveal for humanity all the horror of Bolshevism in its present aspects. Lover of freedom and deep thinker, Leonid Nikolayevich understood that now the struggle must be carried on not only with bayonets, but also with the word, through wide propaganda, in which all reasoning forces should unite in the name of true culture. Saturated with life's contradictions, he was composing his brilliant appeals to humanity, one of which, *S. O. S.,* had already been published; he was also working on his long novel, *Satan's Diary,* which apparently was left without a final reading. In Tyursevo, where he then lived, one could see from the shore through binoculars Kronstadt, even Krasnaya Gorka. And each one of the numerous incomprehensible bombardments of those points aroused Andreyev's question: "What if this is Cain's last minute?" [41]

Andreyev had moved for the winter to Tyursevo because at his village, Vammelsu, he found it difficult to provide all necessities, according to Maria Yordansky, who adds that owing to Andreyev's habit of working all night, Tyursevo had to be chosen for its electric-light facilities.[42] In his diary, written early in the fall of 1918, one finds frequent references to the writer's "hunger for light—lack of kerosene oil." This complaint alternates with grumblings about the futility of his creative efforts. He labors over his last attempt, *Satan's Diary,* a story of the devil who assumes a human aspect for amusement, and who discovers in the end how inferior his tribe is in cruelty and cunning to the human race. His state of mind during this work can be imagined from the following scattered notes in his diary: "Have written seven pages—threw them aside: I don't like it. Superficial. No music, no sorrow, no love. Words, invention. . . . But then, I cannot write about

[41] N. K. Roerich, "To the Memory of Leonid Andreyev," *Native Land—II*, p. 37. New York, 1921.
[42] *Ibid.*, p. 52.

the shooting and drowning of officers, which the Reds are carrying out at Vyborg! . . . Only one lamp in the study—I must put a period. . . . I am working over my Devil with less zeal than over the little wheelbarrow [which he was making for his son, Valentin] . . . Catastrophes are not good for art. Only tricksters are in need of tangible material. Fakirs and miracle workers do without it. Messina [the earthquake] is a banality. Moses, Dostoyevsky—there is something. . . . Have written fifty pages—cheap satire. Poor Shchedrin and poor Andreyev . . . Have changed it to the first person. . . . Eight new pages . . . Nervous impotence." At the same time his complaints about his head and heart become more frequent. On December 18 of that year he suffered a prolonged heart attack, and Mme. Andreyev feared that it was the end.

In February, 1919, Maria Yordansky visited Andreyev at Tyursevo, and found him "considerably thinner, older. Around his eyes and mouth had appeared new, sad lines." [43] He eagerly inquired about the conditions of the Intelligentsia in Russia, and was grieved to hear of their want and humiliation, of the omnipotence of Gorky, who at times interceded with the authorities for his unfortunate colleagues. Andreyev doubted Gorky's sincerity, and said, according to Maria Yordansky:

How many times during the years of my acquaintance with Gorky did I find myself arguing about him, warmly discussing his sincerity! Do you remember, I used to tell you about a circle of writers at Moscow [the "Wednesdays"]? . . . We discussed literature, read our new stories, argued, and toward the end of the evening, when there remained only a close circle, the conversation inevitably turned on Gorky and his sincerity. Once Veresayev, on the evening when the gathering took place at his home, lost his patience at the futility of these arguments, and made a motion: "Gentlemen, once for all let us resolve not to touch on accursed problems. Let us not talk of Gorky's sincerity." We all laughed and, indeed, never spoke of this again. It is the same at present. One hates to talk of the subject. One reads Gorky's statements to foreign correspondents. He declares that he is not a communist, does not sympathize with the Soviet policy, condemns terror—yet he works with them. For enormous sums he sells them his works, takes from them millions for the official Soviet publication house, covers their abominations with his name. He does not trust them, does not believe in them, yet this [attitude] he calls "following the people." . . . No, it is better for us not to "touch accursed problems." [44]

Maria Yordansky further quotes Andreyev to the effect that a representative of Gorky came to see him, and offered to buy his works for a large sum of money, in the name of the state publication house. "Of course, I refused to enter into any negotiations with them," [45] he said. Nicolas Roerich also told me of this, emphasizing the fact that the Soviet authorities endeavored not so much to buy Andreyev's works (since according to the new Russian legal code nothing could prevent them from reprinting his writings at their will), as to secure his good feelings by saving him from hardship and starvation. Andreyev's firmness in declining to deal with the new rulers of Russia does credit to the strength of his convictions, though it remains an "accursed problem" whether Bolshevism should have been fought from within, through spreading enlightenment, in Gorky's manner, or from without, as Andreyev thought fit. The latter preferred to serve his truth by helping the interventionists, by arousing public opinion in the West, by circulating his *S. O. S.*, in the efficacy of which he seemed to have gained faith. Maria Yordansky quotes him as saying:

A certain person has given ten thousand rubles for the purpose of translating this article, and cabling it to the Paris and London press. This money will serve as a foundation for a propaganda fund, which is very greatly needed. . . . Every one who has read *S. O. S.* places great hopes

[44] *Ibid.,* p. 51. His mistrust of Gorky began some time previously. In an undated letter to Nemirovich-Danchenko, written probably during the war, he said: "Once again I find myself at variance with Gorky. Innerly we have parted already, and our outward separation will probably come before long. . . . How full of absurdities is Gorky's head, and how little candor, straightforwardness, and truth has remained in all his actions and in his life. There was a time when I greatly loved and respected this man, and had hoped to preserve these sentiments to the end—but it is impossible!"

[45] *Ibid.,* p. 54.

in it. I am told that the public opinion of Europe cannot help responding. Yes, it cannot help responding.[46]

Andreyev's ardent desire to devote his pen to anti-Bolshevik propaganda met with no enthusiasm on the part of those who should have welcomed his powerful alliance, as we shall see presently. On the other hand, he was prevented from doing much work by the condition of his health. Toward the end of February, 1919, Andreyev met in Finland a prominent refugee, I. V. Gessen, a leader of the Cadet party and an experienced journalist. Andreyev urged Gessen to become the editor of a Helsingfors Russian newspaper, and to make it serve as a disseminator of information. "He believed," writes Gessen, "that once we acquaint Europe with the true condition of affairs in Russia, then the civilized world cannot help coming to its aid in the name of saving Russian culture, so full of promises." [47] For some time Gessen declined the suggestion (so he states), but when he finally yielded to the entreaties of his friends, and communicated with Andreyev, requesting his promised coöperation, the writer's health did not permit him to fulfill his promise. About two months after his meeting with Gessen, he wrote in his diary: "Both my body and my spirit are wretched. Frozen is my soul, and it will probably not revive till my very death" (April 8). During Passion week he entered: "My condition is no worse than that of Christ at this time. But He rose again!" (April 19). After the receipt of Gessen's request, he wrote to him:

Dear Iosif Vladimirovich: I am now in the position of that student who for two nights waited in line for an opera with Shalyapin in it, obtained a ticket, and in his seat, when he got warm, and the music began to play, fell asleep, and slept soundly through the whole evening, until the usher woke him up, and declared that all was finished. But whereas that lucky fellow got some repose, sleep and warmth, I am just ill. Ill and, at least for the present moment, an invalid. For two years I have lived under an excitement which had no outlet; all last winter I craved

---

[46] *Ibid.*, pp. 54, 55.
[47] I. V. Gessen, "The Last Days of Leonid Andreyev," in *Archive of the Russian Revolution—I*, p. 309.

in vain for systematic activity (not artistic): it failed to come to me. The end of it was that the entire store of excitement and emotions was spent on myself—and my heart gave out. I cannot write. The slightest strain of thought, a bit of excitement in front of my typewriter—and I collapse: my heart begins to bump, then it stops, I gasp for breath—and feel the approach of death.

My physician finds my heart "weakened," and forbids all activity, mental and even physical. In this manner I have lived for nearly two months, "neither a candle for God, nor a poker for the devil." I am employing every measure for my recuperation. I have moved back to my home on the Black Rivulet, and have begun to exercise little by little, working in the garden and putting up fences. I feel somewhat better, but in so small a measure as yet that a chance talk about politics, or a newspaper, may at once bring back my heart attacks. I write no letters, try to see as few people as possible—and read fairy tales. This is why I have not written to you; I felt guilty, yet I did not write, intending to explain the reason later.

And here Burtsev invites me to work, then Kartashev,[48] finally your letter has reached me. Woe! Again I try not to fall to pieces, I fill my lungs with air and sun, and endeavor to prove to myself that my ailment is not serious and will pass. Otherwise—what then? I console myself with the consideration that I shall not be too late anywhere, since there are mountains of work ahead of us.

This is how things are with me, dear Iosif Vladimirovich. It goes without saying that as soon as I am strong enough for even a little work, I shall get in touch with you. In the meantime I shall listen to the cannonade which occurs every day, and at times comes from three directions; I mount to the tower to watch naval battles through my binoculars, I make guesses and divinations. Last night there were such imposing salvos and rumblings, somewhere beyond Ino, that our house shook. I must say that all of us have become accustomed to cannonading, as if it were a mere noise, only my most peace-loving dog, Marquis, hides indoors, unable to stand it. The battle at Sestroryetsk excited us somewhat—the machine guns barked distinctly; but this is of the past.

[48] V. Burtsev, once a rabid revolutionary (in writing), has become the mouthpiece of every anti-Bolshevik interventionist. He has been publishing an hysterical paper in Paris, in which he has supported in turn Kornilov, Youdenich, Denikin, Kolchak and Wrangel. N. Kartashev was Minister to Public Worship in Kerensky's cabinet, and later also became a supporter of the interventionists. Since the collapse of the Wrangel affair he has been advocating the maintenance of the remnants of the general's army in Gallipoli and elsewhere, to be kept in readiness for the moment when it may strike again at Soviet Russia.

To-day I received an unexpected and joyous message: a telegram from my officer brother [Andrey] who disappeared last fall, to the effect that he is alive and well. And do you know, from where? From Omsk! "Omsk to Terioki"—those are the very words on the envelope. For me it is simply a miracle. And this miracle was brought by the most ordinary slip of a postman. Well, this means that my brother has reached Kolchak and is serving under him, which gladdens me. Perhaps it is due to my wretched life, but I believe in Kolchak firmly. He is the only one. I have heard about the English version of *S. O. S.,* and I am exceedingly happy that Pavel N. [Milyukov] has written its preface. With all his "mistakes," I consider him the greatest statesman of Russia. Personally, too, he has the greatest attraction for me. And how he works! I am envious. I know, you also work splendidly, and . . . but why stir my wounds.

I press your hand firmly. Farewell, may you have strength and vigor, work on, and remember me not with a word of reproach but with a sigh of friendly commiseration.

June 9, 1919.   LEONID ANDREYEV.[49]

When one recalls Andreyev's caustic satire against the Cadet party and its leaders (*The Pretty Sabine Women,* 1912), and compares it with his sympathetic attitude toward Gessen and Milyukov, expressed in the letter just reproduced, one concludes that war and revolution make strange bedfellows. The necessity of overthrowing the Bolsheviki became an *idée fixe* with Andreyev, a great goal which justified all means. He greeted every counter-revolutionary general as the potential savior of Russia. Thus he rejoiced at the formation, about August 1919, of the "North-Western Government" at Revel, Esthonia, headed by General Yudenich. That he was not completely blinded by his joy, is evident from the sense of national humiliation which he experienced, when considering that this "government" was made up *by the order of the English General March.*[50] Yet he continued to advocate intervention, knowing

[49] *Archive of the Russian Revolution,* v. I, pp. 310, 311.
[50] Cited by Maria Yordansky, *Native Land—I,* p. 57. She quotes him further as remarking with bitterness that the destiny of Russia concerned the Entente less than that of Esthonia, Latvia, Karelia. Did he not know that the concern of the Entente in these countries was due to their forming the links of the "cordon sanitaire" prescribed by Clemenceau as a means for forcing Russia into submission?

that intervention inevitably meant national humiliation. His uncompromising hatred for the Bolsheviki impelled him to compromise a great deal in his unqualified support of their enemies.

One wonders how much of his rectilinear obstinacy fraught with inner contradictions he owed to his mental and physical state during that period. His diary entries became ever blacker in tone, with such refrains as "I feel as though I were in a grave up to my belt," "I am thinking of suicide, or is suicide thinking of me?" "I am living in a jolly little house with its windows out on a graveyard." Worst of all, he became aware that his thinking faculty, once so alert and brilliant, had lost its flexibility. "I feel as though a fat buttock has settled on my head, and softly presses it," he commented on the state of his thoughts. Maria Yordansky relates from the words of Andreyev's mother and wife that in August, 1919, "he ate little, slept not at all, only occasionally took a short nap in the daytime; not long ago he had a fainting spell." [51] She found Andreyev at the end of August "strikingly thin, sick, and exhausted, with deeply sunken sad eyes, and extremely nervous." [52] The last photograph of Andreyev [53] shows plainly traces of suffering and anguish in the deep lines around the mouth, in the vertical furrow on his brow, and especially in the indescribable sadness of the eyes full of pain, self-reproach, and despair. From the verbal descriptions as well as from the even more eloquent photograph, it appears that in the summer of 1919 Andreyev was already a doomed man. His wistful yearning for activity, for struggle, for warfare at any price—does it not suggest the desperate clinging of a drowning man to a straw?

In spite of his poor health, Andreyev found in himself enough energy during the month of August to negotiate with the "North-Western Government" in regard to propaganda work.

[51] *Ibid.*, p. 56.
[52] *Ibid.*, p. 57. Toward the end, his diary abounds in complaints about petty disturbances—the noise of the children, the mooing of the cow, the faces and voices of the neighbors. He moved from village to village, fretting about the unæsthetic interiors of the houses he had to abide in.
[53] Reproduced in *The Fire Bird* (*Zhar-Ptitsa*), No. 2, September, 1921. Paris-Berlin.

"He came to Helsingfors," relates Gessen, "and stayed with me two weeks. A thirst for activity gripped him, and he dreamt of heading an organization for anti-Bolshevik propaganda. However, his plan met with no sympathy on the part of those on whom its realization depended, and the disappointed Leonid Nikolayevich resolved to go to America." [54] This laconic account tells volumes of the tragedy of Russia's ill-fated writer. Nicolas Roerich spoke to me with profound indignation about the treatment of Andreyev by the Whites. When one of the greatest national writers offered all of himself to the "saviors of Russia," pleading for permission to sacrifice his last fire and energy for what he considered a sacred cause, the authorities of the ephemeral government curtly declined the offer. They informed Andreyev, states Roerich, that his work was not needed, since they had a regular "chinovnik" (clerk) for the performance of the propaganda work. At this point I wish to quote the Academician Roerich on a germane matter. According to the painter, Finland was swarming with wealthy Russians, opponents of the new régime and ardent lip-patriots. Yet they refused to come to Andreyev's aid. Some of the writer's friends pleaded with the rich Whites for their help in publishing Andreyev's works, in order to obtain some means for his subsistence, but met with no response. "If Leonid Nikolayevich did not die from actual starvation"—I am quoting Roerich verbatim—"it was due to an ordinary lumber merchant, Samuel Lazarevich Gurevich."

Failing in his negotiations with the army of Yudenich, Andreyev decided to go on a lecture tour to the United States. "We sent a cablegram to a common friend of ours, a prominent American journalist," writes Gessen, "and Leonid Nikolayevich returned home, to wait for an answer and prepare for the long journey." [55] This American journalist must have been

[54] *Archive of the Russian Revolution—I*, pp. 309, 310. According to Mme. Andreyev, I. V. Gessen ultimately was appointed Minister of Propaganda in the Yudenich government. In conversation with me Gessen spoke rather disparagingly of Andreyev, and made light of his *S. O. S.*

[55] *Ibid.*, p. 310.

Mr. Herman Bernstein, who mentions this matter in his preface to *Satan's Diary*.[56] In a letter to the New York *Times*, Mr. Bernstein quoted Andreyev's proposal, to the effect that the purpose of his trip to the United States was "to combat the Bolsheviki, to tell the truth about them with all the power and conviction within him, and to awaken in America a feeling of friendship and sympathy for that portion of the Russian people which is heroically struggling for the rejuvenation of Russia." [57] The nervous strain and bewildering confusion experienced by Andreyev during those trying days may be gauged from his letter to Nicolas Roerich, dated August 23, 1919:

Behold three roads open before me at this moment—such is life. One —"I take upon myself entirely" the whole work of anti-Bolshevik propaganda, as I have written and proposed to Kartashev and to others, and enter the local government with the portfolio of Minister of Propaganda and the Press. Understand: "entirely!" The organization in all its immensity, beside my own writing for it. It will mean that I live at Revel or wherever else chance may ordain, that I travel to and fro, talk for days, search out persons and bring them into the proper mood, and that at night I write, combat inertia and faint-heartedness. This is an activity which requires an iron constitution, while I am sick, sick. My compensation will be a few copecks, not enough to live on with my family, so that I shall be compelled to continue the painful quest for credit, wasting the remnant of my strength—and ahead of me are sickness, insecurity, sleepless nights, the Writers' Asylum. But duty obliges me to work for Russia, so to-morrow I am journeying to Helsingfors, to plead for what will prove my indubitable end as an artist and as a living creature. I say, "am journeying," while my heart is so bad that yesterday I was scarcely able to move from one room to another. I say, "to plead," yet I am too weak to exert my tongue and ask for a glass of tea.

The second road. Getting no hearing in Helsingfors, I journey to America. There I deliver lectures against the Bolsheviki, travel through

---

[56] "A year ago Leonid Andreyev wrote me that he was eager to come to America, to study this country and familiarize Americans with the fate of his unfortunate countrymen. I arranged for his visit to this country and informed him of this by cable. But on the very day I sent my cable the sad news came from Finland announcing that Leonid Andreyev died of heart failure."—*Satan's Diary*, Preface, p. v, dated September. New York, 1920.

[57] New York *Times*, November 9, 1919, part III, p. 2.

the States, produce my plays, sell my *Satan's Diary* to a publisher, and return a multimillionaire to Russia for a care-free, venerable old age. This sounds better. The trip may turn out a failure (I may be sick, and collapse after the first lecture, or the Americans simply may not care to listen to me), but, under happy conditions, it may prove a "triumphant march": I shall meet people who love me, shall receive impulses for new artistic work, and, having healed my mind, I may perhaps also pull up my body, which always lags behind. America! But how to get there? How find a good and generous manager, not a swindler? How to get along, until such a man is found? How procure some money, enough at least to maintain the family during my absence? I intend to travel with my wife and our little son; the rest will stay here.

I have been robbed of my trousers and my boots—how shall I manufacture new ones, and of what style must they be for America? These are questions both grave and insignificant, at all events trifles for a sensible and practical person—but for me they are accursed, thoroughly insoluble problems. Ah, only now I see to what extent I am childishly helpless in life. Yet to-day is my birthday: forty-eight years I have been walking on the earth, and have so little adapted myself to its ways.

The third, the most probable, road is—the hospital. But this road is so gloomy, and in general I am here approaching such thoughts and decisions, that I had better stop.

As to what it means to work against your conscience, Gorky demonstrates that. In the last issue of the *Liberator,* an American Bolshevik journal which for some reason is being sent to me, he has an article, "Follow Us!"—that is, Soviet Russia and its wisdom. And what a miserable, wretchedly flat and insignificant article it is! When a poet and a prophet begins to prevaricate, God punishes him with impotence—such is the law of eternal justice.[58]

[58] The article of Gorky, referred to by Andreyev, appeared in the *Liberator* for June, 1919, page 3. In it Gorky accuses Mr. Wilson of being "the leader of the campaign against Russia," and he calls upon "the workers and honorable men in all the world": "Follow us to a new life, for the creation of which we are working without sparing ourselves or anything or any one else. For this we are working, erring and suffering with the eager hope of success, leaving to the just decision of history all our acts. Follow us in our struggle against the old order, in the work for a new form of life, for the freedom and beauty of life." To make clear his personal stand in regard to the Soviet régime, Gorky says: "I will not deny that this constructive work has been preceded by an often unnecessary destruction. But I, more than any one else, am justified and in a position to explain that the cultural metamorphosis which is going on under particularly difficult circumstances, and which calls for heroic exertions of strength, is now gradually taking on a form and a compass which has up to the present

'Tis night, and I must pack my things for to-morrow's trip. Through the windows I can see over the dark sea—I live on the very shore—searchlights cutting the stormy sky. Yesterday at sunrise, in a pale-blue sky amidst fading stars, I heard the buzzing of an aëroplane, and saw two bright-red flashes of explosions. How beautiful they were, and how beautiful was the pale sky in its early freshness and peace, and how wonderful must have seemed to the aviator the earth and the sky, and how splendid all this is, splendid to live, to fly, to see stars at dawn.[59]

This letter, the last utterance of Andreyev to end with such wistful buoyancy, was written at Tyursevo, whither he had moved once more from Vammelsu, in his ever increasing restlessness. Early in September he was obliged to leave Tyursevo, where he enjoyed so intensely the proximity of his beloved sea. According to Maria Yordansky, "the incessant raids of aëroplanes at Tyursevo disturbed his peace, and rendered all work impossible. The family was in constant alarm." [60]   He decided to spend the last few days before his departure for America at the summer home of the playwright Falkovsky, at Mustamyaki—also in Finland, but more remote from the frontier. Here he sorely missed the sea, became more irritable and fretful. His black despondency was reflected in his last letter to Roerich, which came to the painter as a posthumous message:

September 4, 1919.
All my misfortunes converge in one: I am homeless. I used to have a little home: my house and Finland, to both of which I had grown accustomed. With the coming of autumn, of dark nights, it was a joy to think of my house with its warmth, its light, and the study which preserved the traces of ten years' work and thought. And it was a joy to flee from the city to the quiet and intimacy of my home. Then there was

been unknown in human history. This is not an exaggeration. But a short time ago an opponent of the Soviet government and still in many respects not in agreement with it, I can yet say that in the future the historian, when judging the work which the Russian workers have accomplished in one year, will be able to feel nothing but admiration for the immensity of the present cultural activity. . . ." It is a question of taste as to the literary quality of Gorky's appeal. To be sure, it differs in its blunt straightforwardness from the picturesque metaphors and images of Andreyev's S. O. S.
[59] Native Land—II, pp. 38–39.
[60] Ibid., p. 60.

a big home: Russia, with its powerful foundation, force, and expanse. Then, too, there was my most spacious home: creative art, which absorbed my soul. Now all this is gone. In place of a cozy home—a cold, freezing, plundered summer house, with broken window panes, surrounded by a sullen and hostile Finland. Russia is no more. And my creative power is gone too. Like chains, I drag along with me the Bolshevik and my sorrow. My articles—are not art. I feel so grippingly empty and frightened without my kingdom, as if I had become utterly defenseless against the world. And I have no place to hide either from the autumnal nights or from my sorrow, or from my illness. I am threefold an exile: from my home, from Russia, and from my art. I am most terribly pained by the loss of the last; I experience a nostalgia for "fiction," similar to homesickness for one's motherland. And it is not that I have no time to write or that I am not well—nonsense! Plainly, what constituted my creative power has simply gone, vanished, perished together with perishing Russia. Like heat lightnings flicker the silent reflections of distant storms, but of the storm itself with its life—there is nothing. When I reread an old work of mine, I wonder: How could I do this? Whence did it come into my head? Well, I feel like chatting now; I shall attend to business to-morrow. Regarding my *Black Maskers*. Only in the days of the Revolution did I understand that this was not only the tragedy of the individual, but the tragedy of the whole revolution, its genuine sad countenance. Behold the Revolution, which has kindled lights amidst darkness, and is expecting those invited to her feast. Behold her surrounded by the invited . . . or uninvited guests? Who are these maskers? Chernovs? Lenins? But these know at least Satan. While here, lo, are those others, particles of the great human darkness, which extinguish the torches. They creep from everywhere, the light is not bright for them, the fire does not warm them, and even Satan they know not as yet. Black maskers. Then the end of noble Lorenzo. Yes, one may draw a complete analogy, by using quotations. How did it happen that the tragedy of the individual, which my play was intended to express, has become the tragedy of the history of the Revolution? There is much that is interesting in this. . . .[61]

This is a letter of a broken man and of an artist fallen into decay. When a writer looks admiringly back on his old productions, there must be something stationary and flaccid about his present creative power. In life we begin to reminisce and

[61] *Ibid.*, pp. 40, 41.

to ruminate over our past when we are no longer active and too busy living for looking backward. In the case of Andreyev this observation holds true, in particular: during his active period he paid no attention to what he had written and published, but thought and spoke only of what he was going to do in the future.[62] The war and the revolution must have dried the spring of Andreyev's talent, if he could "wonder" retrospectively at his former productions, and become his own commentator. The consciousness of being a "threefold exile," and an exile from art above all, weighed heavily on his mind, accelerating the end. The last pages of his diary reveal his utter despondency and lack of will to live on. The aëroplane raid which took place during his last night at Tyursevo (he stayed there that night on purpose, "to test his fate," which reminds one of his escapade on the railroad tracks, *supra*, p. 29) shook him deeply. The next day, September 8, at Mustamyaki, Andreyev recorded this raid in his diary, but felt reluctant to relate the event—"so repulsive is everything in the world, so unbearably tedious to live, to talk, to write, that I lack the strength and the desire to scribble down even a few lines. For whom? For what purpose?" The entry on the next day began in the same key: "What one might call a genuine disgust with life. Everything even in the slightest degree suggesting silliness or ugliness provokes in me a revulsion, at times a feeling of physical nausea." Yet the end of that entry contained a faint flash, like heat lightning, of the former Andreyev: "But the place is beautiful. We live high on the hill, all around is a sea of woods, over whose smoothness, as though across a real sea, are flitting at this moment shadows of clouds. Below is the lake, and in the distance are seen N. Kirka, Rayvola. An almost mountainous freshness in the air. . . . If my mind only permits me, I may work and prepare for America." The contemplation of nature had evidently a bracing effect on Andreyev to his very end. One recalls his letter to Lvov-Rogachevsky, in which he spoke of the salutary significance of nature for him: "Nature and

---

[62] See Chukovsky's statement to this effect, *supra*, p. 117, and Andreyev's letter to Nemirevich-Danchenko, *ibid.*, footnote 80.

nature alone brings me back to the lost equilibrium." [63] So now, three days before his death, broken in body and spirit, loathing life and man, Andreyev, at the touch of nature, regained his "equilibrium," and even began again to plan his trip to America. His very last entry, on September 10, was a fitting conclusion to his literary life, for it presented a description of the aëroplane raid at Tyursevo, written with the freshness, simplicity, and fine suggestiveness which he displayed in his best days. [64]

Andreyev died two days later, suddenly. On the last day he felt better than usual, joked with the children, and conversed with their teachers about their studies. At four o'clock in the afternoon he went to his bedroom to take a rest. Presently his wife, who was working on his notes in the adjacent room, heard his call, rushed in, and found him sliding off the bed and gasping for breath. His last words were: "Anna, I am ill." He remained unconscious till the very end, at six o'clock. His death occurred from a hemorrhage of the brain, as had been the case with his father. Maria Yordansky, from whose reminiscences these details are taken, describes the body of the writer:

Already arrayed for the coffin, with his head high on white pillows, covered to his neck with a white sheet, lay Leonid Nikolayevich. No longer were there bitter lines around his mouth, the deep furrow on his forehead had smoothed out, his thick black hair showed no grayness. It was as if there had not been those heavy years, the oppressive tortures of the last days—so young had his face become. Handsome, calm and majestic, it did not seem yet dead—only a deep, complete peace reposed on it. His shut eyes rested. [65]

At the age of forty-eight, having reached fame, success, and comparative comfort after a youth of poverty and loneliness, Andreyev, like his prototype in *The Life of Man*, had been hurled down to the lower depths. He died a forsaken exile,

[63] *Supra*, p. 82.
[64] A translation of this entry appeared in my article, "The End of Andreyev," The *New Republic*, June 28, 1922, pp. 134-135.
[65] *Native Land—I*, p. 59.

suffering privation, leaving not enough money for his burial expenses.   A small group accompanied his body to its last rest, most of the mourners, according to Maria Yordansky, consisting of accidental emigrants, who never had any relation to Russian literature.   This friend of his quotes the following lines from the page she found inserted in Andreyev's typewriter— the passage was interrupted by the author's last call for his wife:

Revolution is as unsatisfactory a method for solving differences as war is.   Once you cannot defeat a hostile idea in any other way than by smashing the skull which contains it; once you cannot subdue a hostile heart except by piercing it with a bayonet—then, of course, fight.[66]

In this last utterance of his Andreyev proved consistent to that despondent outlook which was his throughout his conscious life, with the exception of the few brief moments, when he clutched pathetically at illusions.   He died with hatred for the Bolsheviki, with chagrin at the besotted Whites, with indignation against the Allies, with contempt and scorn for all mankind.

[66] *Ibid.*, p. 62.

PART II

THE MOTIVES AND BACKGROUND OF
ANDREYEV'S WORK

I

INFLUENCES AND KINSHIP

Avowed influences.—Their nature.—Negative views of Pisarev and Tolstoy, of Schopenhauer and Nietzsche.—Andreyev not a consistent
philosopher.—Kinship of the two philosophers to Andreyev.—
Their common attitudes.—Nietzsche's *memento vivere* versus
Schopenhauer's resignation.—Coëxistence of contradictory elements in Andreyev.—His nearness to Nietzsche's passionate restlessness and unreservedness.—His nearness to Schopenhauer's
ethical ideal.—Résumé: Andreyev's aptness for adopting negative rather than positive views.

IN a letter to Lvov-Rogachevsky, written in 1908, Andreyev
stated that he had been "strongly influenced by Pisarev, then
by Tolstoy's 'What Is My Faith?'—then by Schopenhauer, then
by Nietzsche." He went on to say: "The influence of books
has ended, the one remaining influence being apparently that of
Schopenhauer. At present I am living—this is my surmise—
under the sign of *Die Welt als Wille und Vorstellung.*" [1] This
statement is to be understood in the sense that the four named
thinkers, though divergent in their ultimate conclusions, contributed in common to Andreyev's critical attitude toward life's
existing forms. Andreyev was hardly susceptible to any other
kind of influence. Of a solitary, introspective, brooding disposition, possessed of a restless, questioning, analytical mind,
he yielded only to such influences as harmonized with his mental
make-up. This is evident from his testimony in regard to the
effect which Tolstoy had on him. [2] He rejected Tolstoy's positive doctrine as "something foreign" to him, and was moved
only by the negative side of his teaching. Again, like nearly all
of Russia's youth, he was stimulated by Pisarev, the fiery champion of Nihilism during the eighteen-sixties, in the direction of

[1] *Two Truths,* p. 24.
[2] *Supra,* p. 29.

doubting everything and "smashing right and left"—Pisarev's cardinal tenet. Out of his cell in the fortress of St. Peter and Paul, Pisarev preached not only destruction, but, what seemed to him most constructive, the ideas of Büchner and Moleschott. Yet the fact remains that Pisarev appealed to his contemporaries and to the following generations primarily and largely as a negator and destroyer of conventional beliefs. Andreyev, toward the end of his life, even went so far as to charge "Pisarevism" with having poisoned the Russian Intelligentsia, and with having laid "the foundation for the great Russian Mob Spirit," [3] by which he signified Bolshevism.

The influence of Pisarev and Tolstoy on Andreyev's views, in the limited sense just indicated, did not last beyond his boyhood years,[4] and being of a purely general character, it did not perceptibly manifest itself in his writings. Even Schopenhauer and Nietzsche appealed to Andreyev largely and most lastingly[5] through their destructive critique. Their positive precepts he never accepted wholly, as will be seen later. Thus, we may conclude that whatever effect certain thinkers may have had on Andreyev, it was not of the sort which changes extant points of view or generates new outlooks. Rather did he adapt congenial ideas and opinions of certain kindred spirits, for the enhancement and ramification of the basic idea which had been apparently inherent in him. This was a predominantly negative attitude.[6]

---

[3] Diary, dated April 30, 1918.

[4] Mme. Andreyev, in describing for me some of her husband's youthful frolics, cited an experience from his Gymnasium days, when he hoaxed his teacher of composition by obtaining from him an excellent mark for a paper which was cribbed from Pisarev. At college he shook himself free from Pisarev and Tolstoy.

[5] Mme. Andreyev showed me a set of Schopenhauer's main work, in Russian, which her husband had preserved since his student years, and cherished to the end, proud of the neat bindings of the volumes—an extravagant luxury during those days of semi-starvation. I was also shown a volume of *Zarathustra*, in one of the early Russian versions, which was considerably marked and underscored, indicating the owner's repeated ramblings through the pages.

[6] Toward the end of his life, Andreyev reproached himself for having created a few positive characters. "I have been a traitor to myself. Born to curse, I have distributed indulgences," he wrote in his diary, April 20, 1918 (*Supra*, p. 161.

In his letter to Lvov-Rogachevsky, quoted at the beginning of this chapter, Andreyev conjectured that he was "apparently" under the influence of Schopenhauer, and that he lived under the sign of *Die Welt als Wille und Vorstellung*—such was his "surmise." The circumspect words in inverted commas are characteristic of Andreyev's honesty with himself. Disliking labels of all sorts,[7] he was particularly wary of applying philosophic terms in his works as well as in his private correspondence, for Andreyev usually avoided subjects which he could not absorb so as to discuss them with the ease of authority. Philosophy did not lie within his versatile field. He lacked the calm and the methodicalness of a student of philosophic systems, who can grasp them, compare them, finally select one system, and adhere to it. His mind, all aflame with problems such as we call philosophic—life and its value, man, his place in the world and his goal—could contemplate and visualize only chaos, eschewing order and system. One should therefore take his "surmise" with the reserve which the timidity of its tone invites.

The "influence" of Schopenhauer and Nietzsche, of which Andreyev speaks in his letter, is to be understood as the stimulating effect which these thinkers exercised on Andreyev, in developing and strengthening his latent notions and nascent views. His extraordinary power of intuition, which we have noted in the foregoing pages,[8] prompted him to turn to Schopenhauer and Nietzsche, in whom, of all modern philosophers, he could find the closest congeniality with his own outlook. Theoretic speculation *per se* did not interest Andreyev, and what drew him to these thinkers was the vitality of their ideas, their direct concern with earthly life and with the problem of the concrete individual. "The main question is, Where does man come in?" he wrote to Amfiteatrov [9] anent isms and classifications. Man was to him the pivot of the universe, the cardinal problem, and

---

7 ". . . I am not a realist. What am I, then? A mystic? I do not know. And, when all is said, I simply do not understand, and—pardon me—I do not accept *this* classification, it appears ridiculous to me." From his letter to Amfiteatrov, *supra*, p. 121. In a similar vein he wrote to Nemirovich-Danchenko, Goloushev, and in his diary.

8 *Supra*, p. 116 ff.

9 *Supra*, p. 121.

in this respect he was typical of Russia's Intelligentsia. In Schopenhauer and Nietzsche he found a kinship not only because their powerful critique of life as it is corresponded with his own attitude, but also because their ideas were, in the main, not astral or abstract but applicable to flesh-and-blood human beings.

We may say, then, that Andreyev's "surmise" is, on the whole, correct, as are most of his "intuitions." Allowing the reservation that he was not a rigid disciple and consistent follower of Schopenhauer, we can still accept his conjecture of living "under the sign" of Schopenhauer's Weltanschauung. Consciously or unconsciously—the latter is more probable and plausible—Andreyev imbued nearly all of his writings with a spirit which is unmistakably Schopenhauerian-Nietzschean. To put it more precisely, Andreyev's negative attitudes—and these are his predominant attitudes—tally with the views of the two philosophers, often appearing as comments upon them and illustrations of them.

In fusing the critical attitudes of Schopenhauer and Nietzsche, in so far as they correspond with those of Andreyev, no violence is done to either of the two thinkers. Andreyev could find in them many common starting points. Thus, both of them reject the duality of matter and spirit, of body and soul, both emphasize the unity of life's driving force, which presents a combination of volition, instinct, impulse, intellect, of our mental and physical faculties. One calls this force Will-to-live, the other, Will-to-power, a difference of great importance in regard to the ultimate value or valuelessness of life, but one which is ungermane at this juncture of our discussion, where we indicate merely points of departure. Again, both of them regard this will as a blind driving force, interminable and insatiable, because of the limitlessness and endlessness of our wants. Hence both of them consider happiness as a negative quantity, as a temporary elimination of a want, and both look upon pain as the only positive element in life. Both, then, present life as composed overwhelmingly of misery, suffering, slavery. Slaves of their will, men are on the whole narrowly selfish, greedy, cowardly, stupid, in constant need of illusions. Both philosophers express contempt for state, society, church, and other institutions whose *raison d'être* is purely negative, namely the control of men's inherent selfish and brutal impulses, and, secondly, the alleviation of men's anxiety and fear by means of narcotic beliefs and illusions. Both, finally, emphasize the limitation and impotence of our intellect—Schopenhauer's "Sufficient Reason," and Nietzsche's "Small Reason."

This general statement will be illustrated presently, when we come to the analysis of Andreyev's works. In the chapter on his early period we shall see that in his treatment of the individual in his relation to life and the world, Andreyev voices motives which are obviously Schopenhauerian, with an occasional hint at Nietzsche's influence (notably in *The Abyss, Thought,* and *Life of Vasily Fiveysky*). In the next chapter, dealing with his reaction to public events, where the individual problem broadens into collective problems, we shall find Andreyev still in accord with the negative attitude of the two philosophers toward the intrinsic value of social institutions and mass-movements—the church, the state, and such of the latter's concomitants as war and revolution. It is in the following chapter, in the discussion of Andreyev's postulation of general problems, that we shall observe his wavering between the positive ideal of Schopenhauer and that of Nietzsche. For at this point the divergence between the two thinkers becomes irreconcilable.

Like Andreyev, Nietzsche was a disciple of Schopenhauer. He had to immerse himself in the cool waters of Schopenhauer's disillusioning and disenchanting teaching, as a prerequisite for his ascension to the heights of Zarathustra, the forerunner of the Superman. But Nietzsche "overcame" his master, freed himself from the "Fluch Schopenhauers." [10] While accepting his master's view on our existence as composed of pain and folly; while even enchancing Schopenhauer's critique of our standards

---

[10] *Nachgelassene Werke—XI*, p. 380, No. 580. My quotations from Nietzsche are based on the eleven-volume pocket edition of the Alfred Kröner Verlag, Stuttgart, 1921. For Nietzsche's posthumous writings I have used their more complete version in the *Nachgelassene Werke*, in 8°, Verlag Naumann, Leipzig, 1901–1903. For *Der Wille zur Macht*, however, I have used volumes IX and X of the Kröner edition, where this posthumous work is presented in much fuller form.

and illusions, by making it more sweeping and inclusive (to wit, in regard to morality), Nietzsche proclaimed his vigorous affirmation of life, his *memento vivere*. By replacing the Will-to-live with his Will-to-power as the all-mighty driving force of the universe, Nietzsche changed the aspect of a dreary existence, monotonous and unchangeable, into that of an exuberant process of incessant striving for more life, for a more intense and more beautiful life. This conception of a dynamic, everlasting evolution—what Simmel calls "die dichterisch-philosophische Verabsolutierung der Entwicklungsidee Darwins" [11]—enabled Nietzsche not only to be hopeful of the future, but even to justify the past and the present as continuous stages in the onward and upward procession, though each stage had to be denounced and overcome as inferior to the stage next in succession. Having absorbed Schopenhauer's negative attitude to the forms of life as it is, Nietzsche ultimately used this attitude as a basis for his passionate hymn to ever-changing, ever-growing, ever-to-be-surpassed life.[12]

In Andreyev one often feels a passionate love for life, even in some of his lugubrious writings, whenever he lends life the dignity of tragedy, and does not merely present it as a silly farce. In such cases—and these are many, as we shall see—one is inclined to question Andreyev's professed adherence to Schopenhauer. It were closer to the truth, however, to admit the coëxistence in Andreyev of contradictory elements. Logi-

---

[11] Georg Simmel, *Schopenhauer und Nietzsche*, p. 5 (2nd edition, München, 1920). Nietzsche would have hardly subscribed to Simmel's compliment. In his *Streifzüge eines Unzeitgemässen*, 14 (v. X, pp. 303, 304), and in *Der Wille zur Macht*, No. 647 (v. IX, pp. 475, 476) ff., Nietzsche definitely condemns Darwin. Not struggle for existence, but struggle for power—such, in the main, is Nietzsche's argument, not against evolutionism, of course, but against Darwin.

[12] "Wer, gleich mir, mit irgend einer rätselhaften Begierde, sich lange darum bemüht hat, den Pessimismus in der Tiefe zu denken und aus der halb christlichen, halb deutschen Enge und Einfalt zu erlösen, mit der er sich diesem Jahrhundert zuletzt dargestellt hat, nämlich in Gestalt der Schopenhauerischen Philosophie . . . der hat vielleicht ebendamit, ohne dass er es eigentlich wollte, sich die Augen für das umgekehrte Ideal aufgemacht: für das Ideal des übermütigsten, lebendigsten und weltbejahendsten Menschen, der sich nicht nur mit dem, was war und ist, abgefunden und vertragen gelernt hat, sondern es, *so wie es war und ist*, wieder haben will, in alle Ewigkeit hinaus, unersättlich *da capo* rufend" . . .—*Jenseits von Gut und Böse*, No. 56 (v. VIII, p. 80).

cally he "lived under the sign of *Die Welt als Wille und Vorstellung*," while by sentiment and temperament he was akin to the spirit of *Die fröhliche Wissenschaft*. Like Nietzsche he was in his life as in his art, all passion, yearning, restlessness, transpierced with an aching love for life, its drawbacks and defects notwithstanding. His style never attained the epic calm and the cool beauty of Schopenhauer's, nor could he ever achieve the blissful stage advocated by the philosopher in the following characteristic passage:

. . . so ist es dagegen der, in welchem die Verneinung des Willens zum Leben aufgegangen ist, so arm, freudelos und voll Entbehrungen sein Zustand, von aussen gesehen, auch ist, voll innerer Freudigkeit und wahrer Himmelsruhe. Es ist nicht der unruhige Lebensdrang, die jubelnde Freude, welche heftiges Leiden zur vorhergegangenen oder nachfolgenden Bedingung hat, wie sie den Wandel des lebenslustigen Menschen ausmachen; sondern es ist ein unerschütterlicher Friede, eine tiefe Ruhe und innige Heiterkeit, ein Zustand, zu dem wir, wenn es uns vor die Augen oder die Einbildungskraft gebracht wird, nicht ohne die grösste Sehnsucht blicken können, indem wir ihn sogleich als das allein Rechte, alles andere unendlich überwiegende anerkennen, zu welchem unser besserer Geist uns das grosse sapere aude zuruft. Wir fühlen dann wohl, dass jede der Welt abgewonnene Erfüllung unserer Wünsche doch nur dem Almosen gleicht, welches den Bettler heute am Leben erhält, damit er morgen wieder hungere; die Resignation dagegen dem ererbten Landgut: es entnimmt den Besitzer alle Sorgen auf immer." [13]

We do not find this majestic Nirvana mood in Andreyev. Rather does he suggest the flaming outbursts of Nietzsche, the feverish staccato of his aphorisms hastily proclaimed between prolonged periods of suffering. "Was heisst Leben? Leben —das heisst: fortwahrend etwas von sich abstossen, das sterben will; Leben—das heisst: grausam und unerbitterlich gegen alles sein, was schwach und alt an uns, und nicht nur an uns, wird. . . ." [14] This dynamic tone, if not exactly the thought behind it, might belong to some of Andreyev's characters, be it

[13] *Die Welt als Wille und Vorstellung*, No. 68, p. 437 (v. I, Weichert edition, which is used throughout this essay).
[14] *Die fröhliche Wissenschaft*, No. 26, p. 94 (v. VI).

Dr. Kerzhentsev, or the workman Treich, or the astronomer Ternovsky, or Savva, or Haggart. In place of quietism Andreyev championed creative energy, "movement, movement, movement," as he wrote with enthusiasm concerning Kellerman's *Der Tonnel*.[15] He would subscribe to Nietzsche's words: "Das einzige Glück liegt im Schaffen: ihr alle sollt mitschaffen und in jeder Handlung noch dies Glück haben."[16] And he would understand the "divine tremor" of the hero of never-ceasing creativeness, about whom Nietzsche tells us succinctly:

"Wie will ich Atem holen und die Glieder strecken, wenn ich meine Last auf die letzte Höhe getragen haben werde!"—so dachte oft der Held unterwegs. Aber als er oben war und die Last niederwarf, da tat er nicht so,—da bezwang er auch noch seine Müdigkeit: und hierbei lief ihm ein göttlicher Schauer über den Leib.[17]

For temperamentally Andreyev could not bear mental repose. Maxim Gorky tells us with what hatred Andreyev used to recall one of his high-school teachers who was fond of quoting a certain philosopher, to the effect that "true wisdom is reposeful." "But I know," protested Andreyev, "that the best men of the world are painfully restless. To the devil with quiet wisdom!"[18]

Beside his general tone and temperament, Andreyev came closer to Nietzsche than to Schopenhauer in his critique of established standards, notably with respect to the moral problem. Where Schopenhauer stood in awe before man's "mysterious" feeling of sympathy,[19] and prescribed it as a positive precept in man's conduct, supplementing the negative maxim of harming no one (Neminem laede; omnes, quantum potes, juva[20]), Andreyev expressed his contempt for conventional

[15] *Collected Works of Andreyev—XV*, p. 239 (*Enlightenment* edition which is used throughout this essay, unless otherwise indicated).

[16] *Nachgelassene Werke—XII* p. 361, No. 685.

[17] *Ibid.*, p. 255, No. 93.

[18] Gorky's reminiscences, in *A Book on Andreyev*, p. 9.

[19] He speaks of Mitleid as "erstaunenswürdig, ja, mysteriös," "das grosse Mysterium der Ethik, ihr Urphänomenon." *Grundlage der Moral*, No. 16, p. 355 (v. III).

[20] *Ibid.*, pp. 360, 372,

goodness and justice, and for degrading pity (*Judas; Darkness*). Yet it was precisely on the ethical question that Andreyev eventually diverged from Nietzsche and attempted to join Schopenhauer. In *The Ocean*, Haggart cuts a poor figure as the protagonist of Nietzsche's Will-to-power, who tramples upon truth, justice and pity, when these interfere with his onward march. On the other hand, Andreyev's positive characters, such as Werner and Musya, in *The Seven That Were Hanged*, or David Leiser, in *Anathema*, approach Schopenhauer's ideal of the man who, having resigned his Will-to-live, and having thereby renounced his selfish motives and desires, rises triumphant over life, and merges with his fellow beings in an all-absorbing feeling of love and compassion.

Thus we shall find Andreyev frequently recalling to our mind the two keen evaluators, now fusing their negative appraisals, now obviously coming closer to one than to the other, now wavering between the two. For, to sum up, Andreyev was not of a philosophic mind, which performs a double function—of setting up questions, and of solving them in a logical and systematic way. Andreyev's mind had an aptitude for the first part of this function, and it could find itself in accord with a variety of queries and doubts. But whenever he attempted to introduce harmony into the chaos that he had visualized all his life, he vacillated. He quailed before the task of answering questions and reconciling contradictions. Hence his ultimate divergence from the thinkers whose negative views he so readily adapted and assimilated.

II

EARLY PERIOD: PROBLEMS OF THE
INDIVIDUAL

Andreyev's first stories "made to order."—Gorky's discernment.—Andreyev's individuals compared with those of Gorky, Dostoyevsky, Chekhov.—Fear of life.—Loneliness, isolation, chasm between man and man.—Illusionism and disenchantment.—Solution?—Zarathustra's suggestion.—The leper's attitude.—Symbolism of *The Wall.*—Andreyev's broadening skepsis.—The slumbering brute in *The Abyss.*—Thought the traitor.—The tragedy of faith in *Life of Vasily Fiveysky.*—Schopenhauerian motives.—Their epitome in *The Life of Man.*—Someone-in-Grey=Will-to-live.—Man's curse and deliverance in death.

ANDREYEV's first attempts at fiction bore the stamp of "made to order" literature. Requested to write a story for Easter or Christmas, he followed the traditional path. Like Dostoyevsky and Tolstoy, he would endeavor to regenerate a soul by awakening the supposedly ever-present albeit dormant good in man's heart. Thus in his first story, *Bargamot and Garaska,* a callous policeman of a rough neighborhood and a hopeless drunkard and law offender are both of a sudden ennobled by Easter sentiments, and experience the sensation of genuine brotherhood. A similar motive is treated in *From the Life of Captain Kablukov,* where the drinking, swearing officer forgives his orderly, who has pocketed, for family purposes, the money given him for the purchase of drinks and provisions. The sight of the sleeping servant, with his bovine face and protruding bare toes, suddenly makes the captain realize the humanness of one whom he has been maltreating and utterly ignoring as a fellow being. Altogether one may indicate about half a dozen sketches of that period which reiterate the motive of man's good impulse coming to the fore and triumphing. But this motive, so powerful and compelling in Dostoyevsky, sounds "to order" and almost maudlin in Andreyev. The uplifting effect of the church service on an embittered youth (*A Holiday*) ; the energizing and reconciling influence upon a misanthropic roughneck, of the task of performing aid and service during a public calamity (*On the River*) ; the noble indignation of the young lawyer when told by his cynical senior partner that the defendant whose case has just been won by able and sincere pleading is as a matter of fact guilty (*His First Fee*) ; the pathetic grief of the journeyman bringing a present to his sick little assistant, and finding that he has died in the hospital (*The Present*) ; the predicament of a thief setting out for a prearranged robbery, and being prevented from committing it by the pitiful yelping of a puppy which persistently follows him, and which he is finally obliged to take into his arms and carry back home (*A Robbery Planned*)—these are more or less felicitous subjects for a psychologist, and are within the range of Andreyev's talent. But in these stories and sketches the author appears to force the issue for the sake of the moral, a fault practically absent in his more mature productions.

Yet it was *Bargamot and Garaska* which drew Maxim Gorky toward Andreyev, and served as the starting point for the long and mutually meaningful friendship of the two writers. In his reminiscences Gorky relates how he felt in that ordinary story, beside the presence of a "robust talent," "the author's hidden smart smile, a smile of mistrust in the fact—and that smile easily reconciled one to the inevitable, forced sentimentalism of Easter and Christmas literature." [1] Gorky detected the hidden clue to Andreyev's true self, and, indeed, helped his protégé to extricate himself from journalistic hackneyed sham, and to express his genuine personality.

The stories of Andreyev's early period reflect both his personal state of mind (constitutional and enhanced by adverse circumstances) and the mood of the Intelligentsia at the end of the last century, politically oppressed and doomed to inaction,

[1] *A Book on Andreyev*, p. 5.

seeking in introspective analysis a way out of mental chaos. His note differed greatly from that of Maxim Gorky, his senior by two years, and already internationally famous at the time of Andreyev's début. Gorky knew more hardship and want than Andreyev, but his early life was spent largely out of doors, in vagabondage, on the boundless steppes, on wide seashores, in contact with freedom-loving, nomadic men and women. Gorky emerged from the crucible of misery and penury full of love for life, which he regarded as potentially good and fair, and full of hatred for those who make life ugly and mean. His optimism called for vigorous activity, for a thorough cleansing of the Augean stables of tsaristic Russia, and it appeared as a stimulating relief from the melancholy apathy of Chekhov's ne'er-do-wells. But Leonid Andreyev had been a typical poverty-stricken Russian intellectual, leading an anæmic existence within the walls of his ill-ventilated and poorly heated room, silent, introspective, knowing life through books and contemplation rather than from direct contact and personal experience, and by his whole make-up incapable of optimistic moods and notions. Hence his gloomy observations and rayless conclusions. Gorky idolized Man ("Che-lo-vyek! Eto zvuchit gordo!" M-a-n! This sounds loftily![2]), and appealing to man's dignity and self-respect he spurred one to deeds, to revolt, to struggle. Andreyev flattered no man or idol, but questioned everything and everybody, and in irritating one's mental peace he stimulated self-analysis.

In such a mood Andreyev approached the subject matter of his early stories—lonely, miserable wretches. With keen analysis he dissected individuals, "turned their souls inside out," to borrow a favorite phrase from Dostoyevsky. Like Dostoyevsky, he chose the crushed personalities, the morbid, the pathological, the "humiliated and offended." But whereas Dostoyevsky surrounded disease, crime and suffering with the halo of love and compassion, Andreyev failed to mollify life's festering sores with the balsam of sympathy and pity. His characters, like

[2] From Satin's monologue in Gorky's play, *At the Bottom* (*A Night-Lodging*, or *The Submerged*), Act V.

most of Gorky's, were solitary individuals, but while the latter breathed rebellion, and appeared victorious even in defeat, those of Andreyev exuded impotent despair and writhed under the whip of circumstance. Again, to make one more comparison, both Chekhov and Andreyev endowed their heroes or rather victims with a hypertrophied self-consciousness. Yet there is an important difference in the mode by which these writers had their characters manifest their "ailment." In Chekhov atmosphere, mood, always prevailed. His sad, luckless individuals suffered from the sense of their futility and will-lessness; they succumbed to impotent Sehnsucht. In Andreyev the dominant factor was not feeling but thought. His unfortunate individuals went through all sufferings, pains, and passions in the torture-chamber of vivisecting thought; they perished as victims of self-analysis. Into the existence of a gray, commonplace, cowed person he would introduce a moment of intense thinking, which suddenly illuminated the drab sordidness, and lent significance and redemption to the momentarily sublimated thinker.

Andreyev's denizens of the cellars do not speak in the loud, self-assertive tones of Gorky's ex-men. They are weak, crushed. They lie in the dust, burdened with fear of life (*In the Basement*). Life appears to them as blind, inexorable, malignant Chance. Andrey Nikolayevich (*At the Window*) represents what Whitman glorifies as the "divine average," hence a generic type. His whole life is a series of fears and melancholy conjectures. Life to him is "a strange and terrible thing" replete with incomprehensible surprises. To-day we are alive, not suspecting that to-morrow a chance carriage may run over us and crush us to death. The wife of his fellow clerk goes to church, to give thanks to God for the monetary reward her husband had received at the office, and this very money is stolen from her in the church.

And wherever you turn, you encounter coarse, noisy, bold persons who ever push ahead and are prone to grab everything. Cruel-hearted and ruthless, they storm their way forward, whistling and howling, and trample upon others, upon weak folk. Only a squeak comes up from those who are crushed, but no one cares even to listen. That's just what they deserve.[3]

And when Chance knocks at the window of Andrey Nikolayev-ich, and tempts him to turn a new page in his monotonous drudg-ery—to marry a handsome girl from across the street, the man "at the window" hesitates and finally spurns the opportunity. One cannot trust Chance. It—Chance, life—is not merely a potential alternative of good or bad luck. It is a certain calam-ity. Andreyev's individuals share the attitude of Thomas Hardy toward malicious fate. This mistrust of life is subse-quently symbolized in the last scene of Andreyev's *Life of Man,* where the Drunkards prefer delirium tremens to life: "Better horror than life." Only the discerners, those who perceive the world with the eyes of Schopenhauer, may overcome this fear of life. Savva, the destroyer, for instance (in *Savva*), when asked by his sister whether he is afraid, answers:

I? So far I haven't been, and I don't ever expect to be afraid. Nothing can be more awful than having once been born. It's like ask-ing a drowned man whether he is afraid of getting wet. . . . No. If thus far I haven't become frightened, though I have peered into life, then there can be nothing more frightful in store. Life, yes. I embrace with my eyes the earth, the whole of it, all this paltry globe, and I can find nothing more terrible on it than man and human life.[4]

Gorky's individuals are solitary, with the solitude of the strong, of the self-sufficient. Andreyev's characters are lonely, with a pathetic loneliness. Communion with others is an essen-tial need for them, but they are forced to the conclusion that communion is impossible, that human interrelations are skin deep, that mutual understanding is unrealizable. This loneli-ness is felt not only by the submerged outcasts doomed to vege-tate in some dank corner of a cellar, but even by those who ap-parently luxuriate in sociability. The prominent dignitary (in *Peace*) seems particularly happy and amiable toward his guests;

[3] *Works—V,* p. 323.
[4] *Works—VI,* pp. 177, 178.

he takes a lively part in the jolly, friendly conversation, laughs abundantly, even to the point of tears.   But

> he scarcely thought for himself how happy he was, when he was drawn to solitude.   Not to his study, nor to his bedroom, but to the most solitary place, and lo—he hid himself in the place whither one goes only in time of need, hid himself like a boy afraid of punishment.   In this solitary place he spent several minutes, hardly breathing from fatigue, delivering his spirit and body to death, communing with it in silence, sullen as the silence of the grave.[5]

Loneliness in the midst of multitudes is a characteristic trait of city life, and Andreyev uses this theme again and again in demonstrating the fallacies of civilization (*The City, The Curse of the Beast*).   People meet one another, rub elbows, transact affairs, perform together all sorts of functions, yet remain ignorant of one another and mutually indifferent.   Here are four persons meeting regularly once a week for a game of whist (*The Grand Slam*).   For years these human beings have spent several hours each week in close proximity, yet all they know of one another is their names.   One of them causes an unforeseen annoyance and upsets the monotonous regularity, when he suddenly falls dead at the card table.   The remaining players realize for the first time that they know nothing about their dead companion, not even his address, nor whether he has any kin.   The dramatic effect of death is shown when back at the table one of the players opens the cards of his dead partner, and discovers that for the first time in their long experience these cards formed that rare hand in whist—a grand slam. "And my partner will never know that he has a grand slam!"

Solitude is most oppressive for those who eagerly crave communion, who seek to understand and to be understood.   The poor lover who pours out his heart before the girl of his dreams, is jeered at by her and by the multitude at the masquerade ball (*Laughter*).   He wears a mask, a funny mask of a Chinaman, which grotesquely belies the sincerity of his assertions.   This lack of mutual understanding, this solitude of the soul, is a trag-

[5] *Works—XII*, pp. 251, 252.

edy not infrequent among persons externally intimate with one another. In vain does the lover try to probe the conscience of his mistress (*The Lie*). In spite of her assurances and his own ardent wish to believe her, he is tormented by uncertainty, by the impossibility of proving whether she is telling the truth or lying. In his agony he kills her, hoping thus to destroy the source of his doubts. Alas, death does not end bewildering dilemmas, it makes them infinitely more sinister by clamping on them the mystery of silence. His mistress is dead, but the Lie is intangible, and will forever hiss into his ears like "a little snake" (the Russian word for "lie" is "lozh," a terse and hissing syllable), driving him mad. The excruciating pain of silence brings Father Ignaty, too, to the verge of insanity (*Silence*). Silence is enveloping the grave of his daughter, whose reason for committing suicide he can never know. Silence conceals the thoughts and feelings of his wife, whose tongue has become paralyzed at the news of her daughter's death. And he madly runs about, lashed by silence; he rushes from the wide-open inscrutable eyes of his speechless wife to the dumb grave of his daughter, and back again to the silent walls of his house, crying, screaming for a word, for an answer to his anguished query.

This tragedy of the chasm between parent and child appears in many of Andreyev's stories. Great is the solitude of adolescent Pavel (*In Fog*), ill with an unclean disease, the result of indiscretion, promiscuity, but primarily the result of the prudish wall between parents and children in regard to the mysteries of sex. Alone in his room, tearing his heart in vain yearning for the irrevocable purity of his past feelings and sentiments, Pavel is yet not so pathetically lonely as when his father enters, and engages him in conversation. Suspecting something abnormal behind Pavel's moroseness, his enlightened father delivers himself of a diplomatically cautious statement on the dangers of commercialized vice, quoting eloquent figures and statistics. This attempt at communion, at coming closer to his son, is too clumsy and—too late. Still more tragic is the wall between members of the same family, when such attempts at mutual harmony prove hopelessly futile, as in the masterly sketch, *Into the Dark Faraway*. The prodigal son returns after a long absence. His father, his little sister, his grandmother, the old servant, the whole home environment, are conspiring to win back and assimilate the strange young man who has rebelled against his luxurious surroundings and has renounced them for the life of a vagabond. During the few days of his sojourn with the family the air in the home becomes heavy with unuttered antagonism between the two categories, that of complacent smugness and that of free abandon. One is made to feel keenly the incompatibility, the irreconcilability of the two elements, mainly because they are unable to understand each other's sentiments and predilections. In the scene between the father and the son we perceive the impassable chasm which can yawn between individuals, no matter how close their blood relation may be.

From this reality, this life of pain, misery, impotent fear and unbridgeable solitude, Andreyev prompts his characters to attempt an escape into an illusory world. Thus, in *The Foreigner*, the gentle-hearted student, weary of his coarse, brutal environment, of his vodka-swilling, balalaika-strumming, fist-fighting colleagues, closes his eyes to the actual present, and lives in his phantasmagoric Abroad, where life and men are noble and exceedingly beautiful. In *Once There Lived* we encounter two doomed hospital patients, a hard taciturn merchant and a gushing jolly deacon, both of whom are desperately clinging to rapidly vanishing life, and whose disillusionment is pathetic. The pathos appears dual, that of embracing an illusion, and that of disenchantment. When the universally kicked and abused dog, Snapper, in the story by that name, is treated with unexpected kindness by transient summer folk, and is gradually converted to faith in human beings, we are moved by the ardent gratitude and ecstatic joy displayed by the erstwhile misanthrope. Then autumn comes, the kind people return to the city, naturally without their newly acquired canine friend, and once again we are moved by the emotion of the dog howling in despair on the forsaken porch. A bitter complaint is heard in that howling against some unknown Deceiver responsible for our flights and falls.   The same note is felt in *Little Peter in the Country*.   The anæmic, scrofulous urchin, Peter, languishing in the barber shop where his life consists of an interminable fetching of hot water and constant abuse at the hands of his superiors, weaves a dream of another world.   He does not visualize this world in any concrete form, but he endows it with delightful negative features, such as the absence of a master and of bullying assistants.   One morning his mother takes him to the country place of the family where she serves as a cook.   The dream assumes shape and form.   The city-bred child is struck with amazement at the sudden opening of wide vistas, of fields and forests.   Peter gradually overcomes the awe inspired by the new world, makes friends with the mysterious forest, enjoys the sensation of soft earth under his bare feet, goes bathing in the cool stream, and even obtains a fishing rod from a fellow adventurer.   The new life regenerates the sickly lad, becomes convincing reality to him.   Just then a note from the barber arrives, demanding the immediate return of the boy.   It requires a few grave moments for little Peter to distinguish between reality and fantasy.   When he finally realizes that the blurred image of the far-away master is a fact, while the fishing rod in his hands is but a phantom, he naturally falls to the ground and bawls vehemently.   He, too, has been deceived, led to believe in a "different" life which turns out to be a mirage lasting but a brief moment.   Brief is the duration of earthly illusions, too brief for possessing any value as an escape from sordid reality.   Its value is symbolized in *The Little Angel*. Sashka, a naughty boy embittered against all nice people, becomes enraptured with a wax doll, an angel, hanging on a Christmas tree at a charity party.   He obtains the toy by wheedling, and brings it to his home reeking with profanity and alcohol. Before lying down to sleep on his bunch of rags, he hangs the angel up over the stove, so as to have a full view of it from his corner.   The angel embodies for him all that is kind and good and beautiful, all that is not of this wretched world, and in blissful contemplation he falls asleep. In the meantime the Great Illusion, warmed up by the stove, begins to melt, slowly shrinks in size, drips, and is eventually reduced to a greasy spot on the floor. *Sic transit.* . . .

Does Andreyev offer any solution at this stage of his development? There is a suggestion of suicide as a way out, in *Sergey Petrovich,* which, incidentally, is the first of his stories to contain a definitely Nietzschean note. Sergey Petrovich is one of the many-too-many, weak, diffident, gray, amorphous. As in most of Andreyev's early stories, this insignificant existence is suddenly sublimated by the stimulus of intense thinking. A copy of Nietzsche's *Also sprach Zarathustra* has fallen into his hands. The boldness, vigor, newness and brilliance of this unique book strike Sergey Petrovich as if by lightning. He is regenerated by the new vision which flares up in the grayness of his life:

It was the vision of the Superman, of that inconceivable yet human creature that had realized all its latent possibilities, and was full master of power, happiness and freedom. It was a strange vision. Brilliant to the point of hurting one's eyes and heart, it remained dim and vague in its features. Wondrous and ineffable, it was yet simple and life-like. And in its bright light Sergey Petrovich examined his life, and it appeared to him quite new and interesting, like a familiar face in the glare of a conflagration.[6]

Andreyev does not belong to those facile pseudo-Nietzscheans who endow their characters with the Zarathustra phraseology and let them pass as supermen. The contradictory adjectives in the quoted passage show the young author's appreciation of the complexity and esoteric quality of Nietzsche's masterpiece. And so Sergey Petrovich, visualizing the grandeur of the Superman, is sufficiently honest with himself to admit the hopelessness of his aspiring to that dazzling height. Not all who say, Lord! Lord! will be saved. Not all who quote Zarathustra can enter the kingdom of the Superman. Sergey Petrovich finds himself

[6] *Works—II*, p. 246.

capable of executing only one of Zarathustra's precepts, namely: "Manchen misräth das Leben: ein Giftwurm frisst sich ihm an's Herz. So möge er zusehn, dass ihm das Sterben um so mehr gerathe." [7]

But the motive of suicide as an escape from the sad and sick world does not recur in Andreyev. One's personal withdrawal from the vale of tears and folly leaves this vale unchanged, and the problem unsolved. "Though dying every second, we are immortal like the gods," wails the leper in *The Wall*, the gruesome sketch which perhaps sums up Andreyev's attitude toward life at that early period (1901). All struggle seems futile in face of the impregnable indifferent wall towering to the skies. On this side of the wall swarm lepers, idiots, semi-skeletons, brutes, who fight among themselves, gnaw and devour one another, or engage in a ghastly *danse macabre*. Some madmen refuse to succumb to the tyranny of the wall, and attack it with their heads and breasts, bespattering its callous stones with their blood and brains. The wall stands dull and immovable. Is the struggle worth while? One leper cynically observes about those who vainly try to smash the wall or climb over it: "They are fools . . . They think that there is light beyond. But it is dark there also, and there too are lepers dragging themselves along, and entreating to be killed."

This was a dangerous thought, one which was apt to find a hearing among Russian society at the beginning of the twentieth century. Russian life was stifling. The bureaucratic régime loomed like an impregnable wall, rendering all efforts and aspirations futile and hopeless. Education continued to be largely a farce, rigidly circumscribed and so directed that its main purpose seemed to consist in incapacitating the students for mental activity. In protest sporadic disturbances broke out among university students, which made any regular academic work impossible, and which brought about severe punishments upon the students, flogging by cossacks, imprisonment and exile, or forcible recruitment into the army. The press was muzzled and heavily penalized for ambiguous expressions suggesting criticism

[7] *Also sprach Zarathustra:* "Vom freien Tode."

of the Government. Writers and publicists, like Korolenko, Amfiteatrov, Gorky, Peshekhonov, and others, were exiled or silenced or imprisoned. It was difficult for an enlightened person not to be in opposition to the dark forces of the administration, but the number of educated persons was so small that their opposition, unless backed by the masses, amounted to smashing one's head at a stone wall. .The peasantry was still inert in its bulk, apathetically suffering and fatalistically submitting to injustice and oppression. The only class which grew rapidly conscious, intelligent and ready for self-sacrifice, was that of the city workmen. The workshop and the machine proved powerful factors in arousing the simple Russian from his lethargy, and in urging him to replace his passive nonresistance by dynamic struggle. Though small in numbers and of recent birth, the Russian proletariat became the ally of the Intelligentsia in the common conflict with autocracy. But even the combined effort seemed fruitless to skeptical minds, who could not help observing the numerical and material inequality of the two opposing camps. Between the mighty Government bristling with bayonets and sabres, on one hand, and the small group of the revolutionary Intelligentsia and city workmen, on the other, lay the gray mass of indifferent humanity. Gorky and his circle disregarded this apparent inequality of the struggle, and joyfully exalted the "madness of the brave." Andreyev's skepticism, his merciless exposition of life's misery and stupidity, of the "blood-bespattered wall," was apt to exert a chilling effect on the impressionable young generation. Yet, though questioning the reasonableness of the struggle, though doubting the outcome of the unequal conflict, Andreyev did not condemn the efforts of the fighters. There is an illuminating passage at the end of *The Wall:*

And once more a mighty stream of human bodies broke out into a roar, and with all their strength hurled themselves against the wall. And again, and over and over again it was rolled back, until fatigue supervened, and a deathlike sleep, and stillness. But I, the leper, was close to the wall, and saw that it began to quake . . . and that the fear of falling ran through its stones.

"It is falling, brothers! It is falling," I cried.

"Thou are mistaken, leper," replied my brothers.

And then I began to question them:

"Supposing it does stand, what then? Is not every corpse a step toward the top? We are many, and our lives a burden. Let us strew the ground with corpses; upon them let us heap yet other corpses; and so mount to the top. And if there be left but one—he will see a new world."

And I gave a cheerful glance of hope around—and was met only by backs, indifferent, fat, and weary. . . .[8]

This is not very encouraging, but of the two possible attitudes which Andreyev suggests toward life, that of Sergey Petrovich and that of the leper, the latter is surely the braver and socially more beneficial alternative. If life is senseless and cruel, then let us at least perish in battle, that our bodies may—perhaps— fertilize the ground for coming generations. And even if this last hope is but an illusion, who can dare to scorn the audacity and resignation of the wall assailants? In Russia even the conservative elements regarded with respect the Decembrists, the Narodovoltsy, the Social-Revolutionary terrorists, those men and women who were absolutely free from selfish motives, and joyously mounted the scaffold for the sake of the mysterious "people." Russian youths, particularly college students, were looked upon as the pride and hope of the nation, as the advance guard in the endless battle for freedom and equality. *Noblesse oblige.* Owing to the fact that the public expected much from the students, worshipped and flattered them, the students were imbued with a feeling of responsibility, and endeavored to maintain their banner high and unsullied. The socially minded student presented, indeed, a fine, almost ascetic type, noble, idealistic, self-sacrificing.

But the skepticism of Andreyev knows no bounds, and it attacks our holiest beliefs. His story, *The Abyss* (1902), aroused a storm of indignation and protest. The author was accused of slandering Russian youth and human nature in general.

[8] *Works—III,* p. 100.

The Abyss is a moral catastrophe from which, according to Andreyev, none can boast immunity. In the first half of the story we are charmed with the purity and integrity of a couple of college students, Nemovetsky and his girl friend. They are on a stroll in the city outskirts. Though in love with each other, in their chaste modesty they discuss everything on earth except that which absorbs their entire beings. They dream aloud of lofty castles, and lose their way in the oncoming twilight. Rambling through the field they come upon three tramps, who let them pass, but soon leap in pursuit. Nemovetsky is knocked unconscious and thrown into a ravine. Before quite losing his senses he faintly hears the shrieks of horror and despair coming from his companion. Late in the evening he revives, realizes what has happened, and goes in search of his friend, shouting, screaming, half mad with grief. Finally he stumbles upon her numb body. In vain does he try to bring her back to consciousness. While stroking her hands and face, and trying to cover up her body with the tattered clothes, Nemovetsky becomes aware of the beast arising in him. He is horrified, he shouts at the top of his voice, as if entreating some one to save him from his unsuspected self; he frantically endeavors to resuscitate his comrade for self-defense, for his defense. The brute proves the stronger, and he plunges into the Abyss.

The sordidness of the story need not befog the problem it raises. *The Abyss* is the first of Andreyev's attempts at broadening and deepening the range of his themes. Henceforth he will time and again probe our inner self, analyzing our motives and impulses, and endeavoring to gauge the relative strength of our instinct and intellect. In this, and in the two stories to be discussed next, we find an adumbration of the later Andreyev, the postulator of such general problems as reason and faith. Nemovetsky thinks he knows himself, but it is only his intellectual, thinking, reasoning self that he may wager on. He is unaware and therefore horrified at the advent of his dormant self composed of brutal instincts, of animalistic impulses, which slumber under the flimsy mask of intellect and morality, but emerge unexpectedly, and, unleashed, drag him irresistibly into the Abyss. The fact that Nemovetsky is not at all extraordinary but represents the average, rank and file young Intelligentsia, lends the question a general, public import. Are all of us potential Nemovetskys? Does the Abyss yawn, under a thin cover, for any one of those beautiful, saintly, altruistic, heroic persons who constitute the wonderful Russian youth? The affirmative answer implied in Andreyev's story provoked the resentment of a considerable portion of society who reproached the young writer for depicting the sordid and filthy instead of portraying the beautiful and uplifting.[9] More than once did Andreyev dare to attack popular fetiches and dethrone acclaimed idols, at the risk of arousing enmity and resentment. This was not an iconoclastic tendency for the sake of iconoclasm, or *pour épater les bourgeois,* but an earnest motive which continually grew in intensity—to explore man, to understand and explain one's inner self.

In the same year Andreyev wrote his profound study, *Thought,* which became the subject of serious discussion in circles of psychologists and psychiatrists. This is another demonstration of man's deceit and conceit in presuming self-knowledge. Dr. Kerzhentsev is the victim of a hypertrophied intellect. He has been a proud believer in the omnipotence of his reasoning faculty, in the absolute authority of his thought over all his actions and manifestations. Even his passions and emotions he believes to be motivated by his reason, for experimental purposes. "How foreign I am to all these human beings, and how lonely in the world—I, forever incarcerated in this head, in this prison," he observes in one of those moments when the weight of thought oppresses him to the point of madness. Thought! Thought! He has loved and worshipped it, has used it and played with it, has learned to bend and thrust it, to brandish and control it, as a skilful fencer masters his rapier. Coldly he resolves to murder the husband of the woman who once rejected him. Not from jealousy and vindictiveness (he spurns the suggestion of being impelled by mere impulses), but from a desire to test the power of his intel-

[9] *Supra,* p. 71 ff.

lect. With mathematical precision he works out a triplex plan: to gain the complete confidence of the marked victim, to mislead public opinion into believing him, Dr. Kerzhentsev, subject to fits of insanity, and thus to escape punishment for the crime, and thirdly, to have the prospective widow feel, though unable to prove, the sanity and cold scheming of the murderer. His thinking apparatus works faultlessly, and with immense satisfaction he convinces himself of his power over ordinary beings guided not by reason alone. He triumphs over all obstacles by the sheer force of his steel-hard, obedient, supple thought, which (he says)

lifted me upon the summit of a high mountain, and I saw how far below me swarmed little people with their petty animal passions, with their eternal dread of life and death, with their churches, liturgies and prayers. Was I not great and free and happy? Like a mediæval baron secluded in his impregnable castle, as though in an eagle's nest, proudly and imperiously surveying the valleys below—so was I, invincible and proud in my castle, behind these cranium bones. Tsar over myself, I also was a tsar over the world.[10]

The grandiose "castle" collapses, however, at an unexpected moment. The complex psychological problem brilliantly solved, his victim killed with meticulous adherence to the plan, the public duped by his clever simulation of insanity, the victor remains alone in his room, with his faithful slave—thought. And here occurs the "betrayal." The castle turns into a prison, the slave into a master. Reason no longer serves him, but mocks, tyrannizes over, maddens him. A terrible thought enters his magnificent cranium, a hideous suggestion that he is actually insane. Like a "drunken snake" this thought glides through his brain, stings and poisons his infallible system, and makes him a perpetual slave to an insoluble dilemma: has he simulated insanity in order to kill, or is the act of murder a result of his insanity? Dr. Kerzhentsev is hopelessly entangled in the maze of rebellious thoughts, slaves turned masters. He is at the mercy of his intellect, one of his faculties which he himself has cultivated

10 *Works*—III, p. 251.

and cherished and aggrandized and set up as an absolute ruler over his other faculties.   A grim paradox: reason enhanced to madness.

One feels an autobiographical note in Andreyev's attitude toward thought.   Nearly all his works have as their central idea, one might say as their hero, thought.   The typical scheme of a story by Andreyev consists of the drab life of a commonplace person suddenly illuminated by a flash of thought, which sublimates gray existence to tragedy.   The author seems to regard thought with a mixed feeling of reverence and awe.   He sees in it a merciless surgeon apt to destroy the disease together with the body in which it is lodged.   He considers it a double-edged sword which may slash the hand that wields it.   Yet, whatever the perils that lurk in the tortuous paths of thought, Andreyev follows this path with the passion and abandon of a lion hunter, who pursues his quarry at the risk of being devoured by it.

About a year after depicting the tragedy of Dr. Kerzhentsev, Andreyev drew another life destroyed as a result of being "sicklied o'er with the pale cast of thought."   In *Life of Vasily Fiveysky* we are shown faith firm as a rock yet ultimately corroded and consumed by thought.   Vasily's faith is being bruised and tempted exceedingly, yet it is not shaken.   It remains solid and erect in face of Job-like misfortunes.   His boy drowns in the river, while bathing.   His wife succumbs to grief, and drinks heavily.   There is a harrowing scene one winter night when the half-demented woman demands of the priest that he give her back her son, at least another son.   She flings herself on the floor, tears the garments off her body, entreats and curses, whines amorously and shrieks in anger, until the priest yields. The product of this union of madness, alcohol, passion and pity is an idiot boy.   Again the unfortunate mother tries to quench her aching heart in drink, again the priest stands up in the middle of the field, and gravely, laconically declares, "I believe." The Fiveyskys decide to leave their village, to seek a "luckier" place.   For a time the illusion revives the woman, she even stops drinking.   But one hot summer day, Vasily, on the way home from the field, sees a conflagration.   Even without being told he feels that once more he has been chosen as a victim. In a state of intoxication his wife has set the house on fire, and her body is reduced to a "gigantic bubble." But the idiot is saved. "I believe!" insists Vasily. Yet his reason begins to tempt him with whys.

Vasily's personal sorrows render him more susceptible to the sorrows of others. Eagerly he conducts the confessionals, probes the hearts of his parishioners, makes them reveal to him their most secret thoughts and feelings, their sufferings and sins. Sins, to be sure. Like his flock the priest believes in sin, in punishment, in rewards, in a God who metes out justice according to one's deserts. Those wretches who creep up to confess before the mediator between man and God are urged to tell their sins, to relate the wrongs they have done, for surely they have deserved their afflictions. In this naïve conception of a mathematically correct divine justice, Vasily merely voices the average believer, the average seeker after truth, after an understanding of the ways of God. But

he soon realized that all these people who were telling him the whole truth, as though he were God, were themselves ignorant of the truth of their life. Behind the thousands of their trifling, scattered, hostile truths, he dimly saw the shadowy outlines of the one great and all-solving truth. Every one was conscious of it, every one longed for it, yet no one could define it with a human word—that enormous truth of God and of men and of the mysterious destinies of human life.[11]

Father Vasily listens to the woes and tears of his flock, becomes saturated with human grief and pain, of which there is no end, no limit. "Like unto an altar was his soul aflame." Gradually it dawns upon him that the balance of sin and punishment is monstrously uneven, that the misdeeds confessed to are so puny, so trivial, in comparison with the suffering and misery inflicted upon the wretched transgressors. His faith is being jeopardized by the dangerous symptom of reflection. But he still believes, with the persistence of Brand. And when one of his parishioners, a healthy and inoffensive peasant, is killed,

[11] *Works—IV*, pp. 165, 166.

while at work, by an avalanche, leaving a widow and three children in utter helplessness, Vasily's faith reaches its breaking
point, and makes a final effort to stifle the small voice of reason
which has been feebly but consistently stirring to rebellion. A
new thought flashes through the outraged mind of the priest:
this life of his that has been a long series of calamities, heartaches, losses, disappointments, temptations—has it not been a
crucible wherein God has been forging Vasily's soul for the
great test? Is he not the chosen victim-hero through whom
God wishes to manifest his power and beneficence? All night
long the priest meditates his desperate thought-illusions, prop-
ping up his faith with biblical passages that relate miracles and
resurrections. He reads aloud and comments with ecstasy and
fervor, while his audience—the little idiot son—guffaws sense-
lessly at his agitated father. Vasily believes, strenuously,
boundlessly, and he decides to demonstrate the power of faith
by performing a miracle. At the funeral service over the killed
workman, Vasily solemnly commands the dead body to rise, and
calls upon God to help him, to reward him for all his trials,
for his fortitude and loyalty. Faith reaches its climax, and
thwarted it snaps, as does Vasily's life.

The somewhat melodramatic setting of this story may be explained by Andreyev's desire to lend it a universal significance;
hence he conventionalizes the drama of Vasily. The hero lacks
the epic calm of Job, neither does he possess the rock-like
strength and poise of Brand; but he is endowed with the trait
common to most of Andreyev's characters, that of the "divine
average." The tragedy of Father Vasily is likely to be lived
through by an ordinary, commonplace person, once by the whip
of circumstances he is lashed to thought. Thought versus belief. Faith is shown here as the deadly enemy of reason.
Faith keeps the unfortunates in obedience and submission, by
justifying the unjustifiable, by lulling discontent to sleep with
the aid of such narcotic illusions as sin and penalty, virtue and
reward, God and future life.

We have come to the end of what we may consider the first

period of Andreyev's career, the period of a realistic analysis of individual man, in his attitudes toward life and the world. By nature and temperament solitary, sad and skeptical, Andreyev possessed at the same time a keen power of analysis. In the mental chaos which enveloped Russian society at the end of the nineteenth century, his critical eye looked at life clear and undimmed as that of a hawk. He observed the everyday existence of his contemporaries and found it sunless, empty, futile. He pronounced this diagnosis without equivocation. He doubted everything, our dearest beliefs and most sacred tenets. Armed with sharp thought, he brandished it mercilessly over our heads, not concealing his own dread of this weapon. And as his thought matured, the field of his analysis and examination grew ever wider and deeper, establishing his position as that of a consistent critic and severe evaluator of our ideas and actions.

The epitome of his views at that period may be seen in his play, *The Life of Man,* though chronologically this belongs to the next stage (it was written in 1906). Here Andreyev sets forth a popular exposition of Schopenhauer's Weltanschauung, and at the same time a summary of his own attitudes, hitherto expressed fragmentarily. For at this stage as well as later Andreyev lives largely "under the sign of *Die Welt als Wille und Vorstellung,*" and his own views on the whole coincide, temperamentally and intellectually, with those of Schopenhauer. This does not imply any conscious and consistent adherence on the part of Andreyev to Schopenhauer's system. He was a dilettante in philosophy, as he was in all his variegated interests outside of literature proper, be it painting or color photography or yachting or war propaganda. Yet one has no difficulty in tracing a definite Schopenhauerian thread through *The Life of Man.* In fact, nearly all of Andreyev's early writings are saturated with Schopenhauerism of the more obvious variety. Misery, squalor, monotony, fear, loneliness, futility, illusion, disillusionment—these are the elements which in the writings discussed previously, compose Andreyev's vale of tears. Life is on the whole an excess of pain over pleasure, "a disappoint-

ment, nay, a cheat." [12] Man's life is more painful than that
of animals or plants, because it alone possesses the element of
boredom, and because man lives in constant fear of death, of
whose inevitable advent he *knows*.[13] Life is an illusion, a
dream,[14] as is one's striving for happiness—something negative in its very nature, being the absence of pain, or the fulfillment of a desire, to be followed by an endless chain of succeeding desires.[15]

A summarized, systematized exposition of Schopenhauerian
motives we find in *The Life of Man,* Andreyev's morality play.
Here we witness generalizations of Man, Wife, Child, Friends,
Enemies, Fates, and of life's stages in their normal sequence—
the Birth of Man and Mother's Travail, Man's Love and Marriage, Struggle for Existence, Success-Riches, Misfortune, Solitude, Death. Throughout the action in a corner of the stage
remains motionless Someone-in-Gray, the inscrutable master of
life and its vicissitudes. In his hands is a burning candle whose
size and flame increase and diminish in proportion to Man's
progress and regress. We are not told who he is, the moving
factor of life—tedious life composed of childish conflicts, of
aimless struggles and sufferings, of petty achievements, of com-

[12] ". . . das es [life] a disappointment, nay, a cheat ist, oder Deutsch zu reden,
den Charakter einer grossen Mystification, nicht zu sagen einer Prellerei, trägt."—
Paregra und Paralipomena, § 156, p. 274 (*Werke—IV*).

[13] ". . . auf der Seite der Leiden tritt bei ihm [man] die Langweile auf, welche
das Thier, wenigstens in Naturzustande, nicht kennt . . . denn freilich sind Noth
und Langweile die beiden Pole des Menschengeschlechts" . . . "in Menschen wächst
das Mass des Schmerzes . . . und wird noch speciell dadurch gar sehr vergrössert,
dass er von Tode wirklich *weiss.*"—*Ibid.,* § 153, p. 270.

[14] " 'es ist die *Maja,* der Schleier der Truges, welcher die Augen der Sterbli-
chen umhült und sie eine Welt sehen lässt, von der man weder sagen kann, dass
sie sei, noch auch, dass sie nicht sei: denn sie gleicht dem Traume, gleicht dem
Sonnenglanz auf dem Sande, welchen der Wanderer von ferne für ein Wasser
hält, oder auch dem hingeworfenen Strick, den er für eine Schlange ansieht.' "—
Die Welt, etc., No. 3, p. 30 (v. I).

[15] "Alle Befriedigung, oder was man gemeinhin Glück nennt, ist eigentlich und
wesentlich immer nur *negativ* und durchaus nie positiv." *Ibid.,* No. 58, p. 362.
"Die unaufhörlichen Bemühungen, das Leiden zu verbannen, leisten nichts
weiter, als dass es seine Gestalt verändert. Diese ist ursprünglich Mangel, Not,
Sorge um die Erhaltung des Lebens. Ist es, was sehr schwer hält, geglückt, den
Schmerz in dieser Gestalt zu verdrängen, so stellt er sogleich sich in tausend andern ein, abwechselnd nach Alter und Umständen, als Geschlechtstrieb, leidenschaft-
liche Liebe, Eifersucht, Neid, Hass, Angst, Ehrgeiz, Krankheit usw. usw."—*Ibid.,*
No. 57, p. 357.

monplace pleasures, of dead monotony, of shallow pitfalls and snares culminating in the inevitable silly end—death.[16] It is not a mere accident that He is "in gray." Life is not a grand tragedy of romantic colors and titanic dimensions, but rather a stale flat farce.[17] Man is presented here as an Average—not too good nor too bad, moderately clever and gifted, moderately virtuous and philistine. His utter bondage and helplessness, and the futility of his efforts, are summarized in the speech of Someone-in-Gray, in the prologue. It is worth quoting in toto, as a rather complete doctrine:

Look and listen, ye who have come hither for mirth and laughter. Lo, there will pass before you all the life of Man, with its dark beginning and its dark end. Hitherto nonexistent, mysteriously hidden in infinite time, without thought or feeling, utterly unknown, he will mysteriously break through the barriers of nonexistence and with a cry will announce the beginning of his brief life. In the night of nonexistence will blaze up a candle, lighted by an unseen hand. This is the life of Man. Behold its flame. It is the life of Man.

After birth he will take on the image and the name of man, and in all respects he will be like other people who already live on the earth, and their cruel fate will be his fate, and his cruel fate will be the fate of all people. Irresistibly dragged on by time, he will tread inevitably all the steps of human life, upward to its climax and downward to its end. Limited in vision, he will not see the step to which his unsure foot is already raising him. Limited in knowledge, he will never know what the coming day or hour or moment is bringing to him. And in his blind ignorance, worn by apprehension, harassed by hopes and fears, he will complete submissively the iron round of destiny.

[16] Cf. Schopenhauer: "Es ist wirklich unglaublich wie nichtssagend und bedeutungsleer, von aussen gesehen, und wie dumpf und besinnungslos, von innen empfunden, das Leben der allermeisten Menschen dahinfliesst. Es ist ein mattes Sehnen und Quälen, ein träumerisches Taumeln durch die vier Lebensalter hindurch zum Tode, unter Begleitung einer Reihe trivialer Gedanken. Sie gleichen Uhrwerken, welche aufgezogen werden und gehen, ohne zu wissen warum; und jedesmal, das ein Mensch gezeugt und geboren worden, ist die Uhr des Menschenlebens aufs neue aufgezogen, um jetzt ihr schon zahllose Male abgespieltes Leierstück abermals zu wiederholen, Satz vor Satz und Takt for Takt, mit unbedeutenden Variationen."—*Ibid.*, No. 58, p. 364.

[17] Cf.: . . . "das Treiben und die Plage des Tages, die rastlose Neckerei des Augenblicks, das Wünschen und Fürchten der Woche, die Unfälle jeder Stunde, mittelst des stets auf Schabernack bedachten Zufalls, sind lauter Komödienszenen.
—*Ibid.*, p. 365.

Behold him, a happy youth. See how brightly the candle burns. The icy wind blowing from infinite space puffs and whirls about, causing the flame to flutter. The candle, however, burns clearly and brightly, though the wax is melting, consumed by the fire. The wax is melting.

Lo, he is a happy husband and father. Yet look! How dim and strange the candle glimmers, as if the flame were a yellowing leaf, as if the flame were shivering and shielding itself from the cold. For the wax is melting, consumed by the fire. The wax is melting. Lo, now he is an old man, feeble and sick. The path of life has been trodden to its end and now the dark abyss has taken its place, but he still presses on with tottering foot. The livid flame, bending toward the earth, flutters feebly, trembles and sinks, trembles and sinks, and quietly goes out.

Thus Man will die. Coming from the night he will return to the night. Bereft of thought, bereft of feeling, unknown to all, he will perish utterly, vanishing without trace into infinity. And I, whom men call He, will be the faithful companion of Man throughout all the days of his life and in all his pathways. Unseen by Man and his companions, I shall unfailingly be near him both in his waking and in his sleeping hours; when he prays and when he curses; in hours of joy when his free and bold spirit soars high; in hours of depression and sorrow when his weary soul is övershadowed by deathlike gloom and the blood in the heart is chilled; in hours of victory and defeat; in the hours of heroic struggle with the inevitable I shall be with him—I shall be with him.

And ye who have come hither for mirth, ye who are doomed to die, look and listen. Lo, the swiftly flowing life of Man will pass before you, with its sorrows and its joys, like a far off, thin reflection.[18]

Who is He, the inseparable companion of Man in all his walks and tribulations? From the general nature of the play one may judge that Andreyev has wished to symbolize in this mysterious Being the Will, in Schopenhauer's sense. Will, or

[18] *Works—VII*, pp. 35–37. I have used the fine translation of Meader and Scott—*Plays by Leonid Andreyev*, pp. 67–69 (New York, 1920; first edition, 1915). Cf. the opening speech of the Messenger, in *Everyman:*

"I pray you all gyve your audyence
And here this matter with reverence.
By fygure a morall playe;
The somonynge of Everyman called it is,
That of our lyves and endynge shewes
How transitory we be all daye." etc.

Edited by Montrose J. Moses, New York, 1903.

Will-to-live, which to Schopenhauer are synonymous,[19] is responsible for Man's actions and impulses, for it generates all his desires and his futile strivings for the fulfillment of these desires—an unattainable goal, since desire means want, and one want is followed by an interminable series of succeeding wants.[20] There remains only one dignified step for Man, once he becomes aware of the fact that in his race for happiness he is playing the rôle of a mouse in a running wheel—to curse. To curse, according to Dostoyevsky, is "man's only privilege, which differentiates him from other animals."[21] In Schopenhauer's terminology, man revolts against his Will-to-live, rejects it, denies it, and thereby sets himself free.[22] Enraged by the senseless cruelties inflicted upon him, Man in Andreyev's play rises in protest and rebellion against the cause of his sufferings, and turning to the corner where he feels the presence of Someone-in-Gray, he proclaims his "curse of Man," in which he "rises victorious" over life, with its joys and sorrows, and over life's driving force—the mysterious Someone. In defying the moving power of life, in his abnegation of the Will-to-live, Man emerges from his trials and calamities a free and independent being. He has nothing to lose, nothing can be taken away from

[19] ". . . so ist es einerlei und nur ein Pleonasmus, wenn wir statt schlechthin zu sagen, 'der Wille,' sagen 'der Wille zum Leben.' " *Die Welt*, etc., No. 54, p. 315 (*Werke—I*).

[20] "Alles *wollen* entspringt aus Bedürfnis, also aus Mangel, also aus Leiden. Diesem macht die Erfüllung ein Ende; jedoch gegen einen Wunsch, der erfüllt wird, bleiben wenigstens zehn versagt: ferner, das Begehren dauert lange, die Forderungen gehen ins Unendliche; die Erfüllung ist kurz und kärglich gemessen. Sogar aber ist die endliche Befriedigung selbst nur scheinbar: der erfüllte Wunsch macht gleich einem neuen Platz: jener ist ein erkannter, dieser noch ein unerkannter Irrtum. . . . So liegt das Subjekt des Wollens beständig auf dem drehenden Rade des Ixion, schöpft immer im Siebe der Danaiden, ist der ewig schmachtende Tantalus."—*Ibid.*, No. 38, p. 231.

[21] *Notes from Underground* (*Zapiski iz podpolya*), end of chapter VIII, p. 463. Berlin, 1922, Ladyschnikow.

[22] "Wann aber äusserer Anlass, oder innere Stimmung, uns plötzlich aus dem endlosen Strome des Wollens heraushebt, die Erkenntnis dem Sklavendienste des Willens entreisst . . . dann ist die . . . Ruhe mit einem Male von selbst eingetreten, und uns ist völlig wohl. Es ist der schmerzlose Zustand, den Epikur als das höchste Gut und als den Zustand der Götter pries: denn wir sind, für jenen Augenblick, des schnöden Willensdranges entledigt, wir feiern den Sabbat der Zuchthausarbeit des Wollens, das Rad des Ixion steht still."—*Die Welt*, etc., No. 38, pp. 231, 232. (*Werke—I*).

him! In the last scene we observe Man, with his towering "gray, beautiful, terribly majestic" head, rising above the sordid surroundings through ignoring them with complete indifference. He dies a victor, in the Schopenhauer sense of the word, as one who has overcome the world.[23]

The Life of Man presents a disenchanted view of life and man. "Limited in vision and in knowledge," man fussily wriggles during the brief span of his existence, pursuing his small activities, craving for petty, selfish achievements, conceitedly regarding himself as the centre of the universe. Only through suffering does man arrive at the bitter knowledge that his choices and preferences are an illusion, that he is a slave, in bondage to his Will, and that only through destroying this Will, through overcoming life, can he become free. We shall see how Andreyev develops at times Schopenhauer's idea of the will-free man who lives the life of a contemplator or of a saint (e. g., the Astronomer in To the Stars, Werner in The Seven That Were Hanged, David Leiser in Anathema). In The Life of Man, however, he does not go beyond liberating man from his bondage to will, and terminating his futile struggle in peace eternal—death. It is for this reason that Andreyev's first symbolical play forms a fitting climax for the early period of his writings, the period of unrelieved negation and hopelessness. It sums up his fragmentary indictments against life's monotony, cruelty, stupidity, illusoriness, in one sweeping condemnation of man's existence under the tyranny of his Will.

[23] Cf. ". . . dass die grösste, wichtigste und bedeutsamste Erscheinung, welche die Welt aufzeigen kann, nicht der Welteroberer ist, sondern der Weltüberwinder, also in der Tat nichts anderes, als der stille und unbemerkte Lebenswandel eines solchen Menschen, dem diejenige Erkenntnis aufgegangen ist, infolge welcher er jenen alles erfüllenden und in allem treibenden und strebenden Willen zum Leben aufgibt und verneint, dessen Freiheit erst hier, in ihm allein, hervortritt"—Ibid., No. 68, pp. 432, 433.

III

PROBLEMS OF COLLECTIVE HUMANITY

Two kinds of social writers in Russia.—Andreyev's place.—His response to contemporary events: extracting their essential significance.—*The Red Laugh*—indictment of war.—The background of the story.—The disastrous war with Japan, and its resultant upheaval in Russia.—The "bloodless revolution" of 1905.—Public unity and disunity.—*The Governor*, and its background.—Suggestive power of thought, individual and collective.—*Thus It Was*—disparagement of revolutions and of mass intelligence.—Inner slavery.—*To the Stars.*—The Astronomer's outlook *sub specie æternitatis.*—Marusya—attached to the earth.—Encouraging notes of the play.—The Workman.—The year 1906, and *Savva.*—Uncompromising destruction: *Ignis sanat.*—Rationalism versus faith.—Official recognition of Andreyev's influence.—The background of *The Seven That Were Hanged.*—Condemnation of capital punishment.—Triumph over death.—Terrorists in actual life.—Sacrificing one's soul, not only one's body: *Darkness.—Sashka Zhegulev* and its background.—The 20th century Repentant Noble.—Andreyev's sentiment in *From the Story Which Will Never Be Finished.*—Epitome of his social writings in *Tsar Hunger.*—The working class.—The Lumpenproletariat.—The bourgeoisie and its subservient science, art, church, courts.—The Intelligentsia.—Andreyev's attitude consistent with the views of Schopenhauer and Nietzsche.—Yet, unlike them, he fails to justify state institutions as a necessary evil.—Torn between reason and sentiment.

SINCE literature in Russia was the sole outlet for the pent-up and suppressed national aspirations, the Russian writer found himself the spokesman for the inarticulate millions. He was expected to fulfill the high social obligation of furnishing his compatriots with a clear interpretation of contemporary events and ideas, by presenting them in the form of more or less crystallized images. Turgenev in particular distinguished himself as an interpreter of social currents, projecting on large canvases such burning problems as serfdom (*Notes of a Huntsman*), as Slavophilism and Westernism (*Smoke*), as Nihilism (*Fathers and Sons*), as the To the People movement (*Virgin Soil*). Such a writer bore the responsibilities, and enjoyed the disadvantages, of a prophet in his own country. He held the pulse of his people, he kept his ear close to the breast of his land, he inhaled its air and anticipated atmospheric changes—and announced the diagnosis and the prognosis. On the other hand, such writers as Dostoyevsky and Tolstoy reacted to the present in a somewhat different way. Equally sensitive and responsive to contemporary conditions and upheavals, these writers usually failed to reflect them as mass movements and group-phenomena, but employed them as frameworks for individual introspective experiences. *Crime and Punishment* and *The Possessed,* by Dostoyevsky, are chronologically related to the same contemporary events as *Fathers and Sons* and *Virgin Soil,* respectively. Yet Raskolnikov, Svidrigaylov, Stavrogin, Shatov, Verkhovensky, remain sharply individualized characters rather than typical representatives of the young generation during the sixties and seventies. *War and Peace* and *Anna Karenin* are laid at definite periods in nineteenth century Russia, yet their leading characters, Prince Andrey, Pierre, Levin, represent not so much the Napoleonic age or the Russian gentry after the emancipation of the serfs, as they reflect the personal mental experiences of the chief hero in nearly all of Tolstoy's works, namely, Tolstoy himself. In other words, the writers of Turgenev's type aim at interpreting the present objectively and specifically, within the limits of temporal and local conditions, while those of the Dostoyevsky-Tolstoy mode seek to invert social phenomena into subjective and generalizing reflection and speculation.

Leonid Andreyev belongs with the second category of Russian "social" writers. Spurning the "splendid isolation" of the Russian Symbolists, Decadents, Mystics, and other modernists who shut themselves up in their ivory towers and applied the ostrich policy to the palpable horrors of the present, Andreyev remained, like Ezekiel, "among the captives"—"and the hand. of the Lord was there upon him." The last two decades of Russian history, so replete with upheavals, catastrophes, transformations—in a word, so dramatic, have been reflected profoundly and many-sidedly in Andreyev's works. War, revolution, terroristic acts, class struggle, hunger, executions—these and other phenomena were recorded and echoed in his stories and plays, giving some critics a pretext for accusing him of being a mere chronicler, a journalist. But while Gorky has recorded these years in novels and plays that present mass movements, the awakening of mass conscience, of class consciousness, the growth of the revolutionary proletariat, the disintegration of the old order (*Mother, The Spy, The Confession, Okurov Town, Matvey Kozhemyakin*), Andreyev fails to portray these shifting changes, these transient events, these portentous processes, in themselves. Out of these turbulent phenomena he extracts their essence, their absolute significance, their value beyond time or place, thus lending the phenomena a general, universal importance. For this reason his reaction to the Russo-Japanese war becomes a symbolization of war in general, just as his observations of the revolution and of its various concomitants acquire a scope far beyond their local and temporal limits.

Nowhere in literature is the horror of war presented as amply as in *The Red Laugh*. Stendhal's *Chartreuse de Parme* and Tolstoy's *Sevastopol* are more artistic delineations of war's cruelty, injustice and absurdity. But for sheer horror, for the cumulating effect of howling, shrieking horror, *The Red Laugh* has no equal. In passing one may observe that in his fondness for the morbid and pathological, Andreyev has always been on the right side of scientific probability in depicting unusual manifestations. Thus his *Thought* was discussed by a conference of psychiatrists, and declared psychologically unimpeachable.[1] Similarly his portrayal of the state of mind of those convicted

[1] I cite this from memory, unable to locate the source. Mme. Andreyev supports my recollection.

to death was regarded, we may recall, as uncannily correct by men who had gone through such an experience.[2] Andreyev's sailors, aviators, madmen, brigands, Esthonians, Jews, Italians, men in various walks of life and under divers physical and mental circumstances, were drawn by him with the sure stroke of first-hand experience, though he seldom left his study, villa or yacht. We may also recall Gorky's wonderment at Andreyev's intuitive power for grasping with precision remote and difficult subjects,[3] and Chukovsky's description of Andreyev's faculty of impersonating his characters and spontaneously assimilating their traits and emotions [4]—that we may explain in part the convincing effect of the world created by his imagination.

In his portrayal of war Andreyev crushes our senses with the realistic tone of veracity, when presenting such details as bodies torn by barbed wire, or blood streaming from a beheaded body, "as out of an uncorked bottle, such as is drawn on badly executed signboards." One involuntarily compares *The Red Laugh* with the two characteristic productions of the last war, Barbusse's *Under Fire*, and Latzko's *Men in War*, and one concludes that the horrors visualized by the mind of Andreyev are at least as nerve-racking and as convincing as those depicted by the Frenchman and by the Austrian from supposedly personal experiences in the trenches and on the field of battle. "Madness and horror. Horror and madness" is the persistent motive ringing through the bleeding "Fragments" of the war-outraged mind. Seen through the eyes of a sensitive intellectual, shell-shocked and mutilated, war is deprived of all sense and justification, and is reduced to an insane orgy of madmen annihilating one another without knowing why. He sees red, a "red laugh"—"something enormous, red and bloody . . . laughing a toothless laugh." And when death mercifully delivers the unfortunate from the clutches of red agony, his brother, who has stayed at home, becomes infected with the horrors brought back by those returning from the trenches.

[2] *Supra*, p. 98.
[3] *Supra*, p. 116 f.
[4] *Supra*, p. 53 f.

His mind collapses under the tragedy of his brother, under the numerous tragedies witnessed by him day after day, as that commonplace tragedy of a mother receiving tender letters from her soldier boy, long after a telegram has announced his death in battle. But the greatest horror of war is found in the deranged minds of its participants. In the morbid imagination of the writer of the "Fragments," dementia appears the normal state of those in war. He tells about trains full of mad soldiers passing the railroad station, and he describes one face seen through the window of the moving car:

Fearfully drawn, the color of a lemon, with an open black mouth and fixed eyes, it was so much like a mask of horror that I could not tear myself away from it. And it stared at me, the whole of it, and was motionless, and so it swam by together with the moving car, without a stir, without shifting its gaze.[5]

Alongside the tragic horror of war, Andreyev draws nis favorite situation, that of thought struggling with darkness, striving for understanding, and pitifully breaking down under the inexorable force of the inexplicable. Again and again we feel the author's mixed attitude toward thought, this delicate, complex, ruthless apparatus, which may turn against its possessor and destroy him, as it did Dr. Kerzhentsev. Doomed to the fate of his brother, this war victim has but one desire—to hasten the advent of the inevitable darkness which will put out the last flicker of his shocked thought.

I do not understand war [he says], and I must go mad, like my brother, like hundreds of men that are brought from there. And this does not frighten me. The loss of reason seems to me honorable, like the death of a sentinel at his post. But the expectation, this slow and sure approach of madness, this momentary feeling of something enormous falling into an abyss, this unbearable pain of tormented thought . . . My heart is numb, it is dead, and there is no new life for it, but my thought—still alive, still struggling, once powerful as Samson but now defenseless and feeble as a child—I feel sorry for my poor thought. There are minutes when the torture of these iron hoops compressing my brain becomes un-

[5] *Works—V*, p. 137.

bearable; I have an irresistible desire to run out into the street, into the public square, and cry out to the people:

"Stop the war at once, or else . . ."

But what "else" is there? Are there any words which might bring them back to reason, words that might not be met with other words, as loud and lying? Or shall I fall on my knees before them and break into tears? But do not hundreds of thousands fill the world with their tears, and is it of any avail? Or shall I kill myself before their eyes? Kill! Thousands are dying daily—and is this of any avail?

And when I feel thus my impotence, I am seized with rage—the rage of war which I hate. . . .[6]

Ten years later Andreyev's stand implied that to him there were wars and wars. In August, 1914, he found himself not with Romain Rolland and Gorky and Bernard Shaw—"above the battle," but with Maeterlinck and Anatole France and Hauptmann and d'Annunzio and other champions of "la voie glorieuse." But in 1904, when *The Red Laugh* was published, very few thinking Russians could condone the slaughter on the plains of Manchuria.[7] Even the subservient press was at a loss in endeavoring to clothe the adventure with high-sounding phrases of patriotic camouflage. Society knew that the Government had provoked hostilities by breaking its repeated promises to evacuate the Russian troops from Manchuria, and by encroaching on Japan's "sphere of influence" in Korea. It was also known that behind this adventure were greedy speculators and investors hunting for markets. By the year 1903 Russian industry, created and artificially cultivated by the Government, had reached a critical point. The time came when the Government could no longer father the home manufacturers both as guarantor of profits and as chief consumer, besides employing the famous panacea of a protective, or rather prohibitive, tariff. In order to lead a normal existence and to develop naturally, Russian industry needed a market, internal or foreign. The first was out of the question, for the reason that rural Russia,

[6] *Ibid.*, pp. 133, 134.

[7] The historical background presented in this chapter, and elsewhere in the essay, is based on my *Russia under Nicolas II*, appended to volume II of Kornilov's *Modern Russian History* (New York, 1917), unless otherwise stated.

eighty-five per cent of the population, famished, backward, overtaxed, possessed no purchasing power, especially in view of the exorbitant prices on the "protected" commodities. Instead of endeavoring to improve the condition of the peasants, and thus build up an enormous domestic market, the Russian get-rich-quicks preferred to pursue what seemed to them the direction of lesser resistance—the grabbing of timber concessions along the Yalu River, and the grandiose exploitation of the Far East in general. When Japan, exasperated by the endless procrastinations and by the insolent tone of St. Petersburg, began hostilities, Russian liberals and revolutionists anticipated with regret the further increase of the autocratic power through what General Kuropatkin, then Minister of War, predicted would prove a "triumphant military promenade." But the war revealed not only the rapacious greed of the two-headed eagle; it also demonstrated the utter corruption and rottenness of the bureaucratic structure. To the universal astonishment, small and poor Japan dealt the Russian giant blow after blow, on land and on sea, conceding to the Russian arms not one victory. Russia lost in the end, besides Port Arthur and Port Dalny and Manchurian concessions, the southern half of Sakhalin, millions of rubles and hundreds of thousands of men, and well-nigh its entire fleet. The disastrous débâcle of Russia's army and navy did not signify the seriousness of the "yellow peril," one of the numerous hobbies of the versatile Wilhelm Hohenzollern. In that conflict an occidentalized state defeated a semi-Asiatic, archaic, clumsy, corrupt, mismanaged despotism. The lesson was obvious, and however high and dear the price paid for it, it served a great purpose. The nation was aroused. Although the war with Japan was never popular, the Government had hoped to drown the voices of opposition by a patriotic tattoo and by easy victories. But when the uncalled-for war was coupled with disgraceful defeats and with the customary revelations of graft and theft in various departments of the military machine, the cup of endurance became overfilled. Throughout the years 1904 and 1905 the country resembled a volcano whose sporadic eruptions threatened to sweep away the ancient institutions that clung to the precarious crust of the lava. Anti-mobilization riots, labor strikes and sabotage on such a large scale as the burning of the oil fields in the Baku district, agrarian disorders and violence against landowners, soldier and sailor mutinies, the avowed opposition—though only verbal—of the middle class, of professionals, of liberals, of genuine patriots, the active propaganda by word and deed carried on by the Marxian Social-Democrats and by the Narodnik Social-Revolutionists, all this mass of inflammable material required only a spark to burst into a huge conflagration. The Government reluctantly granted concessions, usually after some terroristic act, such as the assassination of Minister of Interior von Plehve, or the assassination of Grand Duke Sergey, uncle of the tsar. But the concessions were half measures which satisfied no one, and only whetted the appetite for real freedom. The press was given more freedom of expression, but not enough. The universities received the right of self-government, a privilege that was at once utilized for throwing the doors of the academic institutions open to revolutionary assemblies and headquarters. The general clamor for a Constituent Assembly which would work out a new form of government was met with a typically bureaucratic proposal for convening a carefully selected Duma with consultative powers only, a proposal that was met with derision and indignation by the larger part of the public. Not one of the least important reasons for the Government's consent to the humiliating conditions of the Portsmouth treaty with Japan was its inability to cope with the internal situation and its desire to have an armed force at home in case of need. But the troops that began to pour across the Urals into European Russia after the conclusion of peace were imbued with such bitterness against the dishonest and stupid authorities that their loyalty seemed far from dependable. Autocracy felt isolated and at bay. The *coup de grace* was administered to it, however, in a peculiarly Russian fashion—in a mode of nonresistance. In place of a traditional armed uprising, with guns and barricades, there took place a general strike of unprecedented dimensions, unanimity and effectiveness. Without any preliminary organization, without any party leadership, Russia united spontaneously in a determination to cease all social functions until the obsolete tyranny was gone. Factory workmen, railwaymen, postmen, telegraphists, bank clerks, opera singers, actors, ballet dancers, journalists, were joined voluntarily by men of independent professions—by lawyers, shopkeepers, publishers, bankers, factory owners, who often urged their employees to strike, with the assurance that their wages would be paid regularly during the time of idleness. Not a wheel turned, not a wire stirred, not an office button buzzed, for nearly a week. The Government faced financial and moral bankruptcy at home and abroad, and had to yield. On October 30, 1905, the tsar signed a manifesto granting the people freedom of speech, of assembly, of organization, of confession, personal inviolability, and a liberal franchise for a Duma without whose sanction no law could become valid.

This "bloodless revolution" caused great national rejoicing, signifying the conquest of those rights and liberties for which the best sons and daughters of Russia had been sacrificing their lives in a century-long struggle. It was a short-lived joy, however. The revolution proved to be only a revolt, if by the first we understand a successful overthrow of an established order, and by the second, an unsuccessful attempt at such a subversion. To be sure, the October manifesto signed the death of the old régime, but the fact that the signature was "granted" by the tsar, the very symbol of that régime, presented a proof that the celebrated death was "an exaggeration," to borrow Mark Twain's comment upon his rumored demise. History hardly knows an instance of an outgoing order voluntarily surrendering to its successor, performing self-decapitation. Autocracy managed to revive shortly after the temporary collapse, and to carry on its existence for another dozen years. Its main strength lay in the weakness of its opponent. Russia in 1905 was not yet ripe for a revolution. The city proletariat, assisted and led by representatives of the Intelligentsia, was too small numerically to offset the inertia of the masses, the unreasoning loyalism of the majority of the army, the opportunism of the liberals, the standpattism of the conservatives. The national unity displayed during the dramatic days of passive resistance was disrupted immediately after the publication of the Manifesto. All groups and classes, with the exception of the mercenary bureaucracy and some purblind reactionaries, were interested in the passing of the archaic semi-feudal order which oppressed not only the peasant and the workman, but the privileged classes also, impeding the progress and natural growth of capital, of commerce and industry. But as soon as it became evident, as early as October, that the political changes implied also economic reforms; as soon as alongside of the slogan "Down with Autocracy" was sounded the demand for an eight-hour working day, and the ancient cry of the peasants for land assumed an ominous intensity, the representatives of the propertied classes and the liberal professions largely withdrew their support from the fighting workmen. They were willing to forgo even the political concessions, if these could not be had without at the same time granting industrial and agrarian reforms. The Government, ever ready to employ the principle of *divide et impera,* hastened to make use of the internecine strife and jealousy among its opponents, and began to withdraw or invalidate the liberal promises and measures granted under pressure and fear. It inaugurated a campaign of vengeance against the people, of wholesale flogging, shooting, hanging. The Duma was reduced to a farce, representing largely the landowners and big manufacturers, with curbed rights and clipped powers. The ideal, for the attainment of which the nation had offered a century of struggle, became cheap and profane. The restoration of the old régime was bound to have a demoralizing effect on Russian society.

In the years of storm and stress outlined in the foregoing paragraphs, it was difficult for a thinking Russian to stay aloof from affairs of the day. Even such a-social poets as Balmont and Bryusov, or such mystics as Merezhkovsky and Minsky, were engulfed by the tide of national upheaval, and were impelled to echo "current events." During these years of hopes and disappointments, of cruel excesses and ruthless vengeance, of mob sentiments and herd actions, Andreyev "sat amidst the captives" and meditated gravely. Though of special significance when regarded in the light of contemporary facts, his works of that period are by no means of a local or temporary value, but present human documents for all times and places.

The Governor, written in 1905, exemplifies this combination of reflecting fleeting modernity with a contemplation of questions deep and eternal. Terror, "red" and "white," furnishes the framework for this study. It brings to one's mind the Red Sunday, January 22, 1905, when thousands of workmen, even women and children, were mowed down on the squares of Petrograd by the tsar's troops. Their crime consisted in being patriotic and public-spirited, their misfortune—in venerating and trusting the crowned father of the people. Armed only with ikons, church banners and crosses, led by a priest, Georgy Gapon, to the singing of religious hymns, thousands of loyal subjects of the tsar marched in procession toward the Winter Palace, in order to present a humble petition about the grievances and needs of the country. The petitioners were not permitted even to approach the palace, and were met with volleys of fire. The snow of the streets was crimsoned with the blood of deceived men, women and children, while the surviving workmen were definitely cured of their faith in crowned fathers of the people.

Few Russian writers have ever attempted to understand and explain the psychology of the tsar's henchmen. Bureaucrats were either caricatured and satirized (as in the works of Gogol and Saltykov-Shchedrin), or treated with undisguised malice (Turgenev's *Smoke*) and contempt (Tolstoy's *Anna Karenin* and *Resurrection*). Andreyev approached his characters with the impartiality of a clinic surgeon toward his patients, with the objectivity of a painter toward beauty and ugliness in his subject matter. Hence his untiring effort to put himself in the place of his character, and to live through the emotions and thoughts of that character, no matter how repulsive they may be. When successful in this endeavor, Andreyev rises, and raises us, to the height of human understanding which is forgiveness. In such cases he proves a worthy disciple of Dostoyevsky, whose treatment of degenerates, criminals, and perverts, illustrates the maxim "tout comprendre c'est tout pardonner."

Andreyev's Governor is a typical official of the old school—an unreasoning mechanical screw in the bureaucratic apparatus. When a crowd of workmen, with their wives and children, march to his mansion with a petition for the betterment of their conditions, the Governor bluntly orders them to go back to work. And when the exasperated wretches linger and give vent to their suffering in shouts, the Governor in annoyance waves his white handkerchief, at which signal the troops fire and kill a number of demonstrants. As usual, the Governor is highly praised by the authorities for his "firmness," and is warmly congratulated by his friends, particularly by his son, an army officer, who regards his father's conduct as exemplary of a loyal "servant of the tsar and the fatherland." But to Andreyev this ordinary, quotidian occurrence serves as a springboard, from which he makes his hero leap into a new existence. He repeats here his favorite scheme, that of introducing into a commonplace life a moment of intense thinking which individualizes this life and makes it dramatic. The Governor, a white-haired general, who has spent his life in receiving and giving orders unquestioningly and unreasoningly, is stirred to the innermost depth of his soul by the sight of the long row of upturned poorly shod feet belonging to the murdered "mutineers," whose corpses have been nicely laid out for the inspection of His Excellency. His whole existence is shocked to its foundations. From the moment of the shooting "time has stopped" for him; his former functions and interests, his family and friends, all that made up the routine of his well-ordered gubernatorial existence, have lost all meaning for him, and he has plunged, as it were, into a dark pit where his mind and memory react only to one image—that single gesture of his hand waving a white handkerchief. Here Andreyev suggests a curious notion, to the effect that red terror is not the response of certain parties or individuals to white terror, but that murder is answered by murder fatally, regardless of the individual will, by force of collective conscience, one might say. With keen psychological analysis Andreyev dissects the mind of the Governor, and reveals its single-track course—toward death. The Governor knows that he is going to be assassinated, that his gesture with the white handkerchief has provoked a power which will repay his deed with inevitable certainty. He devotes the brief span remaining till his doom to an occupation unknown to him in his "normal" days, introspection. With equal subtlety Andreyev presents the state of mind in the town where the drama is being enacted. Since the day of the demonstration, the murder of the Governor has been expected by everybody with the same calm assurance as one expects the rise or the setting of the sun. Foe and friend discuss the question, argue in favor and against the justice of the approaching finale, but no one doubts the unavoidable advent of the judgment of fate. Thus the prospective victim and the community coöperate, so to speak, in forcing upon destiny the foregone decision of the collective conscience. "It was as if the ancient hoary law punishing with death for death, the law which had seemed asleep, almost dead, to those who see not—had opened its cold eyes, perceived the slain men, women, and children, and imperiously stretched out its merciless hand over the head of the man who killed." [8] The masterly handling of the subject and the powerful portrayal of the waves of one definite thought stirring the air of the town act persuasively on the mind of the reader, even though in theory he may regard the theme as a bit fantastic. Certainly those men and women who proudly accepted their appointment by the revolutionary organization to commit an act of terrorism would indignantly spurn the idea that their heroism and self-sacrifice were prompted not so much by their personal views and convictions as by an intangible collective will reflecting an Old Testament sense of justice.

During the same year (1905) Andreyev reacted a second time to the revolutionary movement—in his story *Thus It Was.* Here again, as in *The Governor*, the local and specific are sublimated to the universal and general. Published shortly after the

---

[8] *Works—V*, p. 213.

memorable days of October, when the public mood was at the
highest point of optimism, this story acted on the reader like an
icy shower. Externally it presents a replica of the French revo-
lution·in its early stage, culminating in the execution of the king.
But intrinsically it reflects the author's skeptical contemplation
of his countrymen's passions and emotions, and his disparaging
verdïct concerning political revolution, as such. "Thus it was.
Thus it will be" (in Russian: "tak bylo, tak budet"), tick-tacks
cynically the pendulum of time, while a revolution is taking place
below, a revolution against the king, a symbol of authority, a
generic successor to a long series of ancestors, his very name
being designated merely by a numeral—the Twentieth. How
does a revolution take place? According to the author,

> The people simply unlearned to obey, that was all. And all at once,
> from out the multitude of separate trifling, unnoticed resistances, there
> grew up a stupendous, unconquerable movement. And as soon as the peo-
> ple ceased to obey, all their ancient sores opened suddenly, and wrathfully
> they became conscious of hunger, injustice and oppression. And they
> cried out about them. And they demanded justice. And they suddenly
> reared—an enormous shaggy beast, in one minute of free rage avenging
> himself on his tamer for all the years of humiliation and torture.
>
> Just as the millions of them had not held counsel to decide on obedience,
> so they did not come to an agreement about revolting; all at once the
> uprising rushed on to the Palace. . . .[9]

The rebels then proceed to capture the source of all suffering, the epitome of oppression—the king. He is imprisoned in
a solitary cell, beneath ·the tower where the pendulum indifferently swings its "Thus it was. Thus it will be." Even from
his impregnable cell the king, the mysterious being, by grace of
God inheritor of the all-powerful sceptre, inspires his subjects
with awe and uneasiness. After many weeks of deliberation, the
people's representatives decide on trying the king. On the day
of his trial the king is ceremoniously brought to the court, preceded, surrounded and followed by a whole army—infantry,
cavalry, artillery, watched by thousands of onlookers whose

[9] *Ibid.*, pp. 264, 265.

curiosity is mingled with fear at the notion of a king being tried by ordinary mortals. Finally, in view of the breathless national assembly he appears—the mystery of ages, the king: a commonplace, somewhat stout bourgeois, who in slight embarrassment blows his nose loudly. The people are mystified, insulted. Is this all? Is this what they have venerated for generations, what they have fought to overthrow, what has symbolized authority and tyranny?

The implication is obvious. Man creates his own authority, whether it be God, or king, or priest, but in the course of time he forgets the origin of his creature, and worships it as divine and mysterious. Man creates authorities for himself, in sheer need of surrendering his freedom which is too heavy a burden, too great a responsibility. Of course, Andreyev speaks of the average man, as usual. The average man cannot endure the glare of freedom, for the reason that his slavery is not only external, but also inner. He—the average man—is shocked at the insignificance of his traditional authority, when he visualizes it closely. Yet he is filled with fears. It is out of fear that the people decide to execute the mediocre, helpless person, the possessor of the esoteric title of king. Still the masses are restive, afraid more than ever. The newly acquired, extraneous freedom oppresses them, bewilders them. Everything seems to be in their power, the army is loyal to the new order, the Assembly humbly obedient. But they fear the responsibility bestowed on them by their power, they fear they know not what, a contagious fear spreading like fire, growing into a general panic. Will they not set up a new king, for the sake of cozy comfort and irresponsible ease? Probably so. The shallowness of political revolutions which are not the result of the inner transformation of man's mind is succinctly illustrated in the dialogue taking place between two citizens on the day of the king's execution:

"Authority must be destroyed."

"Slaves must be destroyed. There is no such thing as authority—slavery alone exists. . . ."

"But do they not love freedom?"

"No, they merely fear the whip.　When they shall have learned to love freedom, they will become free." [10]

Andreyev evidently considers that to "unlearn to obey" does not yet mean to be innerly free.　In the phraseology of Nietzsche, it is not sufficient to be free *from* something: one must be able to be free *for* something.[11]　In October, 1905, Russia appeared unanimous in its desire for a negative liberty, namely for freedom from the oppression of the autocratic régime. The unity of purpose, a negative purpose, made its achievement so easy.　But as soon as the acquired freedom had to be molded into positive shape and form, the people proved their utter unpreparedness, in the sense of an inner change.　The average citizen became afraid.　He feared the workmen's soviets which sprang up spontaneously during the general strike, he feared the relaxation of authority, the license of the press, the turbulent mass meetings, he was afraid of himself and still more for himself.　The average citizen in the late fall of that year began to pray for the return of the old order which made life so secure for the unambitious, for one who had no dangerous ideas, or kept them to himself, if he had any.　His prayer was fulfilled.

In contemplating the superficiality of the average human mind, the shallowness of man's strivings, and the ephemeralness of his achievements, one may lose heart and relinquish all attempts at breaking the wall with one's skull.　One may withdraw from this valley of futility into a lofty castle, whence one may soar above the wall bespattered with the blood and brains of the doomed lepers.　Or one may throw one's lot with the wall-smashers, faintly hoping with the half-demented leper that the heap of dead corpses may ultimately serve as a stepping-stone across the Wall.　Andreyev suggests these alternatives in his play of the revolution, *To the Stars,* incidentally his first dramatic attempt to be published (in 1905).

---

[10] *Ibid.,* p. 297.

[11] "Frei nennst du dich? Deinen herschenden Gedanken will ich hören und nicht, dass du einem Joche entronnen bist . . . Frei wovon? Was schiert das Zarathustra? Hell aber soll mir dein Auge künden: frei wozu?"—*Also sprach Zarathustra:* "Vom Wege des Schaffenden," p. 92 (*Werke—VII*).

The action—though there is very little action in the play—takes place in an astronomical observatory, on a lofty mountain peak, where one does not hear the sounds of the life down in the valley. The master of the place is an astronomer, a scientist of international fame, a man of cosmic vision, who regards the universe *sub specie æternitatis*. He seldom leaves his observatory, and remains deaf to the revolution taking place below, though his children are active participants in the movement. In the battle with the government troops his son-in-law loses his legs, and his son, Nikolay, is wounded and taken prisoner. The Astronomer remains unperturbed. He descends upon the agitated family and their friends as they are discussing the tragic events and the ways and means for rescuing Nikolay, the man who does not appear in the play, but whose magnetic personality and radiating nobility are felt all the time. The father languidly wonders: "Do they still kill down there? Are prisons still in existence?" His naïve ignorance of reality is met with sneers on the part of his revolutionary daughter and her wounded husband, who even accuse him of callousness and smugness. But Andreyev displays great talent in compelling us to regard with respect and even sympathy the cold scholar who is unmoved by the heartrending sorrows of the children of earth, because he considers everything through the prism of eternity. For he ceases to be cold when the question of science is concerned. One feels his reserved ecstasy when he speaks of the infinite vistas of the human mind, of such revolutionaries as Galileo and Giordano Bruno, of the road to the stars, *ad astra,* also covered with the blood of seekers. One can see his point of view, whether agreeing with it or not, when he fails to grieve over the death of one man, be it even his son, because he is aware of the fact that "every second a whole world is probably destroyed in the universe." To him all "dark shadows of the earth," such as injustice, suffering, and death, are "vain cares," for in the cosmic aspect life is triumphant, despite all the myriads of those who have perished and who will perish in its endless course. Though his son be lost, life at that same moment restores the balance through the birth of some one as good as Nikolay, "nay—better than Nikolay: nature knows no repetition." He sees the misfortune of the average person in that he "thinks of nothing but his life and his death, wherefore he lives in terror and ennui, like a flea that has lost its way in a sepulchre."

Very few are in a position to mount the observatory of the Astronomer (Schopenhauer's Contemplator or Nietzsche's Higher Man), from whose height the earth and mankind with their problems and interests become dwarfed in size and in significance. Most of us are terrestrials who refuse to be considered as mere cogs in some universal *perpetuum mobile*, serving as means for some higher, imperishable goal. Marusya, Nikolay's betrothed, one of the loveliest woman characters in Russian literature, cannot accept the Astronomer's point of view, for she is a normal human being, attached to the soil, living her life in the midst of, not above, the battle. "I cannot," she says to the Astronomer, "flee from the earth, I do not want to forsake it—'tis so unhappy. It breathes horror and grief, but it gave me birth, and I bear earth's sufferings in my blood. Your stars are alien to me . . . Like a wounded bird my soul ever falls back to the earth." [12]

In Nikolay, Marusya and their comrades Andreyev lovingly depicts those ardent dreamers who live and die for their dreams, and thus beautify both life and death. What matter if their struggle and sacrifice amount to the leper's hallucination at the wall? With his wonted skepticism, ever present or felt in his writings, Andreyev nevertheless invariably pays tribute to these moths plunging into fire. Nikolay, absent in flesh from the stage, dominates it with his beautiful spirit of giving all of himself for the sufferers of the earth, and only an author with a feeling of reverence for his subject matter could endow this invisible character with such a powerful charm. The climax of contrasts comes in the last act, when we learn that the prison has robbed Nikolay not only of his bodily freedom, but also of his mind, as an effect of the beating administered to him and to his comrades by the jailers. Andreyev records here one of

[12] *Works—VI*, pp. 140, 141.

the habitual horrors in tsaristic Russia—the torture of political prisoners in ways both painful and humiliating. A number of interpellations were introduced in the Dumas, charging the gendarmerie and police with employing torture chambers where political suspects were subjected to limb-breaking, hair-pulling and nail-tearing, and to other inventions of man's depraved mind which would turn Torquemada's henchmen green with envy.[13] There is therefore no exaggeration in Marusya's description of the jailers breaking into the cells of the arrested revolutionists, and beating them up, one after another, boxing their ears, trampling them under their feet, mutilating their faces.

They beat them long and terribly [she narrates to the Astronomer]—dull, cold brutes. Nor did they spare thy son: when I saw him, his face was horrible. The dear, beautiful face that smiled to the whole world! They tore his mouth, the lips that never uttered a word of falsehood. They nearly gouged out his eyes—his eyes that saw only the beautiful. . . .

It was then that this terrible, deathly sorrow awakened in him. He reproached no one, he defended his jailers before me—his assassins, but in his eyes grew this black sorrow: his soul was dying. Still he kept on reassuring me, consoling me. Only once he said: "In my soul I bear all the sorrow of the world." [14]

She ends her gruesome narrative with the statement that Nikolay, this brilliant, soulful, magnetic man, has plunged into chaos, has become an idiot, an indifferent creature that will probably grow stout and live long. For a moment Marusya seems about to follow the counsel of Job's wife—curse God and die. What justification is there in a life where the best perish! Even the Astronomer loses his imperturbability for a few moments: his scientific, mathematical sense is outraged by the folly of the race, the madmen, the suicidal blind murderers of their prophets. "Were the sun suspended lower, they would put the sun

[13] Cf. *The Stenographic Reports* (*Stenograficheskiye otchoty*) of the second Duma (Petrograd, 1907), for the following sessions during the year 1907: April 2 (v. I, pp. 1775-1777); April 3 (I, pp. 1542-1562); April 5 (I, pp. 1602, 1603); April 9 (I, pp. 1825, 1826); May 15 (II, pp. 597-599).

[14] *Works—VI*, pp. 132, 133.

out—that they might expire in darkness," he exclaims with contempt. But after this momentary weakness, both the Astronomer and Marusya regain their strength, and appear even hardened, forged anew in their convictions. The mad folly of mankind enhances the Astronomer's contempt for things terrestrial and temporary, and reassures him of the wisdom of his course in pursuit of imperishable truths, of eternal goals. Moreover, when Marusya, prompted by her nostalgia for the earth, determines to descend once again and carry on the struggle in which Nikolay has perished, the man of science gives her his blessing. He predicts that she, too, will perish, but that in her death she will acquire immortality, for like Nikolay she will join the children of eternity. "Only beasts die," he says . . . "Only those who kill, die, but those who are killed, who are torn to pieces, who are burned—those live forever. There is no death for man, there is no death for the son of eternity!" [15]

To the Stars sounds the first encouraging note in Andreyev's important works. Written in the revolutionary days of 1905, this play strikes a dissonance from *Thus It Was*, composed about the same time.[16] It is true, Andreyev seems to say in the drama, that "thus it was, thus it will be"; that the mass of humanity is steeped in slavery, inner slavery which cannot be cured through changes of ruling systems. In *To the Stars* we also hear that "thus it was," that men have *ever* killed their prophets. But here a new note is introduced, to the effect that life is not futile, that struggle and sacrifice for the good and beautiful are not absurd and aimless, but possess an eternal value in the endless progress of the universe. The author appears to have discovered a harmony between the detached point of view of the Astronomer who soars in eternity and seeks his friends among the past and future explorers of scientific truth, and the point of view of Marusya who gravitates toward the earth and longs to give herself for those who suffer in the present. Both have found a goal to strive for. They stand in the observa-

---

[15] *Ibid.*, p. 141.

[16] Gorky comments on Andreyev's "painful" duality: "During one and the same week he was capable of chanting 'Hosannah' to the world, and of hurling an 'Anathema' at it."—*A Book on Andreyev*, p. 16.

tory, up in the heights, and while the Astronomer, his arms out-stretched toward the stars, sends his greeting to his "distant, unknown friend," Marusya, extending her arms toward the earth, sends her greeting to her "dear, suffering brother."

Another encouraging feature in *To the Stars* may be found in the character of the workman, Treich. This is the only time that Andreyev pays his tribute to the revolutionary proletariat, presenting in Treich a powerful creator of new life, an indomitable forger of destiny, reminding one of Gorky's Nil (*Smug Citizens*) and Pavel (*Confession*). To be sure, that was a time when the phrase "His Majesty the Russian Workman" reflected a formidable fact. The workmen were responsible not only for the success of the general strike, but also for the creation of the first Soviet, a labor parliament which arose spontaneously in the days when the Government lost its head. During the fall of 1905 the Petrograd Soviet of Workmen's Deputies was the only public organ that enjoyed the confidence and respect of the country. Even after the publication of the constitutional Manifesto, Count Witte, the premier, repeatedly consulted with the Soviet through its first president, Hrustalev, soliciting its forbearance and coöperation. It was an impressive demonstration of the organization and class consciousness of the Russian proletariat, numerically so insignificant (counting less than three million throughout the Empire). Andreyev reflected the general conception of the workingman's power at the time, by putting into the mouth of Treich these words of calm self-reliance:

We must go ahead. There has been some talk here about defeats, but there is no such thing. I know only victories. The earth is wax in the hands of man. We must maul, press—create new forms. But we must go ahead. If we meet a wall—we must destroy it. If we meet a mountain—we must remove it. If we meet a precipice—we must fly across it. If we have no wings—we must produce wings! . . . But we must go ahead, so long as the sun is shining.[17]

And when one of the Astronomer's melancholy assistants ob-

[17] *Works—VI*, pp. 70, 71.

serves that the sun will be extinguished, Treich retorts nonchalantly: "Then we must kindle a new one."

This major note, constructive, vigorous, hopeful, does not reappear in Andreyev. *To the Stars* was finished in November 1905.[18] Events of deep disappointment followed this month. The Government soon discovered that it had overrated the intelligence of the people, particularly that of the people in uniform, the army. The Government probed the people's resistance, and found it feeble. Hrustalev, president of the Petrograd Soviet, was arrested—and the only reaction on the part of this body was a tactfully worded resolution, and the election of Leon Trotsky to that high post. In the meantime the conservatives and liberals grew impatient with the haughty tone of His Majesty the Workman, and became restive because of His Majesty's demand for economic reforms. The average citizen began to sigh aloud for firmness and order. In response to the growing disintegration of the opposition, the Government arrested the Petrograd Soviet in full session. A general strike was declared. But the country proved weary of continuous strain and privations. Even the working class, the advance guard of the revolution, had exhausted its power and endurance, and responded to the summons without enthusiasm or unanimity. The strike was by no means general, which fact enabled the administration to crush it with the aid of trustworthy troops, notably the Life Guards. The last brilliant page in the revolution of 1905 was turned by Russia's ancient capital, Moscow. For nearly two weeks revolutionary squads of this city resisted the army. Unorganized, armed precariously, at best with Brownings and Mausers, these impractical dreamers attempted to resist from behind romantic barricades a modern military organization equipped with rifles, machine guns and cannon. Christmas found the city of many churches thoroughly pacified, silent as a graveyard. For Russia came a period of reckoning for the few weeks of freedom. Punitive expeditions were sent to various parts of Russia, led by officers who had gained no glory on the fields of Manchuria, and who

---

[18] The authorities forbade its production on the stage.

now tried to distinguish themselves in assaults against their own villages and towns. Martial law practically ruled the country. The Government, the reactionary press and the Church encouraged the organization of the so-called Black Hundred societies, like the Union of True Russian Men, or the Union of Archangel Michael, which employed the most unscrupulous means for the attainment of their aim—the persecution of those who disagreed with the Government's policy, and of non-Orthodox citizens, particularly Jews. Russia suffocated in a torrent of violence, rapine, obscurantism—and disillusionment.

In his play, *Savva*, Andreyev expressed the mood of the year 1906. Treich's tone of calm assurance, of patient and resolute force that defies obstacles and marches on, ever forward, ever creating new forms—was gone, like the snows of yesteryear. Savva is nervous, he sorely lacks poise. His slogan is: *Ignis sanat*. Thorough disgust with the order of things in the world prompts him to find the only solution in destruction, in fire. He scorns all other methods of opposition, and has contempt for all parties and organization. Indeed, which of the Left parties then in existence in Russia could he join? Surely not the Cadets, the liberals, professional opportunists who haggled and bargained and compromised with the Authorities. Both factions of the Social-Democratic party, the Bolsheviki and the Mensheviki, limited their activity to propaganda by word, preparing the revolution through an educational process—too slow for such a fiery temper as that of Savva. The parties that did admit propaganda by deed, the Social-Revolutionists, the Maximalists, the Anarchists, were too deliberative in the eyes of Savva, too "orderly" and "narrow-minded." His estimate of their terroristic acts against individual oppressors he expresses by way of a parable, the favorite style of the common people in Russia, to which Savva too belongs:

They meet and meet, and weigh and consider a long time, and then—bang!—a sparrow drops dead. The next minute there is another sparrow in its place, hopping about on the very same branch.[19]

[19] *Works—VI*, p. 176.

And a few lines below:

> Now you can't clear a dense forest by cutting down one tree at a time, can you? That's what they do. While they chop at one end, it grows up at the other. You can't accomplish anything that way; it's labor lost.[20]

No, Savva has no patience with evolutionary stages, with compromises. He is a typical Russian Nihilist, with not too large a cultural background, one who has found a truth, and is bent on forcing it upon everybody else in its entirety—*aut Cæsar aut nihil*. His truth is neither new nor very deep, it is uncouth and elementary. To the question, Who is he that dares defy everything and all? he replies:

> Who am I? A man who was once born. Was born, and went out to look about. I saw churches—and penitentiaries. I saw universities—and houses of prostitution. I saw factories—and picture galleries. I saw palaces and filthy holes. I reckoned up, you see, how many jails there are to each gallery, and resolved: Everything must be annihilated.[21]

Everything. With the rectilineal simplicity of a child or a savage Savva deals in absolutes only. Modern civilization is to him a gigantic accumulation of stupidities that has grown into a mountain. In place of engaging in futile attempts at building new forms on the mountain, he proposes a more radical remedy—to erase the whole mountain, to lay the earth bare. He is jealous for the earth which "is worthy of kingly purple, yet is clad in convict clothes." The earth must be freed from its hideous excrescences—the cities with their "stone graves." All the old institutions must go, old literature, old art, all "hideous rags." Savva's programme calls thus for the liberation of man through the destruction of the ages-old fetiches and authorities that have kept him enslaved. First of all, God must be destroyed, the greatest enemy of freedom. Savva is an average Russian, hence concrete. He intends to explode with a bomb a tangible divinity, a miracle-working ikon in a famous monastery. At the time when thousands upon thousands of pil-

---

[20] *Ibid.*
[21] *Ibid.*, pp. 230, 231.

grims come from all over Russia to the monastery, to find cure and consolation through contact with the holy image, Savva induces a friar to place a bomb behind the divinity. The explosion would open the eyes of the people to the shameful traffic carried on by the monks at the expense of credulity and piety (even one of the faithful pertinently remarks that were not God immortal, His servants would have long sold him out piece by piece). More than that, the people would become convinced that dynamite is stronger than their God, and would proceed to conclude that man is the creator of both.

Of course Savva fails utterly in his plan and purpose. One recalls the idea suggested in *Thus It Was*, that slavery is not the product of authority, but its creator. Savva fails to realize that man does not wish to be unchained. Man fears freedom, fears the responsibility of it. He craves for the supernatural, for miracles, for a heaven of bliss that would compensate him for earthly sorrow. The monks are better psychologists of the crowd, and ably supply the demand for sweet dupery. Informed as to Savva's plot, they manage to remove the ikon just before the explosion, and to replace it quietly after the deafening blast. The masses are granted a new miracle. The monks make excellent use of the situation, and manufacture abundant enthusiasm, devotion, fanaticism, and—generosity. Savva and his devout sister, Lipa, watch the thousands of pilgrims who march by them singing hymns and shouting in ecstasy and joy. Says Lipa:

Don't you see what is passing by us? Human grief is going by. And you wanted to deprive them of their last possession, of their last hope, last consolation. And why, in the name of what? In the name of some savage, ghastly dream of a "bare earth" . . . To destroy Golgotha! To put out the brightest light that ever shone on earth! [22]

In the final scene of this powerful play Andreyev shows the collapse of unalloyed rationalism before the gregarious believers, who willingly, blissfully allow themselves to be duped, to be lulled. At the same time the author expresses here his hor-

[22] *Ibid.*, pp. 270, 271.

ror and contempt for the mob, this consolidated blind brutal
force that surges like an elemental torrent, roars and thunders,
and sweeps everything in its violent course. One shudders at
the scene of the murder of Savva by the fanatical mob who torture him and mangle his body—*ad majorem Dei gloriam,* shouting at the top of their voices the beautiful words: "Christ has
risen from the dead. He has conquered death with death and
given life to those who lay in their graves. . . ." [23]

Like *To the Stars, Savva* was denied the right of presentation on the Russian stage. The Russian Government has ever
been sensitive to "pernicious" influences. It gauged correctly
the significance of Andreyev, more correctly than some professional critics who scornfully dubbed him a-social, anti-social,
and even reactionary.[24] However aloof Andreyev held himself

---

[23] Maxim Gorky was deeply chagrined at Andreyev's treatment of the subject,
which was based on an actual incident of a revolutionist attempting to destroy
a popular ikon (see his reminiscences, in *A Book on Andreyev*, p. 29). As if in
refutation of Andreyev's portrayal of mobs, of Black Hundreds, who kill their
friends, their prophets and saviors, Gorky published shortly after the appearance
of *Savva* his own *Confession.* Here too a miracle-working ikon is worshipped.
Throngs of sick and cripples are lined along the procession, fervently hoping
to be restored to health by the passing image. The ikon is carried aloft by the
singing, ecstatic multitude. And here Gorky states his faith in mass action.
So powerful is the united will of the people, so potent their concentrated faith,
that the miracle actually takes place, and the narrator bursts out in a panegyric
of God—the people: "Thou shalt have no other gods but the people."

There is another angle in this picture of mass movement and action that invites comparison with other Russian writers. Tolstoy in *War and Peace*, describing the inspection of the troops by Emperor Alexander I, presents the marching
men as united in common worship of their tsar, and in their readiness to die
for him. The emotion produced in men at the sight of their monarch is suggestively explained by Vsevolod Garshin in his *Reminiscences of Private Ivanov,*
the autobiographical sketch which contains a few masterly pages describing the
military inspection by Alexander II. As in *War and Peace*, the soldiers are
mad with ecstatic joy, and are ready to plunge into fire at the merest hint of
their ruler. One word in that description suggests the reason for this sensation
—"irresponsibility." Once you are a part of the mass, of the mob, of the herd,
you become free from the terrific burden of responsibility, of individual thinking
or acting. On the other hand, you show your reverence and admiration for him
who assumes responsibility for your actions—be it a tsar, or a commander, or a
god, or a party leader.

[24] Arabazhin, on pages 95 and 96 of his book on Andreyev, quotes to this effect
Messrs. Filosofov and Merezhkovsky. Curiously enough, these two writers, who
accused Andreyev of reactionism, threw in their lot, after the Bolshevik revolution,
with the blackest anti-Soviet forces, and even went so far as to assist the Poles
in their attack against Russia.

from political groups and from any movements, however skeptical sounded his estimate of these and of all skin-deep revolutions, the fact remained that he bore a social message. More profoundly and efficiently than revolutionary propagandists did Andreyev sow seeds of discontent with existing conditions and institutions. More than any other contemporary writer did he succeed in generating a critical attitude in his readers, a criticism that affected the very root of things, hence so dangerous in the eyes of the perspicacious authorities.

By way of illustration. The years that followed 1905 were stigmatized with the sobriquet of "Stolypin's collar." The premier's policy was laconically defined by himself from the Duma tribune: "First pacification, then reforms." Russia was subjected to a process of pacification which amounted to martial law. The ordinary apparatus of justice, corrupt and servile though it was, appeared too slow and complicated for Stolypin, who inaugurated therefore a régime of field court-martial, a simple and speedy affair, seldom exceeding twenty-four hours, and usually resulting in the same verdict—to be hanged. The average citizen, eager for firmness and the restoration of law and order, was furnished with an appetizer for every meal by the press accounts of the number of persons hanged in various parts of the Empire at the dawn of each day. In time of war or revolution the average person grows callous and accustomed to swallow with his bread the news about the slaughter of the nation's best sons and daughters. ("Man gets used to everything, the scoundrel," says Dostoyevsky's Hobbledehoy.) At such times it remains for the few to wake the conscience of the slumbering herd. The octogenarian Tolstoy came out with his stirring *I Cannot Be Silent,* a powerful arraignment of the governmental hangmen, a pathetic offer of his own "old neck" for the executioner's noose. Yet this direct appeal of the greatest man of Russia did not possess as indelible, as haunting an influence as Andreyev's *Story Of The Seven That Were Hanged.* For whatever greatness of spirit and nobility of purpose Tolstoy's protest possessed, it lacked the one indisputable quality of Andreyev's *Story*—suggestive art.

In simplicity of style, in keen psychological analysis, in humane sympathy, and in its lasting effect, this story is probably Andreyev's best. The deep conviction which the reader is bound to carry out of this work is that there can be no justification in taking another's life. This conviction grows on you gradually and irresistibly as you commune wth the seven doomed persons in the last ‚hours of their earthly existence. Not only are you shocked by the slaying of the five political terrorists, young idealists sacrificing themselves for an idea; your feelings are outraged even by the execution of the two common criminals who happen to be tried by a military court—the elemental rover, Tsiganok, and the stupid, somnolent Esthonian, Yanson, who brutally killed his master under the influence of liquor, and who mutters in broken Russian one and the same refrain: "You must not hang me." It sounds like the cry of human blood, since times primordial setting forth the unanswerable question: Who gave man the right to judge and to take the life of his fellow man?

Aside from discrediting capital punishment, the *Story* raises another interesting problem—the meaning of death for those who have sacrificed their life. To one of the five terrorists, Vasily Kashirin, death is that horrible scarecrow that appears on man's forward march, hissing into his ear the paralyzing, What's the use? In spite of all his efforts to be brave to the end, Vasily loses all his vitality from the moment of the announcement of the death verdict: he is killed outright. The spectre of nonexistence deprives him of his reflective faculty, robs him of his habitual idealism and fearlessness in action, turns him into a corpse. Human justice is accomplished: a beautiful vessel, a fair form, is reduced to dead clay. But not so with the other four. To them death is painful only in the aspect of earthly relations; as, for instance, in the scene where Sergey Golovin's aged parents come to say good-bye to their son on the eve of the execution. But, left alone with themselves, these four face the approaching end without fear or regret. Sergey's father is a retired colonel, and he admonishes his son, also a former officer, to die like a soldier. Indeed, they die rather like the early Christians, imbued with love and happiness. Sergey's healthy, muscular body rebels for a moment against its oncoming destruction, but Sergey's spirit easily conquers the carcass, and he meets death as gallantly and unostentatiously as he has lived. Of the two girls, Tanya Kovalchuk remains to the end the mother protectress of her comrades, utterly self-oblivious, caring to the very last moment for the little comforts of her "children," bestowing a friendly smile on one, an encouraging stroke on another. The other girl, Musya, radiates with the fire of immortality. Still in her teens, she blushes at the perspective of joining the glorious martyrs of the revolution. And when she succeeds in persuading herself that in spite of her youth and brief service she may be worthy of the halo about to descend on her head, there is no limit to her joy. So,

she has been taken into the pale. Rightfully she has entered the ranks of those bright heroes who go to heaven through flames, tortures and executions. Serene peace and quietly radiating, infinite happiness. She seemed already to have departed from the earth, to have drawn near to the mysterious sun of truth and life, and, disembodied, she hovers in its light.[25]

And as Musya reflects on her destiny, her heart overflows with a wave of ardent love for all humanity, for the whole earth, and she experiences keen bliss. "Is this really death?" she asks herself in happy amazement. "My God, how beautiful it is! Or is it life?" She falls asleep, an ecstatic smile on her lips.

To-morrow, when the sun shall rise, this human face will be distorted in an inhuman grimace, the brain will be inundated with thick blood, and the glassy eyes will protrude from their orbits—but to-day she sleeps peacefully, and smiles in her great immortality.[26]

She has become a "child of eternity," as the Astronomer would say, a sister of Giordano Bruno. The chapter on Musya bears the title, "There Is No Death." In the chapter, "Walls

[25] *Works—VIII*, p. 59.
[26] *Ibid.*, p. 65.

are Crumbling," we encounter a more complex personality, that of a hardened terrorist passing under the name of Werner. Throughout his revolutionary activity he has obeyed his intellect rather than his emotion. In the course of his collisions with his enemies, and of his contact with his comrades, Werner has acquired a deep contempt for all men, himself included. Haughty, cruel, reserved, bored, he has mechanically continued to carry out his hazardous work of a terrorist, and as coldly and indifferently he meets the expected end. During the court proceedings and the reading of the verdict, Werner is all absorbed in a complicated game of chess which he plays on an imaginary board. But in his solitary cell, awaiting execution, the hard misanthrope becomes surprisingly aware of a sensation of joy and liberty:

> Yes, of liberty. I think of to-morrow's execution, and it seems not to exist. I look at the walls, and they seem not to exist either. And I feel so free, as though I were not in prison, but had just come out of some prison in which I have been confined all my life.[27]

Life and men assume a new aspect in his transformed vision. All the baseness and meanness, all the evil and ugliness, all the traits and phenomena that caused his erstwhile contempt for the race, appear to him now in the light of pathetic naïveté, of childlike awkwardness, to be pitied and pardoned. Werner, considered by his comrades as flint-like in his severe reserve, feels his heart bursting with emotion and his eyes overflowing with tears as he addresses humanity in an ecstatic whisper: "My dear friends. My dear comrades." His love, like that of Musya, expands and soars above time and space, becomes cosmic, and thereby lifts Werner above the walls of his prison, above the fear of death, above the contempt for life, lifts him to the heights of Schopenhauer's "conqueror."

> With that wondrous illumination of the spirit, which in rare moments descends upon a person and raises him to the highest peaks of contemplation, Werner suddenly perceived both life and death, and was struck with

[27] *Ibid.*, p. 84.

the magnificence of the unique spectacle. He seemed to be walking along the crest of a tremendously high mountain, as narrow as the edge of a blade. On one side he saw life, and on the other he saw death, like two sparkling, deep, and beautiful seas, merging into one another at the horizon in a single infinite vista.[28]

Thus the revolutionists prove victorious over death in the last moments of their life, and at the very execution. Unostentatiously they exchange light friendly remarks before being strung up, and spontaneously echo Musya, who recalls at random a fragment from a song:

> The shores of life cannot contain
> My love, as broad as the sea.[29]

At dawn seven lives were snuffed out. "Thus did men greet the rising sun," Andreyev concludes the gruesome paragraph about the dead bodies "with elongated necks, bulging eyes, and blue tongues protruding from their mouths." Yet in spite of the gloomy conclusion, the *Story* is most exhilarating and stimulating, in that it justifies life, struggle, striving, self-sacrifice, through the exalted feeling of immortality.

One must bear in mind that to Russians, and to those who know Russia, the *Story* is not mere rhetoric, not a purely imaginative piece of writing about something that does not exist in life. Before 1917, Russian revolutionary terrorists ranked with saints in public sentiment, and with good reason. Those men and women who were chosen by the central revolutionary committee for the highly responsible work of terror had to undergo a long and thorough test as to their moral integrity, devotion to the cause, and fearlessness. When one turns to the biographies of Russian terrorists, one finds invariably that they were gentle souls, incapable, in their private life, of harming a fly. How great must have been their faith in the justness of their cause, and how deep their conviction of the correctness of their methods, to turn them into cold-blooded homicides and bomb throwers. One who was chosen for the action considered

[28] *Ibid.*, p. 85.
[29] *Ibid.*, p. 106.

himself or herself, as the case might be, at the apogee of achievement, at the grand finale of life. For surely none of those who went into action expected to survive it; all anticipated either being blown up by their own explosive when hurling it at the victim, or executed by the authorities after the usual, perfunctory trial. Thus the prospective homicide became *eo ipso* a suicide. Of great human interest are the farewell letters or diary notes of the convicted terrorists, which were occasionally smuggled through by friendly or mercenary jailers. In them the men and women, very few of whom ever passed their twenty-fifth year, who were about to die, parted with life without rancor or remorse, proud of their martyrdom, hopeful about the future of humanity, and pathetically tender toward their surviving relatives and comrades. One need only recall the last utterances of such revolutionists as Zhelyabov, Zotov, Kogan-Bernstein, Balmashev, Kalyayev, Konoplyannikova— words spoken at a moment when affectation is unthinkable, when one's self is revealed crystalline and purged.[30]   Thus Andreyev's saint-like heroes appear real and convincing not only because of the artistic power with which they are drawn, but also because one meets in them familiar features, features of Russia's best sons and daughters, however erring they may have been in their means or aims.

In the generous spirit of Russia's revolutionary youth, Andreyev perceived a readiness to sacrifice not only their bodies, but even their souls. In the year preceding the composition of *The Seven That Were Hanged,*—that is, in 1907,—he had written a story, *Darkness,* wherein the hero, a proud terrorist, becomes ashamed of his moral loftiness on encountering a prostitute, who hates him for his purity, spits at him, and hurls into his face the severe maxim: " 'Tis a shame to be good, when such as I exist." Andreyev lets his hero be persuaded, not quite logically, of the weightiness of the prostitute's argument. He concludes that moral privileges are as unjust as economic

---

[30] Some of these letters may be found in English, e. g., in Olgin's *The Soul of the Russian Revolution,* p. 338 ff. (New York, 1917), or in A. J. Sack's *The Birth of the Russian Democracy,* p. 88 ff. (New York, 1918).

or political privileges, and he casts away his glorious life of danger and resignation, even his "immortality," to plunge into "darkness," to merge with filthy humanity, with the Lumpen-proletariat. Not quite logically, because in his very decision that it is not "right" to be "good," and in his resolution to be "bad" out of solidarity and sympathy, he deals in purely ethical values, and thus continues to be good and self-sacrificing in spite of his rational self. The story caused considerable discussion at the time, as it fitted the atmosphere of general disappointment in the revolution, on one hand, and of the spreading filth and crime in life and letters, on the other. As has already been mentioned, the failure of the revolution disheartened the Intelligentsia, and drove them either into the ranks of mystics and religionists, or in the direction of carnality and pornography. But aside from its timely appeal, *Darkness* impresses the reader as pure head work, not felt through and lived through by the author, as were his other productions.

Quite different in this respect is Andreyev's *nouvelle, Sashka Zhegulev,* published in 1911. From the first to the last page it breathes a lyrical sadness, a tender sympathy with the character of the story. Indeed, the *nouvelle* presents a poem in prose, beautiful in style and rich in incomparable Russian landscapes and folk scenes. It reflects one of the sad phenomena in Russian life during the "pacifying" régime of Stolypin, the wave of "expropriation." This term was originally applied to the tactics of the "Maximalists," the extreme wing of the Social-Revolutionists, which seceded from the party after the Moscow barricades, and launched a series of grandiose expropriations, or hold-ups, to employ a sound Americanism. The Maximalists limited their activities to state institutions, such as state banks, post offices, army treasuries, carrying out their performances in broad daylight and before public eyes, with the aid of hand grenades and revolvers. Their aim was twofold—to replenish the party funds and to harass the Government. No one questioned their disinterestedness, while their extraordinary bravery spread around them a romantic halo. Impressionable individuals, particularly among young people, were stimulated to follow in the footsteps of the popular heroes, just as Wild West shows work on the imagination of American lads. To this universal trait of youth should be added the fact that Russia was in an extremely nervous state of mind in those years of rousing events—war, revolution, punitive expeditions, field courts-martial, events that impelled sensitive natures to seek unusual sensations and adventures out of the ordinary. Expropriations, so-called, usually perpetrated by amateurish bands of young men, often high-school students, primarily from love of adventure, spread like wild fire through the country. It was only natural, however, for professional brigands and robbers to exploit this morbid sentiment, by frequently joining the puerile dreamers, and infecting them with their own prosaic aims and vulgar tendencies.

Andreyev must have been deeply moved by the daily accounts of these exploits. He was probably stirred in particular, as Lvov-Rogachevsky suggests,[31] by the wide-open staring eyes on the death photograph of Savitsky, a gentle lad who for three years terrorized the authorities in an Ukrainian district. He led a band of peasants, attacked wealthy landowners, divided the spoils among the needy, and was worshipped by the population. Finally he was betrayed, and discovered by the police lying sick in a barn. He fought to the end, until his body was "literally like a sieve from the bullets that pierced it." In his coat pocket was found a copy of *The Seven That Were Hanged.* The case of Savitsky was by no means unique, and Andreyev's story possesses, aside from its psychological value, the value of a social phenomenon in the turbulent Russian reality.

Sashka Zhegulev treats the same theme as *Darkness,* only emotionally instead of intellectually. A note of pathos rings through the entire work. While *Darkness* gives the impression of a labored problem in dogmatic ethics, here we are swept away by hardly definable emotions. In *Darkness* the revolutionist commits a moral harakiri when his intellect proves to him, somewhat sophistically, that he has no right to be "good" so long as there are "bad" people in this world. In the *nou-*

[31] *Two Truths,* p. 123.

velle, Sasha Pogodin becomes transformed into Sashka Zhegulev.[32] The first, Pogodin, is a genteel, noble youth, with an
austere countenance and severe dark eyes, resembling a Byzantine ikon. This pure, tender boy, deeply loved by his mother,
also resembling a Byzantine ikon, turns into a brigand by the
nickname of Zhegulev. What impels him to commit this painful metamorphosis is not quite clear. The author gives us poet-
ical hints as to certain voices, voices of Russia, calling to Sasha
in his beautiful home surroundings, under the loving care of his
mother, the chummy friendship of his sister, and the awakening,
still vague, feeling between him and a schoolmate, Zhenya.
The opening of the story, written in a style reminding one of
the later Sologub, suggests the leit-motif of the drama:

Love thirsts for quenching, tears seek for respondent tears. And when
the soul of a great people sorrows, then all life is in a turmoil, every living
spirit quakes, and the pure of heart go to slaughter.

So it was even with Sasha Pogodin, a youth beautiful and pure: life
had chosen him for the quenching of its passions and pangs, had opened
his heart for prophetic voices, unheard by others, and with his sacrificial
blood it filled a golden cup to the brim. Sad and tender, beloved by all
for the beauty of his face and for the austerity of his ideas, he was quaffed
to the bottom of his soul by thirsting lips, and died early; by a lonely and
terrible death did he die. And he was buried together with evil-doers
and murderers, whose lot he shared of his own free will; and he left no
good name, and there is no cross on his unknown grave.[33]

In the voluntary "fall" of Sasha Pogodin to the lower depths
of Sashka Zhegulev who leads, and fraternizes with, social
dregs and outcasts, who tramples his own gentle soul in pools of
human blood shed by him, in this sacrifice of one's all—tastes
and attachments and dear ones and traditions—Andreyev symbolizes the terrific price which young Russia had to pay for the
sins of their fathers. For Pogodin is the son of a general, he
belongs to that small group of cultured, well-to-do, European-

[32] Both Sasha and Sashka are derivatives from Alexander, but Sashka is employed in a somewhat depreciative connotation, and is used among the common
people.
[33] *Wild-Rose Almanacks,* No. 16, p. 11. Petrograd, 1911. (*Works—XIV,* p. 1).

ized Russians who have acquired their elegance and comfort at the expense of the sweat and blood of the millions of inarticulate, illiterate, poverty-stricken, oppressed and persecuted beasts of burden—the peasants. Pogodin (if we may so interpret Andreyev's rather vaguely expressed idea) is the twentieth century prototype of the Repentant Noble of the seventies in the preceding century. He feels the need of atoning for the crimes of his fathers, of giving back to the people what he owes them. But he is no longer the worshipful Narodnik who sees in the people only angelic traits, meekness and tolerance, communistic equality and brotherly love. Pogodin is the Narodnik grown wise and sober. The voices that call him are the elemental voices of primitive humanity unfettered by codes and precepts. In the Volga forests, at the campfire, the youthful chief watches his merrymaking band, listens to their songs of abandon, to the frantic balalaikas, to their nonchalant remarks about violence committed and to be committed—and he feels himself in the grip of a powerful Russia, anarchic, nihilistic, destructive, avenging itself on those who are good and beautiful and wise. Like the terrorist in *Darkness*, Pogodin is ashamed of being good, and he, too, has plunged into darkness.

What renders the darkness still blacker and gloomier is the inevitable profanation of Pogodin's ideal. He left his clean environment in obedience to the powerful urge that emanated from the mysterious voices of Mother Russia, and he set forth to lead the submerged masses in an amateurish campaign of revenge against those to whom he belonged by birth and bringing up. With fire and sword he has terrorized the land, burning and killing and expropriating those surcharged with earthly possessions and power, in favor of the dispossessed. But soon there appeared false Sashka Zhegulevs, ordinary brigands, who engaged in rank robbery, making no discrimination in regard to the victim's status, and using the spoils for themselves. And when Pogodin-Zhegulev tried to uphold his own, higher standard, his band failed to appreciate the fine line of demarcation between regular brigandage and elemental popular revenge.

Broken in spirit and heart, he is finally betrayed to the police, and meets his death bravely, like Savitsky.

So on a day preordained by those who lived before him and had burdened with their sins the Russian land—there died a shameful and terrible death, one Sasha Pogodin, a noble and unfortunate youth.[34]

From the Russo-Japanese war, through the Red Sunday, the October revolution, the wholesale executions, the wave of organized and unorganized terror, through the whole gamut of the national drama that served as a prelude to the greater drama, to come a decade later, Andreyev watched and listened and meditated. His utterances were seldom hopeful or encouraging, more often skeptical and melancholy, yet the Russian public owes him a debt of gratitude for having kept his post at the watch tower, indefatigably ringing the bell of alarm, stirring the conscience and stimulating the thought of his countrymen. Moreover, Andreyev did not remain altogether objective and impartial. Despite reason and logic, and doubts notwithstanding, his heart was with those who struggled against the Wall. *From a Story Which Will Never be Finished,* written in 1909, is a most beautiful tribute to man's readiness for sacrifice in the name of a fine cause. Barricades are being constructed in the street in the dead of the night, and the blows of the hammers sound like music to the wife who sends her husband out to meet the wonderful adventure, and the little son wakes, and puts his warm little arms around his father's neck, gravely whispering his adieu into his ears. Lightly steps the husband and father into the night, a new being, oblivious of his everyday attachments and bonds, elevated above time and space, obedient to the ineffable impulse to gain immortality through giving oneself for an ideal. One cannot read this brief sketch without emotion and hopeful pride for the human race. As long as our race is versatile, variegated in tendencies, tastes, aspirations, points of view; as long as we are what we are—conflict is unavoidable. And as long as there is conflict, and

[34] *Ibid.,* p. 195.

as long as there are men willing to fall in conflict, the glorious story of human advance will, indeed, never be finished.

But the major note of this story sounds rather like a dissonance in the writings of Andreyev. The revolution, with its display of personal heroism and altruism, appeals to the author's feeling, and he pays homage to Russia's noble fighters in such of his works as *To the Stars, The Seven That Were Hanged, From a Story Which Will Never be Finished,* and allegorically perhaps even in his early sketch, *The Wall.* But in Andreyev the doubting intellect prevails against feeling, even when he rebels against "thought." "Thus it was; thus it will be" is his predominant attitude toward collective humanity, its activity and intelligence. Inner slavery is what he regards as the root of all our evils, religious, social, political, economic. This thesis is formulated in his play, *Tsar Hunger,* which may be considered the climactic summary of his social writings, in the same way as *The Life of Man* culminates his first period—of the individual and his problems.

Andreyev's *Tsar Hunger* (1907) is a personification of modern society, with emphasis on its economic interrelations. The very title suggests the author's notion as to the *primum mobile* of human actions, the insatiable Desire which serves simultaneously as the master of the needy and as the lackey of the opulent. [35] Hunger motivates the workmen's acquiescence as well as their rebellion. In the gigantic factory, to the deafening blows of the sledgehammers, workmen worship the almighty Machine, sing hymns and pray to it. The men have lost their individual personalities: some of them have become wheels, others screws, belts, joint-pins, hammers. Upon the entrance of their all-powerful, autocratic leader, Tsar Hunger, the slaves eagerly surround him and pour out their grievances. Andreyev presents three categories of workmen. The First Workman is of Herculean build, of overdeveloped muscles and oppressive physical strength, wearing on his huge trunk a tiny head

---

[35] THIRD WORKMAN: ". . . Here you are a tsar, but there you are a lackey about their tables. Here you wear a crown, but there you walk about with a napkin."—*Tsar Hunger,* First Scene. *Works—IX,* p. 30.

with dim eyes conveying servility and dullness. Old as the
earth, he has performed since time immemorial gigantic toil,
altering the appearance of the earth. But he cannot think, he
cannot comprehend the wherefore of his existence, he only
threatens to lift his enormous hammer and "crack the earth as
a hollow nut"—as a relief from his overwhelming strength and
stupidity. This category is a sphinx pregnant with unmensur-
able possibilities, whose nature may depend largely upon the
Œdipus that will try to read the riddle. The third group appears hopelessly dehumanized. Its representative, the Third
Workman, is "a vapid, blanched man, as if long, all his life, he
had been drenched in corroding solutions. His voice is also
colorless; and when he talks, it seems as if millions of wan,
colorless beings, almost shadows, were whispering." Between
this cog of a machine and the pin-headed muscular giant, Andreyev places the Second Workman, the dreamer, the idealist,
who visions beauty and love. Though young, he is already
wasted, and coughs. He resents the gloomy point of view of
his comrades, slaves of Hunger and the Machine, and he pities
the dullness of the First Workman. He is loth to follow Tsar
Hunger's call to revolt, he believes that there is another tsar,
a different moving power than the despair of want; but when
pressed to name this other tsar, he is unable to name him.
Who, indeed, can lead and direct and urge slaves, machine cogs,
more surely than hunger?

Andreyev's judgment of the working class may be too severe.
The three varieties he introduces are too sweeping generalizations. To be sure, one may find a happy combination of the
First and Second Workmen, of great physical power with noble
idealism. In the fall of 1905, the Russian workman presented
such a combination, and Andreyev paid him tribute in Treich,
of *To the Stars*. But while the latter play is realistic, *Tsar
Hunger* is symbolic, the kind of drama which permits the author
to deal in broad abstractions and in large generalities, overlook-
ing exceptional particulars. In this work Andreyev sets out
with the purpose of showing the shallowness and meanness of
society as a whole, in all its ramifications. In his treatment the

working class does not fare worse than other classes. Up and down the conventional hierarchy of social strata we encounter nothing but negative traits. At the very bottom swarms the micrencephalous mob composed of the scum of modern life, "the most horrible that poverty, vice, crime and eternal insatiable hunger of the soul can create." At the meeting of these creatures the chairman calls to order the "Misses harlots and carrion, and Messrs. hooligans, pickpockets, cutthroats, and pimps," and opens the discussion as to the methods of universal destruction, the motive for this being revenge for the state in which the assembled find themselves. Suggestions are made to poison the aqueducts, to release the wild beasts in the zoölogical gardens, to infect society with the diseases of the mob, to burn all books, which they hate. But their Father, Tsar Hunger, helps them to realize their sinister power in the very fact of their existence.

TSAR HUNGER: "Who is then powerful, if not you, beloved children of Hunger? . . . Even now . . . are you not the darkness which quenches their lights? Do you not, in expiring, effuse the venom that poisons them? You are the soil of the city, you are the groundwork of their life, you are the sticky carpet to which their feet adhere. Great darkness emanates from you, my children, and their miserable lights hopelessly quiver in the gloom." [36]

With glee the mob hears the tsar's announcement of the coming revolt and his invitation for them "to sneak among the people softly, like black shadows—and ravish, slay, steal and laugh, jeer!" This flotsam and jetsam, this indictment of society, always participates in public upheavals, clings to mass movements, exploits social calamities and festivities, "catches fish in muddy water." Revolutions, however great of purpose and lofty of intention, are seldom spared the profanation inflicted on them by the filthy touch of hooliganism. The unenviable reputation of the Bolsheviki, to cite an instance, is due in part to the fact that their leaders unleashed, for a time at least, the passions of the mob, in consequence of which numerous crimes perpe-

[36] *Ibid.*, pp. 56, 57.

trated by professional malefactors have been laid at the door
of those responsible for the revolution of November, 1917.

Nor does Andreyev flatter the classes in power. He has no
faith either in the proletariat or in the bourgeoisie. Democracy (*Thus It Was*) inspires him with as little respect as plutoc-
racy. The latter state is so virulently drawn in *Tsar Hunger*
as to leave no doubt as to the author's deep aversion and contempt for the triumphant money classes. The masters of the
revolting slaves buy with their money every institution, every
product of the human mind that may help them to maintain
slavery. We witness in the drama the prostitution of justice,
the subjugation of the church, the monopolization of art productions, the domination over science—by and for the moneyed
class. At the moment of the revolt the masters involuntarily
reveal their real selves, and pressed by fear for their safety
and even life, they display base cowardice, vulgarity, absurd
selfishness, utter disregard for those moral and æsthetic values
which they so boastfully claim to uphold in normal times. They
abuse the priest, whose God appears bankrupt, and who has
failed to befog the minds of the slaves into pious obedience and
submission. With indignation they jeer at the artists who be-
wail the destruction of works of art in the museum set afire
during the battle (not by the mob, to mark in passing, but by
the cannon of the masters). And disdainfully they turn their
backs upon the Professor who appears half-demented from
grief at the sight of the books being destroyed by the infuriated
mob. They discard all their alleged virtues, sentiments, and
devotions, at this moment of frankness, when they shout vocifer-
ously: " 'Tis we, we, we, who may perish . . . Do you understand? We, we, we," implying that nothing else matters.
Their mortal fear is allayed only at the appearance of the Engineer, who represents science, one of the handmaids of the
masters. The Engineer reports the successful end of the revolt owing to the latest product of science, an improved type of
cannon, which has performed excellent service mowing down its
producers, the rebels.

Does Andreyev find a single hopeful element in modern society? Hardly. The artists and the Professor, it is true, appear in the end as the only persons who care for higher interests, and not merely the safety of their physical selves. But even these are in the grip and at the mercy of the bourgeoisie in time of peace and "normalcy." From time to time there appears in the drama the Girl-in-Black, who evidently represents the Intelligentsia, those who are endeavoring to rise above class selfishness and greed. Her attempts are pathetic in their futility. She is aware of the violence and injustice practiced by her class—the possessors—over the dispossessed, and is trying to make amends by expressing her sympathy with the latter, even her readiness to share their fate. But she recoils from the low-browed youth who frankly admits that he would ravish and kill her if he had a chance. And she is infuriated when her proffered hand is refused with hatred by the young woman whom circumstances have compelled to drown her own child. The Girl-in-Black finds it impossible to merge with, or even to be trusted by, the lower strata. At least she rises above the rest in the rebellion scene, indignant at the egotistic cowardice of the bourgeoisie. Abandoned as a madwoman, she asks for music, she is determined at least to die beautifully! The tragedy of the Girl-in-Black is in a large measure the tragedy of the Russian Intelligentsia, the gruesomeness of which has been displayed most strikingly since the revolution of 1917.

Andreyev's attitude toward collective humanity is a logical consequence of his attitude toward individual man; it is as consistent as that of his admired philosopher, Schopenhauer (and, indeed, of Nietzsche). Once we accept the view that man is a slave of his blind, despotic will, we are bound to arrive at the conclusion that the will of the state or of society presents individual will multiplied. Man's institutions are instruments of the will, designed for the furtherance of its unlimited power and absolute authority. Since man is by nature brutal and selfish,[37] his government and public institutions present organ-

[37] "Der Egoismus ist eine so tief wurzelnde Eigenschaft aller Individualität überhaupt, dass, um die Tätigkeit eines individuellen Wesens zu erregen, egoist-

ized selfishness and pettiness, for the purpose of preserving injustice and violence, and of maintaining might at the expense of right.[38] Clashes between one organized violence and another —that is between states—naturally result in wars, since life presents *bellum omnium contra omnes*.[39] Within the state, violence is organized in the form of social and economic inequality, the exploitation of the toil and sweat of the slaves by their masters, for the production of variegated and multiple commodities designed to quench (temporarily) man's bottomless Will, grown complex and jaded, by those who are afforded a minimum of these products. This economic slavery exists in every state, whether an oriental despotism or a democratic republic.[40]

ische Zwecke die einzigen sind, auf welche man mit Sicherheit rechnen kann."— *Die Welt*, etc., II, Chapter 44, p. 556 (*Werke—II*). Or this satanic sentence: "Mancher Mensch wäre imstande, einen andern totzuschlagen, bloss um mit dessen Fette sich die Stiefel zu schmieren."—*Grundlage der Moral*, No. 14, p. 346 (*Werke —III*).

[38] "Der Staat ist . . . so wening gegen den Egoismus überhaupt und als solchen gerichtet, dass er umgekehrt gerade aus dem sich wohlverstehenden, methodisch verfahrenden, vom einseitigen auf den allgemeinen Standpunkt tretenden und so durch Aufsummirung gemeinschaftlichen Egoismus aller entsprungen und diesem zu dienen allein da ist, errichtet unter der richtigen Voraussetzung, dass reine Moralität, d. h. Rechthandeln aus moralischen Gründen, nicht zu erwarten ist; ausserdem er selbst ja überflüssing wäre. Keineswegs also gegen den Egoismus, sondern allein gegen die nachteiligen Folgen des Egoismus, welche aus der Vielheit egoistischer Individuen ihnen allen wechselseitig hervorgehen und ihr Wohlsein stören, ist, dieses Wohlsein bezweckend, der Staat gerichtet."—*Die Welt, etc.— I*, No. 62, p. 390 (*Werke—I*).

[39] "Diese Raubtiere des menschlichen Geschlechts sind die erobernden Völker, welche wir, von den ältesten Zeiten bis auf die neuesten, überall auftreten sehn, mit wechselndem Glück . . . daher eben Votaire Recht hat zu sagen: Dans toutes les guerres il ne s'agit que de voler. Dass sie sich der Sache schämen, geht daraus hervor, dass jede Regierung laut beteuert, nie anders, als zur Selbstverteidigung, die Waffen engreifen zu wollen."—*Paregra und Paralipomena*, No. 124, p. 222 (*Werke—IV*).

[40] "Zwischen Leibeigenschaft, wie in Russland, und Grundbesitz, wie in England, und überhaupt zwischen dem Leibeignen und dem Pächter, Einsassen, Hypotheken-schuldner und dgl. m., liegt der Unterschied mehr in der Form, als in der Sache." —*Ibid.*, No. 125, p. 222.

"Armuth und Sklaverei sind also nur zwei Formen, fast möchte man sagen zwei Namen, derselben Sache, deren Wesen darin besteht, dass die Kräfte eines Menschen grossenteils nicht für ihn selbst, sondern für andere verwendet werden; woraus für ihn teils Ueberladung mit Arbeit, teils kärgliche Befriedigung seiner Bedürfnisse hervorgeht. . . . So . . . entspringt also jenes Uebel, welches, entweder unter dem Namen der Sklaverei, oder unter dem des Proletariats, jederzeit auf der grossen Mehrzahl des Menschengeschlechts gelastet hat. Die entfern-

Thus far Andreyev's views coincide with those of Schopenhauer. Nietzsche's solidarity with Schopenhauer in regard to the state is well known. To him the state is the "coldest of all cold monsters," [41] "organized immortality," [42] born of violence.[43] Andreyev, as we have said before, fuses the negative views of the two philosophers, and since he professes to be much nearer to Schopenhauer, we need not, at this juncture, discuss Nietzsche's views. What should be noted here is that Andreyev fails to follow either of them in their final evaluation of the state from the aspect of expediency. He never utters a word of justification for the existence of this "monster," whereas both Schopenhauer and Nietzsche consider the state as a necessary evil. Because of the inherent egotism of human beings, it is for their own good that the authority of the state should regulate their interrelations and keep them from mutual destruction. Schopenhauer refuses to grant the state a positive moral value,[44] but he justifies its existence as a "Schutzanstalt," [45] as a protection against aggression from without, and individual violence from within. Nietzsche also credits the state with exercising a salutary control of human passions, with substituting justice for revenge, and he even bestows on the state the privilege of super-moral actions.[46]

tere Ursache desselben aber ist der Luxus. Damit nämlich einige wenige das Entbehrliche, Ueberflüssige und Raffinierte haben, ja, erkünstelte Bedürfnisse befriedigen können, muss auf dergleichen ein grosses Mass der vorhandenen Menschenkräfte verwendet und daher dem Notwendigen, der Herforbringung des Unentbehrlichen, entzogen werden."—*Ibid.*, pp. 223, 224.

[41] "Staat heisst das kälteste aller kalten Ungeheuer."—*Also sprach Zarathustra:* "Von neuen Götzen," p. 69.

[42] *Wille zur Macht*, No. 717 (*Werke—X*, p. 2).

[43] *Zur Genealogie der Moral—II*, No. 17 (v. VIII, pp. 381, 382).—Also, *Wille zur Macht*, No. 755 (v. X, pp. 23, 24).

[44] "Der Staat und das Reich Gottes oder Moralgesetz sind so heterogen, dass ersterer eine *Parodie* des letzteren ist, ein bitteres Lachen über dessen Abwesenheit, eine Krücke statt eines Beines, ein Automat statt eines Menschen."—*Neue Paralipomena*, p. 142, § 212, v. IV of *Handschriftlecher Nachlass* (Reclam, Leipzig).

". . . Hieraus folgt, dass die Notwendigkeit des Staats, im letzten Grunde, auf der anerkannten *Ungerechtigkeit* des Menschengeschlechts beruht: ohne diese würde an keinen Staat gedacht werden. . . ."—*Paregra, etc.—II*, No. 123, p. 220 (*Werke—IV*).

[45] *Die Welt, etc.—II*, Chapter 47, pp. 614 ff. (*Werke—II*).

[46] *Zur Genealogie der Moral—II*, No. 11 (*Werke—VIII*, pp. 364, 365); *Wille zur Macht*, No. 734 (v. X, pp. 11, 12).

Similarly, in his indignation against governmental oppression, violence and executions, Andreyev parts company with both philosophers. For it follows from their utilitarian conception of the state, that its preservation warrants coercive measures and Machiavellian methods.[47] The author of *The Seven That Were Hanged* digresses from Schopenhauer, who definitely approves of capital punishment as a means for the security of the state.[48] The state cannot afford to tolerate attempts at the subversion of its established forms and interrelations, hence it is justified in punishing individual transgressions and in suppressing mass uprisings. Andreyev's Governor has merely performed his duty, in ordering the slaughter of the rebellious workmen. The bourgeoisie in *Tsar Hunger* are within their rights when they employ cannon against the slaves in revolt. The state is in danger when such occurrences take place as the one described in *Thus It Was*. Between despotism and anarchy Schopenhauer chooses the first.[49] Moreover, he prefers monarchy to any other form of government, because he regards human beings as similar to beasts and insects, in that they need a single leader.[50]

Andreyev is frequently torn between his reason and his feel-

[47] "Das Recht an sich selbst ist machtlos: von Natur herrscht die *Gewalt* . . . Unmittelbar kann immer nur die physische Gewalt wirken; da vor ihr allein die Menschen, wie sie in der Regel sind, Empfänglichkeit und Respekt haben. . . . Also allein die physische Gewalt vermag sich Respekt zu verschaffen."—*Paregra—II*, No. 127, pp. 228, 229 (v. IV). On Machiavelli—*ibid.*, end of No. 126, p. 228. Nietzsche's "organizierte Unmoralität," *Wille zur Macht.* No. 717 (v. X, p. 2).

[48] "Der dem Gesetze zufolge der Todesstrafe anheimgefallene Mörder muss jetzt allerdings und mit vollem Recht als blosses *Mittel* gebraucht werden. Denn die öffentliche Sicherheit, der Hauptzweck des Staates, ist durch ihn gestört, ja sie ist aufgehoben, wenn das Gesetz unerfüllt bleibt: er, sein Leben, seine Person, muss jetzt das *Mittel* zur Erfüllung des Gesetzes und dadurch zur Wiederherstellung der öffentlicher Sicherheit sein, und wird zu solchem genmacht mit allem Recht, zur Vollziehung des Staatsvertrages . . ."—*Die Welt*, etc., I, No. 62, p. 394 (*Werke—I*).

Nietzsche emphasizes the point that a state, like an organism, must "excrete" (exkretiren) criminals and anarchists. *Wille zur Macht*, No. 50 (*Werke—IX*, p. 43). Also Nos. 52, 81, 237, 238 (*ibid.*, pp. 44, 66, 182, 183, 184).

[49] *Neue Paralipomena*, p. 177.

[50] "Ueberhaupt aber ist die monarchische Regierungsform die dem Menschen natürliche; fast so, wie es den Bienen und Ameisen, den reisenden Kranichen, den wandernden Elefanten, den zu Raubzügen vereinigten Wölfen und andern Tieren mehr ist, welche alle *einen* an die Spitze ihrer Unternehmung stellen."—*Paregra*, etc.—*II*, No. 127, p. 233 (*Werke—IV*).

ing. His reason tells him of the stupidity and inner slavery of
the masses, and leads him to declare the futility of revolution
(in *Thus It Was*, for example), wherein he agrees with
Schopenhauer and Nietzsche.[51] Logically, he should proceed
to defend the state and its institutions, as indispensable for the
protection of the slaves from themselves and from outsiders.
But, inconsistently, Andreyev goes over on the side of emotion,
which dictates his unreserved hatred for the "cold monster"
and its various agencies, and warm admiration for the futile
fighters. Temperamentally Andreyev belongs to the rank and
file of humanity, however strongly his intellect prompts him to
align himself with the "few," the "higher men."

[51] "Die Revolution hat neue Hausnummern gemacht; das einzige von ihr, was zu
bleiben verdient."—Letter to Frauenstadt, September 26, 1851, *Schopenhauers
Briefe*, p. 179 (Reclam, Leipzig).

" 'Freiheit' brüllt ihr Alle am liebsten: aber ich verlernte den Glauben an
'Grosse Ereignisse,' sobald viel gebrüllt und Rauch um sie herum ist. Und glaube
mir nur, Freund Höllenlärm! Die grössten Ereignisse—das sind nicht unsre laut-
esten, sondern unsre stillsten Stunden."—*Also sprach Zarathustra:* "Von grossen
Ereignissen," p. 193.

Nietzsche's aversion to subversive movements grows out naturally from his contempt for democracy, socialism, the idea of equality. Cf. *Wille zur Macht*, Nos.
752, 753, 755 (*Werke—X*, pp. 23, 24).

IV

PROBLEMS OF REASON AND MORALITY

Apparent contradictions in Andreyev's outlook.—He exalts reason as a perpetual quest.—Rejects dogmatic, presumptuous reason.— "Man according to Schopenhauer"—Schopenhauer's Sufficient Reason.—Nietzsche's Small Reason.—Mystery of Self.—*The Black Maskers.*—Duke Lorenzo's castle.—Courage of self-analysis.—Reason versus faith.—Religion as an expedient.— Value of suffering: "King Herod."—Dogmatic reason: Judas and the Apostles.—Dogmatic common sense: *My Memoirs.*— The formula of the Iron Grate.—A caricature of Tolstoy?— Adaptability—a modern fetich.—Peace and war.—Restless intellect: Judas's "test."—Repetition of theme: *Anathema,* seeker of phenomenal knowledge.—Success of Anathema's "test." —Small Reason versus Great Reason.—Immortality.—Schopenhauer's liberating, transcendental knowledge.—Immortality through altruism: David, Musya, Werner.—"Heroic" life.— Andreyev's adherence to Schopenhauer's positive ideal implies his divergence from Nietzsche.—Nietzsche's "overcoming" of Schopenhauer.—Will-to-power, ruthless creative force.—Acceptance of life and pain.—Masters and Slaves.—Rejection of pity, altruism, equality.—Personalism.—*The Ocean.*—Haggart—superman, Mariet—humanity, Horre—brutal force.—Haggart's adaptability.—The rejection of Nietzsche's moral standard.—Andreyev's duality.—His quest of a synthesis.—Resemblance to Nietzsche.

ANDREYEV lacks unity of outlook. He is torn with discordant ideas and with discrepant sentiments. As a result his attitudes appear at times mutually contradictory, particularly with regard to intellect, thought. Explicitly, he disparages human thought, demonstrates its treachery, futility and impotence (as, for example, in *Thought, Anathema*). At the same time one is aware of his passion for searching, probing, never-resting

259

thought. In presenting the victims of thought, he adorns them, by implication, with the thorny crown of heroes. Defeat does not prove the wrongness of endeavor. As will be shown in the course of this discussion, the duality of Andreyev's attitude toward man's reasoning faculty is not altogether contradictory. He exalts reason in its function of uncompromising quest after ultimate goals and meanings. He rejects reason when it presumes to solve and settle problems dogmatically. The former attitude goads him on to question and doubt, to destroy and overturn, causing him and his readers heartbreaking disappointments and disillusions. Indeed, it is this attitude which brings him so near to Schopenhauer and Nietzsche. His contempt for mental peace and quiescence, his readiness for interminable battle with established conceptions, his willingness to forgo popularity, and to enjoy the unenviable reputation of a crank and *advocatus diaboli,* make him eligible to the rank of "Man according to Schopenhauer," in the expression of Nietzsche. This man, to use the words of Henri Lichtenberger, "insoucieux de sa propre souffrance, insoucieux aussi des souffrances qu'il cause autour de lui, soutenu dans sa marche douloureuse par l'inébranlable volonté d'être vrai et sincere a tout prix," [1] or, in Nietzsche's own words:

Der *Schopenhauerische Mensch nimmt das freiwillige Leiden der Wahrhaftigkeit auf sich,* und dieses Leiden dient ihm, seinen Eigenwillen zu ertödten und jene völlige Umwälzung und Umkehrung seines Wesens vorzubereiten, zu der zu führen der eigentliche Sinn des Lebens ist. Dieses Heraussagen des Wahren erscheint den andern Menschen als Ausfluss der Bosheit, denn sie halten die Conservirung ihrer Halbheiten und Flausen für eine Pflicht der Menschlichkeit und meinen, mann müsse böse sein, um ihnen also ihr Spielwerk zu zerstören. Sie sind versucht, einem Solchen zuzurufen, was Faust dem Mephistopheles sagt: "so setzest du der ewig regen, der heilsam schaffenden Gewalt die kalte Teufelsfaust entgegen"; und der, welcher Schopenhauerisch leben wollte, würde wahrscheinlich einem Mephistopheles ähnlicher sehen als einem Faust— für die schwachsichtigen modernen Augen nämlich, welche in Verneinen immer das Abzeichen des Bösen erblicken. Aber es giebt eine art zu

---

[1] *La Philosophie de Nietzsche,* p. 53.

verneinen und zu zerstören, welche gerade der Ausfluss jener mächtigen Sehnsucht nach Heiligung und Errettung ist, als deren erster philosophischer Lehrer Schopenhauer unter uns entheiligte und recht eigentlich verweltlichte Menschen trat. Alles Dasein, welches verneint werden kann, verdieent es auch verneint zu werden; und wahrhaftig sein heisst: an ein Dasein glauben, welches überhaupt nicht verneint werden könnte und welches selber wahr und ohne Lüge ist . . . Gewiss, er [der Schopenhauerische Mensch] vernichtet sein Erdenglück durch seine Tapferkeit, er muss selbst den Menschen, die er liebt, den Institutionen auss deren Schosse er hervorgegangen ist, feindlich sein, er darf weder Menschen noch Dinge schonen, ob er gleich an ihrer Verletzung mitleidet, er wird verkannt werden und lange als Bundesgenosse von Mächten gelten, die er verabscheut, er wird, bei dem Menschlichen Maasse seiner Einsicht ungerecht sein müssen, bei allem Streben nach Gerechtigkeit. . . .[2]

One can hardly doubt Andreyev's predilection for this type of thinking and feeling. He, indeed, filled the office of a Mephisto in the eyes of society, with his incessant efforts to smash its "toys." Nietzsche's words to the effect that whatever can be denied deserves to be denied, coincide with the opinion of another thinker whose influence Andreyev acknowledges, namely, Pisarev, who preached the desirability of smashing right and left, without fear of destroying something worth saving, since only those things that will survive the smash-up will thereby prove their right to exist. Furthermore, Andreyev fits Nietzsche's definition of the Schopenhauerian man, in that his denial and destruction also emanated from a "powerful aspiration for holiness and deliverance," the motive which impels him to "take upon himself voluntarily the pain of telling the truth," to be "an enemy to the men he loves and to the institutions in which he grew up," "to spare neither person nor thing."

Andreyev's negative attitude to presumptuous reason, omniscient and dogmatic, harmonizes in the main with the views of Schopenhauer and Nietzsche. Both of these philosophers scoff at the pretensions of our intellect to independence and power. Schopenhauer limits our knowledge to the world of appearances, and even then it is incomplete. "Sufficient Reason" is

---

[2] *Unzeitgemässe Betrachtungen—III:* "Schopenhauer als Erzieher," pp. 251–253 (*Werke—II*).

governed by the all-powerful Will, is its tool and toy, and is bound to be defeated when it attempts to understand and interpret the unknowable, the Thing-in-itself, that which is beyond mere appearances.[3] Nietzsche calls our intellect "Small Reason," a plaything of the "Great," mysterious Reason, which is our Self—our body, our feelings, and our thoughts combined.[4] The mystery of our Self, our ignorance of its elements and motives, and the demonstration of the resulting poverty of our knowledge, are illustrated in several of Andreyev's works, notably in *The Abyss, Thought, The Black Maskers*. The first two stories have been mentioned before (pp. 200–204). In *The Abyss*, the student Nemovetsky, pure and idealistic in the eyes of the world, as well as in his own opinion, is hurled into an abyss by his brutal instinct, whose dormant existence he has not suspected. This was Andreyev's first attempt at probing man beneath mere appearance, and it was followed by the subtler study of the unknown and unknowable Self, in *Thought*.

[3] "Nun aber ist der *Wille* allein das Beharrende und Unveränderliche im Bewusstsein. Er ist es, welcher alle Gedanken und Vorstellungen, als Mittel zu seinen Zwecken, zusammenhält, sie mit der Farbe seines Charakters, seiner Stimmung und seines Interesses tingiert, die Aufmerksamkeit beherrscht und den Faden der Motive, deren Einfluss auch Gedächtniss und Ideenassoziation zuletzt in Tätigkeit setzt, in der Hand hält: von ihm ist im Grunde die Rede, so oft 'Ich' in einem Urteil vorkommt. Er also ist der wahre, letzte Einheitspunkt des Bewusstseins und das Band aller Funktionen und Akte desselben: er gehört aber nicht selbst zum Intellekt, sondern ist nur dessen Wurzel, Ursprung und Beherrscher."—*Von den wesentlichen Unvolkommenheiten des Intellekts*, in *Die Welt*, etc., II, p. 145 (*Werke—II*), and practically the entire Chapter 15. Professor Höffding regards Schopenhauer's philosophy as "a systematized doctrine of the limitation and impotence of reason."—*History of Modern Philosophy—II*, p. 215. New York, 1915.

[4] "Der Leib ist eine grosse Vernunft, eine Vielheit mit einem Sinne, ein Krieg und ein Frieden, eine Herde und ein Hirt. Werkzeug deines Leibes ist auch deine kleine Vernunft, mein Bruder, die du 'Geist' nennst, ein kleines Werk—und Spielzeug deiner grossen Vernunft. 'Ich' sagst du und bist stolz auf dies Wort. Aber das Grössere ist—woran du nicht glauben willst—dein Leib und seine grosse Vernunft: die sagt nicht Ich, aber tut Ich . . . Werk—und Spielzeuge sind Sinn und Geist: hinter ihnen liegt noch das Selbst . . . Hinter deinen Gedanken und Gefühlen, mein Bruder, steht ein mächtiger Gebieter, ein unbekannter Weiser—der heisst Selbst . . . Dein Selbst lacht uber dein Ich und seine stolze Sprünge. "Was sind mir diese Sprünge und Flüge des Gedankens? sagt es sich. Ein Umweg zu meinem Zwecke. Ich bin der Sängelband des Ichs und der Einbläser seiner Begrieffe!"—*Also sprach Zarathustra:* "Von der Verächtern des Leibes," pp. 46-47 (*Werke—VII*).

In the drama of Kerzhentsev we see a proud, masterful, seemingly self-sufficient and independent intellect come to grief through its betrayal by one unaccountable thought, which has nestled in his brain and destroyed his lordly "castle." This one thought could not be controlled by the Doctor's brilliant intellect, it came from the obscure regions of the Self, and brought mockery and ruin upon the "Small Reason," the "Sufficient Knowledge." The theme evidently pursued Andreyev. Eleven years after the publication of *Thought* (1902) he dramatized it, under the same title and without essential changes, and had it produced at the Moscow Art Theatre (season of 1913–1914). Between these two moments he wrote (in 1908), and presented on the stage, one of his most baffling plays, *The Black Maskers*.

The symbols of this play, beyond the understanding of the average theatrical audience, are quite comprehensible in the light of the ideas we are now discussing. Duke Lorenzo di Spadaro, a knight of the Holy Grail, graceful, generous, poetic, beloved, gives a ball in his castle which he orders illuminated in the brightest manner possible, that his guests may see their way in the night. Generous and hospitable, amiable and charitable, the Duke expects nothing but joy and pleasure. For is he not worthy of happiness, his conscience clear, his thoughts lofty and beautiful, his desires modest and proper, his heart true and sound, his devotion to his people integral, his love for his wife, Francesca, boundless and irreproachable? To his chagrin the guests appear wearing hideous, repulsive masks representing monstrous thoughts and brutal passions, crime and pettiness, falsehood and treachery. The Duke does not recognize his strange visitors, but they declare themselves to be none other than his thoughts, his desires, his heart, his mind, his unuttered sentiments. His horror and bewilderment become climactic when he perceives in the throng a mask of himself, his *alter ego*. He challenges the impostor and kills him, but the wound is visible on his own breast. The ball ends in confusion, since beside the invited guests who have appeared in allegorical masks, the castle is gradually filled with black creatures, children of the night, who are lured by the light and the fires, and who quench all light with their bodies. Duke Lorenzo discovers many new things. His soul—his castle—illuminated with the powerful light of analysis and experience, he becomes cognizant of numerous unsuspected brutes and imps slumbering within his Self, and also of the nameless, shapeless passions and impulses which emerge out of the darkness at the call of the light. He also discovers that the very nobility of his birth is dubious, as he learns of the illicit relations between his mother and their stable groom. At the coffin of his double he overhears the peasants relating his own misdeeds, his maltreatment of rustic maidens, the ruin brought on their sons and fields by his crusading campaigns. He even fails to recognize Francesca, for he is approached by several maskers closely resembling the woman whom he has considered unique, unrivaled, unmistakably his.

Bewildering in its multiplicity appears the Great Reason with the strong light turned on it. Indeed, it requires reckless courage to project such a merciless light on one's castle, for the very existence of the castle is then jeopardized. The tragedy of the magnificent Duke is the tragedy of Andreyev, of Nietzsche,[5] of any bold spirit fond of perilous brinks and indifferent to possible consequences. Such as these spurn the common-sense maxim formulated by Pushkin: "Dearer to us than bitter truths is deception which exalts our self." They do not wince before danger, nor do they blink their eyes in face of the dazzling light, but greet it as a savior from debasing complacency. Duke Lorenzo, rather than bear in his heart snakes and monsters, rather than suffer the coëxistence in him of masks and doubles, purges himself in the all-powerful fire which consumes his castle, that while perishing in the blaze he may exclaim: "But I assure you, Signor:

[5] I have it on the authority of Mme. Andreyev that in creating Duke Lorenzo her husband had in mind the tragic personality of Nietzsche. On the other hand, Andreyev's diary contains material hinting with indubitable transparency at the author's personal experiences, revelations and discoveries during the eventful year of 1908, which he reflected in the drama of Lorenzo.

Lorenzo, the Duke of Spadara, has no snakes in his heart."[6]
With all his disbelief in the effectuality of Small Reason, of
autonomous intellect, Andreyev is drawn time and again to
present it rather sympathetically, hereby confirming his duality.
Even in *Thought* we feel that the author himself is lured to
the dizzy heights where Dr. Kerzhentsev is performing his
mental acrobatics. In *The Life of Vasily Fiveysky* reason battles with faith, and proves victorious. Here Andreyev shows
the incompatibility of the two elements in a sincere person.
Like Schopenhauer, he thinks that knowledge and belief cannot
harmoniously coëxist in one mind, the former being sure to devour the latter.[7] As long as reason is silent in Vasily, he
stoutly believes together with his flock. Mankind is in need of
some formulation of universal truth and justice and power, of
some symbol of supreme authority guiding them, responsible
for their destiny, atoning for and justifying their sufferings and
death. Such a formulation the masses find in popular religion,
which requires implicit faith untouched by the worm of reason.[8]

[6] Did Andreyev have in mind the self-burning of Nietzsche in his own flame?
One recalls Nietzsche's glowing lines:

Ecce homo—
Ja! Ich weiss, woher ich stamme!
Ungesättigt gleich der Flamme
Glühe und verzehr' ich mich.
Licht wird alles, was ich fasse,
Kohle alles, was ich lasse:
Flamme bin ich sicherlich!
—*Die Fröhliche Wissenschaft*, p. 56 (*Werke—VI*).

The symbolic pregnancy of *The Black Maskers* is shown by the breadth of the
play's applicability. Thus we find that shortly before his death, when his creative
urge gave place to rumination upon his former works, Andreyev discussed the resemblance of Lorenzo's tragedy to the tragedy of Russia under the Bolsheviki *supra*,
p. 174. See also *supra*, p. 109–110, for Andreyev's "explanation" of the *Black Maskers*.

[7] "Glauben und Wissen vertragen sich nicht wohl im selben Kopfe: sie sind
darin wie Wolf und Schaf in *einem* Käfig; und zwar ist das Wissen der Wolf,
der den Nachbar aufzufressen droht."—*Paregra, etc.:* "Ueber Religion," pp. 360,
361 (*Werke—IV*).

[8] Cf. Schopenhauer: "Die Religion ist das einzige Mittel, dem rohen Sinn und
ungelenken Verstande der in niedriges Treiben und materielle Arbeit tief ein-
gesenken Menge die hohe Bedeutung des Lebens anzukündigen und fühlbar zu machen . . . Die Religion ist die Metaphysik des Volks . . . Wie es eine Volkspoesie
gibt und, in den Sprichwörtern, eine Volksweisheit; so muss es auch eine Volks-
metaphysik geben; denn die Menschen bedürfen schlechterdings einer *Auslegung
des Lebens,* und sie muss ihrer Fassungskraft angemessen sein. Daher ist sie
allemal eine allegorische Einkleidung der Wahrheit, und sie leistet in praktischer
und gemüthicher Hinsicht, d. h. als Rischtschnur für das Handeln und als Beruhi-

But as soon as experience jolts Vasily out of the slough of contentment, and he begins to question and to evaluate and probe, desperately endeavoring to prove to himself the justness and wisdom of our world of tears and pain, his equilibrium is destroyed, and he perishes. Vasily cannot endure the dazzling light of reason which kills faith, destroys comfort and generates doubt and despair. But the majority of men escape this tragedy, through spurning reason. The instinct of self-preservation urges them to close their eyes to logic, and to seek refuge under the wing of authority. The masses fear responsibility more than anything else, and they eagerly entrust it to some other power, be it king or god. In *Thus It Was* we see the people terrified by the newly acquired freedom, and they appear like helpless sheep bereft of their shepherd. Savva, endeavoring to open the eyes of the blind believers to the fraud practised on them by the monks, is stoned to death. They reject Savva's terrible gift—cold reason, and choose the warm comfort of faith in miracles and supreme authority.

Vasily fails to see any reason in human suffering, when this is not regarded as a punishment by a just God for some sin. But to Andreyev, as to Schopenhauer,[9] suffering is the essence

gung und Trost im Leiden und im Tode, vielleicht ebensoviel, wie die Wahrheit, wenn wir sie besässen, selbst leisten könnte." *Ibid.*, pp. 296–297. Nietzsche agrees with Schopenhauer in crediting religion with serving as a disciplinary medium for mankind, keeping them content with their condition, giving them "vielfachen Frieden des Herzens, eine Veredlung des Gehorsams, ein Glück und Leid mehr mit Ihres-Gleichen und etwas von Verklärung und Verschönerung, etwas von Rechtfertigung des ganzen Alltags, der ganzen Niedrigkeit, der ganzen Halbtier—Armut ihrer Seele."—*Jenseits von Gut und Böse*, No. 61, pp. 85–87 (*Werke—VIII*). Also *Wille zur Macht*—II, No. 135, pp. 108, 109 (*Werke—IX*).

[9] "Jedoch, wie unser Leib auseinanderplatzen müsste, wenn der Druck der Atmosphäre von ihm genommen wäre;—so würde, wenn der Druck der Not, Mühseligkeit, Widerwärtigkeit und Vereitelung der Bestrebungen vom Leben der Menschen weggenomen wäre, ihr Uebermuth sich steigern, wenn auch nicht bis zum Platzen, doch bis zu den Erscheinungen der zügellosesten Narrheit, ja, Raserei.—Sogar bedarf jeder allezeit eines gewissen Quantums Sorge, oder Schmerz, oder Not, wie das Schiff des Ballasts, um fest und gerade zu gehn.

Arbeit, Plage, Mühe und *Not* ist allerdings, ihr ganzes Leben hindurch, das Los fast aller Menschen. Aber, wenn alle Wünsche, kaum entstanden, auch schon erfüllt wären; womit sollte dann das menschliche Leben ausgefüllt, womit die Zeit zugebracht werden? Man versetze dies Geschlecht in ein *Schlaraffenland*, wo alles von selbst wüchse und die Tauben gebraten herumflögen, auch jeder seine Heissgeliebte alsbald fänds, und ohne Schwierigkeit erhielte.—Da werden

and sense of life. With the greater number of Russian writers, he regards suffering as an ennobling factor, as a redemption from sordidness, and in this he approaches Nietzsche more closely than he does Schopenhauer, whose remarks on the subject are somewhat sneering. Nietzsche, who knew keen suffering, physical as well as mental, from personal experience, considered the discipline of suffering responsible for "all the elevations of humanity."[10] Andreyev puts Savva, the rational Nihilist, face to face with Yeremy, a wretched pilgrim nicknamed "King Herod" for having accidentally killed his own child. Eaten by remorse, the father burns his guilty hand, puts heavy chains on his body, and becomes a perpetual wanderer from monastery to monastery, fasting, tormenting himself, not for a moment forgetting his sorrow. So enormous does his woe appear to him that the whole world shrinks in his eyes to a "poppy seed," and cannot contain it. He does not belong to Nietzsche's "higher men," but is one of Andreyev's Averages—a peasant, a believer in Christ, in the Russian Christ humanized through His suffering. Far from inviting pity and sympathy, Yeremy takes great pride in possessing his precious burden, which has taught him the "truth," and which he would not exchange for "all the kingdoms of the earth," even if God Himself should offer them to him in exchange for his "sweet sorrow." Deprived of his woe, Yeremy would sink to the level of a normal peasant, while as its possessor he approaches the stage of which the aristocrat Nietzsche speaks, upon his temporary recovery from acute, prolonged pain: "Ich zweifle, ob ein solcher Schmerz 'verbessert'—; aber ich weiss, dass es uns vertieft." [11] Suffering makes one deeper—and richer. Nothing can buy Yeremy's treasure—surely not Savva's reason—and should his son be resurrected he would probably kill him once more, as one of his listeners remarks. Man needs, however irrationally, faith and suffering to fill his life and to lend it meaning.

die Menschen zum Teil von Langerweile sterben, oder sich aufhängen, zum Teil aber einander bekreigen, würgen und morden, und so sich mehr Leiden verursachen, als jetzt die Natur ihnen auflegt.—Also für ein solches Geschlecht passt kein anderer Schauplatz, kein anderes Dasein."—*Paregra, etc.,* No. 152, p. 268 (*Werke—IV*).

[10] *Jenseits von Gut und Böse,* No. 225, pp. 179-181 (*Werke—VIII*).

[11] *Die fröhliche Wissenschaft: Vorrede,* 3, pp. 34, 35 (*Werke—VI*).

Thus our reason, though it may wreck the faith of individual persons, proves helpless in face of mass faith, the instinctive, elemental medium for self-protection. But in describing the manifestations of blind faith as a weapon of self-defense in the hands of the masses shrinking before freedom and responsibility (the believers in *Life of Vasily Fiveysky,* the people in *Thus It Was,* the pilgrims in *Savva*), Andreyev is not so resentful as when he attacks beliefs that savor of the head, of the intellect, whether it be in religion or in philosophy or in social conduct. While pitying blind faith (recall the moving words of Lipa, anent the light of Golgotha for humanity, in *Savva*), he hates rationalizing faith, all attempts to base beliefs on logic, to explain everything through reason.

Andreyev has suggested, in *Darkness,* the absurdity to which one may arrive in the effort to base one's moral conduct on logical reasoning. The ascetic revolutionist, "convinced" by the harlot that he has no right to be good as long as there are bad persons like herself, determines to renounce his moral privileges and to join the children of darkness, whose father is Tsar Hunger. Whether the author has intended it or not, he leads one to detect an intrinsic fallacy in the reasoning of the revolutionist, namely, in his very determination to sacrifice his moral superiority in the name of absolute equality, he continues to be hopelessly good, hence a privileged aristocrat, ethically speaking. More outspoken is Andreyev in *Judas Iscariot and the Others.* Here he gives free vent to his contempt for dogmatic "oughts," for those persons whose life is simplified to a series of definite duties, whose conduct is dictated not by the heart but by the head, in the sense in which Schopenhauer uses these words. [12] It appears that the author even doubts the honesty

<hr>

[12] "Mit vollem Recht ist das *Herz,* dieses primum mobile des tierischen Lebens, zum Symbol, ja zum Synonym des *Willens,* als des Urkerns unserer Erscheinung, gewählt worden und bezeichnet diesen, im Gegensatz *des Intellekts,* der mit dem Kopf geradezu identisch ist. Alles, was im weitesten Sinne, Sache *des Willens* ist, wie Wunsch, Leidenschaft, Freude, Schmerz, Güte, Bosheit, auch was man unter 'Gemüth' zu verstehen pflegt, und was Homer durch φίλον ἦτορ ausdrückt, wird dem *Herzen* beigelegt . . . Hingegen bezeichnet der *Kopf* alles, was Sache der *Enkenntniss* ist . . . Herz und Kopt bezeichnen den ganzen Menschen. Aber der Kopf ist stets das Zweite, das Abgeleitete; denn er ist nicht das Zentrum,

of conviction in those who act according to dogmatic duty, suspecting that they use their fixed moral code as a screen for the concealment of their impulses and motives. Thus he makes us feel his dislike for John, the beloved disciple of Christ, mainly because he is so definitely certain of the infallibility of his ethical standard. It is about such as John that Andreyev has Judas say:

> They are called "good" who know how to hide their deeds and thoughts. But should you take hold of one of these worthies, embrace him, pet him, and draw him out, there will ooze from him, like pus from a boil that has been pricked, all sorts of evil, nastiness and falsehood.[13]

Judas exaggerates, with his customary malice. But one is inclined to agree that there can be no spontaneous truth in a life led not in accordance with one's instinctive preferences and choices, but rather on the basis of an established code, a double-entry bookkeeping system, where the good and the bad are designated and labeled in advance and once for all. In such a life one may expect contradictions between the "oughts" dictated by one's intellect and the "oughts" emanating from one's whole Self or Will, one may foresee collisions between the head and the heart. We have seen how the revolutionist, in *Darkness*, violates his Will—that is, the whole system of his inclinations, tastes, and desires—in favor of an alleged logical dogma. In *Judas Iscariot* the faithful disciples of Christ justify their nonresistance to the capture and execution of the Master, by their obedience to His command, by the predestination of the great sacrifice, by the fact that were they to perish in the unequal struggle with the Roman soldiers, there would be no one to preach the Gospel. Their argument sounds correct and reasonable. Yet more convincing by far appears the harangue of Judas, the traitor, when he calls on the disciples on the morrow of the crucifixion, and finds them sane and sound, quietly sorrowing, after having normally slept and eaten. He ques-

---

sondern die höchste Effloressenz des Leibes."—*Die Welt, etc.—II*, Chapter 19, p. 246 (*Werke—II*).
[13] *Works—VII*, p. 160.

tions their love for Christ, since those who love act spontaneously, before reasoning out the logicalness of their action. "If
your son were drowning, would you go into the city and inquire
of the passers-by: 'What must I do? My son is drowning!'
No, you would rather throw yourself into the water and drown
with him. One who loved would!" Unreserved love should
have prompted them to risk their bodies and souls, to fall upon
the Roman soldiers, to die in the hopeless battle, and even to
earn the torments of hell by disobeying the command of their
Master. "Why are you alive, when He is dead? Why do
your feet walk, why does your tongue talk trash, why do your
eyes blink, when He is dead, motionless, speechless? How do
your cheeks dare to be red, John, when His are pale? How
can you dare to shout, Peter, when He is silent?" [14]

Historically, one may object, the conduct of the Apostles has
proved to be beneficial for the spread of the Gospel. One may
further disparage Judas's vehemence, by observing that it takes
more courage to control one's passions, to check one's impulses,
to refrain from reflex action, than to be "just human." One
may praise the iron discipline of the "Others" in their setting
out upon the mission of practising, and not only preaching, the
doctrine of nonresistance to evil by evil. But Andreyev is not

[14] *Ibid.,* pp. 240, 242. There is a curious analogy between Judas's judgment of
the "good" and Andreyev's view of the Russian nonresisting "democrats," an
analogy retrospectively observed by the author himself.

When Judas negotiates with the high priest about the betrayal of Jesus, Annas
asks him whether the disciples may not raise a rebellion when their Master is
taken from them.

"Judas laughed long and maliciously: 'Who, they? Those cowardly dogs,
who run if a man but stoop to pick up a stone. They, indeed!'

" 'Are they really so bad? . . .'

" 'But surely it is not the bad who flee from the good; is it not rather the
good who flee from the bad? Ha! They are good, and therefore they will flee.
They are good, and therefore they will hide themselves. They are good, and
therefore they will appear only in time to bury Jesus. They will lay Him in the
tomb themselves; you need only execute Him.'

" 'But surely they love Him? You said so yourself.'

" 'Men always love their teacher, but better dead than alive. . . .' " (p. 193.)

On the margin of this page in his personal copy of *Judas,* Andreyev has inscribed in pencil: "The betrayal of October 26 [November 9], 1917." On this
date the Bolsheviki overthrew the provisional government, meeting with no serious
resistance, since Kerensky had been abandoned by all the "good" patriots. (See
supra, p. 151 f.

concerned here with the drama of the Golgotha *per se*. He
utilizes certain situations for the illustration of the dogmatic
fallacy, and he does not hesitate about deviating from the traditional version, and interpretation of, the story. He makes
the disciples appear beaten by Judas's argument, implying their
admission that the "ought" advocated by Judas corresponds
with their true Selves, with their Wills, rather than the dogmatic "ought" presented by John.

It is clear that Andreyev denies the Head the power to dom-
inate or even to explain life. Reason, a thing of the head, is
unable to coëxist with faith, and it is bound to devour it, as
Schopenhauer suggests, or to render it soulless, as Andreyev
makes it appear in the Apostles. Still less does he allow reason
the ability to reign supreme, "unalloyed." The tragedy of Dr.
Kerzhentsev, in *Thought*, consists in his betrayal by his reason,
which has failed even in explaining himself to himself. Savva,
who sets out with the apparently simple task of clearing the
minds of his fellow men by inoculating them with reason, is
crushed by the avalanche of unreasoning faith. Yet those who
perish because of their faith in reason acquire a redeeming feature in their martyrdom. Utterly obnoxious, on the other
hand, appear the "successful" ones, those who thrive on reason,
who succumb to it, and willingly become its slaves, as is the case
of the Prisoner, the author of *My Memoirs*. Here we see reason reach the lowest grade of corruption, of mental prostitution,
of adaptability. Andreyev presents in the writer of the
Memoirs the type he hates most, the dogmatist of common
sense, the justifier of life at any cost, the champion of the doctrine that all is well on earth and in heaven. In a language
unctious and oily, ingratiating yet full of conceit, the writer
creeps into your soul with his ambiguous confessions. Ambiguous, because their author serves logic, not truth. He cleverly
manipulates his logical deductions and seductions, until you are
bewildered and unable to tell whether or not the writer has
actually committed the crime for which he is imprisoned.

It so happened [he insinuates] that in the game of circumstances the truth concerning my actions, which I alone knew, had assumed all the features of an infamous and shameless lie. However strange it may seem to my indulgent and serious reader, not through truth but only through falsehood could I establish and affirm the truth of my innocence.[15]

Convicted as a parricide and fratricide, he begins to serve his life term in prison, gradually adapts himself to the régime, and turns into its apologist. The warden appreciates his loyalty, and enlists his coöperation in improving prison regulations, in making the life of the prisoners safe, sane and immune from escape. The writer modestly admits his authorship of the peephole in cell doors, the invention which has placed the prisoner under the incessant observation of his jailer. As he grows old, he becomes more and more enamored of his prison, and begins to preach his views to audiences especially invited by the warden. His doctrine is compressed in the Formula of the Iron Grate, which he discovers while observing the blue sky outlined through his cell window:

"Why is the sky so beautiful through these bars?" I reflected . . . "Is not this the effect of the æsthetic law of contrasts, according to which azure stands out prominently beside black? Or is it not, perhaps, a manifestation of some higher law, according to which the infinite may be conceived by the human mind only when it is brought within certain boundaries, for instance, when it is enclosed within a square?"

When I recalled that at the sight of a wide-open window, which was not protected by bars, or of the sky, I had usually experienced a desire to fly, which was painful because of its uselessness and absurdity—I suddenly began to experience a feeling of tenderness for the bars; tender gratitude, even love. . . .[16]

By way of sophistry, or plausible logic, the old man tries to convince his readers and hearers that a prison has a salutary effect on man's soul. Man is restless and vainly seeking. His sufferings and misfortunes arrive chiefly as a result of excessive

---

[15] *Works—VIII*, p. 116. In his article on the Jewish question, Andreyev again differentiates between truth and logic, no longer in the form of fiction. Cf., e. g., the sentence: "Of course, logic was on my side, but a certain dim *truth* stood behind him."—*The Shield (Shchit)*, p. 4. Moscow, 1916, 3rd edition.

[16] *Ibid*, pp. 133, 134.

freedom. His soul demands fetters. The Iron Grate is a "simple, sober, honest, mathematical formula" based on the solid foundations of "strictly logical reasoning," a scheme containing all universal laws "which do away with chaos, substituting in its place strict, iron, inviolable order." Let all sufferers and all those who are restless of spirit embrace the bars of the Iron Grate, and they will find peace for their souls and healing for their ailments. The preacher has an opportunity for proving the strength of his convictions, when upon being granted pardon for his loyal conduct, and released, he finds freedom too hazardous and disquieting an element. He has a strong cell constructed, where he incarcerates himself, and hires an experienced jailer to guard him day and night, to watch him through the peephole, and to prevent him from transgressing any of the strict regulations drawn up by himself after the model of his former happy abode.

That this moralist is a caricature of Tolstoy, as it has been assumed in Russia, is not too far-fetched a conjecture. There are some details in the *Memoirs* which carry one's thoughts to Yasnaya Polyana. The portrait of the patriarchal prisoner is one of these details. In the lower part of his face kindness, authoritativeness, and calm dignity are harmoniously blended. But the eyes have a "fixed immobile gaze; madness glimmering somewhere in their depth; the painful eloquence of a deep and infinitely lonely soul." Tolstoy's "Aye"-saying to the God-ruled world, his asceticism in later years, his advocacy of suppressing one's natural instincts—may have served Andreyev as the basic elements for the Iron Grate Formula. Again, Tolstoy's effort to rationalize faith invites comparison with the abuser of logic in *My Memoirs*. Tolstoy had no patience with mystics and with all those who place faith outside, or even above, reason. "Man," he wrote, "has been given directly from God only one instrument for knowing himself and his relation to the world—there is no other—and this instrument is reason . . . Without reason man cannot even believe . . . If the meaning of man's life does not appear clear to him, then this proves not that reason is unfit for clarifying this meaning, but only this, that too much of the irrational has been accepted on faith, and one should cast aside whatever is not confirmed by reason." [17]

The philosopher of adaptability describes in his *Memoirs* the confidence with which the warden has revealed to him all the details concerning the prison, its architecture, its rules and regulations. Translated, this means that the prison—our life—is not unknowable. The Warden—God—allows us to see, to understand everything. Reason is the basis of our faith and loyalty. But is absolutely everything open to the inspection of reason?

> To my request for a precise plan of the prison, the warden answered with a polite refusal.[18]

This break in the perfect harmony of reason and faith does not, however, provoke a rebellion in the warden's loyal prisoner. His sense of adaptability prompts him to retreat quietly whenever some wall blocks his facile logic.[19] For such as he "a wall has something soothing, calming, morally absolving and final," in the words of the arch-enemy of rationalism, Dostoyevsky.[20] Such rationalistic jugglers are concerned not about finding truth, at the probable risk of smashing their logical structure; rather are they in search of some sort of pliable truth that may be bent and molded and conveniently squeezed into ready frames and formulæ. Peace and "happiness" at any price, is the pottage of lentils for which these Realpolitiker in morals are ready to sell their birthright to free investigation and endless questioning. And do not such artful dodgers compose the bulk of our contemporary shepherds and priests of omnipotent Common Sense?

[17] From a letter, dated November 26, 1894, reproduced by I. Teneromo in his *Reminiscences about L. N. Tolstoy, and His Letters* (*Vospominaniya o L. N. Tolstom i yevo pisma*), pp. 146, 147, 149, 150 (Petrograd, ?).

[18] *Works—VIII*, p. 136.

[19] Tolstoy also had to admit the shortcomings of reason in explaining certain questions. He used the following metaphor: "Your reason is like an opera-glass: you may turn it up to a certain point, but thereafter things look wrong. So it is with questions about life, and its purposes. . . ."—Quoted in *History of Russian Literature in the 19th Century* (*Istoria russkoy literatury XIX veka*), v. V, pp. 380, 381. Moscow, 1910.

[20] *Notes from Underground—I: III*, p. 440. Berlin, 1922.

There is no gainsaying the peace that the Memorist's cell may bring to the weary and restless. The closer the cell, the less of life and movement penetrates this refuge—the greater the peace, the deeper the calm, the nearer is death. This bliss will hardly tempt a free, self-respecting person. The seeker, the one thirsty for knowledge, will prefer perpetual war to deadening peace, will greet life-intensifying storm rather than stifling calm, and will regard "the overhanging clouds of trouble as an udder from which he shall draw milk for his refreshment," in the expression of Nietzsche.[21] Disenchanted in his quest, finding the goal unattainable, the honest prober will admit his defeat, will perhaps bow his head before the impossibility of achieving absolute knowledge, but he will scorn patched-up compromises and sweetened nostrums of quack logicians. Rather will he hail suffering. "Suffering—but this is the sole cause of consciousness," cries Dostoyevsky,[22] in whose works only those who suffer lead an intense, self-justifying life. Suffering does not prevent the free man from striving forward. Even though he cannot break the wall of his cell, the man who is above the domesticated animal will go on smashing his head and bruising his breast against the iron grate, if only in protest, if only in order to proclaim through his suffering his refusal to acquiesce in commonplace contentment.

Andreyev does not believe in the ability of man to acquire absolute knowledge, either about himself or about life and the world outside of himself. Not one of his fervent seekers achieves his aim. Intellect is a tool and plaything of the will, of the self, and is bound to be defeated in its presumptuous

---

21 "So hast du noch nicht gelernt, dass kein Honig süsser als als der der Erkenntniss ist, und dass die hängenden Wolken der Trübsal dir noch zum Euter dienen müssen, aus dem du die Milch zu deiner Labung melken wirst."—*Menschliches Allzumenschliches—I*, No. 292, p. 267 (*Werke—III*).

It is in this sense that Nietzsche preaches "war" as against "peace," in his much-abused and misrepresented aphorisms, such as these: "Euren Feind sollt ihr suchen, euren Krieg sollt ihr führen. . . . Ihr sollt den Frieden lieben als Mittel zu neuen Kriegen. Und den kurzen Frieden mehr als den langen. . . . Ihr sagt, die gute Sache sei es, die sogar den Krieg heiligt? Ich sage euch: der gute Krieg ist es, der jede Sache heiligt."—*Also sprach Zarathustra:* "Vom Krieg und Kriegsvolke," p. 67 (*Werke—VII*).

22 *Notes from Underground—I: IX*, p. 467.

attempt to interpret the cause and source of all. But the attempt in itself, however futile, has an intense charm for Andreyev, who returns to this theme time and again. It is evident from the preceding discussion that intellect, reason, is obnoxious and hateful to Andreyev only when it pretends to have arrived at a definite solution of all questions, when it dictates precise Thou shalt's and Thou shalt not's. In other words, he is opposed to dogmatic reason. But the quest in itself is dear to his heart, and we recognize Andreyev himself in his passionate, often Quixotic, hunters after absolute knowledge and perfect understanding of the universe and its laws.

This restless intellect, incessantly questioning, ever searching and probing, is presented by Andreyev with particular force in his story, *Judas Iscariot and the Others,* and in his play, *Anathema.* As can be seen from the very title of the story, the author places Judas above the "Others." Indeed, he succeeds in convincing us that the traitor, who is ugly, who lies, steals, and betrays, is yet far higher and bigger intellectually than the twelve faithful disciples. In argument he easily gets the best of the lovable but limited Peter and the dogmatic, almost academic, John, let alone the simple Thomas who "looked so straight with his bright, transparent eyes, through which, as through a pane of Phœnician glass, was visible a wall behind, with a dismal ass tied to it." We have seen how Judas forces the Apostles to feel the superficiality of their dutifulness, when after the crucifixion he comes to deride and reproach them for their nonresistance policy during the perpetration of the greatest crime on earth. What raises Judas above the ordinary good or bad is the perpetual restlessness of his spirit, his faculty of merciless analysis, of seeing far and deep beyond appearances. There is a baffling duality about his thoughts and actions, even about his external features—the nape of his neck split by a sword cut, and one side of his face distorted by a blind, wide-open, never-blinking eye. Dual, too, appears his attitude toward Christ, who remains significantly silent throughout the story. Judas loves his Master with the love of an hysterical mother for her doomed child. Outside the guardhouse where

Jesus, betrayed by him, is being scourged and abused by the Roman soldiers, crouches Judas, the traitor, and suffers physical pain and mental anguish from each blow and insult administered to his victim. Yet he fears Him, is uneasy in His presence, and deliberately delivers Him into the hands of His enemies. Judas is, naturally, misunderstood, is lonely and wretched. He is consumed by a passion, an intellectual passion, for analyzing, dissecting, revealing and demonstrating truth—that is, what appears as mathematical truth to the "unalloyed" reason [23] of Judas. No defect, no flaw, no allusion, no veil, no falsehood, can escape his one, evil-looking, evil-seeing eye. He is the skeptic incarnate. He doubts everything and everybody. The disciples arouse in him contempt and annoyance, the masses of humanity do not deserve the love and redemption bestowed on them by Jesus. One is led to believe—in Andreyev's later works one cannot get along without hypothetic conjectures— that Judas sets out on a mad adventure to prove the justness of his skepticism. He will test the priests, the enemies of Him who is transvaluing their old values. Do they appreciate the significance of their adversary? He will test the intelligence and the sense of the populace. Will they or will they not revolt against the betrayal and crucifixion of their greatest treasure, their Savior? He will test the devotion and love of the disciples. Will they endure the loss of their Master, who has talked with them, and has shared their bread and lodging, and has cast pearls before them? He will test God, heaven, the sun, the earth. Will they allow the mad catastrophe to take place? In carrying out his grotesque analysis, Judas often seems to hope against hope that he may be proved wrong. To the very last minute of the Golgotha tragedy he craves for a miracle, for a

[23] This expression is used here in the sense of Dostoyevsky and Nietzsche, who allow for a small admixture of reason in all things. Dostoyevsky asserts that man must "alloy all positive rationality with the pernicious element of the fantastic. Precisely his fantastic dreams, his most trivial folly, will he wish to retain, solely in order to assert for himself that men are still men, and not keys in a keyboard . . ." *Notes from Underground—I: VIII*, p. 462. Zarathustra, on the other hand, permits "ein *wenig* Vernunft zwar, ein Same der Weisheit zerstreut von Stern zu Stern,—dieser Sauerteig ist allen Dingen eingemischt: um der Narrheit willen ist Weisheit allen Dingen eingemischt!"—*Also sprach Zarathustra:* "Vor Sonnen-Aufgang," p. 243.

refutation of his misanthropic theory, for the salvation of Him whom he loves and fears. But his skepticism wins in the gruesome test. The priests set the price of Jesus at thirty pieces of silver. The populace, always cruel and blood-thirsty,[24] ever eager to witness crime, at all times craving for either bread or shows, and invariably hostile to, and suspicious of, the great and the original, until after they are dead, clamor for the crucifixion of their noblest Friend. The disciples prove dogmatically obedient and reasonable: they do not break down under the calamity, they do not go mad, or attack the captors of their Master in an uneven battle. Jesus is crucified, and God does not smash the savage world into fragments, neither does the earth quake and spit out its murderous inhabitants. "Nothing has happened. Nothing has changed." [25]

Judas has proved right, terribly right. He has proved *his* truth. But is it *the* truth? Does his being "right" signify that Christ, his antipode, is "wrong"? Andreyev does not answer in the story about Judas, but he suggests an answer in his play, *Anathema*. Here we may discern variations on old themes. Someone-Guarding-the-Gates reminds us of Someone-in-Gray, while Anathema resembles none other but Judas. Again, David Leiser is a popular edition of Jesus, an approachable, speaking Jesus. But the variations are of a considerable degree. Someone-in-Gray delivers long monologues on the Life of Man, voicing the negative side of Schopenhauer's outlook upon the world. The words of Someone-Guarding-the-Gates are few, but they are pregnant with ethical significance, as we shall see presently. Then, too, Anathema is a departure from Judas in that he, the accursed one, is not so much a skeptic, a doubter, as he is a passionate fanatic of knowledge, yearning for the unveiling of all mysteries, aspiring for limitless power—through knowledge:

[24] Cf. Nietzsche: "Der Mensch nämlich ist das grausamste Tier. Bei Trauerspielen, Stierkämpfen und Kreuzigungen ist es ihm bisher am wohlsten geworden auf Erden; und als er sich die Hölle erfand, siehe, da war das sein Himmel auf Erden."—*Also sprach Zarathustra:* "Der Genesende," 2, p. 318 (*Werke—VII*).

[25] Scene 7 of *Anathema*, p. 165 (*Wild Rose* edition). Petrograd, 1909.

And I shall know, and become a God, become a God, become a God![26]

The Guardian-of-the-Gates frankly admits that what Anathema is seeking after is unknowable and unnamable. But the searching spirit never retreats before a wall, as does the inventor of the Iron Gate Formula. Anathema cannot acquiesce in accepting life with closed eyes, unable to explain its course, its why and wherefore. For this rebelliousness of spirit he has been banished and anathematized. Yet time and again he creeps up to the Gates, in his unquenchable thirst for knowledge, his efforts ever breaking at the immovable will of the Guardian. In impotent rage Anathema threatens to raise the earth in revolt against heaven, against the Guardian of the iron Gates, behind which dwells the "Beginning of every being, the Great Reason of the universe." Like Judas, he is going to *prove* the cruelty, absurdity, ugliness, painfulness, and injustice of earthly life, so that the outraged universal sensibility will storm the Gates, demanding the revelation of the Mystery ruling the world in such dark inexplicable ways.

Anathema's "test" is in its essence similar to the one of Judas. He reënacts the drama of Christ on a miniature scale, in the form of a conventionalized allegory. Anathema, disguised as a lawyer, Nullius, comes to a small town stricken with poverty and filth, and announces to a sickly dreamy Jew, David Leiser, that he is heir to two million dollars left for him by his brother who has died in America. At first the pious dreamer refuses to accept the gift, which he feels to come from an evil source. But Anathema (Small, Sufficient Reason) *proves* to David how much good can be accomplished through his money. David then issues a call to all the needy, to come and share in the blessing that has been bestowed on him. Human misery begins to flow toward David. To the long-awaited call are drawn all unfortunates, all afflicted, cripples, blind, bereaved, all who have some sorrow or want, expecting miracles, demanding miracles. Andreyev evidently refers to the appeal which Christianity bears for all who are weak and miserable rather than for the strong

[26] *Ibid*, p. 15.

and joyous ones of humanity. One recalls the words of St. Paul concerning those invited to be saved:

. . . not many wise after the flesh, not many mighty, not many noble are called: but God chose the foolish things of the world, that he might put to shame them that are wise; and God chose the weak things of the world, that he might put to shame the things that are strong; and the base things of the world, and the things that are despised did God choose, yes and the things that are not, that he might bring to nought the things that are: that no flesh should glory before God.[27]

The meek in spirit and weak in body swarm along the path leading to the luring will-o'-the-wisp. A bitter reproach is heard in the words of David's beautiful daughter, Rosa: "I have heard you call everybody. . . . But did you call the beautiful?" and scornfully she leaves the Mecca of the ugly. There remain only life's stepchildren, life's outcasts, those who are doomed to perish, moribund mankind.[28] But generous David finds himself unable to meet the ever-growing requests and demands. His love, his kindness, his sympathy cannot still the hunger, or heal the sick, or make the blind see. As to his "capital," his great American fortune, it is swiftly frittered away, and when divided among the applicants, amounts to one copeck per person—the net effect of Christian charity on misery and suffering! David grows despondent. Anathema drives into his tormented mind mathematically unanswerable questions, such as this: "Why love, when it is impotent?" His money,

---

[27] *I. Corinthians*, 1: 26–29.

[28] Georg Simmel quotes a little known passage from St. Francis, also affirming the predilection of Christianity for the base and lowly: "Du willst wissen, warum mir die Menschen nachfolgen? Weil es die Augen des Höchsten also gewollt haben. Da sie unter den Sündern keinen geringeren, keinen unzulänglicheren, keinen sündigeren Menschen gefunden haben als mich, so haben sie mich auserwählt, um das wunderbare Werk zu vollbringen, das Gott unternommen hat; mich hat er erwählt, weil er keinen Niedrigeren finden konnte, weil er also Adel, Grösse, Kraft, Schönheit und Weisheit der Welt zuschanden machen wollte."—*Nietzsche und Schopenhauer*, p. 200.

Nietzsche objects to Christianity mainly on this account—its being a religion of the weak, of the slaves, and its trying to preserve that "which should have perished." See, e. g., *Jenseits von Gut und Böse*, No. 62 (*Werke—VIII*, pp. 87–90), *Wille zur Macht, Book Two—I* (v. IX, pp. 107–195), *Der Antichrist* (v. X, pp. 359–456).

his tears, his heart, cannot quench the insatiable human want.
The disappointed mass becomes restive and threatening. They
accuse David of having deceived and betrayed them, and stone
him to death.

Anathema has won on all points. But no revolt takes place
as a protest against the crime perpetrated. As with Judas after
the Crucifixion, "nothing has happened. Nothing has changed.
As before, the earth is weighed down by iron gates, closed from
time immemorial, behind which dwells in silence and mystery
the Beginning of every being, the Great Reason of the universe.
And as silent and gravely motionless is Someone-Guarding-the-
Gates. . . ." Anathema comes to demand an exact answer.
He has just been instrumental in demonstrating beyond doubt
the reign of stupid injustice on earth, and as a victor he is en-
titled to the spoils—the knowledge of "the name . . . the
name of him who has ruined David and thousands of men."
He rages against the immutability of the Guardian, and plain-
tively enumerates the achievements of his "test": Has he not
shown the powerlessness of love, in David, stoned to death by
those for whom he gave his soul? Has he not proved the evil
which love and altruism may cause? For not only has David
failed to help the sufferers, but in his name people are committing violence and mutual slaughter, waging persecution and war.
The Guardian grants Anathema's claim:

> Yes, David has done that which thou sayest; and the people have done
> that of which thou accusest them. And the numbers do not lie, and the
> scales are correct, and every measure is what it is.[29]

At this answer Anathema feels triumphant. For he is Sufficient, Small Reason, hence "immortal in numbers." He is
strong in mathematics and in logic, he can prove everything—except the mystery of life and its governing forces. His symmet-
rical mind requires exact figures, sharp outlines, clear definitions,
fixed quantities, and he refuses to believe in the words of the
Guardian that what he craves to know "is not measured with
a measure, and is not calculated in numbers, and is not weighed

[29] Scene 7, p. 168.

on scales." At the very outset of his quest, Anathema is warned by the Guardian that the mystery of truth and love is above and beyond "proofs," that in the sight of Great Reason nothing is definite, nothing is absolute:

> There is no name for that which thou askest, Anathema. There is no number by which to count, no measure by which to measure, no scale by which to weigh that which thou askest, Anathema. Whoever hath said the word, Love—hath lied. Whoever hath said the word, Reason—hath lied. And even he who hath uttered the word, God—hath lied an utmost and terrible lie. For there is no number, no measure, no scale, no name for that which thou askest, Anathema.[30]

Andreyev thus asserts the illusoriness of attaining absolute knowledge by means of our limited intellect. But though Anathema is defeated, he is not subdued. In his refusal to submit to the impregnable wall, he rises above the calculating logic of Small Reason, the logic of adaptability, and voices the instinct of all searching minds, the longing for certainty (dass Verlangen nach Gewissheit), which, in the words of Nietzsche, separates higher from lower men. For Nietzsche, not to question perpetually while living amidst uncertainty and multiplicity, is contemptible.[31] And Anathema is the spirit of interminable search, and will live as long as there remain mysteries in life— that is, eternally.

The Guardian, besides the idea of the unknowability of absolutes, suggests yet another motive. He proclaims after the murder of David that

> David hath attained immortality, and he liveth forever in the deathlessness of fire. David hath attained immortality, and he liveth forever in the deathlessness of light, which is life.[32]

David's sufferings and errors, so mathematically proved by

---

[30] Scene 1, p. 19.

[31] "Aber inmitten dieser rerum concordia discors und den ganzen wondervollen Ungewissheit and Vieldeutigkeit des Daseins stehen *und nicht fragen,* nicht zittern vor Begierde und Lust des Fragens . . . Das ist es was ich als *verächtlich* empfinde . . ."—*Die fröhliche Wissenschaft: 2.* Das intellektuale Gewissen," p. 64 (*Werke—VI*).

[32] Scene 7, p. 167.

Anathema to be futile, senseless, and misleading, are raised to a high tragedy of redemption through immortality, immortality in the sense in which Schopenhauer employs this word, namely the destruction of the illusion of individual consciousness and independence from the rest of the world.[33] This motive is suggested in several of Andreyev's works, showing the influence of Schopenhauer's ethical views, and pointing to the possibility of a positive ideal in life.

Schopenhauer disparages sufficient reason which can grasp only phenomena within the limits of time, space, cause and effect. He distinguishes immanent knowledge, obtained by means of sufficient reason, from transcendental knowledge of the true knowledge of things, of what he calls Platonic Ideas. As individuals, subject to the Will, we can know only particular things; in order to be in a position to apprehend Ideas, we must divest ourself of our individual Ego, and regard ourself as a part of the whole, of the universal. But in order to attain this stage it is necessary for us to abnegate our Will, to rise above it, and thus become a *subject* rather than an object. Then we are capable of freeing ourself from petty and selfish motives and strivings—for these are dictated by our Will-to-live—and to perceive the unity of the world and of the species, of which we are an integral part. Once released from the principium individuationis, the Scholastic term used by Schopenhauer to denote our egoistic notions arrived at by our sufficient reason, we may rise to the heights of sublime altruism.

Wenn nämlich vor den Augen eines Menschen jener Schleier der Maja, das principium individuationis, so sehr gelüftet ist, dass derselbe nicht mehr den egoistischen Unterschied zwischen seiner Person und der fremden macht, sondern an den Leiden der anderen Individuen so viel Anteil nimmt, wie an seinen eigenen, und dadurch nicht nur im höchsten Grade hilfreich ist, sondern sogar bereit, sein eigenes Individuum zu opfern,

33 "Denn zwar ist jeder nur als Erscheinung vergänglich, hingegen als Ding an sich zeitlos, also auch endlos; aber auch nur als Erscheinung ist er von den übrigen Dingen der Welt verschieden, als Ding an sich ist er der Wille, der in allem erscheint, und der Tod hebt die Täuschung auf, die sein Bewusstsein von dem der Uebrigen trennt: dies ist die Fordauer."—*Die Welt, etc.*—*I*, No. 54, p. 323.

sobald mehrere fremde dadurch zu retten sind; dann folgt von selbst, dass ein solcher Mensch, der in allen Wesen sich, sein innerstes und wahres Selbst erkennt, auch die endlosen Leiden alles Lebenden als die seinen betrachten und so den Schmerz der ganzen Welt sich zueignen muss. Ihm ist kein Leiden mehr fremd. Alle Qualen anderer, die er sieht und so selten zu lindern vermag, alle Qualen, von denen er mittelbare Kunde hat, ja die er nur als möglich erkennt, wirken auf seinen Geist, wie seinen eigenen. Es ist nicht mehr das wechselnde Wohl und Wehe seiner Person, was er im auge hat, wie dies bei dem noch im Egoismus befangenen Menschen der Fall ist; sonder, da er das principium individuationis durchschaut, liegt ihm alles gleich nahe. Er erkennt das Ganze, fasst das Wesen desselben auf, und findet es in einem steten Vergehen, nichtigen Streben, innerm Widerstreit und beständigem Leiden begriffen, sieht, wohin er auch blickt, die leidende Menschheit und die leidende Tierheit, und eine hinschwindende Welt. Dieses alles aber liegt ihm jetzt so nahe, wie dem Egoisten nur seine eigene Person. Wie sollte er nun, bei solcher Erkenntniss der Welt, ebendieses Leben durch stete Willensakte bejahen und eben dadurch sich ihm immer fester verknüpfen, es immer fester an sich drücken? Wenn also der, welcher noch im principio individuationis, im Egoismus befangen ist, nur einzelne Dinge und ihr Verhältniss zu seiner Person erkennt, und jener dann zu immer erneuerten *Motiven* seines Wollens werden; so wird hingegen jene beschriebene Erkenntniss des Ganzen, des Wesens der Dinge an sich, zum *Quietiv* alles und jedes Wollens. Der Wille wendet sich nunmehr vom Leben ab; ihm schaudert jetzt vor dessen Genüssen, in denen er die Bejahung desselben erkennt. Der Mensch gelangt zum Zustande der freiwilligen Entsagung, der Resignation, der wahren Gelassenheit und gänzlichen Willenslosigkeit.[34]

Only a few can arrive at this stage—the saint, or the true artist. But Schopenhauer asserts that even the average person possesses in a certain degree altruistic feelings. In his essays on ethics he speaks with great reverence of that psychological mystery—sympathy, common to the majority of men. This feeling is possible only when one identifies himself with others, when one can regard others' pain, misfortune, sorrow, as one's own, when one ceases to consider oneself in the aspect of the principium individuationis, when one approaches the maxim of the Vedas: *Tat twam asi* (This thou art). Schopen-

34 *Die Welt, etc.—I*, No. 68, pp. 425, 426 (*Werke—I*).

hauer expresses his moral code in the precept, *Neminem laede; imo omnes, quantum potes, juva.* The first part of the precept, the negative, he calls justice. The second he regards as the positive virtue of charity, of sympathy, than which he knows no surer pledge for public well-being.[35] A mystery, he calls this universal feeling, because "reason cannot give a direct account for it."[36] Indeed, our virtues emanate from a peculiar source of knowledge—"nämlich von einer unmittelbaren und intuitiven, die nicht wegzuräsonnieren und nicht anzuräsonieren ist, von einer Erkenntniss, die, eben weil sie nicht abstrakt ist, sich auch nicht mitteilen lässt, sondern jedem selbst aufgehen musst, die daher ihren eigentlichen adäquaten Austruck nicht in Worten findet, sondern ganz allein in Taten, im Handeln, im Lebenslauf des Menschen."[37]

Schopenhauer's lingering influence, admitted by Andreyev, is recognized without difficulty in those few works of Andreyev where he appears to be on the verge of uttering an ethical "Aye." Opposing dogmatic precepts, he portrays on several occasions with evident sympathy such deeds of virtue as result from the heart rather than from the head, this virtue being the one Schopenhauer places above all others—*caritas.* While he lets his Judas and Anathema display all the infallible force of their reason, he makes them shrivel into nothingness in the face of the reason-defying sublimity of their "victims." The greatness of Christ's conduct is most impressive through his silence. In *Anathema,* the Guardian declares David's achievement of immortality. Indeed, David becomes aware of his immortality while still alive. He rises above things measurable and weighable, and in face of lonely death at the hands of those to whom he has given all, he perceives the immortal fire glowing in his

---

[35] "Denn grenzenloses Mitleid mit allen lebenden Wesen ist der festeste und sicherste Bürge für das sittliche Wohlverhalten und bedarf keiner Kasuistik. Wer davon erfüllt ist, wird zuverlässig keinen verletzen, keinen beeinträchtigen, keinem Wehe tun, vielmehr mit jedem Nachsicht haben, jedem verzeihen, jedem helfen, so viel er vermag, und alle seine Handlungen werden das Gepräge der Gerechtigkeit und Menschenliebe tragen."—*Grundlage der Moral,* No. 19; 4, p. 380 (*Werke—III*).

[36] *Ibid.,* No. 18, p. 374.

[37] *Die Welt—I,* No. 66, p. 416 (*Werke—I*).

heart, the fire of love which destroys solitude and annihilates death.

Am I alone [he exclaims in ecstasy]? Am I a pauper and near death? . . . There is no death for man. What death is there? What is death? . . . Perhaps it does exist, I do not know—but I . . . I am immortal . . . Oh, how terrible it is: I am immortal. Where is the end of the sky—I have lost it. Where is the end of man—I have lost it. I am immortal. Oh, the breast of man aches from immortality, and his joy burns him like fire. . . .[38]

First to relinquish your personal Will-to-live, with its self-ish little ambitions and aspirations for success, for wealth, for fame (*The Life of Man*), then to merge with the rest of beings and things, to accept their sorrows as your sorrows, to love them as the whole, the universal—this is the way of immortal-ity, according to Andreyev, when he follows Schopenhauer. Anathema finds David a sick old pauper, utterly indifferent to life, free from all earthly desires. From this point there is only a step to immortality through embracing all mankind, all life, all the world, in whose perpetual course you are but an infinites-imal atom, the existence and the passing of which cannot have any isolated, individual importance. Thus Musya and Werner, in *The Seven That Were Hanged*, sentenced to death and in-wardly resigned to die, without regrets or longing for the con-tinuation of their personal existence, rise above the will, and gain immortality by fusing their consciousness with that of the cosmos. It is then that "the shores of life cannot contain their

[38] Scene 4, p. 108.
The idea of losing your solitude when merging your individuality with the mass of humanity, was suggested by Andreyev as early as in *The Life of Vasily Fiveysky*. Speaking of the effect produced on Father Vasily by the tales of woe and misery related by his parishioners during their confessions, he wrote: "Here-tofore it was thus: There existed a puny earth, on which lived an enormous Father Vasily with his enormous grief and enormous doubts, with no other people living about, as it were. But now the earth had grown immense, boundless, and had become peopled with multitudes of men like Father Vasily. Each one of them lived in his own way, suffered, hoped, doubted in his own fashion. In their midst Father Vasily felt like a solitary tree in a field, around which had sud-denly grown up an endless and dense forest. His solitude was gone . . ."— *Works—IV*, pp. 164, 165.

love, broad as the sea." It is then that Werner perceives the
beauty of the spectacle of life and death, sparkling like two
seas melting into one another at the horizon. Werner's rising
above his ego enables him to regard the flaws of the human race
with compassion and forgiveness, in the manner of the man of
"sublime character" described by Schopenhauer:

> Ein solcher character wird demnach die Menschen rein objektiv be-
> trachten, nicht aber nach den Beziehungen, welche sie zu seinem Willen
> haben könnten: er wird z. B. ihre Fehler, sogar ihren Hass und ihre
> Ungerechtigkeit gegen ihn selbst, bemerken, ohne dadurch seinerseits zum
> Hass erregt zu werden . . . Denn er wird in seinem eigenen Lebenslauf
> und dessen Unfällen weniger sein individuelles, als das Los der Mensch-
> heit überhaupt erblicken. . . .[39]

He who succeeds in throwing off "the veil of Maja," and in
placing his person properly in regard to the universe, will not
fear death. In *Eleazar* (or *Lazarus*) Andreyev powerfully
depicts the paralyzing effect of death on human activity.
Those who look into the eyes of the resurrected Lazarus, the
man who spent three days and three nights in the grave, perceive the horror of the infinite, and lose all joy and ambition.
The terrible knowledge lurking in the eyes of Lazarus kills the
love in the lovers who dare look into them; it destroys the
thought-impulse in the thinker; it cripples the sense of beauty in
the artist. The divine Augustus confronts those eyes, and is
also dragged to the verge of nothingness, but at the moment
of apathetic despondency, when peering into the abyss of death,
the emperor feels in his heart a spark flare up into a flame:
his love for his people. The thought of others saves him from
destruction, as the religion of altruism saved Tolstoy from suicide. Augustus comes back to life, "to find in its suffering and
in its joys a shield against the darkness of the void and the
horror of the Infinite." According to Schopenhauer, to him
who regards his own person as something apart from other persons, who regards the rest of the world as "not myself" (*Nicht-
Ich*), who exists therefore exclusively within his own self, death

[39] *Die Welt—I*, No. 39, pp. 242, 243 (*Werke—I*).

appears as the end of all reality, of the whole world. On the other hand, he who sees in his own existence a close link with the existence of other living beings, loses in his death only a small part of his existence, for he will be continued in all those in whom he has seen and loved his own existence. He looks upon death as "the blinking of an eye, which does not interrupt the vision," [40] or as the setting of the sun, which does not sig· nify the extinction of the sun,[41] or as upon a deep sleep.[42] Andreyev uses Augustus, rather freely from the point of view of historical truth, as a symbol of an individual whose life is intertwined with the lives of others. Once Augustus realizes that his existence is of import only in so far as it is linked with that of others, he concludes further that with his disappearance there is not going to ensue a "void darkness," but that the session will proceed. Life, objectively, is eternal. "That evening," the author tells us, "the divine Augustus partook of his meats and drinks with particular joy." The horror he has envisaged in the eyes of Lazarus will remain with him for the rest of his days—a "black shadow" dulling from time to time the brightness of his own eyes. Those eyes have disillusioned him forever concerning individual happiness or purposefulness. But with this knowledge has also come the consciousness of being a part of the cosmos, of living with others, through others and for others. Augustus rises above personal disenchantment, and determines to live and act for his people. Altruism, love and life for others, sounds strongly in this lugubrious story, and it sounds more or less faintly in *The Seven That Were Hanged,* in *Judas Iscariot,* in *Anathema.* The author does not suggest that altruism can in any way alter conditions, transform life into something less silly and cruel and ugly, or bestow happiness. What one may infer is that since we are where we are, in this vale of tears, the only way that remains for us to follow

[40] *Grundlage der Moral,* No. 22, p. 412 *(Werke—III).*

[41] ". . . wenn ein Mensch den Tod als seine Vernichtung fürchtet, es nicht anders ist, als wenn man dächt, die Sonne könne am Abend klagen: 'Wehe mir! Ich gehe unter in ewige Nacht.' "—*Die Welt, etc., I,* No. 54, p. 321 *(Werke—I).*

[42] "Der tiefe Schlaf ist vom Tode . . . gar nicht verschieden. . . . Der Tod ist ein Schlaf, in welchem die Individualität vergessen wird: alles andere erwacht wieder, oder vielmehr ist wach geblieben."—*Ibid.,* No. 54, p. 318.

is the noble way of unselfish love and sympathy. "A heroic life," is what Schopenhauer prescribes for one who knows that happiness in life is impossible:

> Ein *glückliches Leben* ist unmöglich: das Höchste, was der Mensch erlangen kann, ist ein *heroischer Lebenslauf*. Einen solchen führt der, welcher, in irgendeiner Art und Angelegenheit, für das allen irgendwie zugute Kommende, mit übergrossen Schwierigkeiten kämpft und am Ende siegt, dabei aber schlecht oder gar nicht belohnt wird. Dann bleibt er, am Schluss, wie der Prinz im Re corvo des Gozzi, versteinert, aber in edler Stellung und mit grossmütiger Gebärde stehn. Sein Andenken bleibt und wird als das eines *Heros* gefeiert; sein *Wille,* durch Mühe und Arbeit, schlechten Erfolg und Undank der Welt, ein ganzes Leben hündurch, mortifiziert, *erlischt* in der *Nirvana.*[43]

In suggesting such a positive ideal in life, Andreyev chooses the way of Schopenhauer, and, by implication, rejects that of Nietzsche. We have observed Andreyev's destructive analysis of existing institutions, of man's individual follies and collective foibles, of the frailty of faith' and of reason's futility. In this analysis he was able to follow, consciously or not, both philosophers, who agree in the main in their critique of life and man. But in drawing conclusions from their critique, the two part company. Andreyev's further course is indicated in his statement, to the effect that after remaining for some time under the influence of Nietzsche, he ultimately reverted to Schopenhauer.[44] For our purpose it will suffice to point out succinctly the divergences between the two philosophers, in so far as Andreyev's views are involved.

As has been stated previously,[45] Nietzsche owed his analysis of the world to Schopenhauer, who formed the theme of his early work, *Schopenhauer als Erzieher.* Even later, after declaring himself emancipated from his former master, Nietzsche affirmed the Schopenhauerian view that "das ganze menschliche Leben ist tief in die Unwarheit eingesenkt; der Einzelne kann es nicht aus diesem Brunnen herausziehen, ohne dabei seiner

[43] *Paregra, etc.,* No. 172, a, p. 295 (*Werke—IV*).
[44] *Supra,* p. 179.
[45] *Supra,* p. 183.

Vergangenheit aus tiefstem Grunde gram zu werden, ohne seine gegenwärtigen Motive, wie die der Ehre, ungereimt zu finden und den Leidenschaften, welche zur Zukunft und zu einem Glück in derselben hindrängen, Hohn und Verachtung entgegenzustellen." [46] But whereas Schopenhauer proceeded to say "No" to this life of error and absurdity, Nietzsche declared his passionate "Yes" to it. Himself a sufferer from physical and mental ailments, Nietzsche emerged from his trials a believer in life as it is, with all its negative traits.[47] He arrived at this view by way of replacing the Will-to-live by the Will-to-power as life's chief motive and factor. Once we live, we are prompted in our strivings not merely to continue this process of living,[48] but to live more, better, to excel, to surpass, to intensify our faculties, to advance infinitely, to create unceasingly. Life is Will-to-power, a never-ending creative process of the growth and improvement of whatever possesses surplus energy, at the expense of the weak.[49] This driving force brushes aside all considerations which do not lead to the achievement of its goal. When truth, for example, may appear harmful to the growth of life, truth shall perish; [50] error and illusion have often served for the enhancement of life and for the progress of humanity.[51]

[46] *Menschliches Allzumenschliches—I*, No. 34, p. 52 (*Werke—III*).

[47] In his preface to *Menschliches Allzumenschliches—II*, p. 9 (*Werke—IV*), he says: "das hier ein Leidende und Entbehrender redet, wie als ob er *nicht* ein Leidender und Entbehrender sei. Hier *soll* das Gleichgewicht, die Gelassenheit, sogar die Dankbarkeit gegen das Leben aufrecht erhalten werden, hier waltet ein strenger, stolzer, beständig wacher, beständig reizbarer Wille, der sich die Aufgabe gestellt hat, das Leben *wider* den Schmerz zu vertheidigen und alle Schlüsse abzuknicken, welche aus Schmerz, Enttäuschung, Uberdruss, Vereinsamung und andrem Moorgrunde gleich giftigen Schwämmen aufzuwachsen pflegen."

[48] "Es giebt keinen Willen zum Dasein. Was Dasein hat, kann nicht zum Dasein wollen; was kein Dasein hat, kann es auch nicht." *Nachgelassene Werke*, v. XI, p. 190. The same idea is expressed also in *Also sprach Zarathustra:* "Von der Selbst-überwindung," p. 168: " 'Wille zum Dasein': diesen Willen gibt es nicht!"

[49] "Ich lehre das Nein zu Allem, was schwach macht,—was erschöpft. Ich lehre das Ja zu Allem, was stärkt, was Kraft aufspeichert, was das Gefühl der Kraft rechtfertigt."—*Wille zur Macht—I*, No. 54, p. 46 (*Werke—IX*). The idea of Will-to-power runs through all the works of Nietzsche after his rupture with Wagner.

[50] *Fröhliche Wissenschaft*, Forrede, 4, p. 37 (*Werke—VI*); *Nachgelassene Werke —XIII*, p. 124.

[51] *Menschliches Allzumenschliches—I*, No. 29, p. 46, 47; No. 31, pp. 48, 49 (*Werke—III*); *Morgenrothe*, No. 248, p. 230; No. 307, pp. 251, 252 (*Werke—V*).

The question of moral or immoral does not exist, for life is essentially unmoral.[52] This dynamic doctrine prompts Nietzsche to oppose vigorously Schopenhauer's conclusions, even though he continues to accept his diagnosis. Yes, life is composed of pain and misery, but this fact need not dictate to us the negation of life. On the contrary, to Nietzsche pain is one of the essential conditions of intense living, since it provokes the resistance of our Will-to-power, tests its endurance, probes its vitality.[53] Pain and suffering have been responsible for the advancement of the race.[54] We have seen that Andreyev, like most Russian writers, regards pain in a similar way—as a significant and enriching element of life.[55] Subtract this element of suffering from the lives of Andreyev's characters (or from those of Dostoyevsky), and you rob them of their very *raison d'être*. In this respect, then, Andreyev is closer to Nietzsche than to Schopenhauer. It is in his postulation of the ethical problem that Nietzsche estranges Andreyev.

Nietzsche opposes Schopenhauer's moral precepts on the same ground that he abhors all Jewish-Christian morality—as "slave morality," designed for the weak and plebeian, and as the antithesis of the Greek-Roman "master morality," the expression of the strong and the noble. Moral codes and impulses are to Nietzsche means employed by the Will-to-power for the furtherance of its aims, individual or collective. Christianity has been adopted by the masses, the "slaves," the weak, the ignoble, the cowardly, because it furthers their cause, by

---

[52] "Denn dieses Dasein ist *unmoralisch.* . . . Und dieses Leben ruht auf unmoralischen Voraussetzungen: und alle Moral *verneint* das Leben."—*Wille zur Macht—II*, No. 461, p. 351 (*Werke—IX*).

[53] "Ich schätze die Macht eines *Willens* darnach, wie viel von Widerstand, Schmerz, Tortur es aushält und sich zum Vortheil umzuwandeln weiss; ich rechne dem Dasein nicht seinen Bösen und schmerzhaften Charakter zum Vorwurf an, sondern bin der Hoffnung, dass es einst böser und schmerzhafter sein wird, als bisher. . . ."—*Wille zur Macht—II*, No. 382, p. 282 (*Werke—IX*).

[54] "Ihr wollt . . . *das Leiden abschaffen;* und wir . . . wollen es lieber noch höher und schlimmer haben, als je es war! . . . Die Zucht des Leidens, des *grossen* Leidens—wisst ihr nicht, dass nur *diese* Zucht alle Erhöhungen des Menschen bisher geschaffen hat?"—*Jenseits von Gut und Böse*, No. 225, p. 180 (*Werke—VIII*).

[55] *Supra*, p. 266 ff.

proclaiming the equality of all before God, and by championing such virtues as love (even for your enemy), humility, nonresistance, pity—virtues which would have been considered vices by "masters," by the noble and aggressive.[56] And Nietzsche definitely allies himself with the "masters." The Christian virtues are to him life-reducing, life-denying, as are those advocated by Schopenhauer. Pity, altruism, self-denial, are prescribed by Schopenhauer for a resignation diet, as means for the annihilation of our selfish desires and instincts, and for merging our illusory individuality in the Nirvana of human equality. Nietzsche rejects both pity and equality. Pity is an impertinence on the part of its bestower, and is offensive to its recipient,[57] unless both of them be slaves. Pity poisons and depresses life, negates life, this being the reason for Schopenhauer's enthusiasm for this sentiment.[58] As to equality, the very idea of it sounds "unjust" to Nietzsche.[59] He sees a "Rangordnung" in every phase and walk of life; it is to him a biological as well as a spiritual fact. Even our body has higher and lower functionaries—an "oligarchic arrangement." [60] Similarly the social organism is based on inequality, consisting of rulers and ruled, of masters and slaves, of those who command and those who obey.[61] Inequality, variability, gradation, distance between rank and rank, relieve life of the monotony which Schopenhauer sees in it, and lend it color, perpetual movement, conflict and

[56] Nietzsche's views on morality are scattered through practically all his works. In a matured form they are made particularly clear in his *Zur Genealogie der Moral; Der Antichrist; Der Wille zur Macht.*

[57] "Ein Erraten sei dein Mitleiden: dass du erst wissest, ob dein Freund Mitleiden wolle. Vielleicht liebt er an dir das ungebrochene Auge und den Blick der Ewigkeit."—*Also sprach Zarathustra:* "Vom Freunde," p. 82 (*Werke—VII*). "Wahrlich, ich mag sie nicht, die Barmherzigen, die selig sind in ihrem Mitleiden: zu sehr gebricht es ihnen an Scham."—*Ibid.,* "Von den Mitleidigen," p. 127.

[58] "Das Mitleiden steht im Gegensatz zu den tonischen Affekten, welche die Energie des Lebensgefühls erhöhn: es wirkt depressiv. Mann verliert Kraft, wenn man mitleidet . . . Schopenhauer war in seinem Recht damit: durch das Mitleid wird das Leben verneint, *verneinungswürdiger* gemacht . . ."—*Antichrist,* No. 7, pp. 363, 364 (*Werke—X*).

[59] ". . . Denn so redet *mir* die Gerechtigkeit: 'die Menschen sind nicht gleich.' " —*Also sprach Zarathustra:* "Von den Taranteln," p. 146.

[60] *Genealogie der Moral—II,* No. I, p. 344 (*Werke—VIII*).

[61] *Wille zur Macht—IV: I:* "Rangordnung," No. 854 ff., p. 105 ff. (*Werke —X*).

incentive. Nietzsche not only asserts the existence of this condition of inequality: he exalts it, regards it as a mark of every
"strong time," [62] as a pledge for evolution and progress, as a
stimulus for perpetual self-surpassing. Life presents an endless series of stages, each one superior to some one stage and
inferior to some other stage, the Will-to-power imbuing all and
everything with a striving forward. Thus the present society
may have its justification not in its existence for its own sake,
but as a means for a "stronger race," [63] and man in general
must accelerate his own disappearance, in order to give room
to the superman, for whom he serves as a bridge.[64]

Schopenhauer's ideal man emanates from resignation, from
indifference to life and all desires. Through pity for others
he frees himself from the burden of individual personality (an
illusion in itself), and melts in the sea of suffering humanity.
Nietzsche's superman is to be the product of overbrimming life,
of excessive energy and Will-to-power. He is endowed with
a distinct personality, fully developed, immune from pettiness
and weakness, from all such sentiments as may impede his
further, never ceasing growth. The superman need not be considered as an ultimate goal, since in the light of Nietzsche's doctrine he is to be regarded merely as a rung in the evolutionary
ladder which leads into the infinite. Georg Simmel justly
names Nietzsche's ideal "Personalism," [65] for the superman is

[62] Nietzsche considers the Renaissance as the last "great" time, whereas ours
is to him petty and weak, with its virtues and aspirations. "Die 'Gleichheit,'
eine gewisse thatsächliche Anähnlichung . . . gehört wesentlich zum Niedergang:
die Kluft zwischen Mensch und Mensch, Stand und Stand, die Vielheit der Typen,
der Wille, selbst zu sein, sich abzuheben—Das, was ich *Pathos der Distanz* nenne,
ist jeder *starken* Zeit zu eigen."—*Götzen-Dämmerung*, No. 37, p. 324 (*Werke*
—X).

[63] *Wille zur Macht*, No. 898, p. 134 (*Werke*—X).

[64] "Der Mensch ist ein Seil, geknüpft zwischen Tier und Übermensch—ein Seil
über einem Abgrunde. . . . Ich liebe Den, welcher lebt, damit er erkenne, und
welcher erkennen will, damit einst der Übermensch lebe. Und so will er seinen
Untergang. Ich liebe Den, welcher arbeitet und erfindet, dass er dem Über-
menschen das Haus baue und zu ihm Erde, Tier und Pflanze vorbereite: denn so
will er seinen Untergang."—*Also sprach Zarathustra:* Vorrede, 4, p. 16.

[65] Simmel rejects the popular view that Nietzsche's teaching is egoistic. "Der
Egoismus will etwas haben, der Personalismus will etwas sein. Damit stellt er
sich jenseits des Gegensatzes von Eudämonismus und Moralismus, in dem die
Kantische Moral aufging. Der Eudämonismus fragt: Was gibt mir die Welt?

the ideal of a relatively complete, fully expressed, creative personality.

Andreyev refuses to accept Nietzsche's positive ideal. With all his contempt for the average man, for the herd, Andreyev cannot subscribe to a doctrine primarily designed for the few and the exceptional,[66] ignoring humanity in favor of the superman.[67] We have inferred (page 289) this stand of his from the fact of his apparent acceptance of Schopenhauer's positive ideal. The Ocean offers an opportunity for interpreting Andreyev's direct attitude toward the idea of the superman.

The Ocean (subtitle: "A Tragedy") is one of Andreyev's most cryptic productions. Through its symbolic maze one may discern the perplexed mind of the author, torn in twain between contempt and sympathy for men, between denial and acceptance of life, between the "shore" where abide the many-too-many, and the "ocean," the unknown expanse whither bold spirits venture in quest of new horizons.[68] In this drama Andreyev draws one of his conceptions of the superman, that "strange vision" which has been pursuing him since his student years. He personifies him in Haggart, the captain of a pirate vessel flying under black sails—evidently symbolizing Great Reason. For some cause or other—is it his nostalgia for the herd life?—Haggart lingers on the shore, below the lighthouse of the Holy Cross, amidst the ruins of an Old Tower. He openly despises the villagers, greedy fishermen for whom the ocean is only a supplier of fish. They are ruled by the Abbé, who while also despising the fishermen pities them at the same time, and who, like Dostoyevsky's Grand Inquisitor, tries to make life easier for them by deceiving them, by not afflicting them with truth. The

Der Moralismus: Was gebe ich der Welt? Für Nietzsche aber handelt es sich überhaupt nicht mehr um ein Geben, sondern um eine Seinsbeschaffenheit . . . insoweit sie eine bestimmte Entwicklungshöhe des Typus Mensch darstellt."—Schopenhauer und Nietzsche, p. 245.

[66] "Wir Anderen sind die Ausnahme und die Gefahr . . . es lässt sich wirklich Etwas zu Gunsten der Ausnahme sagen, vorausgesetzt dass sie nie Regel werden will."—Die fröhliche Wissenschaft, No. 76, p. 132 (Werke—VI).

[67] "Nicht 'Menschheit,' sondern Übermensch ist das Ziel!"—Wille zur Macht, No. 1001, p. 188 (Werke—X).

[68] Cf. Nietzsche's aphorism on the "ocean of becoming"—Morgenröthe, No. 314, p. 254 (Werke—V).

ambiguity of his compromising tenets is apparent from the presence of his "adopted" daughter, Mariette; it is an open secret that he is her real father. His is a convenient religion, adapted to the requirements of a weak and cowardly race. But Mariette is drawn to Haggart, to his bold black sails. To her the greedy fishermen are dead, and the religion of her father false. "A God who makes corpses out of men, is no God. We shall go in search of a new God," cries Mariette, the embodiment of yearning humanity. Her heart is torn by contradictions, by conflicting emotions, by shreds of beliefs poisoned with acid doubts, by hatred of the present, and hope mingled with fear for the future. She clings to Haggart, she would trust him, for is he not truthful and courageous? Has he not freed himself from the chains of all dogmas, and is he not flying under the rebellious Black Sails? Haggart is not only negatively free. He seems to know not only from what but also for what he is free. Says he:

Had I a ship, I should race after the sun. And however many golden sails it might set, I should overtake it with my black sails. And I should force the sun to outline my shadow on the deck of my ship. And I should plant my foot on it—like this! [69]

This race after the sun may be a vague venture, but at all events it stands for striving away and up from the miserable existence on the shore. Away from the Old Tower—old codes and standards, this once strong shelter from violent breezes which is now a peril and a risk for those who would venture under its battered roof. Away from the lighthouse of the Holy Cross: its light is too faint, too dim, too gentle, to be of any aid in storms. Haggart is determined to start out on the boundless ocean, in search of new horizons, of unlimited vistas. He is to be accompanied by Mariette who is weary and sick of the shore, and by the little son she has borne him. Under the Black Sails, Haggart will lead Mariette and the product of their union onward to race with the sun. One recalls Nietzsche's fine lines:

[69] *Works—XIII*, p. 19.

Saht ihr nie ein Segel über das Meer gehn, geründet und gebläht und zitternd vor dem Ungestüm des Windes? Dem Segel gleich, zitternd vor dem Ungestüm des Geistes, geht meine Weisheit über das Meer— meine wilde Weisheit! [70]

But just at the moment when the ship is to set out on the great adventure, an "accident" takes place. The Abbé, the dispenser of hope and life among the fisherman, is killed by Haggart's boatswain, old Horre. No reason is given for the murder, but Horre insinuates, and the crew second him, that it has been committed by Haggart's order. The captain has never given such an order, yet one feels that he is responsible, indirectly, for the act of Horre, a mere tool of Haggart's will. The situation resembles the murder of old Karamazov, in Dostoyevsky's story, where the actual slayer, Smerdyakov, justly ascribes the guilt to Ivan Karamazov, whose philosophy of "Everything is permitted" has generated in him the idea of murder. Horre nursed Haggart in his infancy, and now he is his faithful though unthinking follower, his devoted servant, his blind slave. He has no ambition for racing with the sun. His only slogan is: "Hit 'em on the head!" Under the Black Sails there is room for many varieties of Great Reason—for Nemovetskys and Lorenzos, for Haggarts and Horres. The "freedom" of Horre is not of the kind that may benefit the evolution of the race, it is of that brutal, vulgar variety, concerning which Zarathustra feels so uneasy:

Bist du ein Solcher, der einem Joche entrinnen *durfte?* Es gibt manchen, der seinen letzten Wert wegwarf, als er seine Dienstbarkeit wegwarf.[71]

Mariette is indignant. She still clings to some traditions of the Old Tower, such as justice. Can they start their glorious journey, with crime at their heels? But Haggart reassures her. He overcomes his devotion to his old slave, Horre, and orders him hanged. Mariette is ecstatic over this act of

---

[70] *Also sprach Zarathustra:* "Von den berühmten Weisen," p. 152 (*Werke —VII*).

[71] *Ibid.,* "Vom Wege des Schaffenden," p. 92.

justice. She admits that heretofore she has been afraid of Haggart's power, but now she cries:

> Thou art strong and just . . . Gart, may I shout to the sea: Haggart the Just?
> HAGGART. That is not true. Silence, Mariette . . . I know not what justice is! [72]

Which he proceeds to demonstrate. The crew perform a flimsy manœuvre with a broken rope, so as to save their comrade, with whom they are in perfect harmony. Haggart yields to the half-truth, and frees Horre. Under the Black Sails there is no such thing as absolute truth, as truth at any cost. Nietzsche scoffs at the "metaphysical belief" of Plato and Christianity that God is truth and truth is divine.[73] Truth and falsehood are to be regarded from the point of view of their usefulness or harmfulness to the preservation and intensification of life. In the eyes of a Nietzschean, will-to-truth may be equivalent to will-to-death, since it implies the maxim of *Pereat vita, fiat veritas.* Haggart knows only the truth of Great Reason, the truth taught to him by his father:

> There is but one truth and one law for all: for the sun, for the wind, for the waves, for the beast—only man has a different truth. Beware of the truth of man! [74]

But humanity is not ripe for the reign of Reason unalloyed, be it even Great Reason, because humanity is not morally in the same category with the sun and the wind and the waves. Humanity cannot endure Haggarts any more than it can tolerate Kerzhentsevs. Hence Mariette's ideal is shattered. So even Haggart yields to compromising lies! She will not follow him. And while the Black Sails are raised over the pirate vessel, Mariette remains on the shore and flings her curse at Haggart.

Andreyev's solidarity with Mariette is felt unmistakably. He is with her when she is infatuated with Haggart's strength,

---

[72] *Works—XIII,* p. 145.
[73] *Die fröhliche Wissenschaft,* No. 344, p. 298 ff. (*Werke—VI*).
[74] *Works—XIII,* p. 118.

bigness, directness, and superiority over the petty herd of fishermen. He is ready to greet Haggart's venture into the ocean, in quest of unknown opportunities for the expression of his personality, with the intention of forcing the sun to "outline his shadow" on the ship's deck. But the champion of "Personalism" cannot apparently live up to Simmel's expectation— that he manifest his creative existence, outside of giving and taking [75]: he is impelled to blaze a path for his aggressive personality, even if it lie across the bodies of others. And here Andreyev refuses to follow Haggart, one of the superman's personifications. He rejects Haggart's application of the Will to-power, wherein he becomes undistinguishable from Horre. Haggart appears quite consistent in brushing aside the consideration of truth, when it interferes with Great Reason. Has not Zarathustra asserted that his Will-to-power walketh even on the feet of the Will-to-truth? [76] One may, indeed, question whether Nietzsche would approve of Haggart as a protagonist of the superman, remembering the sterling nobility he demands from him. [77] Haggart is a vulgarized edition of the superman. The broken rope as an argument for the release of Horre is worthy of that arch-logician and high priest of Small Reason, the writer of *My Memoirs*. But Andreyev is justified in demonstrating one of the multifarious aspects of the Great Reason, one of the numerous potential variants of the superman.

Andreyev rejects the superman, the ideal of the few, because he is largely concerned with, and speaks for, the average rank-and-file modern man of reflective faculties. Knowing as he does all the failings and follies of men, and with all his contempt for those who cling to old values and illusions, he nevertheless sides with Marusya as against the Astronomer (in *To the Stars*) and sympathizes with Mariette in her refutation of the pragmatic superman, Haggart. "Strong *and* just" is what

---

[75] See *supra*, p. 294.

[76] ". . . wahrlich, mein Wille zur Macht wandelt auch auf den Füssen deines Willens zur Warheit!"—*Also sprach Zarathustra:* "Von der Selbst-Überwindung," p. 168.

[77] Cf. *Wille zur Macht*, Nos. 935, 943, 944, p. 154 ff. (*Werke—X*).

Mariette, and with her yearning humanity, hopes for in the ideal man. Not finding this combination in Haggart she refuses to follow him. Rather than race the sun under the Black Sails covering up small falsehoods, she will stay on the shore, close to the ridiculous Old Tower, in view of the pathetically feeble light of the Holy Cross. To remain on the shore, to live with the miserable fishermen, to share their sufferings, while knowing the drawbacks and the futility of such a life, is the lot of him who follows the ethical precepts of Schopenhauer.

To avoid misapprehension, we must remember that it would be hazardous to ascribe to Andreyev fixed conclusions and definite solutions. By pointing out wherein he approaches the ideal of Schopenhauer, and wherein he departs from Nietzsche, we are suggesting certain leanings in Andreyev's wavering, unity-lacking mind, farther than nailing down any ultimate decisions on his part. For Andreyev neither accepts nor rejects wholly. Like Dostoyevsky, he contains within himself multiple contrasts and discrepancies. "Particularly striking was the coëxistence in Leonid Nikolayevich of two contradictory attitudes to the world, and their everlasting conflict, under the burden of which he often languished," is the testimony of Mme. Andreyev (in a letter to me), than whom no one understood him better. Not infrequently he presents antipodal characters in his works, without perceptibly tilting the balance of judgment to one side or another. His Astronomer and Marusya (in *To the Stars*) voice mutually exclusive views, yet both are drawn by the author with evident sympathy. Similarly, in juxtaposing Jesus and Judas (*Judas Iscariot*), Leiser and Anathema (*Anathema*), Haggart and Mariette (*The Ocean*), Storitsyn and Telemakhov (*Professor Storitsyn*), Judea and Philistia (*Samson Enchained*), Andreyev does not ally himself unreservedly with either side. Even when the characters are obviously "negative," as, for instance, Judas, Anathema, Haggart, the author emphasizes their "positive" features lovingly and impartially,[78]

[78] Mme. Andreyev tells me that occasionally she would question her husband, while he was creating one of his "dualistic" works, as to how he could contain

and through making them suffer he raises them to the heights of
atoning tragedy.

This faculty of seeing simultaneously both sides of the coin
is not apt to grant peace and comfort to its possessor. Andreyev groaned under the yoke of this double vision. Time and
again he sought escape in an attempted fusion of opposing
views, in a synthesis. One of his paintings—the one he cared
most about—resembles a Byzantine ikon, and presents Jesus
and Judas crucified on the same cross, with a common wreath of
thorns on their heads.[79] This seemingly sacrilegious idea is
suggested also by the words of Judas (*Judas Iscariot*), addressed to the mother of Jesus, whom he perceives weeping at
the cross: "Thou weepest, mother? Weep, weep, and long
will all the mothers of earth weep with thee: until I come with
Jesus and we destroy death." [80] Throughout the story we are
made to feel Judas's yearning for his antithesis, Jesus, as a com-
plementary counterpart. Andreyev seems to dream from time
to time of an utopian combination of antipodal traits. A synthesis of gentle Jesus, with his love condoning human frailties
and follies, and of the ruthless *advocatus diaboli* of the one
never-closing, ever-accusing eye; a harmonious union of Aye
and Nay, of spontaneous acceptance of life, creative and constructive, and of alert analysis, dissecting and destructive. A
similar synthesis is suggested in *Anathema*, where the Guardian
addresses the futile seeker as an "unfortunate spirit, deathless
in numbers, eternally alive in measures and in weights, but as
yet unborn to life." [81] As yet! Like Judas, he is one-eyed.
He lacks spontaneous feeling, he is all intellect. Life eschews
such hypertrophy. A combination of Anathema and David,
of head and heart, of keen analysis and unreasoning love, is
once more inferred as an ideal solution. Again, in the final

two contradictory attitudes. He would answer jocosely: "I am a lawyer. For a
poltinnik [half a ruble] I can plead the case of the defendant as readily as that
of the plaintiff."

[79] Andreyev often mentions this painting in his diary and in his letters (especially to Goloushev). Cf. also Chukovsky, in *A Book on Andreyev*, p. 43, and
Two Truths, p. 89.

[80] *Works—VII*, p. 233.

[81] Scene 7, pp. 169, 170.

scene of the *Black Maskers* there is a hint at some synthesis in the words of Francesca concerning the child she feels under her breast. She promises to tell her child of its father, Duke Lorenzo, who has burned himself alive in the purging fire of truth. Francesca symbolizes beauty and purity, Lorenzo merciless analysis. Will the offspring of the two combine both characters? The same motive sounds at the conclusion of *The Ocean*. Mariette lifts her baby toward the sea, where the pirate ship is ready to start under its Black Sails, and shouts to Haggart that their son, little Noni, will grow up and hang his father at the mast-head. Their son—again a synthesis, a combination of Haggart and Mariette, of will-to-power and justice-truth.

The kinship between Nietzsche and Andreyev, their differences notwithstanding, has been shown in the course of this essay. One may recall that the synthetic motive is common to both of them. To Zarathustra the "Great Noontide," the ripe hour when the advent of the superman becomes possible, is announced by a significant "sign," the communion of the lion and the doves. The hardness of the diamond, the fearlessness of the lion, the wisdom of the serpent, the flight of the eagle, these virtues Zarathustra deems indispensable for building up the superman, for overcoming the bedwarfing temptation of the "last man." Yet he admits that these virtues are not sufficient for the consummation of the ideal, that they must have their complement in the gentleness of the dove. "It is the stillest words which bring the storm. Thoughts that come with doves' footsteps guide the world." [82] Andreyev may have noted Zarathustra's exclamation at the sight of the lion and the doves: "Meine Kinder sind nahe, meine Kinder." [83] The ideal man will be personified not in Jesus or in David Leiser, not in Haggart or Judas or Anathema, not even in Zarathustra—the forerunner, but in their "children," in their problematic, utopian syntheses. Toward the land of the children yearns the seeker:

---

[82] "Die stillste Worte sind es, welche den Sturm bringen. Gedanken, die mit Taubenfüssen kommen, lenken die Welt."—*Also sprach Zarathustra:* "Die stillste Stunde," p. 217 (*Werke—VII*).
[83] *Ibid.,* "Das Zeichen," p. 474.

Ach, wohin soll ich nun noch steigen mit meiner Sehnsucht! Von allen Bergen schaue ich aus nach Vater-und Mutterländern. Aber Heimat fand ich nirgends; unstet bin ich in allen Städten und ein Aufbruch an allen Toren. Fremd sind mir und ein Spott die Gegenwärtigen, zu denen mich jüngst das Herz trieb; und vertrieben bin ich aus Vater-und Mutterländern. So liebe ich allein noch meiner *Kinder Land,* das unentdeckte, im fernsten Meere: nach ihm heisse ich meine Segel suchen und suchen. An meinen Kindern will ich es gut machen, dass ich meiner Väter Kind bin: und an aller Zukunft—*diese* Gegenwart! [84]

Hope in a better future, in a synthetic man relegated to the "land of the children," brings Andreyev once more closer to Nietzsche than to Schopenhauer, who could see no chance for the world's amelioration. We have been able to observe Andreyev's kinship to both these philosophers, through a common critical evaluation of life as it is, and a common quest for a dignified *modus vivendi* for man. Finding it possible in the main to follow both of them in regard to the first problem, Andreyev was forced to vacillate between the two in his examination of the second question. Should man's ideal be the reduction of the life-impulse to a minimum, or its augmentation to the *n*th degree? Is man's mission to abnegate his self, and live for others, or is man to practice the teaching of Personalism, and to ignore everything and everybody in favor of his personal growth and expression? Andreyev does not come out decidedly for one solution or the other. His treatment of these questions suggests a painful effort to reconcile Schopenhauer and Nietzsche, to arrive at a synthesis.

[84] *Ibid.,* "Vom Lande der Bildung," p. 177.

V

RECAPITULATIONS

Variants of former themes.—Maturity of tone and conceptions.—Contemporary social life at a standstill.—Pseudo-parliamentarism.—Cadets, and *The Pretty Sabine Women*.—Political adaptability.—Merit of the Cadets.—Demoralizing effect of official policy.—Reign of pettiness and vulgarity, portrayed in *Professor Storitsyn, Katherina Ivanovna, Thou Shalt Not Kill*.—Storitsyn and Savvich.—Mentikov, omnipotent pettiness.—Yakov, the Russian people.—*He Who Gets Slapped*.—Intellect and beauty profaned.—*The Waltz of the Dogs*.—Solitude motive.—*Samson Enchained*, Andreyev's triumph.—Man's inner conflict.—Andreyev's decline, in *Satan's Diary*.—A characteristic close to Andreyev's career.

DURING the last years of his life (1912–1919) Andreyev created nothing that was new in form or in motive. His writings of this period present largely repetitions or elaborations of former themes, and further illustrations of his basic points of view. His premise is the same: a negative attitude toward life, man, human intellect and institutions. What he proceeds to draw is merely one detail or another, one situation or another, for the substantiation of the premised idea. Only he no longer vacillated in the direction of hope and encouragement, as he did on occasion in the preceding period: the picture he now projects on his canvas is consistently gloomy, whether it reflects the opportunism of the Russian liberals (*The Pretty Sabine Women*), or the reign of vulgarity in life (*Professor Storitsyn*), or the omnipotence of pettiness (*Katherina Ivanovna*), or the tragedy of misplaced force (*Thou Shalt Not Kill*), or the eternal drama of man's solitude (*The Waltz of the Dogs*), of man's inner discord (*Samson Enchained*), or of man's prodigious villainy (*Satan's Diary*). Andreyev's last

303

period resembles his first period, both by its unrelieved gloom and by the realistic style of the writings that fall within it. But, needless to say, the later Andreyev has acquired maturity and greater depth in his evaluations as well as in his style. Toward the end of his life he speaks with the sad wisdom of experience, and he speaks in the sure tones of a realism understandable to all, yet pregnant with symbolic significances.

Coincidentally, Russian life during the years preceding the war was at a standstill, at least on the surface. Apathy and stagnation seemed to have taken the place of the recent intense activity which had spurred Russia to live through in weeks events, hopes and disappointments, normally requiring years and generations. The public was weary of the strenuous years of war, strikes, revolts, broken promises and shattered hopes, punitive expeditions, wholesale executions and political noise in general. Life seemed to have become normal again, differing but little from the state of affairs before 1905. The liberties solemnly granted in the October Manifesto (namely, personal inviolability, freedom of conscience, speech, meetings, and associations, equal franchise, and the "immutable rule that no law can ever come into force without the approval of the State Duma"), were withdrawn, explained away, "modified" into nothingness. When the first and second Dumas, despite governmental interference and police coercion, gave an overwhelming majority to the opposition, Premier Stolypin perpetrated a *coup d'état*. In June, 1907, the electoral law was modified in such a way that the majority of seats in the third and fourth (last) Dumas belonged to the landowners and to the large capitalists. Even the "desirable" Duma had little power, however: its measures had to be sanctioned by the Council of State (the upper house), half of which consisted of the tsar's appointees. The "parliament" was reduced to a pliable tool in the hands of the Government. When one of the chambers had the audacity to oppose Stolypin, the latter did not scruple to prorogue the "parliament" for three days, during which time he promulgated the rejected law as an emergency measure. In 1912 P. N. Milyukov admitted that "the five years of the third

Duma had sufficiently clarified the situation. In order to acquire one single right—to *exist*, the Duma had to become one of the wheels in the bureaucratic machine." [1] Count Witte, the author of the Constitutional Manifesto, bitterly attacked Alexander Guchkov, leader of the Octoberist party, for hailing Stolypin as the protagonist of the "new order." "I assert," wrote Witte, "that in the new, renovated order, which Guchkov champions at present, only the corpse of October 30 is preserved, that under the banner of a 'constitutional régime' . . . they [the Government] have augmented their own power to unlimited, absolute, unprecedented arbitrariness." [2]

The revolutionary forces were once more driven underground. No political party to the left of the Octoberists was permitted to function legally. Consequently not only the socialist groups but even the liberals existed "illegally." The latter, namely the Constitutional-Democratic party, better known as the Cadets, occupied a very delicate position. This party contained the most cultured men of Russia, liberal-minded professors, lawyers, physicians, engineers, journalists, landowners, manufacturers and average middle-class persons. Though opposed to the Government, the Cadets did not approve of the principles and tactics of the revolutionists, and endeavored to follow a middle course, which was most difficult under the circumstances. Composed of various elements, the party wavered from the right to the left and back again, shifting its policy time and again. The Cadets formed the largest group in the first two Dumas, but while in the first Duma they demanded the subordination of the Government to the parliament,[3] in the second

---

[1] *Yearbook of the Daily Speech* (*Yezhegodnik gazety Ryech*), p. 94. Petrograd, 1912. Though a prominent figure in the Duma, Milyukov grew more and more pessimistic in his view of the value of this institution. Cf. his article on "The Representative System in Russia," in *Russian Realities and Problems*, pp. 25–46. Cambridge, England, 1917. Also p. 5 of his book, *Russia To-Day and To-Morrow*. New York, 1922.

[2] *Speech*, October 8, 1911. Quoted in *Russia's Riches*, October 1911, p. 118, footnote.

[3] V. Nabokov: "The executive power shall submit to the legislative power." In his speech in the first Duma, May 13, 1906.—*Stenographic Reports—I*, p. 326. Petrograd, 1906. I. I. Petrunkevich: "Popular representation in Russia can exist only when there shall be a ministry responsible before the Duma . . . The ulti-

Duma they pursued the "siege tactics" advocated by their able leader, Paul N. Milyukov.[4] Though legally a forbidden party, they tried to coördinate their words and acts with the existing laws. The legalistic opportunism of the Cadets was satirized by Andreyev in *The Pretty Sabine Women*.[5]

The Cadets are the husbands of the Sabine women—the liberties declared in October 1905—abducted by the Roman soldiers—the Government. The leader of the bereaved husbands assembles them to march to the camp of the kidnappers, armed with heavy volumes of laws, enactments and decisions, and with four hundred tomes of investigations compiled by their jurists on the question of the legality of their marriages and the illegality of the kidnapping. The just Sabines reject other weapons and violent methods as unworthy of their dignity: "Our weapons are a clear conscience and the justice of our cause." The leader has some difficulty in training the Sabines how to march, for they are not quite sure of their right and of their left. Moreover, he has a special system of marching:

Two steps-forward, one step backward; two steps forward, one step backward. The first two steps are designed to indicate, Sabines, the unquenchable fire of our stormy souls, the firm will, the irresistible advance. The step backward symbolizes the step of reason, the step of experience and of the mature mind. In taking that step we ponder the outcome of our acts. In taking it we also maintain, as it were, a close bond with tradition, with our ancestors, with our great past. History

mate result . . . will be either a *coup d'état*, the withdrawal of the constitutional charter of October 30 and the abolition of popular representation, or the complete victory of the latter, and the establishment of a responsible and parliamentary ministry."—In *The First State Duma* (*Pervaya gosudarstvennaya duma*). Petrograd, 1907.

4 "Not by storm, but by regular siege . . . Not hopeless 'demands,' but a systematic effort to conquer the position occupied by the enemy . . . No need to hurry: the conflict will be serious and lasting."—*The Second Duma* (*Vtoraya Duma*). Petrograd, 1908.

5 During the season of 1915–1916 this play ran with considerable success at the Chicago Little Theatre, under the direction of Maurice Browne. Though a political satire, the play was enjoyed for its genuine humor even by those who knew nothing about the Cadets. As in the case of *He Who Gets Slapped*, the uninitiated audience liked the play for its visible value, regardless of its underlying meaning —an acid test for a symbolistic play.

makes no leaps, and we, Sabines, at this great moment, we are history. Trumpeters, trumpet![6]

One recognizes in Martius, the leader of the husbands, Andreyev's pet aversion—the dogmatic preacher of common sense. He speaks in the turgid style of the slimy author of *My Memoirs,* also dragging in reason and logic to cover his cowardly adaptability. "Two steps forward, one step backward" was the way Lenin characterized the policy of opportunistic revolutionists, in a pamphlet of the same title, published about 1902. In employing this slogan for the Cadets, Andreyev voiced the opinion of those opposed to the tactics of Milyukov and his party, both from the conservative and from the radical sides. It is the fate of mediators, of reconcilers, of neutrals, of neither-one-thing-nor-the-other, to be disliked and despised by their antagonists on either side. The Cadets pleased none of their opponents by their splendid oratory, their erudite arguments, their forceful exhortations, their pathetic appeals to justice, right, and humanity. Of what avail are the efforts of the Sabine husbands to prove the legality of their marriages and the illegality of the abduction of their wives? The Roman soldiers do not even attempt to deny either of these postulates. To touch the conscience of the Government was as easy as to make a Cossack blush. The government of Stolypin and his successors acted as victors by virtue of superior force, and they used force without stint in subduing the vanquished. Russia presented two sharply divided camps—the Government, with those of the landowners and manufacturers who supported the drastic policy of Restoration, and the broad layers of the people, robbed of the concessions they won in October, 1905. The balance of power depended on the army. As long as it remained unthinkingly loyal and obedient to the authorities, the people's cause had no chance for success. The revolutionary parties recognized this fact, and concentrated their efforts on revolutionizing the army and the young workmen and peasants,

---

[6] *Works—XIV,* Act II, p. 178 (quoted after the translation of Meader and Scott, *Plays by Leonid Andreyeff,* p. 182).

who were prospective recruits. Meanwhile the eloquent Cadets continued to vie with the laurels of Mirabeau and Parnell. The Government trampled under its heavy boot all considerations of law and justice, cynically destroying any respect for these conceptions, but the Cadets persevered in acting the outraged innocents, and in strictly adhering to the legal code. When the Sabine women suggest that their husbands should reabduct them from the Romans, Martius refuses to commit violence, to jeopardize his "legal conscience," and he beats a grandiloquent retreat:

> Long live the law! Let them take my wife from me by brute violence; let them ruin my home; let them extinguish my hearth; I shall never prove false to the law. Let the whole world laugh at the unfortunate Sabines, they will not prove false to the law. Virtue commands respect, even in rags. Sabines, retreat! Weep, Sabines, weep bitter tears! Sob, beat your breasts, and be not ashamed of tears. Let them stone us, let them mock us, but weep! Let them besmear us with mud! Weep, Sabines; you are weeping for the scorned and down-trampled law. Forward, Sabines. Attention! Trumpeters, strike up the march. Two steps forward, one step backward; two steps forward, one step backward! [7]

Justice demands that one should credit the Cadets with at least one merit—the preservation of the Duma. Since the second Duma their slogan had been: "Spare the Duma," which was by no means an easy task. The Cadets had to steer between the Scylla of revolutionary outbursts on the part of the Left, and the Charybdis of provocative onslaughts by the extreme Right, whose leaders were openly supported and encouraged by the Government in their hostility to the Duma. It is a debatable question as to the net results of the twelve years of the Duma's existence. But one can hardly deny the fact that it performed an educational service in the development of the national political consciousness. For twelve years the politically untrained country watched the performances of the quasi-parliament, and, if anything, it must have gained information as to what is not a true representative form of government.

[7] *Ibid.*, p. 185. (Meader and Scott, p. 194.)

Again, one must remember that the tribune of the Duma was the only place from which the country could be addressed by such speakers as Milyukov, Rodichev, Shingarev, Nabokov, Aladyin, Kerensky, Chkheidze, Tseretelli and others, whose denunciations of the existing order became accessible to millions of eager readers and to even more millions of illiterate listeners. Whether it ultimately pleased Milyukov and his group or not, through their efforts the Duma had played the rôle of a grandiose soap box for the spread of subversive ideas among the Russian population.

At the same time the reigning policy could not but have a demoralizing effect on the public. The adage that a people have the kind of government they deserve does not preclude the possibility that a government may infect, not merely mirror, the governed. And the Russian government, from the end of 1905 to March 1917, reeked with cynicism and falsehood. Before the October uprising official Russia was avowedly autocratic, paternalistic, despotic, a mixture of Byzantine and Tartar traditions. In their struggle against tsarism the people knew definitely that they strove for the substitution of European forms for Asiatic, of Constitutionalism for Absolutism. But after 1905 official Russia presented a Janus. On the one hand a bicameral parliament, on the other a tsar continuing to bear the title of "Autocrat of all the Russias." On the one hand an alleged legislative body, on the other an irresponsible ministry arrogantly playing with the Duma and with the Council of State as with pawns. Partial abolition of the censorship, and multiplied penalties on editors and publishers, confiscations of newspapers, magazines and books. Academic freedom, and wholesale dismissals of deans and professors from the University of Moscow and from the Kiev Politechnicum, and their replacement by "desirables," in "administrative order." "Constitutionalism," and arbitrary arrests, trials, executions, on an unprecedented scale, the prisons and places of exile overfilled with political "offenders." [8] The Government did not scruple about supporting reactionary organizations responsible for the

---

[8] For names and figures, see *Russia under Nicolas II*, pp. 329–331.

assassination of liberal members of the Duma, about organizing and condoning massacres of Jews, about employing in the revolutionary parties agents provocateurs who performed the double function of betraying their comrades and of dynamiting official dignitaries. The atmosphere was saturated with brutality, hypocrisy, perversity. Literature became flooded with pornography. Obscenity permeated the popular stage. Rough sports began to appeal to college youths, replacing their former idealistic predilections. Rude force, the might of the fist, dominated the hour. At the same time numerous religious fads reigned in salons and in saloons, from esoteric mysticism to vulgar Rasputinism. It seemed as if the public, tired of sacrifices and of thwarted idealism, had thrown itself with abandon in an opposite direction—carnal self-gratification and solipsism.

With these conditions as a background, Andreyev's realistic, or psycho-realistic, plays, *Professor Storitsyn, Katherina Ivanovna,* and *Thou Shalt Not Kill* may be regarded as symbolizations of contemporary moods and ailments, or rather of one general phenomenon—life's vulgar pettiness. The loneliness, the insecurity, the impotence of the beautiful and noble, amidst the crude surroundings of modern materialism, is the tragedy of Professor Storitsyn and the tragedy of Katherina Ivanovna. The former dies from a broken heart, unable to survive life's coarseness. The latter is infected with life's coarseness, and becomes a moral ruin. In either case it is the vulgar and the base that triumph, that survive as the fittest. How weak sounds the voice of the æsthetic Professor!

I am a modest, quiet Russian, born with an enormous, and apparently fortuitous, need of beauty, of a beautiful, meaningful life. Every one has his hangman—my hangmen are the coarseness of our life, its ugliness, its meanness.[9]

The still, small voice of Storitsyn is drowned by the husky shouts of his "hangman," Savvich, who demoralizes the Professor's home and bullies the gentle worshipper of beauty.

[9] In *Earth* (*Zemlya*), Miscellany—*XI*, p. 40. Moscow, 1913.

Storitsyn is crushed when he is forcibly drawn from his heights to realize the mire surrounding him.   In vain does he endeavor to ignore the intimate relations between his wife and the coarse Savvich.   The filth accumulates, and bespatters him even in his retreat.   Savvich breaks into his study, reprimands him for scolding his wife, the woman who was once his ideal of pure beauty, and who is now "a lady in a stiff corset, with powder on her beet-like face, with a bosom that might nurse thousands of infants, thousands of martyrs and heroes, but which nourishes only Savvich."   Savvich even threatens to beat him, Storitsyn, an academic luminary, the idol of ecstatic audiences. Why not?   Savvich is proud of his muscular strength, and physical force is what counts most these days.   It is not only Savvich, an outsider, an impudent intruder, who thrusts his dirty boot into the Professor's soul: even his best friend, the soldierly Dr. Telemakhov, and his own son, Volodya, rack his fine mind with their rude manners, when they administer a well-deserved thrashing to the impossible Savvich.   And a potential Savvich appears in his own family, in the person of his younger son, Sergey, who steals and sells his father's books, drinks and smokes, "lives with" a classmate, a high-school girl, prides himself on being a lowbrow, respects a man of "character," like Savvich, and chides his father for carrying a trifling life-insurance policy of only ten thousand rubles.

STORITSYN: . . . You are my flesh and blood, my own son . . . But where am I to be found in this creature?   Stay, stay, it is as though I were seeing your face for the first time . . . sit still, sit still, don't be embarrassed.   So then, this thing here, this flat thing, receding, squeezed in at the temples, is your forehead, my son's forehead?   Strange!   And whence comes to you this low, brutal jaw . . . you probably can bite through very thick bones, yes?

SERGEY: I don't care.

STORITSYN: And whence come these young but already dull and sullen eyes—such sullen eyes!   And then this little parting over your forehead . . . an interesting parting.   And this strange, cheap perfume. . . .[10]

[10] *Ibid.*, p. 62.

It is not the individual, Savvich, that is alarming: it is Savvichism, the vulgarization of all life, that menaces the few fine minds still extant to-day. Pre-war life in Russia—if only in Russia—presents an arena where the victors are invariably bullies, knaves, "practical characters." To the vulgar, the unscrupulous, belong the spoils. To the unscrupulous in particular. The frankly coarse and loudly rude are sufficiently conspicuous to be shunned, but life is infested with unscrupulous parasites whose very power consists in their smallness, pettiness, slickness, adaptability, aptness to sneak in through the tiniest crack and settle on you and yours. Such a pest is Mentikov, in *Katherina Ivanovna*. He is openly despised by all, yet he is ubiquitous; he unfailingly attends exclusive gatherings and artistic parties, lives on his numerous acquaintances, who do not know how to get rid of him, and even succeeds in befouling and utterly ruining Katherina Ivanovna, once a noble and beautiful soul. Her husband remarks that while he is not afraid of battling with strong enemies because they employ equal weapons, he finds himself absolutely powerless in face of an unscrupulous nonentity:

He is so deadly insignificant . . . Like a louse, he exists only because of our own uncleanliness . . . He crawls as long as we let him crawl, and should we block his way, he will crawl in a different direction. He exists always, always on the qui vive, ever ready. Why, one is likely to "catch" him, as one catches an infection, on the street car.[11]

Mentikovs breed where they meet with no strong resistance, they thrive in insanitary places; this is what is tragic. Katherina Ivanovna is dragged down lower and lower, finding no one strong enough to hold her back, to lift her from the mire. She is surrounded with the cream of the nation: her husband is a

---

[11] In *Wild-Rose Almanacs*, No. 19, pp. 179–180. Petrograd, 1913. Cf. Nietzsche's words on pettiness: "Das schlimmste aber sind die kleinen Gedanken. Wahrlich, besser noch bös gethan, als klein gedacht! . . . Wie ein Geschwür ist die böse Tat: sie juckt und kratzt und bricht heraus,—sie redet ehrlich. 'Siehe, ich bin Krankheit'—so redet die böse Tat; das ist ihre Ehrlichkeit. Aber dem Pilze gleich ist der kleine Gedanke: er kriecht und duckt sich und will nirgendswo sein—bis der ganze Leib morsch und welk ist vor kleinen Pilzen."—*Also sprach Zarathustra*: "Von den Mitleidigen," p. 129 (*Werke—VII*).

prominent member of the Duma, their friends are from the intellectual aristocracy, their environment artistic—yet she suffocates in emptiness. Andreyev shows the moral bankruptcy of Russia's intellectuals. They are devoid of chivalry, they lack fastidiousness, they have cheapened life's values. They all tolerate Mentikov, though he steals their wives and their drawings: they are avowed compromisers. No wonder Mentikov has the nerve to treat Katherina Ivanovna's husband with a cigarette, and to offer a Bruderschaft-drink to all these respectable intellectuals. They observe the decaying process of Katherina Ivanovna, they watch her sink ever deeper, some of them make use of her weakness and accessibility, but not one of them possesses moral stamina to save her, to bring her back to her exalted place from which she once slipped. The presentation of this play aroused heated comments among the Russian intellectuals, some of these comments referring to the general emptiness and pettiness of their life during the Duma years. Alexander Benois, a leading critic and painter, wrote:

Somehow the play stirs our dark despair, our helpless grief. Katherina Ivanovna says that they have "killed her soul," but is our common soul sufficiently alive to sympathize with others' woe? Do we not at these terrible words turn involuntarily to ourselves, not individually, but to the self of all of us taken together, and do we not perceive that where we have supposed the existence of a soul, there is only the abomination of desolation? This [the play] is the reflection of our life, this is our spiritual emptiness gazing with dead eyes out of the mirror.[12]

In *Thou Shalt Not Kill* the central figure is Yakov, the handsome janitor who kills the tottering old eccentric landlord. He kills only to please his mistress, the housekeeper, who is heir to the master of the house. The act is committed neither from hatred or malice, nor from avariciousness, not even from love for his mistress. Yakov is overflowing with energy. He does not utilize it, but squanders it on petty things, just to oblige others. Yakov is awfully good-natured, he does not refuse himself to any of the numerous women who are fond of him.

[12] In *Speech*, No. 129, 1913. See *supra*, p. 124.

And he kills just to oblige. He recognizes no law, neither that of God nor that of the Senate. It is this primitive nihilism of the Russian people that Andreyev probably intends to depict. The time of the idealization of the people has passed. It has become evident that illiterate Russia is under the "dominion of darkness," as Tolstoy has named his terrible play based on village life. The enormous stored-up power of Yakov requires an outlet. But unless Yakov be imbued with some ideas, with some knowledge, his good nature may work havoc when made use of by destructive or petty forces. It is a terrible abyss, this nihilistic emptiness of the elemental Yakov, more terrible, indeed, than the emptiness of the upper layers of society, the intellectuals, because it is elemental and chaotic, capable of subverting and destroying and annihilating for no other reason than the need of an outlet. Perhaps it is this Yakov-spirit which has inspired the futuristic sculptor, the author of the monument to Michael Bakunin, recently erected in Moscow. The reproduction of the monument presents a chaotic mass of débris looming upward, with the inscription of Bakunin's words: "The spirit of destruction is the creative spirit." [18]

The impotence of Storitsyn's craving after beauty, in face of triumphant vulgarity; the spiritual wilderness among the Russian Intelligentsia, who through their opportunism and passivity breed legalistic sophists and Mentikovs; the misplaced and misused strength of Yakov—the common people—these are fragmentary motives of Andreyev's Weltanschauung already familiar to us. The war seemed to have transformed Andreyev's outlook, to have generated in him a strong faith in man. But this change was only on the surface, in his journalistic utterings and such semi-journalistic productions as *King, Law, Liberty*. Andreyev tried to drown his never slumbering doubts in the turmoil of the war, to silence his persistent inner No with a violent, blatant Yes. Neither his bombastic war stuff, nor such popular trifles written during the war as *Youth, Dear Phantoms, Requiem* (of these he speaks with contempt in his

[18] The reproduction appeared in Konstantin Umansky's *Die Neue Kunst in Russland*, p. 31. Potsdam, 1920.

diary and in his letters to Goloushev and to Nemirovich-
Danchenko), expressed his true self. For though he was many-
voiced and composed of several contradictory selves, his genuine and dominating self was essentially negative. His actual
attitude to mankind, fragmentarily reflected in the four plays
discussed in the preceding pages of this chapter, was stated more
fully and, one may say, summarily, in *He Who Gets Slapped*,
presented on the stage of the Moscow Dramatic Theatre in
1915.

In this drama life is a grotesque misplacement of forces and
faculties. Intellect, in the person of a celebrated luminary, disgusted with the surrounding stupidity, treachery and vulgarity,
descends into a circus, to serve as a clown. He leaves his great
name behind him, becomes known as He (the Russian word
"tot" means "that one"), and makes the audience roar with
laughter at the sight of him receiving innumerable slaps from
his fellow clowns. A bizarre revenge, this contemplation of
men gaffawing at the spectacle of intellect reduced to a clown
who submits placidly to the slaps of professional jesters. "He"
prefers this open mockery and humiliation to the treatment
great minds are given "out there," where his own, genuine ideas
are successful only after they have been stolen by a popularizer
and rehashed into a vulgar concoction for the crowd. To the
Prince, the man who has taken possession of his wife and his
thoughts, and whose uneasy conscience prompts him to come to
the circus and hold discourse with his master-victim, He says:

You—you great profaner!—you have made my ideas accessible even to
horses. With the skill of a great profaner, of a costumer of ideas, you
have arrayed my Apollo as a barber, you have handed my Venus a yellow
ticket, to my radiant hero you have appended the ears of an ass, and lo,
your career is made, as Jackson [the chief clown] says. And wherever
I go, the whole street grimaces at me with thousands of faces, in which—
what mockery!—I recognize the features of my own children. . . .[14]

[14] *He Who Gets Slapped* (*Tot, kto poluchayet poshchdchiny*), pp. 52, 53. (Ladyschnikow, Berlin, undated.) One recalls Nietzsche's words: . . . "meine *Lehre*
ist in Gefahr, Unkrauten will Weizen heissen! Meine Feinde sind mächtig
worden und haben meiner Lehre Bildniss entstellt, also, dass meine Liebsten sich
der Gaben schämen müssen, die ich ihnen gab."—*Also sprach Zarathustra:* "Das
Kind mit dem Spiegel," p. 120 (*Werke—VII*).

But the vulgarizer is not satisfied with being the "flat shadow" [15] of "He," reaping success and fame by means of the borrowed ideas. Far from being grateful to the man responsible for his prosperity, he hates him, because he is aware of his superiority, of his dominating personality which looms from behind all the stolen and popularized editions of his thoughts. Only the death of the master will reconcile and appease his "flat shadow." But no—

. . . you are not my shadow [says "He"], I was mistaken. You are the crowd. While living a life imbued by me, you hate me. While breathing my breath, you are choking with malice. Yet while choking with malice, while hating and despising me, you drag yourself at the tail of my ideas . . . but advancing hindside forward, advancing hindside forward, comrade! [16]

"He," intellect profaned and abused by the crowd, is not the only tragic character in the drama, though the most obvious one. There is Consuella, the bareback rider, the alleged daughter of a dubious count, pretty of face but ignorant, illiterate, and desperately naïve. "He" discovers under her ordinary husk a sleeping beauty, a goddess born out of the sea foam, who has forgotten her native atmosphere, asleep among wretched mortals. Consuella is stirred by the words of "He," who attempts to awaken her, to lift her above her sordid surroundings, but she is unable to recall clearly her divine origin, and is about to plunge blindly into the net of the spider—to marry the Baron, the incarnation of self-confident vulgarity. "He," who has deliberately placed himself in a grotesque position, cannot endure the gross burlesque which is to be enacted behind the circus scenes, and he rescues Consuella by sharing with her a glass of poisoned wine. For once the all-powerful, never-failing spider-vulgarity is cheated out of a prospective victim. But the circus goes on, the crowd continues to be amused by misplaced tal-

---

[15] Zarathustra, too, was pursued by his "shadow," his imitator, follower and simplifier, to whom the gist of his master's teaching consisted of "Nichts ist wahr, alles ist erlaubt."—*Ibid.*, "Der Schatten," p. 395 ff. In a similar sense, Smerdyakov acted as the shadow of Ivan Karamazov, in Dostoyevsky's novel.

[16] Act III, p. 54.

ent and by misused force, by caged lions and submissive tigers, by intellect become clown, by Bezano—a young god turned circus rider, by Zinida—surcharged with power and passion which she spends in taming and distorting wild beasts.[17]

Our attention need not be detained long by *The Waltz of the Dogs*, a play which harmonizes with Andreyev's mood during this last period, permeated as it is with black sadness. Although the author regards the play as "remarkable! One of the teeth in his lugubrious crown, a black dent,"[18] one has difficulty in sharing his enthusiasm. Andreyev tries to express the depth of the tragedy of solitude—in fact he gives the play the subtitle of "a poem of solitude." This old motive of his, which we have discussed in the chapter on his early writings, increased in intensity toward the end of Andreyev's life, owing to his personal experience. We may understand therefore why this play possessed an intimate value for its author, but the very fact that he found himself obliged to defend it, to battle for it, to explain

[17] Andreyev's personal view of this play was expressed in a letter to Mlle. Polevitsky, the first Consuella at the Dramatic Theatre. A few extracts from this letter are given below:

First of all, Consuella must be in appearance a goddess, according to the exact laws of classic beauty. Tall and graceful, with features regular and severe, softened by the expression of an almost childlike naïveté and charm. Everything about her which savors of the circus and of the commonplace, from her costume to her language and somewhat vulgar manners, is only on the surface, external. One of the most important tasks of the player and of the director, is to show the actual beneath the tinsel of a bareback rider and acrobat. In her character, her psyche, Consuella is lofty, pure, and unconsciously *tragic*. The latter is very important. It is not the extraneous dramatism of the voluptuous Zinida, but the deep and genuine tragicness created by the contradiction between Consuella's divine essence and her external, *accidental* expression.

She is a captive in life, she is enslaved by oppressive reality, by the power of material things, and she suffers. Before the advent of "He," she is asleep, as it were; he awakens her. That moment, when she tries to recall her home—the heaven, and cannot, is replete with great sorrow for her. . . .

There is nothing easier than a drama in which everything is on the surface—in movements, shouts, tears, wails, in the clear visibility of dramatic collisions. But great is the difficulty of that rôle in which the whole tragedy is outwardly based on half-tones, on a sigh, on an expression of sadness in one's face or eyes, when the inner state of mind is hidden even from the person who experiences it. . . . this fairy-tale play tells of beautiful gods tormented by earthly violence, wandering in the labyrinth of man's petty affairs and heavy passions.—From his letter addressed to Elena Alexeyevna [Polevitskaya], September, 1915.

[18] Letter to Goloushev, October, 1916.

and comment, to exhort in its favor even such a keen appreciator as Nemirovich-Danchenko, shows that its intrinsic and universal value is dubious. He endeavors to convince Danchenko of the serious importance of the "poem," of its possession of "the most hidden and cruel sense of tragedy, which denies the meaning and reason of man's existence," through "comparing the world and mankind to dancing dogs which some one is pulling by a cord and tempting with a lump of sugar." [19] Any one trained in reading and interpreting Andreyev cannot fail to grasp this underlying idea in *The Waltz of the Dogs,* but the idea remains dangling in the air, unattached to the ground, disembodied. From the very beginning of the play to its end, the reader, like the dogs in the waltz, is being pulled by a string. The author attempts to hypnotize him, and he shouts into his ear with monotonous repetition that he is witnessing a tragic performance. The actors *tell* us that the new residence of Henry Tille has an atmosphere of crime, that the song of the plasterers expresses Russian sadness, that they are afraid, that they are oppressed with solitude, that they are on the verge of insanity. The character of Henry Tille, the chief personage of the play, is drawn with too obvious, bold strokes, with an exaggerated emphasis on his preciseness and fondness for mathematical figures, deviced for the purpose of making his smashed plans and thwarted expectations appear in high relief. The reader is aware of the author's efforts, and is therefore on the *qui vive,* on the defensive against being hypnotized. *The Waltz of the Dogs,* with its many excellences (such as the character of Alexandrov, or as the entire third act), is one of Andreyev's rare failures to capture the reader and persuade him of the inner reality of the world presented to him. It is not impossible that the author may be more successful with the spectator. Intelligent actors may succeed in conveying the atmosphere of marionettes in *The Waltz of the Dogs,* not so much through the verbal medium, as through other histrionic means. This hypothesis has as yet had no chance to be tested.

[19] From a letter dated September, 1916.

Far more successful than *The Waltz of the Dogs,* was Andreyev's dramatic experiment in his tragedy, *Samson Enchained* (still unpublished). Here, as in *Professor Storitsyn,* in *Katherina Ivanovna,* in *He Who Gets Slapped,* in *The Waltz of the Dogs,* the author attempts a "psycho-realistic" treatment of the subject. Instead of leading up to a climactic action, in the ordinary theatrical fashion, he begins his dramas *after* the external dénouement has taken place. Convinced that the "new theatre" ought to leave exterior action to the cinematograph, and strive for an artistic expression of man's inner experiences,[20] Andreyev reveals the drama of Storitsyn, displayed amidst an environment already corrupted, the drama of Katherina Ivanovna, taking place after her husband's attempt to shoot her, the drama of "He," evolving after his catastrophic collision with life "out there," the drama of Henry Tille, following his betrayal by his betrothed, and the drama of Samson as it develops subsequent to his being captured, blinded, and chained by the Philistines. The problem is to construct the psychic drama on a realistic basis, to present the soul-world of the character not as a disembodied abstraction, but as a concrete reality comprehensible to "Schopenhauer and his cook." Unlike *The Waltz of the Dogs, Samson Enchained* proves Andreyev's ability to cope with this difficult problem. In a letter, presumably to Nemirovich-Danchenko (undated), he gives an interesting estimate of his *Samson:*

. . . Pushkin, like Shakespeare, is not a psychologist. That which we regard as Psyche, is an inseparable combination of spirit and body; in Pushkin and Shakespeare the spirit exists without a body. This lends the aspect of divinity to Pushkin's heroes, but it destroys utterly our precious Psyche. Neither Mozart nor Salieri [in Pushkin's *Mozart and Salieri*], nor even Don Juan [in Pushkin's drama of that name], possesses a body. However wild it may sound, Don Juan lacks the ordinary mark of manhood—Paganini without his violin! In Pushkin we find not feelings, but Platonic *ideas* of feelings; not love and envy and fear, but the ideas of love, envy, fear. . . . *Samson Enchained* presents an experiment in psy-

[20] *Letters on the Theatre. Supra,* p. 119 ff.

chologic tragedy, and an experiment which has succeeded. The spirit remains on a tragic elevation, yet it does not depart from the body, is merged with it as a living unity. The feelings, too, are given as such, not in their idea, not in a divine abstraction beyond time. Samson is a prophet who both performs the functions of nature and converses with God. Here the methods of truth and inner experiences, that is, the psychologic approach, may achieve a full, perhaps an unprecedented, triumph.

Indeed, Andreyev succeeds in blending the exotic historical exterior of the play with the inner, psychic tragedy of its hero. We are transported without effort into the time and place of the drama, we visualize the gorgeous festivities on the streets of Askalon, the splendor of Delilah's palace and of the temple of Dagon; and our ear drinks in the marvelous biblical language, which surpasses even *Judas Iscariot* in its virile simplicity and richness of images. Against this convincing background looms the gigantic figure of Samson, blind and fettered but still inspiring awe in his captors. The drama of Samson is a familiar Andreyev motive—man's inner conflict of opposing wills and contradictory selves, the struggle between the forces of good and evil, of nobility and baseness, of altruism and selfishness. Samson's chains are not those put on him by the Philistines, but the chains of his battling impulses. He is a huge animal, passionately addicted to carnal pleasures, but at the same time he is a chosen instrument of God, for the fulfillment of His will. Dark are the ways of Providence, and Samson cannot understand why he, such an unworthy vessel, has been selected to contain the voice of God. He groans under the burden of his mission, he rebels against his Sender, he craves quiescence. Captured during one of those moments when his carnal self prevails, blinded, beaten, humiliated, thrown into a filthy dungeon and cowed into submission, Samson is tempted to reconcile himself to his new position. The lot of a slave is so light, so care-free; Samson asks for nothing more than a hovel and a woman—"any kind of a woman: for my eyes see naught." We may recall that the idea of freeing oneself from responsibility through renouncing one's noble impulses and merging with the base and lowly has been suggested by Andreyev on several occasions.[21] But Samson is not permitted to find rest and peace in the slough of irresponsible vegetation. He is torn between calls and allurements. Delilah's brothers believe in Samson's divine power, and they desire to use this power for the aggrandizement of Philistia. Knowing of Samson's weakness for earthly pleasures, they release him from his dungeon, array him in royal garments, and bring him to the palace of Delilah, where he feasts on wine and song and Delilah's love. The judge and champion of Israel succumbs to the call of his carnal self. He spurns with contempt the girl of Judea, who comes to exhort him, to entreat him in the name of suffering Israel, to abuse and curse him for having sold himself to the enemies of his people. Samson declares his hatred for Judea, the wretched land of an austere God and a joyless religion. He refuses to be a slave to the Jewish God. He is free. But can the arrow rebel against the archer? In the desert, whither the Philistine nobles take him on a lion hunt, Samson shakes off the narcotic influence of Delilah's arms, wine and perfume. He listens to the wail of the wind, to the roar of the lion, he perceives the voice of God—and submits to it. The chains of the divine will prove stronger than those of woman's arms, of fragrant wine, of splendid garments, of jingling gold. At the Dagon festival Samson is stirred by the humiliations hurled at his nation and at his God, he becomes imbued with his former strength of will, he wills the destruction of his enemies, and proves victorious. Under the débris of the temple he frees himself of his unworthy instincts, even as Duke Lorenzo purges his heart in the fire of his Castle.

Samson Enchained is Andreyev's dramatic masterpiece. It is free from the stylistic eclecticism of *The Life of Man* and *Anathema,* from the baffling obscurities of *The Black Maskers* and *The Ocean,* from the obvious allegory present in most of

---

[21] For example, in his review of Ibsen's *Enemy of the People,* where he tells of his momentary desire to climb to the seat of the drozhki driver and become like him; in *Thought,* where Dr. Kerzhentsev dreams of joining the brotherhood of bandits; in *Darkness,* where the revolutionist throws in his lot with the riffraff; in *Professor Storitsyn,* where Storitsyn asks his brutish son for vodka, and requests him to take him to "bad places"; in *Sashka Zhegulev,* where the pure and noble Sasha descends to a life of robbery and murder, to appease the "voices."

his plays (*He Who Gets Slapped* included), it is free—needless
to say—from the evident laboriousness of *The Waltz of the
Dogs*. In its stylistic unity and clarity, and in its masterful
delineation of character, this tragedy ranks with *Professor Storitsyn, Katherina Ivanovna,* and *Thou Shalt Not Kill,* but it
surpasses these in the titanic grandeur of its scope, in its Attic
majesty.[22] *Samson Enchained* is Andreyev's unique triumph
as an ambitious attempt splendidly executed. Indeed, it presents the climactic peak in Andreyev's art, to be followed by
an indubitable decline. It may be considered, then, as his swan
song.

A striking proof of this decline is given by Andreyev's last
artistic effort, *Satan's Diary*. It was published posthumously,
and one is inclined to doubt whether the author would have
approved of the book's appearance in its present form. It
impresses the reader as slipshod and incomplete.[23] At all
events, the story produces a painful effect on one accustomed
to Andreyev's depth and brilliance, as though one beheld a
costly vase with a crack across its body. The author has lost
his mastery over the subject matter, his sense of proportion, his
subtlety, his felicity of expression. Aware of his failing, he
employs a subterfuge, making Satan blame the human tongue
for its inability to express complex ideas.[24] The Satan proves,
on the whole, a poor spokesman for Andreyev, when compared
with such preceding spokesmen as Kerzhentsev, Savva, Judas,
Anathema, Lorenzo and others. The fault, of course, is not
with Satan, but with the disintegration of his creator's talent.
The author is unable to cope with a plot which in his normal
days would lie precisely within his métier—witness *Anathema*.
His Satan enters the body of Mr. Wandergood, a multimillionaire packer from Illinois, with the intention of amusing himself
by "playing a part" as a human being. In the course of a few
weeks his superior mind and infernal wisdom collapse before human cunning and treachery. A human adventurer "plays his

---

[22] In his letter quoted on p. 129 f., Andreyev wrote that Fyodor Sologub regarded *Samson* as a restoration of the Greek tragedy.
[23] See Roerich's statement, *supra,* p. 162.
[24] Cf. pp. 9, 25, in *Satan's Diary (Dnevnik Satany),* Helsingfors, 1921.

part" more cleverly than Satan, exploits the latter's sentiments and emotions, inveigles him into falling in love with an alleged saintly virgin who turns out to be a depraved harlot, finally robs him of all his millions, and kicks him out of his own home. What an excellent subject for the author of *Judas, Anathema, My Memoirs, He Who Gets Slapped.* But Andreyev in the year 1919 resembles a bird whose wings have been pinioned. Instead of ranking with Andreyev's artistic productions, *Satan's Diary* comes closer to a wordy feuilleton, voicing in an obvious manner its author's disgust with the world and contempt for the human race.

Considered in this light, *Satan's Diary* forms a characteristic close to Andreyev's life and career. In the unevenly and nervously told story of a devil hoodwinked and surpassed by human deviltry one visualizes the pale face of the author in his last days, full of pain and humiliation. In cold and inhospitable Finland, cut off from Russia, living in solitude and privation, condemned by his Red enemies, and abandoned by his White "friends," Leonid Andreyev reaches the stage of complete disillusionment. He has spent forty-eight years on this earth, years of restless seeking, of futile attempts at solving life's riddle, in vain efforts to reconcile contradictions, to find a pacifying and harmonizing synthesis. Time and again he has been tempted by life—Delilah—to acquiesce, to bow down to earthly considerations (to write a popular play, a "best seller," to edit a patriotic daily), to soften his keen vision by rosy spectacles, to escape from reality into the mist of illusions. But, like Samson, he has been impelled to tear off the veil of Maja, and, hearkening to the voice of God, to shake the pillars of Philistia's stronghold, to smash and deny and destroy—and to perish amidst the ruins.

BIBLIOGRAPHY

BIBLIOGRAPHY

A. A CHRONOLOGICAL LIST OF ANDREYEV'S WORKS

Based largely on his *Collected Works*, in eight volumes, given as a premium to the magazine, *The Field* (*Niva*), for 1913, and on his *Collected Works*, in sixteen volumes, between 1910–1915, published by *Enlightenment* (*Prosveshcheniye*), Petrograd, (volumes I–XIII), by the *Moscow Publication House* (*Moskovskoye Knigoizdatelstvo*), Moscow (volume XIV), by the *Wild Rose* (*Shipovnik*), Petrograd (volume XV), and by the *Writers' Publication House* (*Knigoizdatelstvo Pisateley*), Moscow (volume XVI).

A question mark (?) appears after writings the year of whose composition is either unstated or uncertain.

An asterisk (*) denotes works which have been translated into English.

A cross (ˣ) precedes those works which are red-penciled in Andreyev's personal set of the *Field* edition, with the following explanation written with his own hand in the last volume: "The red marks works which I should include in a posthumous edition of my collected writings." One should observe that Andreyev wrote this before the publication of his *Thou Shalt Not Kill*, and of other works published after 1913.

1897–1903. Journalistic articles, sketches and reviews, which appeared largely in the Moscow *Courier*. Most of these were reprinted in volume I of his *Works*, in the *Enlightenment* edition.

1898. * Bargamot and Garaska.—Defense.—From the Life of Captain Kablukov.—Young Men.

1899. His First Fee.—* A Friend.—* Peter in the Country.—Valia.—In Passing.—* Little Angel.—At the Window.—* ˣ The Grand Slam.

1900. * ˣ The Lie.—ˣ On the River.—Mother.—ˣ The Story of Sergey Petrovich.—* Splendid is the Life of the Resuscitated.—A Holiday.—* ˣ Silence.—Into the Dark Faraway.

1901. * Laughter.—The Present.—ˣ Once There Lived.—* Snapper.—The Book.—* ˣ The Wall.—* The Tocsin.—An Incident.—* In the Basement.

1902. In Spring.—ˣ The Abyss.—* The City.—* ˣ Thought.—* ˣ An

327

Original Person.—* The Foreigner.—ˣ In Fog.—* A Robbery Planned.

1903.   * From My Life (autobiographical sketch).—* The Marseillaise.—Promises of Spring.—* At the Station.—* ˣ Ben Tobit. —* ˣ Life of Father Vasily Fiveysky.

1904.   There Is No Forgiveness.—The Thief.—ˣ Phantoms.—* ˣ The Red Laugh.

1905.   * ˣ The Governor.—* ˣ Thus It Was.—* To the Stars (a play).

1906.   * ˣ Lazarus.—Plays: * ˣ Savva.—* ˣ The Life of Man.

1907.   * ˣ Judas Iscariot and Others.—ˣ Darkness.—The Curse of the Beast.—* ˣ Tsar Hunger (a play).—Tales Not Quite for Children.

1908.   Ivan Ivanovich.—* ˣ My Memoirs (Marginal note by Andreyev: "My best story").—* ˣ The Seven That Were Hanged.—* From the Story Which Will Never Be Finished.— * Love, Faith, and Hope.—ˣ Christians.—The Oath.—Stop Thief.—The Giant.—Plays: * Death of Man (a variant of the last act of The Life of Man).—* ˣ The Black Maskers.— ˣ Days of Our Life.—* ˣ Love for Your Neighbor.—The Bat.

1909.   ˣ He.—ˣ Son of Man.—Plays: * ˣ Anathema.—Anfisa.

1910.   ˣ Sincere Laughter.—* ˣ Day of Wrath.—* The Serpent's Story.—Plays: Gaudeamus.

1911.   Gulliver's Death.—ˣ Peace.—ˣ Ipatov.—* ˣ A Flower under Foot.—ˣ Sashka Zhegulev.—* ˣ The Ocean (a play).

1912.   Carelessness (?).—ˣ Rules for Good Deeds.—* A letter on the Theatre.—Administrative Ecstasy (?).—A Cinematographic Story about Luckless John (?).—Plays: Honor.— * ˣ The Pretty Sabine Women.—ˣ Professor Storitsyn.—* ˣ Katherina Ivanovna.

1913.   * Letters on the Theatre (including the first Letter).— Thou Shalt Not Kill (a play).

1914.   The Flight.—Nights.—Resurrection.—The End of John the Preacher.—Herman and Martha.—The Bearers of Horns.— The Return.—Plays: Thought.—* An Event.—The Parrot.— * King, Law, Liberty.—Youth.

1915.   * War's Burden (a play).   * He Who Gets Slapped.

1916.   Dear Phantoms (a play).

1917.   Requiem (a play).

In 1914 Andreyev wrote two plays: * Samson Enchained, and * The

riote. Tr. by S. Persky. Paris, 1914 (Payot).

le la guerre. Confidences d'un petit homme durant le gran
s, 1917 (Collection de la Grande Revue).

d'un prisonier. Tr. by S. Persky. Paris, 1913 (Fontemoing
(contains: The Governor; Snapper; Life of Captai
The Foreigner; Bargamot and Garaska; The Present; A
Life is Splendid for the Resurrected). Tr. by S. Persky
(Monde Illustré).

rouge. La Guerre en Mandchourie. Tr. by S. Persky
(Perrin).

Pendus (includes: La vie d'un pope). Tr. by S. Persky and
d. Paris, 1911 (Fasquelle).

ime de Nietzsche (Histoire de Serguéi Piétrovitch), tr. by Z.
and Fagus. Mercure de France, March, 1903, pp. 620–654.

CH TRANSLATIONS OF ANDREYEV'S WRITINGS

chte. Tr. by S. van Praag. Amsterdam, 1917 (E. Querido).
erneur. Tr. by J. C. Termaat. Nijmegen, 1906 (H. Prakke).
slaapstee. Tr. by J. C. Termaat. (Zie Bibliotheek van
iteratuur, No. 8, 1908).

skarioth en de anderen. Tr. by Annie de Graaff. (Zie
van Russische literatuur, Nos. 13, 14, 1908).
ndige dorpspriester. Tr. by S. van Praag. Amsterdam, 1916
do).

e lach. Tr. by J. C. Termaat. Nijmegen, 1906 (H. Prakke).
Tr. by E. en L. de Haas, 1919 (W. P. van Stockum &

rten van België. Tr. by Oswaldi. Amsterdam, 1918 (J. M.
ff).

en gehangenen. Tr. by S. van Praag. Amsterdam, 1918 (E.

MAN TRANSLATIONS OF ANDREYEV'S WRITINGS

grund. Berlin, 1903 (J. Räde).
bgrund, und andere Novellen. Tr. by T. Kroczek. Halle,
Hendel).
ma. Tr. by C. Ritter. Berlin, 1911 (Ladyschnikow).

Waltz of the Dogs. The former is still unpublished; the latter was printed in the tenth issue of the Paris monthly, *Contemporary Annals,* for the year 1922. Two of Andreyev's unfinished works, A Conversation in the Night, and * Satan's Diary, were published in Helsingfors, Finland, in 1921 (Biblion Company). Satan's Diary appeared in its English version in 1920, in New York (Boni & Liveright) and Samson Enchained, in 1923 (Brentano).

This list does not include Andreyev's contributions to the daily press before and during the war and. the revolution.

B. ENGLISH TRANSLATIONS OF ANDREYEV'S WRITINGS

When the translator's title is too remote from the original title, the literal translation of the latter is given in parenthesis.

Andreyev on the Modern Theatre. Tr. by Manart Kippen. *New York Times* October 5, 1919, IV, 3: 1.

Andreyev on Motion Pictures. Tr. by Manart Kippen. *New York Times* October 19, 1919, VIII, 5: 1.

(The two preceding articles were translated—with excisions—from Andreyev's *Letters on the Theatre.*)

Anathema. Tr. by H. Bernstein. New York, 1910 (Macmillan).

Burglar, The (A Robbery Planned). Tr. by Thomas Seltzer. *Current Literature,* July, 1905, pp. 109–111.

Confessions of a Little Man During Great Days (War's Burden). Tr. by H. Bernstein. New York, 1917 (Knopf).

Crushed Flower, The. Includes also: A Story Which Will Never be Finished; On the Day of Crucifixion (Ben Tobit); The Serpent's Story; Love, Faith, and Hope; The Ocean; Judas Iscariot and Others; The Man Who Found the Truth (My Memoirs). Tr. by H. Bernstein. New York, 1916 (Knopf).

Dear Departing, The. See "Love to Your Neighbor."

Dilemma, A (Thought). Tr. by J. Cournos. Philadelphia, 1910 (Brown Brothers).

Donkeys. Tr. by H. Bernstein. *The Smart Set,* December, 1922, pp. 123–129.

Fallen Angels. Tr. by S. Hoffman. *The English Review,* January, 1914, pp. 181–185.

Governor, His Excellency, The. *Harper's Weekly,* February 9–March 2, 1917, pp. 196–198, 236–239, 270–273, 310–313.

330 Leonid Andreyev

He Who Gets Slapped. Tr. by Gregory Zilboorg. *The Dial,* March, 1921, pp. 250–300. Separately published by Brentano.

Incident, An (An Event). Tr. by L. Pasvolsky. *Poet Lore,* No. 2, 1916, pp. 171–179.

Judas Iscariot. Includes also: Eleazar (see "Lazarus"); Ben Tobit (see "Crushed Flower"). Tr. by W. H. Lowe. London, 1910 (Griffith).

Katerina (Katherina Ivanovna). Tr. by H. Bernstein. New York, 1923 (Brentano).

King Hunger. Tr. by E. M. Kayden. *Poet Lore,* No. 6, 1911, pp. 401–459.

Lazarus. Tr. by A. Yarmolinsky. Boston, 1918 (Stratford Co.).

Lazarus. In *Best Russian Short Stories,* pp. 215–234, New York 1917. (Boni & Liveright).

Life of Man. Tr. by C. J. Hogart. London, 1915 (Allan & Unwin). See also "Savva."

Little Angel, The. Includes also: At the Road Station; Snapper; The Lie; An Original; Petka at the Bungalow (Little Peter in the Country); Silence; Laughter; The Friend; In the Basement; The City; The Marseillaise; The Tocsin; Bargamot and Garaska; Stepping Stones (Splendid is the Life of the Resuscitated). Tr. by H. Bernstein. New York, 1915 (Knopf). See "Silence."

Love to Your Neighbor. Tr. by T. Seltzer. New York, 1914 (Glebe). The same, under the title "The Dear Departing," tr. by J. West, London, 1916 (Henderson).

Luckiest Man in the World, The (Chemodanov). Tr. by H. Bernstein. *World Fiction,* August, 1922, pp. 57–63.

Plays by Leonid Andreyeff: The Black Maskers; The Life of Man (see "Savva"); The Sabine Women. Tr. by S. L. Meader and F. N. Scott, with an introduction by V. Brusyanin. New York, 1915 (Scribner's).

Pretty Sabine Women. *The Drama,* February, 1914, pp. 34–71. See "Plays."

Realm of Roerich, The. Tr. by A. Kaun. *The New Republic,* December 21, 1921, pp. 97–99.

Red Laugh, The. Tr. by Alexandra Linden. London, 1905. See "The Seven," etc.

Samson in Chains. Tr. by H. Bernstein. New York, 1923 (Brentano).

Bibli... 332

Satan's Diary. Tr. by H. B... Liveright).

S. O. S., tr. by J. Pollock. *Nin...* pp. 1061–1071.

Savva. Includes also: The Li... York, 1914 (Mitchell Kennerley).

Seven That Were Hanged, The... 1909 (Ogilvie).

Seven That Were Hanged, The. 1918 (Boni & Liveright).

Silence. Tr. by J. Cournos. P...

Silence. *Lippincott's,* August, 19...

Silence. Includes the same storie... with the addition of The Wall. T... (Griffith).

Sorrows of Belgium, The (King... stein. New York, 1915 (Macmillan...

To the Stars. Tr. by Dr. A. G... 417–467.

Waltz of the Dogs, The. Tr.... (Macmillan).

When the King Loses His Head... Iscariot; Life of Father Vassily (Fi... Flower" and "Judas Iscariot"); Th... and "Silence"); Dies Irae (Day of W... York, 1920 (International).

C. FRENCH TRANSLATIONS

Au pied de l'échafaud. Translatio... ern Russian writers, by J. W. Bienstoc... (*Mercure de France*).

C'Était . . . *Revue Bleue,* January,...

Dans le Sous-Sol. *Revue Bleue,* Oc...

L'Épouvante. Tr. by T. de Wyz... (Perrin et Cie).

Le Gouffre. Tr. by S. Persky. Pa...

Le Gouverneur (together with Ko... Tr. by J. Ferenczy. Paris, 1909 (Fer...

332

Judas Isc...
Le Joug...
jours. Par...
Mémoirs...
Nouvelles...
Kablukov;...
the Station...
Paris, 1908...
Le Rire...
Paris, 1905...
Les Sept...
A. Touchai...
Une Vic...
Yelenkova...

D. DUT...

De geda...
De gouv...
In de...
Russische...
Judas...
Bibliotheek...
De opsta...
(E. Queri...
De rood...
S. O. S...
Zoon).
De sma...
Meulenho...
De zev...
Querido).

E. GER...

Der A...
Der A...
1905 (D...
Anathe...

Der Ausländer und andere Geschichten. Tr. by Anna Lubinow. Berlin, 1903 (Steintz).

Der, der die Maulschellen kriegt. Tr. by A. Scholz. Berlin, 1921 (Ladyschnikow).

Ezrählungen. Tr. by Elissawetinskaja and Y. Georg. Stuttgart, 1902 (Deutsche Verlag).

Es war einmal. Tr. by S. Goldenring. (Includes: Das Schweigen; Das Lachen; Die Lüge). Berlin, 1902 (Neufeld & Henius).

Frühlingsversprechen und andere Geschichten. Tr. by S. Wermer. Vienna, 1904 (Wiener Verlag).

Gaudeamus. Tr. by A. Scholz. Berlin, 1912 (Bong & Co.).

Der Gedanke. Tr. by A. Scholz. Berlin, 1922 (Ladyschnikow).

Der Gedanke und andere Novellen. Tr. by Elissawetinskaja and Y. Georg. Munich, 1903 (A. Langen).

Die Geschichte von den Sieben Gehenkten. Munich, 1920 (Musurion Verlag). See "Die Sieben," etc.

Der Gouverneur. Tr. by A. Scholz. Berlin, 1906 (Ladyschnikow).

Hinter dem Front (ein Teil des Romans "Unter dem Joch des Kriegs"). Tr. by H. v. zur Mühlen. Zurich, 1918 (M. Rascher).

Ignis Sanat (Sawwa). Tr. by D. D. Potthof. Berlin, 1906.

Im Erdgeschoss und anderes. Berlin, 1903 (Globus Verlag).

Im Nebel. Tr. by L. A. Hauff. Berlin, 1905 (D. Janke).

Im Nebel. Tr. by Steinitz. Berlin, 1903.

Im Nebel. Tr. by S. Wermer. Vienna, 1903 (Wiener Verlag).

Im Nebel und andere Novellen. Tr. by Elissawetinskaja and Y. Georg. Stuttgart, 1903 (Deutsche Verlag).

Jekaterina Iwanowna. Tr. by A. Scholz. Berlin, 1914 (Ladyschnikow).

Judas Ischariot und die Anderen. Tr. by O. Buck. Berlin, 1908 (Ladyschnikow).

Das Leben des Menschen. Tr. by A. Scholz. Berlin, 1908 (Ladyschnikow).

Das Leben Vater Wassili Fiwejski's. Tr. by G. Polonski. Berlin, 1906 (Ladyschnikow).

Die Lüge. Ausgewählte Erzahlungen. Tr. by N. Hornstein. Dresden, 1902 (H. Minden).

Die Lüge. Ausgewählte Erzahlungen. Tr. by N. Hornstein. Dresden, 1920 (H. Minden).

Ein Nachtgesprach. Leipzig, 1921 (Renaissance Verlag).

Novellen. Tr. by S. Goldenring. Contains: Once there Lived; Silence; Laughter; The Lie; The Abyss; Valya; Little Peter in the Country; The Grand Slam; The Tocsin. Berlin, 1902 (Neufeld & Henius).

Novellen. Tr. by A. von Krusenstjerna. Leipzig, 1904 (Reclam).

Das Rote Lachen. Tr. by A. Scholz. Berlin, 1905 (Ladyschnikow).

Das Rote Lachen. Tr. by A. Luther (illustrated). Berlin, 1922 (Emphorion).

Die Sieben Gehenkten. Tr. by A. Scholz. Berlin, 1908 (Ladyschnikow).

Die Sieben Gehenkten. Munich, 1908 (R. Piper & Co.).

Der Spion. Tr. by S. Wermer. Vienna, 1905 (Wiener Verlag).

Studentenliebe. Tr. by C. Richter. Berlin, 1909 (Ladyschnikow).

Tagebuch des Satan. Tr. by A. Rabinowitsch. Leipzig, 1921 (Renaisance Verlag).

Zu den Sternen. Tr. by A. Scholz. Berlin, 1906 (Ladyschnikow).

F. ITALIAN TRANSLATIONS OF ANDREYEV'S WRITINGS

L'abisso. Rome, 1920 (Carra & Co.).

Anathema (fragments from the play, supplemented to Dino Provenzal's book: *Una vittima del dubbio: Leonide Andreief*). Rome, 1921 (Bilychnis).

Il Belgio vivrà. Tr. by Markoff and Morselli. Rome, 1915 (Bontempelli). See "Re, legge e libertà."

Un delitto tragico. Tr. by Edm. Corradi. Rome, 1910 (Carra).

Diario di Satana. Tr. by T. Interlandi and B. Gurevich. Bologna, 1922 (Apollo).

Il figlio del'uomo, e altre novelle. Tr. by P. Gobetti and A. Prospero. Milan, 1920 (Sonzogno).

Il giogo della guerra. Milan, 1919 (Sonzogno).

Giuda Iscariota. Tr. by D. Cinti. Milan, 1919 (Sonzogno).

Lazzaro, e altre novelle. Tr. by C. Rèbora. Florence, 1919 (Vallecchi).

Padre Vassili. Includes: Bassi fondi; La Marsigliese. Tr. by C. Castelli. Milan, 1922 (Avanti!).

Il pensiero includes: Le maschere nere. Tr. by the Duchess d'Andtria. Milan, 1921 (R. Caddeo & Co.).

Re, legge e libertà. Tr. by O. Campa. Lanciano, 1916 (Carraba). See "Il Belgio."

Il riso rosso. Tr. by C. Castelli. Milan, 1915 (Sonzogno).

La rivoluzione (così fu). Tr. by C. Castelli. Milan, 1918 (Sonzogno).

Savva (Ignis sanat). Tr. by Gobetti and A. Prospero. Ferrara, 1921 (A. Taddei).

I sette impiccati. Tr. by D. Cinti. Milan, 1919 (Sonzogno).

Sotto il giogo della guerra: confessioni di un piccolo uomo su giorni grandi. Tr. by L. and F. Paresca. Florence, 1919 (Vallecchi). See "Il giogo," etc.

G. SPANISH TRANSLATIONS OF ANDREYEV'S WRITINGS

Los espectros. Novelas breves. Tr. by N. Tasin. Madrid, 1919 (Collección Universal).

Judas Icariote. Tr. by N. Tasin. Madrid, 1920 (Biblioteca nueva).

El misterio y otros cuentos. Tr. by N. Tasin. Madrid, 1921 (Colección Universal).

El Oceano. Tr. by A. Ruste. Madrid, 1922 (S. G. E. de Libreria).

Sachka Yegulev. Tr. by N. Tasin. Madrid, 1919 (Colección Universal).

Los siete ahorcados. Tr. by G. Porthof. Madrid, 1919 (Biblioteca nueva).

H. SWEDISH TRANSLATIONS OF ANDREYEV'S WRITINGS

Djävulens dagbok. Tr. by Jarl Hemmer. Bnr., 1921.

Det röda skrattet. Stockholm, 1906 (Bonnier).

I Taagen u. a. Noveller. Tr. by L. Swendsen. 1909 (E. Jespersen).

This list of translations is by no means complete. Some of Andreyev's writings have been translated into Hebrew, Yiddish, Turkish, Japanese.

———

I. BOOKS ON ANDREYEV, IN RUSSIAN

(A star (*) indicates unverified or inaccessible references.)

*Alman, A. D., *Leonid Andreyev: My Memoirs. A critical Study.* Saratov, 1908.

Arabazhin, K. I. *Leonid Andreyev: A Summary of His Work.* Petersburg, 1910.

* Baranov, I. L., *Leonid Andreyev as an Artist—Psychologist and Thinker*. Kiev, 1907.

Botsyanovsky, F. L., *Leonid Andreyev: A Critical-Biographical Study* Petersburg, 1903.

Brusyanin, V. V., *Leonid Andreyev. His Life and Work*. Moscow, 1912.

* Charsky, L., *In Order*. Petersburg, 1908.

Chukovsky, K., *L. Andreyev—Big and Little*. Petersburg, 1908.

Chukovsky, K., *On Leonid Andreyev*. Petersburg, 1911.

* Churinov, I., *The Tragedy of Thought*. Petersburg, 1910.

* Dobrokhotov, A., *The Career of L. Andreyev*. Moscow, 1908.

* Ettinger, E., *Andreyev's Someone in Grey and Someone in Red*. Kiev, 1908.

Fischer, K., *Anathema as presented by the Moscow Art Theatre*. Moscow, 1910.

Friche, L., *Leonid Andreyev: An Essay in Characterization*. Moscow, 1909.

* Ganzhulevich, T., *Russian Life and Its Currents in the Works of Leonid Andreyev*. Petersburg, 1910.

* Gekker, N., *Leonid Andreyev and His Works*. Odessa, 1903.

Gorky, Maxim; Blok, Alexander; Chukovsky, Korney; Chulkov, Georgy; Teleshov, Nikolay; Zaytsev, Boris; Zamyatin, Evgeny; Bely, Andrey, in their reminiscences, in *A Book on Leonid Andreyev*. Petrograd, 1922.

Ivanov, P., *To the Enemies of L. Andreyev*. Moscow, 1904.

Lvov-Rogachevsky, V., *Two Truths*. Petersburg, 1914.

* M. K., *Leonid Andreyev*. Moscow, 1903.

* Muromtsev, Dr. M., *Psychopatic Traits in the Heroes of L. Andreyev*. Petersburg, 1910.

* Nevedomsky, M. N., *At the Breaking Point*. Petersburg, 1909.

* Prokhorov, C. V., *Individualism in the Works of L. Andreyev*. Petersburg, 1910.

Reisner, M. A., *Andreyev and His Social Ideology*. Petersburg, 1909.

* Smolensky, N., *To the Defenders of L. Andreyev*. Moscow, 1910.

Michael, Father, *To Fathers and Children*. Moscow, 1904.

* Stomyarov-Sukhanov, *Symbolism, and L. Andreyev as Its Representative*. Kiev, 1903.

* Strumilin, S., *Spiritual Aristocracy and Profaners*. Petersburg, 1910.

* Tkachev, G. J., *Pathologic Art*. Harkov, 1913.

* Umius, *L. Andreyev and His Literary Heroes.* Nizhni-Novgorod, 1910.
* Urusov, Pr. N., *Impotent Individuals in Andreyev's Presentation.* Petersburg, 1903.
* Witte, Sophia, *Leonid Andreyev: A Critical Study.* Odessa, 1910.
* Zhurakovsky, E., *Realism, Symbolism, and Mystification of Life by L. Andreyev.* Moscow, 1903.
Zhurakovsky, E., *The Tragicomedy of Modern Life.* Moscow, 1907.

J. ARTICLES ON ANDREYEV, IN RUSSIAN BOOKS AND PERIODICALS

* Adrianov, in *Messenger of Self-Education,* Nos. 35 and 36, 1904 (Petersburg).
* Alexandrov, P., *Maxim Gorky and L. Andreyev: Their Life and Work.* Riga, 1903.
* Amfiteatrov, A., in *Against the Current.* Petersburg, 1908.
Andreyev, Leonid, *From My Life,* in *Everybody's Magazine,* January, 1903 (Petersburg).
Andreyev, Leonid. Autobiography, in Fidler's *First Literary Steps,* pp. 28–33. Petersburg, 1911.
Andreyevich (Solovyev), in *An Essay on the Philosophy of Russian Literature,* Chapter VIII, pp. 499–511. Petersburg, 1905.
* Anichkov, E., in *Messenger of Knowledge,* Petersburg, 1903.
Annensky, I., Judas—A New Symbol, in *Second Book of Reflections.* Petersburg, 1909.
Asheshov, N., *Life of Vasily Fiveysky,* in *Culture (Obrazovaniye),* May, 1904, pp. 81–99 (Petersburg).
Avrely (Bryusov), Andreyev's *Life of Man* at the Moscow Art Theatre, in *The Balance,* January, 1908, pp. 143–146 (Moscow).
Batyushkov, F., *Life of Man,* in *The Contemporary World,* March, 1907.
Batyushkov, F., Notes on the Theatre (*To the Stars*), in *God's World,* July, 1906 (Petersburg).
Bely, A., Reminiscences, see "Gorky."
Blok, A., Concerning Realists, in *The Golden Fleece,* May, 1907 (Moscow).
Blok, A., Reminiscences, see "Gorky."
Boborykin, P., At a Tragic Play, in *Theatre and Art,* No. 42, 1909 (Moscow).

Bostrem, A., What Andreyev's Story [*In Fog*] Tells the Paternal Heart, in *Culture*, December, 1904.

* Botsyanovsky, V., in *Literary Messenger*, January, 1902.

Bulgakov, V. F., in *With L. N. Tolstoy during the Last Year of His Life*, pp. 141–146. Petersburg, 1911.

Burenin, V., Critical Notes, in *New Times*, January, 1902, No. 9666. (Petersburg).

* Chagovets, V., in *The Kiev Gazette*, November, 1903.

Chirikov, E., Leonid Andreyev, in *Russian Miscellanies—II*, pp. 57–75, Sofia.

Chukovsky, K., in *From Chekhov to Our Days*, pp. 129–140. Petersburg, 1908.

Chukovsky, K., Reminiscences, see "Gorky."

Chulkov, G., see "Gorky."

Derman, A., Concerning *Professor Storitsyn*, in *Russia's Riches*, February, 1913, pp. 403–410 (Petersburg).

* Dryer, D., Andreyev's *Anathema*, in the Miscellany *A Black Temple—I*. Moscow, 1910.

Efros, *Anathema*, in *Speech*, October, 1909 (Petersburg).

Eichenwald, Y., Literary Notes, in *Russian Thought*, January, 1908, pp. 3–65 (Moscow).

Eichenwald, Y., in *Silhouettes of Russian Writers—III*, pp. 147–175 (4th edition). Berlin, 1923.

Filosofov, D., in A Spring Breeze, in *Word and Life*. Petrograd, n. d.

Galich, L., The Black Maskers, in *Theatre and Art*, No. 51, 1908.

Gerasimov, in *At the Bellows* (on *Savva*). Petersburg, 1907.

Gorky, Chukovsky, Blok, Chulkov, Zaytsev, Teleshov, Zamyatin, Bely, Reminiscences, in *A Book on Andreyev*, Petrograd, 1922.

Gornfeld, A., Andreyev's Small Tales, etc. (*To the Stars, Savva, Life of Man, Thus It Was, The Thief, The Governor*), in *Books and Men*, pp. 5–18. Petersburg, 1908.

Gornfeld, A., *My Memoirs*, in *Russia's Riches*, January, 1909, pp. 96–120.

* Gurevich, Lubov, in *Literature and Æsthetics*, pp. 61–64. Petersburg, 1912.

Gurevich, Lubov, *Anathema*, in *Russian Thought*, November, 1909.

Gurevich, Lubov, the Miscellany *Znaniye* for 1903 (Life of Vasily Fiveysky), in *Culture*, May, 1905.

Gusev, in *Two Years with L. N. Tolstoy*, pp. 77–81. Moscow, 1912.

Hippius, Z., on *Darkness*, in *The Balance*, February, 1908.

Hippius, Z., The Latest Fiction, in *The Balance*, March, 1903.

Hippius, Z., On *Judas*, in *The Balance*, July, 1907.

Homo Novus, see "Kugel."

Ivanov, Vyacheslav, Andreyev's New Story (*Life of Vasily Fiveysky*), in *The Balance*, May, 1904.

Ivanov-Razumnik, in *On the Sense of Life*. Petersburg, 1908.

Izmaylov, A., in *Literary Olympus*, pp. 235–293. Moscow, 1911.

Kizevetter, A., Notes on the Theatre, in *Russian Thought*, November, 1909.

Kogan, Peter, in *Notes on the History of Modern Russian Literature*, v. I, part I, pp. 1–61. Moscow, 1912.

Kozlovsky, L. S., L. Andreyev, in Vengerov's *Russian Literature of the Twentieth Century*, pp. 251–280.

Kranichfeld, V., in *Culture*, October, 1902.

Kranichfeld, V., *Anathema*, and others, in *Contemporary World*, January, 1910, pp. 82–94 (Petersburg).

Kranichfeld, V., Concerning Andreyev's Latest Production (*To the Stars*), in *Contemporary World*, October, 1906.

Kranichfeld, V., *Darkness*, in *Contemporary World*, January, 1908.

Kranichfeld, V., *Savva*, in *God's World*, April, 1906.

Kranichfeld, V., *The Seven That Were Hanged*, in *Contemporary World*, June, 1908.

Kugel, A., *The Black Maskers*, in *Theatre and Art*, No. 42, 1909.

Kugel, A., *Gaudeamus*, in *Theatre and Art*, No. 38, 1910.

Kugel, A., *Life of Man*, in *Theatre and Art*, September, 1907.

Kugel, A., The Presentation of *Life of Man* at the Moscow Art Theatre, in *Theatre and Art*, No. 17, 1908.

Latsky, E., Andreyev's New Story (*Life of Vasily Fiveysky*), in *Messenger of Europe*, November, 1904 (Petersburg).

Latsky, E., Betwixt Abyss and Mystery (*Judas*), in *Contemporary World*, August, 1908.

* Lenin, A., Our Writers, in Miscellany *A Black Temple—I*. Moscow, 1910.

Lorenzo, To Andreyev's Fifteenth Anniversary, in *Russia's Morning*, No. 79, 1913 (Moscow).

Lunacharsky, A., in *Literary Disintegration*, Petersburg, 1908.

Lunacharsky, A., in *News from Abroad*, No. 3, 1908.

Lunacharsky, A., in *Russian Thought*, February, 1903.

Lunacharsky, A., A New Drama (*Life of Man*), in *Messenger of Knowledge*, March–April, 1907.

Lunacharsky, A., Social Philosophy and Social Mysticism (*Savva*), in *Culture*, May, 1906.

Lvov (-Rogachevsky), V., *Children of the Sun* (by Gorky) and *To the Stars*, in *Culture*, July, 1906.

Lvov, V., *Judas*, in *Culture*, June–July, 1907.

Lvov, V., Steps of Death (*Life of Man*), in *Culture*, March, 1907.

Lvov-Rogachevsky, V., in *Again on the Eve*. Petersburg, 1913.

Lvov-Rogachevsky, V., Concerning Sashka Zhegulev, in *Contemporary World*, January, 1912, pp. 269–281.

Lvov-Rogachevsky, V., A Dead Kingdom, in *Culture*, November, 1904, pp. 73–130.

Lvov-Rogachevsky, V., *Phantoms* and *Red Laugh*, in *Culture*, March, 1905.

Merezhkovsky, D., In the Paws of an Ape, in *Russian Thought*, January, 1908.

Mikhailovsky, N., Literature and Life, in *Russia's Riches*, November, 1901, pp. 58–75.

Minsky, N., L. Andreyev and Merezhkovsky, in *Our Gazette—I*, 1908 (Petersburg).

Mirsky (Solovyev), *Our Literature*, in *Everybody's Magazine*, January–February, 1902.

Mirtov, O., War in the Works of Tolstoy, Garshin, Andreyev, in *Culture*, October, 1905.

Morozov, M., in *Notes on Modern Literature*, pp. 1–70. Petersburg, 1911.

N., Andreyev's Sea Wanderings, in *Russia's Morning*, September 8, 1913.

Narodin, K., Beauty and Ham (*Professor Storitsyn*), in *Contemporary World*, May, 1914, pp. 39–51.

Nevedomsky, M., L. Andreyev, in *History of Russian Literature of the Nineteenth Century—V* (edited by Ovsyaniko-Kulikovsky), pp. 260–272. Petersburg, 1910.

Nevedomsky, M., *Darkness*, in *Contemporary World*, February, 1908.

Nevedomsky, M., *Life of Vasily Fiveysky*, in *God's World*, October, 1904.

Nevedomsky, M., On Art Quests, in *Contemporary World*, January, March, April, 1909.

Nevedomsky, M., On Contemporary Creative Art, in *God's World*, April, 1903, pp. 1–42.

Nevedomsky, M., A Victim of Stilization (*Life of Man*), in *Contemporary World*, December, 1908.

Novik, I., Leonid Andreyev: Reminiscences, in *The Russian Emigrant*, Nos. 3, 4, 1920 (Berlin).

Orlovsky [V. V. Vorovsky], in *From Modern Literature*, pp. 37–58. Moscow, 1910.

Ovsyaniko-Kulikovsky, D., in *Collected Works—V*, Petersburg, 1912.

Ovsyaniko-Kulikovsky, D., Notes on Andreyev's Art, in *Heat Lightnings—II*, pp. 197–214. Petersburg, 1909.

Pavlovich, P., Red Laugh, in *Messenger of Knowledge*, July, 1905.

Petrony, Andreyev's Tenth Anniversary, in *Free Thoughts*, April 15, 1908 (Petersburg).

* Pilsky, P., in *On Andreyev, Kuprin, Sologub, etc.*, Petersburg, 1909.

P-y (Pilsky), P., in *Contemporary World*, April, 1908.

Protopopov, M., Young Sprouts, in *Russian Thought*, March, 1902, pp. 187–206.

Redko, A., *Anathema, etc.*, in *Russia's Riches*, December, 1909, pp. 75–94.

Redko, A., Andreyev's Good and Bad Ones.—*Ibid.*, June–July, 1908, pp. 1–19, 1–17.

Redko, A., Andreyev's *Ocean*. *Ibid.*, May, 1911, pp. 152–163.

Redko, A., Andreyev's *Sashka Zhegulev*. *Ibid.*, January, 1912, pp. 139–147.

Redko, A., An Elegy by Andreyev (*The Black Maskers*). *Ibid.*, April, 1909, pp. 173–183.

Redko, A., Gorky on the Guilty and Andreyev on the Innocent Ones. *Ibid.*, February, 1905.

Rossov, *Anathema*, in *Theatre and Art*, No. 47, 1909.

Rostislavov, *Life of Man*, in *Theatre and Art*, November, 1907.

Rozanov, V., Apropos, in *New Times*, No. 9677, June 2, 1903.

Rozanov, V., Judas Iscariot. *Ibid.*, July 19, 1907.

* Skabichevsky, A., New Talent, in *News*, January, 1902 (Petersburg).

Skabicheysky, A., Degenerates in Our Contemporary Literature (*Life of Vasily Fiveysky*), in *Russian Thought*, November, 1904, pp. 85–101.

Skitalets (Petrov), Reminiscences, in *Russia's Voice*, Nos. 462, 467, 470, 472, 474, February, 1922 (Harbin).

Shulyatnikov, V., On a New Theory of Art, in *The Moscow Courier*, August 16, 1903.

Smirnov, A., The Tragedy of Anarchism (*Savva*), in *Culture*, November, 1906.

Stark, E., *Tsar Hunger,* in *Theatre and Art,* No. 21, 1908.

Teleshov, see "Gorky."

* Tolstoy, L. N., in Miscellany *Italia,* 1909.

Tolstoy, Countess Sophia, Letter to the Editor, in *New Times,* No. 9673, February 7, 1903, p. 4.

Treplev, in *Russian Thought,* April, May, June, September, November, 1905.

* Vartanyan, V., in *L. N. Tolstoy and L. Andreyev, as Ideologists of the Toiling Masses.* Baku, 1909.

Vengerov, S., in Brockhaus & Efron's *Encyclopedic Dictionary,* supplementary Volume I, pp. 115–118. Petersburg, 1905.

Vengerov, S., in *Russian Literature of the Twentieth Century,* pp. 246–251. Moscow, 1917.

Veresayev, V., Reminiscences, in *Morning Breezes,* pp. 79–85. Petrograd, 1922.

* Vladislavov, I., in *Russian Writers of the Nineteenth and Twentieth Centuries,* pp. 13–18. Petersburg, 1913.

* Volsky, A., The Problem of Duty in Russian Literature (*Thought, In Fog, Life of Vasily Fiveysky*), in *Truth,* January, 1905 (Petersburg).

Volzhsky, in *Everybody's Magazine,* July, 1904.

Volzhsky, in *From the World of Literary Quests.* Petersburg, 1906.

* Voytolovsky, L., Social-Psychologic Types in Andreyev's Stories, in *Truth,* August, 1905, pp. 123–140.

Yasinsky, J., in *Monthly Writings,* December, 1901 (Petersburg).

Yordansky, Maria, L. Andreyev's Emigration and Death, in *Native Land,* I, pp. 44–63.

* Zakrzevsky, in *Dostoyevsky; Andreyev,* pp. 4–28. Petersburg, 1911.

Zamyatin, see "Gorky."

Zaytsev, see "Gorky."

Zetlin, M., On the Art of Leonid Andreyev, in *Russia of the Future,* February, 1920, pp. 243–256 (Paris).

K. ARTICLES ON ANDREYEV IN ENGLISH

Anonymous, Apostle of the Terrible, in *Lippincott's,* August, 1912, pp. 235–240.

Anonymous, A New Portent in Russian Literature, in *Current Literature,* September, 1908, pp. 282–286.

Anonymous, A Novelist of Nerves, in the London *Nation,* reproduced in *The Living Age,* February 18, 1911, pp. 434–437.

Baring, Maurice, A Russian Mystery Play (*The Life of Man*), in *The Oxford and Cambridge Review,* reproduced in *The Living Age,* September 26, 1908, pp. 786–792.

Chukovsky, K., L. Andreyev as Seen by a Fellow Russian, in *The Living Age,* June 26, 1920, pp. 776–779 (translated from *The Literary Messenger,* Petrograd, 1919).

Gorky, M., L. Andreyev at Capri, in *The Living Age,* August 26, 1922, pp. 525–529 (translated from the Milan *Avanti!;* a portion of Gorky's reminiscences in *A Book on Andreyev*).

Kaun, A., The Art of Andreyev, in *The Freeman,* September 22, 1920, pp. 35–37.

Kaun, A., Chekhov and Andreyev, in *The Little Review,* September, 1914, pp. 44–49.

Kaun, A., The End of Andreyev, in *The New Republic,* June 28, 1922, pp. 133–135.

Kaun, A., Leonid Andreyev, in the New York *Nation,* October 11, 1917, pp. 393–395.

Kaun, A., Leonid Andreyev's Last Illusion, in *The New Republic,* August 8, 1923, pp. 282–283.

Kaun, A., The Solitude of Leonid Andreyev, in the *Freeman,* June 21, 1923, pp. 356–357.

Kayden, E. M., The Life and Work of L. Andreyev, in *The Dial,* November 15, 1920, pp. 425–428.

Lavretsky, I., A Sketch of L. Andreyev, in *The Independent,* July 29, 1909, pp. 242–245.

Milyukov, P., L. Andreyev and His Appeal to Humanity, in *Struggling Russia,* July 26, 1919, pp. 282–285.

Olgin, M., A Wounded Intellect, in *The New Republic,* December 24, 1919, pp. 123–125.

Pasvolsky, L., L. Andreyev and the Bolsheviki, in *The Review,* December 6, 1919, pp. 638–639.

Persky, S., in *Contemporary Russian Novelists,* pp. 199–245, Boston, 1913.

Phelps, W. L., in *Russian Novelists,* pp. 262–277, New York, 1911.

Seltzer, T., The Life and Works of L. Andreyev, in *The Drama,* February, 1914, pp. 5–33.

Thomson, O. R. H., Andreyev's *Anathema* and the Faust Legend, in *The North American Review,* December, 1911, pp. 882–887.

Witte, Sophia, Russian Literature and the War, in *The Independent,* May 11, 1905, pp. 1043–1045.

A suggestive epitaph appeared in *Life and Letters,* September, 1922, p. 11, by Clarendon Ross:

LEONID ANDREYEV

Walls, walls, walls.
I found myself enclosed by walls:
    The granite wall of natural law,
    The bloody wall of the laws of man,
    The slippery wall of my own mind,
    The murky wall of the unknown,
    The iron wall of fate,
    The gray wall of old age,
    The lofty wall of death.
On these seven walls I pounded
    Till I fell by the wall of death
    At the age of forty-eight.
    Perchance you that now live
    Have gained the way to freedom?

L. NOTES ON ANDREYEV IN FRENCH PERIODICALS

Hippius, Z., in Notes sur la littérature russe de notre temps, in *Mercure de France,* January 1, 1908, pp. 74–75.

Séménoff, E., in Lettres russes, in *Mercure de France:*

April, 1903, pp. 275–281 (apropos of the polemic in connection with *The Abyss* and *In Fog*).

May, 1905, p. 310.

February 15, 1906, pp. 627–630 (*Vers les Etoiles*).

February 16, 1908, pp. 755–756 (*Les Ténèbres*).

May 1, 1908, pp. 175–177 (*Le Roi-la-Faim*).

July 16, 1908, pp. 347–349 (*Les Récits des Sept pendus*).

January 16, 1909, p. 368 (bare mention of *Masques Noirs,* and *Les Jours de la Vie*).

April 1, 1909, p. 561 (bare mention of *Anathema*).

November 16, 1909, pp. 372–374 (*Anfisa*).

October 1, 1910, pp. 568–569 (*Gaudeamus*).

April 1, 1912, p. 660 (*Sachka Gégouleff*).

August 16, 1913, p. 873 (*Les Mémoirs d'un Prisonnier*).

Wyzewa, de, Deux nouveaux conteurs russes: MM. Andréief et Artsi-bashef, in *Revue des deux Mondes,*—May 15, 1909, pp. 458–465.

Persky, Serge, in *Les maitres du roman russe contemporain,* pp. 245–285. Paris, 1912.

M. NOTES IN GERMAN PERIODICALS (ACCORDING TO *BIBLIOGRAPHIE DER DEUTSCHEN ZEITSCHRIFTEN-ARTIKELN*)

Anonymous, in *Landeszeitung* (Beiblatt), No. 23, 1903 (Karlsruhe).
Anonymous, in *Die Zeit,* No. 50, 1903 (Berlin).
Aurich, Lv., in *Die Woche,* No. 47, 1912.
Balte, F. M., in *Morgen,* No. 17, 1908.
Balte, F. M., in *Allgemeine Zeitung,* 10/4, 1909 (Munich).
Bruck, R., in *Masken,* 219, 1908 (Düsseldorf).
Cramer, H. H. (*Du sollst nicht töten*), in *Die Scene,* VIII:31, 1919 (Charlottenburg).
Düsel, F., (*Studentenliebe*), in *Der Kunstwart,* 24. J. II. 200, 1911.
Ernot, F., in *d. literarische Echo—VIII,* 20–21, 1905.
Goldenring, St., in *Norddeutsche allgemeine Zeitung,* No. 260 (Berlin).
Hochdorf, M., in *Sozialistische Monatshefte,* 18: 1035, 1918.
Luther, A. (*Joch d. Krieg*), in *d. literarische Echo,* 86–89, 1918.
Poppenberg, F. (*Zu den Sternen*) in *Der Türmer,* March, 1907, pp. 862–864 (Stuttgart).
Rodef, in *Wiener Fremdenblatt,* 6/6, 1903.
Scholz, A., in *Die Zeit,* No. 411, 1902 (Vienna).
Simchowitz, S., in *Die Kultur,* No. 587, March, 1903, pp. 1066–1072 (Cologne).
Wolschsky, N., in *Nation,* No. 50, 1903 (Berlin).

N. ANDREYEV'S PLAYS

Nearly all of Andreyev's plays (excepting those forbidden by the censorship) were presented throughout Russia and Siberia. Outside of Russia they were played most often in Germany. Next in order come Italy, the Scandinavian countries, and the countries of the Balkan Slavs. At the very end come France, Spain, and the United States of America. American productions comprise: *Anathema, Black Maskers, He Who Gets Slapped, Life of Man, Love to Your Neighbor, Pretty Sabine Women.*

Satan's Diary was dramatized and presented at the Alexandrine Theatre, Petrograd, during the season 1922–1923. It was withdrawn for lack of success. According to the Berlin daily, *Dni, Samson Enchained* is to be produced by the Moscow Art Theatre in the season of 1923–1924.

Three operas were based on Andreyev's plays: *Days of Our Life,* composed by Glukhovetsky. Presented at the People's Palace, Petrograd; during 1915–1916. *The Abyss,* by Rebikov. *The Black Maskers,* by Vladimir Nikolayevich Ilyin.

The late composer Elia Satz wrote the incidental music for *The Life of Man* and *Anathema.*

For the cinematograph Andreyev wrote a part of the scenario for *Anfisa.*

The war prevented the Moscow Art Theatre from producing the projected picture of *Anathema.* This Theatre is at present planning several films of Andreyev's plays; among others, *Katherina Ivanovna,* with Mlle. Germanova in the title rôle. An Italian company is about to produce a film version of *He Who Gets Slapped.*

INDEX

INDEX

Andreyev's writings are indexed under their titles. His personal characteristics, attitudes, views, utterances, and experiences, and also names of persons and works mentioned in his letters and diaries, are grouped under "Andreyev, Leonid Nikolayevich." The characters of his stories and plays will be found under the heading "Characters."

A